DEVIL TAKE THE HINDMOST

DEVIL TAKE THE HINDMOST

A HISTORY OF FINANCIAL SPECULATION

• EDWARD •
CHANCELLOR

MACMILLAN

First published in the United States of America
in 1999 by Farrar, Straus & Giroux, Inc.

This edition published 1999 by Macmillan
an imprint of Macmillan Publishers Ltd
25 Eccleston Place, London SW1W 9NF
Basingstoke and Oxford
Associated companies throughout the world
www.macmillan.co.uk

ISBN 0 333 64824 2

3 5 7 9 8 6 4

A CIP catalogue record for this book is available
from the British Library.

Printed and bound in Great Britain by
Mackays of Chatham plc, Chatham, Kent

To Antonia

CONTENTS

PREFACE: DEVIL TAKE THE HINDMOST

When I was young, people called me a gambler. As the scale of my operations increased I became known as a speculator. Now I am called a banker. But I have been doing the same thing all the time.

Sir Ernest Cassell,
banker to Edward VII

Never before has the subject of speculation attracted as much attention as it does today. Behind much of the contemporary financial and economic news—foreign currency crises, stock market bubbles and crashes, derivatives fiascos, and technological innovations—lurks the speculator. In the United States, millions of individual investors trade stocks daily. The success of the American economy in the 1990s has largely been the product of speculative funds flowing into the stock market. This has enabled new companies to be floated and old ones to be merged and encouraged corporations to invest and investors to spend some of their stock market gains. A great bubble of prosperity has been blown before our eyes and its stability is naturally a cause for anxious concern.

Speculation is a divisive topic. Many politicians—several of them in Asia—warn that the global economy is being held hostage by speculators. In their opinion, the speculator is a parasitical figure, driven by greed and fear, who creates and thrives on financial crises:

an egoist and a slave to his passions, who in his euphoric and depressive moods reflects the limited intellectual outlook of the crowd. To them, the wealth of nations depends on caging this wild beast. Others—mainly Western economists—take a radically different line. They argue that speculation is fundamentally a benign force, essential to the proper functioning of the capitalist system. According to this view, the speculator acts as a conduit enabling new information—whether it be the results of the latest inflation figures or the effects of a hurricane on coffee production—to be fed through into prices. Without the speculator, markets would be full of bottlenecks and economic crises would be even more common. Furthermore, the inception of new technologies, such as the Internet, is heavily dependent on the activity of stock market speculators. Curb the speculator, argue the economists, and capitalism will lose its vitality.

WHAT'S IN A NAME?

Despite the endless discussion that it generates, speculation remains an elusive concept. It acquired an economic meaning only in the late eighteenth century and even then it was a curiously imprecise term. In a letter dated 1 May 1774, Horace Walpole described Sir George Colebrooke, the MP and banker, as a "martyr to what is called speculation," after Colebrooke was bankrupted in a failed attempt to corner the market for alum, a substance used in the dyeing of textiles.[1] Two years later, Adam Smith in *The Wealth of Nations* referred to the sudden fortunes that "are sometimes made . . . by what is called the trade of speculation." Yet Smith's "speculative merchant" was not a financial operator but an entrepreneur who

> exercises no one regular, established, or well-known branch of business. He is a corn merchant this year, or tea merchant the year after. He enters into every trade when he foresees that it is likely to be more than commonly profitable, and he quits when he foresees that its profits are likely to return to the level of other trades.

For Smith, the speculator is defined by his readiness to pursue short-term opportunities for profit: his investments are fluid whereas those of the conventional businessman are more or less fixed. This distinction was retained by John Maynard Keynes, who described "enterprise" as "the activity of forecasting the prospective yield of assets over their whole life," in contrast to speculation, which he called "the activity of forecasting the psychology of the market."

Speculation is conventionally defined as an attempt to profit from changes in market price. Thus, forgoing current income for a prospective capital gain is deemed speculative. Speculation is active while investment is generally passive. According to the Austrian economist J. A. Schumpeter, "the difference between a speculator and an investor can be defined by the presence or absence of the intention to 'trade,' i.e. realize profits from fluctuations in security prices."[2] The line separating speculation from investment is so thin that it has been said both that speculation is the name given to a failed investment and that investment is the name given to a successful speculation. Fred Schwed, a Wall Street wit, declared that clarifying the difference between investment and speculation was "like explaining to the troubled adolescent that Love and Passion are two different things. He perceives that they are different, but they don't seem quite different enough to clear up his problem." Schwed concluded the two could be separated on the grounds that the first aim of investment was the preservation of capital while the primary aim of speculation was the enhancement of fortune. As he put it: "Speculation is an effort, probably unsuccessful, to turn a little money into a lot. Investment is an effort, which should be successful, to prevent a lot of money becoming a little."[3]

Similar problems of definition are encountered in distinguishing speculation from gambling. While a bad investment may be a speculation, a poorly executed speculation is often described as a gamble. The American financier Bernard Baruch was once dismissed from the presence of Pierpont Morgan for uttering the word "gamble" in relation to a business proposition.[4] Later, Baruch recalled that "there is no investment which doesn't involve some risk and is not something of a gamble." The psychologies of speculation and gambling are almost indistinguishable: both are dangerously addictive habits which involve an appeal to fortune, are often accompanied by delusional behaviour and are dependent for success on the control of emotions.*

Speculation has come to mean different things to different people, yet it retains something of its original philosophical meaning; namely, to reflect or theorise without a firm factual basis. According to a seventeenth-century definition, a speculator is "one who indulges in occult observations or studies." The financial speculator still resembles the alchemist in that he is constantly constructing abstruse theories to turn paper into gold, normally with little success.† Occasionally, investors consult astrological tables or spiritual mediums in order to enhance their performance—even today in New York there exists an Astrologer's Fund whose manager promises "naturally stellar returns."

People resort to such measures when they are faced with uncertainty. The name given to financial uncertainty is "risk." Economists differentiate gambling and speculation on the grounds that gambling involves the deliberate creation of new risks for the sake of diversion while speculation involves the assumption of the inevitable risks of the capitalist process.‡ In other words, when a

---

*It is often said that speculation requires a control of both "greed" and "fear." The speculator George Soros ascribes his phenomenal success to a profound sense of his own fallibility. Fyodor Dostoevsky, while suffering from a gambling addiction, wrote in a letter to his wife (of 20 August 1863) that the secret of winning at roulette was "very stupid and simple and amounts to ceaseless self-control at all stages of the game and not getting excited."

†See George Soros, *The Alchemy of Finance: Reading the Mind of the Market* (New York, 1987). Soros maintains that "whereas alchemy has failed as natural science, social science can succeed as alchemy." By this he means that the application of speculators' ideas may actually change the conditions of the market. In other words, speculators may create their own self-fulfilling prophecies.

‡Henry C. Emery claims that "in gambling one party must lose just what the other wins. In speculation this is not necessarily so . . . whereas gambling consists in placing money on artificially created risks of some fortuitous event, speculation consists in assuming the inevitable economic risks of changes in value" (*Speculation on the Stock and Produce Exchanges of the United States*, New York, 1896, p. 188). According to James Grant, "what chiefly distinguishes a speculator from a gambler is that the risk he or she bears comes into existence independently of the speculator's decision to bear it" (*The Trouble with Prosperity* [New York, 1996], p. 222).

gambler places a bet on a horse he is creating a risk, while the speculator who buys a share is simply involved in the transfer of an existing risk. Speculation is generally considered riskier than investment. The securities analyst Benjamin Graham declared that investment requires a "margin of safety" so that the value of the principal is maintained even in unforeseen adverse conditions. An uninformed or spontaneous investment is more speculative than one in which the investor has taken the time to investigate and assess its potential returns. Graham added that buying shares with borrowed money was always speculative. The capitalist is confronted with a broad spectrum of risk with prudent investment at one end and reckless gambling at the other. Speculation lies somewhere between the two.

According to modern economic theory—which holds that markets are efficient, i.e., that share prices reflect intrinsic values, and that speculators are simply rational economic agents intent on optimising their wealth—the history of speculation is a dull affair. In the world of efficient markets there are no animal spirits, no crowd instincts, no emotions of greed or fear, no trend-following speculators, and no "irrational" speculative bubbles. Yet the activities of speculators down the ages appear to me to be richer, more diverse in motivation and extraordinary in result, than anything described by economists. My own approach is closer to that of Charles Mackay, Dickens's friend and the author of *Extraordinary Popular Delusions and the Madness of Crowds* (1841), who provided the first popular accounts of the Tulip Mania, Mississippi, and South Sea bubbles. For Mackay, speculative manias were a manifestation of the occasional tendency of society to succumb to delusion and mass madness: "Men, it has been well said, think in herds; it will be seen that they go mad in herds, while they only recover their senses slowly, and one by one."

Mackay's historical narrative of speculative manias remains the only one readily available. While I felt it was time to examine the subject anew, I have not attempted to produce a comprehensive history of speculation—such a task was likely to yield an unwieldy and repetitious tome whose final page would never be written. Instead, I concentrate on occurrences of speculation in the leading economic powers of the day, from the Dutch Republic in the seventeenth century to Japan in the 1980s, interspersed with the occasional look at speculation in the present day. I believe that speculation can only be understood within a social context and that a history of speculation cannot simply be a description of economic affairs but must also be something of a social history. The behaviour and attitude of politicians towards speculation is especially important, since the laws governing markets are framed and enforced by governments. On numerous occasions we find politicians stimulating speculative manias for their own gain.* Above all, I hope to have retained some of Mackay's enthusiasm so that the reader will come to agree with his observation that the "subject [of speculation] is capable of inspiring as much interest as even a novelist can desire . . . Is it a dull or uninstructive picture to see a whole people shaking off the trammels of reason, and running wild after a golden vision, refusing obstinately to believe that it is not real, till like an *ignis fatuus*, they are plunged into a quagmire?"†

*As Keynes's mentor Alfred Marshall wrote: "Public opinion and private morality have driven home the maxim that if a statesman bases stock exchange speculation on his policy, he will soon base his policy on his speculation." The South Sea Bubble of 1720 and the Japanese "Bubble Economy" of the 1980s derived from just such behaviour. Cited by Marco Dardia and Mauro Gallegati, in "Alfred Marshall on Speculation," *History of Political Economy*, XXIV, No. 3 (1992), p. 591.

†*Ignis fatuus:* the light of combustion of marsh gas, apt to lead travellers into danger; any delusive ideal that leads one astray.

DEVIL TAKE THE HINDMOST

CHAPTER 1

"THIS BUBBLE WORLD": THE ORIGINS OF FINANCIAL SPECULATION*

And when dreams deceive our wandering eyes in the heavy slumber of night, and under the spade the earth yields gold to the light of day: our greedy hands finger the spoil and snatch at the treasure, sweat too runs down our face, and a deep fear grips our heart that maybe someone will shake out our laden bosom, where he knows the gold is hid: soon, when these pleasures flee from the brain they mocked, and the true shape of things comes back, our mind is eager for what is lost, and moves with all its force among the shadows of the past . . .

Satyricon of Petronius Arbiter, *circa* A.D. 50[1]

The propensity to barter and exchange is an innate human characteristic. An inclination to divine the future is another deeply ingrained trait. Together they comprise the act of financial speculation. "All life is speculation," declared the celebrated nineteenth-century American trader James R. Keene, "the spirit of speculation is born with men." For the earliest known historical cases of speculation we must turn to ancient Rome during the Republic of the second century B.C. By this date, the Roman financial system had developed many of the characteristics of modern capitalism: markets flourished because Roman law allowed the free transfer of property, money was lent out at interest, money changers dealt in foreign currencies, and payments across the Roman territories could be made by bankers' draft. Capital

*"What's lighter than the mind? A thought. Than thought? This bubble world." Francis Quarles, *Emblems*, i.iv, 1635.

concentrated in Rome, as it later did in Amsterdam, London, and New York.[2] The idea of credit had also developed, along with a primitive form of insurance for ships and other forms of property. The people of Rome exhibited a passion for the accumulation of wealth, matched by an extravagance in its display and consumption. Gaming was common.

In Latin, the word *speculator* describes a sentry whose job it was to "look out" (*speculare*) for trouble. The financial speculator in ancient Rome, however, was called *quaestor*, which means a seeker. Collectively, speculators were sometimes referred to as *Graeci* or Greeks.* Their meeting place was the Forum, near the Temple of Castor, where "crowds of men bought and sold shares and bonds of tax-farming companies, various goods for cash and on credit, farms and estates in Italy and in the provinces, houses and shops in Rome and elsewhere, ships and storehouses, slaves and cattle."† The Roman comic playwright Plautus describes the Forum as peopled with whores, shopkeepers, moneylenders, and wealthy men. He identifies specifically two unsavoury groups; the first lot he describes as "mere puffers" and the second as "impudent, talkative, and malevolent fellows, who boldly, without reason, utter calumnies about one another."[3] In this description, we find the originals of the bulls and bears of later stock markets.

The Roman state contracted out many of its functions, from tax collecting to temple building, to societies of capitalists, known as *publicani*. Like modern joint-stock companies, the *publicani* were legal bodies independent of their members whose ownership was divided into *partes*, or shares. They had executive managements, produced public accounts (*tabulae*), and held occasional meetings of shareholders. Many were considerable concerns, employing tens

---

*This may have been because many were of Hellenic origin, although for the Romans to call someone "Greek" (especially *graeculus*, a little Greek) was also a form of abuse.

†This description of the Forum as a prototype stock market by the Russian classical historian Mikhail Rostovtzeff is contested by some economic historians. He cites in support Cunningham's *Essay on Western Civilisation* (New York, 1913, p. 164): "the forum with its immense basilicae may be regarded as an immense stock exchange where monetary speculation of every kind was going on." See Rostovtzeff, *The Social and Economic History of the Roman Empire* (Oxford, 1957), p. 31; also Antonin Deloume, *Les Manieurs d'Argent à Rome* (Paris, 1892).

of thousands of slaves. Shares came in two sorts: larger executive shareholdings of the great capitalists, known as *socii,* and smaller shares, called *particulae.* The manner of dealing in unregistered *particulae* shares was informal, resembling the modern over-the-counter stock markets.[4] The *publicani* maintained a system of couriers throughout the Roman territories in order to gather information, enabling them to calculate how much to bid for contracts at auction and how much shares in going concerns were worth.

No evidence remains of the prices for which *partes* sold, and there are no descriptions of stock market behaviour. We do know, however, that shares fluctuated in value. When the Roman consul Vatinius was accused of corruption he was asked: "Did you extort shares, which were at their *dearest* at the time . . . ?"[5] Cicero referred to *partes carissimas* (most expensive shares) and claimed that buying shares in public companies was seen as a gamble which conservative men avoided.[6] Shares in the *publicani* did not attract only politicians and large capitalists. Polybius, the Greek chronicler, describes a widespread popular interest in share ownership: "All over Italy," he writes, "an immense number of contracts, far too numerous to specify, are awarded by the censors for the construction and repair of public buildings, and besides for the collection of revenues from navigable rivers, harbours, gardens, mines, lands—in a word every transaction which comes under the control of the Roman government is farmed out to contractors. All these activities are carried on by the people, and *there is scarcely a soul, one might say, who does not have some interest in these contracts and the profits which are derived from them*" (my italics).[7] Describing the last years of the Republic, Petronius Arbiter wrote that "filthy usury and the handling of money had caught the common people in a double whirlpool, and destroyed them . . . the madness spread through their limbs, and trouble bayed and hounded them down like some disease sown in the dumb flesh."[8] Perhaps these are descriptions of the first speculative "mania," although the evidence is too weak to prove the case.*

*M. Cary and H. H. Scullard write that "this sudden craze for financial speculation we may compare with the speculative fever which swept over Britain in the early eighteenth century" (i.e., the South Sea Bubble of 1720) (*A History of Rome,* London, 1975, p. 609, n. 7).

The Roman *publicani* withered under the Empire, but speculation in property, commodities, and currencies continued.* After fiduciary money—i.e., money created by government decree which has no intrinsic value but depends on public confidence—was introduced in the third century A.D., currency crises became common. The city council of Mylasa in Caria (in modern-day Turkey) complained that as a result of the speculative hoarding of specie, "the very security of the city is shaken by the malice and villainy of a few people, who assail and rob the community. Through them speculation in exchange has entered our marketplace and prevents the city from securing a supply of the necessities of life, so that many of the citizens and indeed the community as a whole, suffer from scarcity."[9] It is a very modern lament.

FINANCIAL SPECULATION IN THE EARLY MODERN PERIOD

The culture of medieval Europe was inimical to financial speculation for both practical and ideological reasons. The feudal system dispensed with many financial transactions of the Roman world, replacing cash dealings with payments in kind. Medieval schoolmen revived the Aristotelian notion of a "just price," following the teaching of St. Thomas Aquinas, who declared that it was unjust and unlawful to "sell dearer or buy cheaper than a thing is worth."† Usury was also condemned. The pursuit of profit was viewed as both morally corrupting and dangerous to the commonwealth. St. Augustine considered the unlimited lust for gain, *appetitus divitarum infinitus*, as one of the three principal sins, alongside the

*According to Rostovtzeff most new fortunes in Imperial Rome were acquired through speculation. (*History of Rome*, p. 17.) Another historian, Jérôme Carcopino, wrote that during the Empire "work might still ensure a modest living, but no longer yielded such fortunes as the imperial favour or a speculative gamble might bestow . . . speculation was the life-blood of an economic system where production was losing ground day by day and mercantilism was invading everything." (Carcopino, *Daily Life*, p. 80.)

†Aquinas declared that exchange "of money for money or of things for money, not to meet the needs of life, but to acquire gain . . . is justly condemned." (See A. E. Monroe, *Early Economic Thought*, London, 1934, p. 15.)

craving for power and sexual lasciviousness. In his City of God, there was no place for the speculator. When famine threatened, the medieval state intervened to supply food, and speculative hoarding was made illegal. These strictures against profiteering and speculation continue to resonate down the ages. When contemporary politicians rise to condemn the pernicious actions of speculators, they perpetuate unconsciously the Scholastic prejudices of medieval monks.

In the later Middle Ages, several Italian city-states began issuing marketable government securities. In Venice, government securities were traded from the middle of the thirteenth century at the Rialto. Speculation seems to have taken its normal course: In 1351, a law was introduced against rumours intended to sink the price of government funds; in 1390, 1404, and 1410, there were repeated attempts to prevent the sale of government obligations on deferred terms (i.e., bond futures); the Doge and members of the Ducal Council also tried to outlaw "insider trading." State loans also were traded at Florence, Pisa, Verona, and Genoa in the fourteenth century. The Italian city-states farmed out the collection of taxes to *monti*, companies whose capital was divided into tradable shares (*luoghi*). These early joint-stock companies appear strikingly similar to the Roman *publicani.**

The great fairs of Northern Europe, which had their origins in the *fora* and *Bacchanalia* of ancient Rome, enjoyed exemption from many of the medieval restrictions on trade and finance. They became, in effect, prototype stock markets. At the Leipzig fairs, shares in German mines changed hands in the fifteenth century; at the St.-Germain fairs near Paris, which opened after Lent, municipal bonds, bills of exchange, and lottery tickets were traded. Antwerp, with its two lengthy annual fairs in spring and autumn and yearlong permission of free trade, was described as a "continuous fair."[10] In the middle of the sixteenth century, the city gave a

*Fernand Braudel asserts that "all the evidence points to the Mediterranean as the cradle of the stock market." To this we might add that if the Mediterranean was the "cradle," then paternity can be traced to ancient Rome. See F. Braudel, *The Wheels of Commerce*, trans. Siân Reynolds (New York, 1982), p. 101; and R. C. Mueller, *The Venetian Money Market* (Baltimore, 1997), pp. 517–19.

home to the first settled bourse, so named after a gathering of merchants at the Hôtel des Bourses in neighbouring Bruges.

From the middle of the sixteenth century, there is more detailed evidence of speculative market conditions. The financial markets had developed a collective notion of credit (the so-called *ditta di borsa*) and bond prices reflected an anticipation of future events such as defaults. Market manipulation appeared in the 1530s, when a syndicate organised by the Florentine Gaspar Ducci led an attempt to suppress prices in the Lyons market (what we would now call a "bear raid").[11] In the middle of the 1550s there suddenly appeared in the markets of Antwerp and Lyons a speculative enthusiasm for royal loans, which came to an abrupt end when King Henry II of France suspended payments on his debts in 1557.*

On an individual level, we find an Antwerp commodity trader, Christoph Kurz, puzzling at the periodic tightness and ease (*strettezza* and *largezza*) of money in the market. He believed that future prices were divinely ordained and discoverable through astrological observation. People bought when prices were at their highest, because "the upper influences so blind the natural reason with affections or desires." Like a modern technical analyst, Kurz rose early in the morning, surrounded "with work as a man in the ocean with water, for our astrologers aforetime have written much, but with little reason; wherefore I trust not their doctrines but seek mine own rules, and when I have them I search in the histories whether it hath fallen out right or wrong . . ."[12] Later Kurz forsook

*Rubys's *Histoire de Lyons* relates the public's enthusiasm for the French loan, the *Grand Parti*, raised by Henry II at the Easter Fair of Lyons in 1555: "God knows how greed for these excessive gains, disguised by the designation *don gratuit*, lured men on. Every one ran to invest his money in le Grand Parti, the very servants brought their savings. Women sold their ornaments and widows their annuities in order to take shares in le Grand Parti. In short people ran for it as if to see a fire." The loan paid 16 percent, which included a 1 percent quarterly contribution to a sinking fund. It was said to have attracted investors from Switzerland, Germany, and even Turkey. Later the Grand Parti fell to a discount of 85 percent. Given the shaky creditworthiness of sixteenth-century monarchs, these events might be described as the first "junk bond mania." (Ehrenberg, *Capital and Finance*, p. 303.)

the market and enjoyed great professional success as a political astrologer, forecasting among other things the imminent extinction of the papacy.

The development of the capital markets in France and Flanders was interrupted in the second half of the sixteenth century by the Wars of Religion and the Revolt of the Netherlands and a succession of state bankruptcies. After 1557, Lyons went into decay as a financial centre. The sack of Antwerp by Spanish troops in 1585 led to the permanent decline of its bourse. Amsterdam benefited at the expense of Antwerp, as thousands of Protestant and Jewish refugees fled the Spanish, bringing capital and trading skills to the Netherlands. The stimulus provided by these immigrants has led historians to refer to the Dutch "economic miracle" of the 1590s. By the early seventeenth century, the Dutch Republic was the most advanced and thriving economy in Europe. Its merchants encircled the globe, buying wood in Norway, sugar in the West Indies, tobacco in Maryland, investing in forges in Wales or estates in Sweden, farming the Russian Tsar's export monopolies, and supplying Spanish America with slaves.[13]

Although the Dutch did not invent the institutions and practices of financial capitalism such as banking, double-entry bookkeeping, joint-stock companies, bills of exchange, and stock markets, they brought together and established them on a secure basis in a mercantile economy organised around a highly evolved profit motive.[14] In 1602, the United East India Company, the first joint-stock company to receive an official government charter, was established with a monopoly on Eastern trade. Nineteen years later, the Dutch West India Company was founded to exploit commercial opportunities in the Americas. Europe's first central bank, the Amsterdam Wisselbank, an institution derived from the Casa San Giorgio in Genoa, was established in 1609. Highly conservative in its operations, the Wisselbank paid no interest on deposits, issued notes only against its gold holdings, and made no loans. Yet its existence allowed Dutch merchants across the globe to settle their accounts bills in a universally accepted currency.[15] The Dutch city authorities raised funds through bond issues and lotteries which attracted great popular interest. By the early seventeenth century, capital from across Europe was invested in a variety of Dutch financial assets, from property to annuities, municipal bonds, bills of exchange, and medium-term loans. Amsterdam was not simply a great entrepôt, it was the financial capital of the world.

All manner of financial products and services were traded on the Amsterdam Exchange (a New Exchange was founded in 1610): "commodities, current exchange, shareholdings, maritime insurance . . . [it was] a money market, a finance market, [and] a stock market."[16] Naturally, the Exchange became a crucible for speculative activities. Futures contracts—agreements to deliver or take delivery of a commodity at a fixed price some date in the future—were common. Since the previous century, futures had been traded in a variety of commodities, including grain, herring, spices, whale oil, sugar, copper, saltpetre, and Italian silks. In the early seventeenth century, they became available in the *actions* (shares) of the East India Company. Speculators could also take out loans on shares at up to four-fifths of their market value (what Americans later called "margin loans"). Stock options—which gave the buyer the right, but unlike the futures contract not the obligation, to buy or sell shares at a fixed price during the contract period—were also traded on the Exchange. Later in the century, *ducaton* shares in the East India Company were introduced; valued at a tenth of the highly priced ordinary shares, they enabled less wealthy speculators to play the market.[17] Futures, options, and *ducaton* shares are all examples of what we call derivatives, namely financial contracts which *derive* their value from an underlying asset, such as a share. Together with stock loans, they created the opportunity for financial leverage, so that small rises in share prices brought larger percentage gains to speculators (with small price declines producing the opposite effect).*

*Leverage in stock derivatives can be explained with reference to a stock option. If we assume a share trades at $100 and an option to buy the share at that price costs $5, then a 10 percent rise in the share price (to 110) will be accompanied by a rise in the value of the option to $10 (i.e., a 100 percent rise from its purchase price).

VEGA'S *CONFUSION*

The first description of stock market activity in Western Europe is provided by Joseph Penso de la Vega in his *Confusion de Confusiones,* written in Spanish (Vega was a Marrano Jew) and published in Amsterdam in 1688. In a series of dialogues between a merchant and a shareholder, he describes the stock market as a madhouse, full of strange superstitions, peculiar practices, and compulsive attractions. *Confusion* provides a definitive picture of the speculative psychology.

The "game [of speculation] is an affair of fools," whose participants show a tendency to ritualistic playfulness:

> A member of the Exchange opens his hand and another takes it, and thus sells a number of shares at a fixed price, which is confirmed by a second handshake. With a new handshake a further item is offered, and then follows a bid. The hands redden from the blows (I believe from the shame that even the most respected people do business in such an indecent manner as with blows). The handshakes are followed by shouting, the shouting by insults, the insults by impudence and more insults, shouting, pushes, and handshakes until the business is finished.*

In the *Compleat Gamester,* first published in London in 1674 and attributed to the poet Charles Cotton, gambling is described as "an enchanting witchery, gotten between idleness and vice; an itching disease, that makes some scratch the head, whilst others, as if bitten by a tarantula, are laughing themselves to death; or, lastly it is a

*Compare Vega's picture of speculators in *Confusion* with a recent description of traders at an American stock exchange: "Gathered in a close ring the traders shake their fists in each other's faces, faces torqued tight, twisted . . . Shouting gets more intense, roaring and echoing despite the sound-absorbing tiles, as the decibels crash in waves and the ears ache from the noise. Fingers flail; arms thrust; the ring knots, bunches, turns . . . A tall spectator waves two fingers, three, shakes his head, nods, waggles his hand just above his hair." (Vega, *Confusion,* p. 21; Gregory Millman, *Around the World on a Trillion Dollars a Day,* London, 1995, p. 2.)

paralytic distemper, which seizing the arm, the man cannot chuse but shake the elbow . . . it renders a man incapable of prosecuting any serious action, and makes him always unsatisfied with his own condition; he is either lifted up to the top of mad joy with success, or plunged to the bottom of despair by misfortune; always in extremes, always in a storm . . . and, as he is transported as he wins, so losing, is tost upon billows of a high swelling passion, till he hath lost sight of both sense and reason."[18] The same mentality was found on the Amsterdam bourse. Vega describes the obsessive-compulsive behaviour of a speculator invoking his luck; he "wavers as to how best to secure a profit, chews his nails, pulls his fingers, closes his eyes, takes four paces and four times talks to himself, raises his hand to his cheek as if he has a toothache, puts on a thoughtful countenance, sticks out a finger, rubs his brow, and all this accompanied by a mysterious coughing as though he could force the hand of fortune."[19] Some speculators are said to be of such a "nervous condition," and their behaviour so restless and fixated, that "even on their deathbed, their last worries are the shares." Many exhibit signs of split personality: "There are many occasions," Vega observes, "in which every speculator seems to have two bodies, so that astonished observers see a human being fighting himself."[20]

Like later stock markets, the Amsterdam bourse in the seventeenth century was dominated by a perpetual conflict between bulls and bears.* Vega contrasted the *liefhebbers* ("lifters-up" or bulls), who were "scared of nothing," with the *contremines* ("underminers" or bears), who were "completely ruled by fear, trepidation, and nervousness." The *contremines* were said to organise themselves into *cabala* (i.e., bear pools) in order to drive prices down. Speculation for a fall was not new to the Amsterdam Exchange of Vega's day.

*The English term "bear," describing "a speculator for a fall," originated in the well-known proverb "to sell the bear's skin before one has caught the bear" (i.e., to contract to sell what you did not as yet own). Defoe in *Anatomy of Exchange Alley*, first published in 1719, refers to "buyers of Bear-skins." The associated "bull," derived from the German verb stem *büllen*, meaning "to roar," appears somewhat later and was perhaps suggested by *bear*. The earliest reference to a bull, as "one who endeavours by speculative purchases, or otherwise, to raise the price of stocks," is found in Charles Johnson's *Country Lasses* (1715): "You deal in Bears and Bulls" (*Oxford English Dictionary*).

Back in 1609, the Flemish-born merchant Isaac Le Maire had organised a bear raid on the Exchange to drive down the price of East India stock.[†] Although his manipulation ended in failure, it led to an edict outlawing sales by speculators who did not at the time own the stock but expected to buy it back cheaper—"cover their shorts"—at a later date. As with most subsequent antispeculative legislation, the ban was roundly ignored.

Vega's stock market was far from being a forum for rational price adjustments. Speculators were, in his words, "full of instability, insanity, pride, and foolishness. They will sell without knowing the motive; they will buy without reason." Their behaviour produced undue movements in stock prices: "the expectation of an event creates a much deeper impression upon the exchange than the event itself."[21] Only the shrewd observer, "who makes it his business to watch these things conscientiously, without blind passion and irritating stubbornness, will hit upon the right thing innumerable times, though not always." Despite all its faults, the market retained a sinister attraction for Vega: "He who has [once] entered the [charmed] circle of the Exchange is in eternal agitation and sits in a prison, the key of which lies in the ocean and the bars of which are never opened . . ."[22]

Vega's speculators exhibit many of the features associated with the full range of manic-depressive behaviour. A manic-depressive experiences violent and uncontrollable mood swings. During his manic phase, he is energetic, grandiose, greedy, sexual, distractible, persuasive, exuding charm and exercising an infectious leadership over others, and above all optimistic. As his expectations grow increasingly unrealistic, the manic becomes careless and this precipitates his downfall. His moods are cyclical, and during a depression he becomes timid, anxious, enervated, shy, indecisive, and lacking in self-confidence. Unable to see the broader picture, he becomes fixated on insignificant details.

---

*Le Maire had been earlier involved in the establishment of the East India Company and was apparently driven to speculation by the need to feed his large family of twenty-four children. For his bear raid, he was provided with information by the company's treasurer—the first individual case of "insider trading" in the stock market known to the author. In 1621, the Dutch made a further attempt to outlaw short sales and the trade in stock futures.

As the stock market itself is, like Hobbes's Leviathan, composed of the actions of individual speculators, these neurotic traits can be found in the mass psychology of bull and bear markets.* During the bull or manic phase, activity is frenetic and expectations become unrealistic.† On the other hand, when the mood of the market is *depressed*, activity—measured by stock market turnover—is lethargic, and universal pessimism replaces unrealistic optimism. According to Benjamin Graham, the author of *The Intelligent Investor*, "Mr. Market lets his enthusiasms or his fears run away with him." Graham's disciple, the investor Warren Buffett, elaborates this description of Mr. Market's instability: "At times he feels euphoric and can see only the favorable factors affecting the business . . . At other times he is depressed and can see nothing but trouble ahead for both the business and the world."[23] The tendency of the market to produce excessive swings can be ignored for investment purposes, as Graham and Buffett advise; or it can form the basis for speculation, as was the successful practice of the nineteenth-century economist David Ricardo, who "made money by observing that people in general exaggerated the importance of events. If, therefore, dealing as he dealt in stocks, there was reason for a small advance, he bought, because he was certain the unreasonable advance would enable him to realise; so when stocks were falling, he sold in the conviction that alarm and panic would produce a decline not warranted by circumstances."[24]

TULIPOMANIA

Conditions in the Dutch Republic in the 1630s were propitious for an outburst of speculative euphoria. It was a period of rising com-

*The journalist Mike Royko has described the market as a manic-depressive: "*The Market.* All you have to do is look at the headlines or listen to the daily broadcasts and you think you are hearing the latest medical report on someone who ought to be in therapy, on tranquilizers, or strapped down by attendants. It sounds like a manic-depressive psycho head case." (*Chicago Tribune*, 16 October 1989, reprinted in Charles D. Ellis and James R. Vertin, eds., *The Investor's Anthology*, New York, 1997, p. 58.)

†According to James Grant, "in bull markets there is no clear demarcation between progress and fantasy." *Minding Mr. Market* (New York, 1993), p. xvii.

mercial optimism, owing partly to the final extinction of the Spanish military threat and partly to the booming Dutch textile trade, which profited from the turmoil in Central Europe at the beginning of the Thirty Years' War. The Amsterdam bourse had moved into a new building in 1631. The East India Company was profitably developing its settlement in Batavia and its shares rose faster than at any time during the century.[25] House prices were also climbing sharply, producing a boom in the construction of suburban mansions. The Dutch Republic lost some of its Calvinist austerity as its people, who enjoyed the highest incomes in Europe, became a nation of consumers. In the tulip, they found an object which enabled them to mix their love of display with the avid pursuit of wealth.

The intense feeling of the Dutch for flowers can partly be explained by the geography of the Netherlands, whose flat terrain and rich soil provided the perfect ground for the cultivation of bulbs, while a shortage of space allowed for only modest gardens, arranged in tiny parterres, at the centre of which were planted prize flowers whose bright colours set off the drabness of the surrounding countryside. Most prized of all flowers was the tulip. In the middle of the sixteenth century, the Imperial Ambassador to Suleiman the Magnificent, Ogier Ghislaine de Busbecq, introduced the first tulip bulbs into Europe from Turkey (its name came from the Turkish *tulipan*, meaning a turban). During its early years in Western Europe, the tulip was confined to the gardens of the nobility and specialist botanists. A few years after Busbecq's return, tulips were observed in the Augsburg garden of the Fuggers, an exotic horticultural novelty for Europe's wealthiest banking dynasty. In 1573, the ambassador presented some tulip bulbs to the famous Dutch botanist Carolus Clusius, who distributed them and described the flower in his *Rariorum plantarum historia.* Clusius, who is said to have charged an enormous price for the sale of his tulip bulbs, became the first victim of the growing passion for this rare plant when one night his bulbs were dug up and stolen.

Collectors classified the tulip varieties according to the colouring of their flowers and gave them splendid militaristic titles to reflect their position in the horticultural hierarchy. At the head of the bulbous troop came the Semper Augustus with its petals streaked in imperial purple; it was followed by Viceroys, Admirals, and Generals. From the time of their earliest appearance tulips had been associated with wealth and in the first quarter of the seventeenth century the more exotic varieties began to attract extravagant prices. In 1624, a Semper Augustus fetched the handsome sum of 1,200 florins, an amount sufficient to purchase a small Amsterdam town house. Ten years earlier, an emblem book by Roemer Visscher was published which contained an engraving of two tulips bearing the prescient motto: "a fool and his money are soon parted."[26]

The tulip lent itself to speculation: uncertainty surrounding its variegations (which, unknown to contemporaries, were caused by a virus that attacked the bulb) opened up a game of chance. A plain breeder tulip might break out into a precious Semper Augustus. The bulbs were relatively easy to cultivate, required little land, and there were no guilds restricting entry into the trade. Those who could not afford to purchase the expensive shares of the great joint-stock companies could instead wager on a bulb. In the past, the market in tulips had taken place during the summer period when the bulbs were out of the ground. As popular interest in tulips grew, arrangements were made for them to be traded throughout the year. The growers marked the rows of bulbs, each bulb was given a number recording its variety and weight at planting, and the individual bulb's trading history was stored on a separate sheet. Precious varieties were sold by the piece, weighed by the *aas* or ace (one twentieth of a gram), while commoner types were sold by the flower bed. The tulip had become as standardised and undifferentiated as a note of the Wisselbank or a share in the East India Company.

The beginning of the *tulpenwoerde*, or what the Victorians called the tulipomania, is associated with the arrival in the tulip market around 1634 of outsiders who were apparently attracted by stories of rising prices for tulip bulbs in Paris and northern France.[27] Among these entrants to the market—later dismissed by Dutch florists as the "new amateurs"—were weavers, spinners, cobblers, bakers, grocers, and peasants. Although the tulip craze grew to embrace most social classes, two parties were absent who might otherwise have brought stability to the trade. The wealthy amateur bulb collectors, who had long shown a readiness to pay vast sums for the rarer varieties, withdrew their custom as prices began to soar, while the great Amsterdam merchants continued investing their trading profits in town houses, East India stock, or bills of exchange—for them, tulips remained merely an expression of wealth, not a means to that end.

The nature of the tulip market changed as the traffic increased. Private negotiations between individuals gave way to informal meetings in the rooms of inns, called Colleges, where traders and speculators could trade in convivial surroundings. A contemporary pamphlet, containing three dialogues between a speculator Gaergoedt (Greedy-Goods) and his friend Waermondt (True-Mouth), introduces the business to the neophyte tulip speculator:

> You must go to an Inn [says Gaergoedt]; I will name a few. I know of few or none, where there are no companies or colleges. Being there, you must ask whether there are any florists. If you then come into their room and because you are a newcomer some will squeak like a duck. Some will say, "A new whore in the brothel," and so on, but don't take any notice; that goes with it. Your name will be put down on a slate. Now the plates go round. That is, everyone who is present at this company has to give plates, beginning with the one at the top of the slate. He who holds the plate must ask for some goods. You may not put up on auction your own goods, but if you drop a hint in conversation, and somebody is interested, you are almost sure to have it bid for or to get the plates on it.

There were two methods of dealing: direct negotiation between two persons or general auction. The former method, called "with the plates" (described above), involved both buyer and seller inscribing an agreed price for a bulb on wooden plates provided by the College. Auctions were referred to as "in the naught" since the seller set a starting price by writing a figure in the middle of a slate circled with a zero. A commission of up to three guilders for "wine money" was paid by the buyer to the College, which was spent on tobacco, alcohol, light, and heating. Pleasure was mixed with profit: "I have been on several journeys," related Gaergoedt, "when I brought home more money than I brought to the inn. And then I had eaten and drunk wine, beer, tobacco, cooked or roast fish, meat, even fowls and rabbits and sweets to finish, and that from the morning till three or four at night . . . and I made a beautiful profit too."[28] Speculators who took their profits or were confident of receiving their dues spent their gains on new coaches and horses. "All grandeurs were imagined. No one knew how high he would rise in his estate."[29]

No actual delivery of tulips took place during the height of the boom in late 1636 and early 1637 as the bulbs remained snug in the ground. A market in tulip futures appeared, known as the *windhandel* (the wind trade): sellers promised to deliver a bulb of a certain type and weight the following spring, buyers took the right to delivery—in the meantime, cash settlement could be made for any difference in market price. Most transactions were expedited with personal credit notes which also fell due in the spring when the bulbs would be dug up and delivered. Gaergoedt boasts of having made 60,000 guilders from his tulip speculations but admits that he has only received "other people's writing." By the later stages of the mania the fusion of the *windhandel* with paper credit created a perfect symmetry of insubstantiality: most transactions were for tulip bulbs that could never be delivered because they didn't exist and were paid for with credit notes that could never be honoured because the money wasn't there.

The average annual wage in Holland was between 200 and 400 guilders. A small town house cost around 300 guilders and the best flower paintings sold for no more than a 1,000 guilders.* Against these values we can measure the extravagance of tulip prices. According to the *Dialogues*, a Gouda bulb of four aces rose from 20 to 225 guilders; a Generalissimo of ten aces which had sold for 95 guilders fetched 900 guilders; a pound of plain yellow Croenen which sold for around 20 guilders rose in a few weeks to over 1,200 (i.e., the price went from the equivalent of one month's pay to five years'). "Yes," Gaergoedt admits, "it has gone so far that the stuff which used to be weeded and thrown in basketfuls on the dung heap has been sold for heavy money."[30] The Semper Augustus retained its position as the most prized bulb. Gaergoedt relates how "about three years ago, it was sold for 2,000 guilders, transferred

*Taylor, *Dutch Flower Painting*, p. 5. Taylor states that the floral arrangements in still-life paintings became so expensive that artists were obliged to share the same flowers.

at once at the Bank," but at the height of the boom it might sell for "even 6,000 and possibly more, even if it be a plant of only 200 aces."[31] A Viceroy that formerly sold for 3,000 guilders doubled in price. A contemporary pamphleteer calculated that the 2,500 guilders paid for a single bulb would have bought twenty-seven tons of wheat, fifty tons of rye, four fat oxen, eight fat pigs, twelve fat sheep, two hogsheads of wine, four tuns of beer, two tons of butter, three tons of cheese, a bed with linen, a wardrobe of clothes, and a silver beaker.* There was little attempt to justify these prices—most speculators entered into contracts with the intention of selling quickly at a higher price. When Gaergoedt advises Waermondt to speculate, he tells him that "you give no money till it's summer, and then you have sold all your stuff."[32] Asked how long the madness will last, Gaergoedt replies: "if it only goes on for two or three years, it is sufficient for me . . ."[33] An anonymous pamphleteer, however, expressed reservations: "if there should ever be more sellers than buyers, which given the number of people involved could easily occur, then the collapse of this mania will be at hand."[34]

On 3 February 1637, the tulip market suddenly crashed. There was no clear reason for the panic except that spring was approaching when delivery fell due and the game would be up. In Haarlem, the centre of the flower trade, rumours circulated that there were no more buyers, and the next day tulips were unsaleable at any price. Contracts were not settled, and one default followed another. The professional florists attempted in vain to extract payment from defaulting speculators.† However, the collapse of the Tulip Mania did not cause a national economic crisis. N. W. Posthumus, the historian of the Tulip Mania, refers to a more modest "upheaval in the whole western part of the Republic."[35] The great merchants, upon

*Sometimes payment was made in part exchange. Gaergoedt describes the sale of "one Branbanson Spoor of 370 aces, for 700 gld., on condition of receiving 200 gld., a cabinet cupboard, made of ebony with a multiple glass in it, and a big picture, being a pot of flowers." (Taylor, *Dutch Flower Painting*, p. 10; and Posthumus, "Tulip Mania," p. 458.)

†Later in the summer, six Haarlem florists recorded a complaint with their lawyer: "They have themselves traded extensively, selling and buying, importing for many thousands, but delivery and payment not being made by many and several, but a few honest people compromised by paying one, two, three, four, yes, even five, which was the utmost, out of a hundred." (Posthumus, "Tulip Mania," p. 464.)

whose credit the economy depended, were largely unaffected. But many of the lower orders were not so fortunate. Those who had mortgaged their properties and exchanged their chattels for a chance of quick gain, must have suffered a permanent loss of wealth. A few individual instances of ruin are recorded, including that of the landscape painter Jan van Goyen, who on the eve of the crash had exchanged 900 guilders and two paintings for a quantity of bulbs—he died insolvent nineteen years later.[36]

Litigation in the tulip market continued until, finally, in May 1638, a government commission declared that tulip contracts could be anulled on payment of 3.5 percent of the agreed price.[37] By this date, amateur bulb collectors had returned to market to pick up rare bulbs at bargain prices, and within a few years the prices of precious tulips, including the Semper Augustus, regained the levels they had traded at prior to the mania. However, the prices for the plain breeder bulbs—known as the *gemeene goed* (common goods) and *vodderij* (rags)—which had attracted the smaller speculators during the boom, never recovered.

BLOWING BUBBLES: THE ALLEGORIES AND LEGENDS OF SPECULATION

In the aftermath of the crisis, tulipomania gave way to tulipophobia—a revulsion analogous to the public distaste for common stocks after the Great Crash of 1929. The professor of botany at Leyden, Evrard Forstius, was said to be so incensed by the flower that he could not see a tulip without attacking it viciously with his stick.[38] By offering reward without effort, the speculative mania had violated the Calvinist work ethic. As Waermondt asked in the *Dialogues*:

> what need is there for merchants to have any style, or to risk their goods overseas, for the children to learn a trade, for peasants to sow and to work so hard on the soil, for the skipper to sail on the terrible and dangerous seas, for the soldier to risk his life for so little gain, if one can make profits of this sort?[39]

Furthermore, by raising some to riches and reducing others to penury, speculation had unsettled relations between the various social classes. According to Gaergoedt, "each [speculator] was a bigger master than the other."* Just as the tulip was well adapted to serve as an object of financial speculation, it now came to represent luxury, wickedness, and superfluity alongside the traditional images of skulls, hourglasses, and books in the allegorical depictions of Dutch *vanitas* painters. The tulip became the symbol of folly in the sense anticipated by Visscher's emblem, its ephemeral beauty seen as a seductive illusion to the unwary.[40] Another common *vanitas* symbol was the bubble, which represented the evanescence of human life: *Homo bulla est,* man is a bubble, the Roman moralist Varro had declared. A bubble grew rapidly, delighting beholders with its reflective brilliance, but disappeared instantaneously. It was sustained only by air or wind, a symbolism recognised both in the seventeenth-century Dutch expression *windhandel* to describe the futures trade and in a contemporary *tulpenwoerde* print depicting the allegorical figure of Flora blown in a wind chariot, and later in the stockbroker's nefarious practise of "puffing up a share."† The bubble metaphor, however, was not applied to speculative excesses until the time of the South Sea Bubble in 1720. In the meantime, the tulip served an identical function: It burst forth in glorious colours, just as suddenly its petals blew off, and the plant withered, only to return with the next cycle of nature.

---

*According to Simon Schama, after the collapse of the mania the Dutch authorities "felt impelled to launch a didactic campaign in tracts, sermons and prints against the folly, since its special wickedness had led the people astray." (*The Embarrassment of Riches: An Interpretation of Dutch Culture in the Golden Age* [London, 1987], p. 362.)

†Schama describes the allegorical print by Crispijn van de Pas, the younger, entitled *Floraes Mallewagen* (Flora's Car of Fools), which portrays the figure of Flora reclining in a wind chariot (representing both a *vanitas* allegory and a satire on the *windhandel*), accompanied by her associates Lekkebard (Sweet Beard) holding a flask to his mouth and drinking to gullible Graagryk (Eager for Wealth) and Leegwagen (Travelling Light). Also seated in the chariot are two girls, one weighing bulbs while the other (named Idle Hope) releases a bird, a symbol denoting the loss of innocence. Behind the chariot follow the people clamouring to come on board. The road is strewn with broken tulips, while in the background a preceding wind chariot is shown sinking beneath the waves. (*Embarrassment,* pp. 327, 364.)

A number of legends developed around the Tulip Mania. The most famous of them provided the inspiration for Alexandre Dumas's novel *The Black Tulip*:

> A syndicate of Haarlem florists, hearing that a cobbler at The Hague had succeeded in growing a black tulip, visited him and after some haggling purchased the bulb for fifteen hundred florins. No sooner was it in their possession than they threw it on the ground and trampled it underfoot. "Idiot!" cried one of them when the astonished cobbler began to protest; "we have a black tulip, too, and chance will never favour you again. We would have given you ten thousand florins if you had asked for it." The wretched cobbler, inconsolable at the thought of the wealth which might have been his, took to his bed and promptly expired.[41]

This legend—it is impossible to cultivate a black tulip, the closest achievable colour being dark brown—reflects the corruption and cupidity that the Tulip Mania provoked. The Black Tulip and a number of other legends from later periods have entered the popular history of speculation. Out of the Mississippi Bubble came stories of lackeys who rose to fortune so rapidly that when they picked up their new coaches, they forgot themselves and mounted to their old accustomed postilion positions. Another tale from the same period relates how a doctor, while taking the pulse of an elderly female patient, murmurs to himself, "Oh good God, it falls, it falls," nearly scaring the lady to death, who is only saved when she discovers that he is referring to the Mississippi stock rather than her heartbeat.* From the South Sea Bubble and the Great Crash of 1929 came exaggerated tales of speculators' suicides.[42]

---

*A similar legend derives from the land speculation fever in Chicago in the 1830s, which centred on lots of land sold by the Illinois and Chicago Canal: A physician busy selling town lots was reluctantly called away to visit a sick lady and hurriedly wrote a prescription before proceeding to leave: "Why, Doctor," the lady called after him, "you don't state here how I shall take the medicine." "Oh," he called back over his shoulder, "Canal terms. One-quarter down, and the balance in one, two, and three years." (John Philip Wood, *The Life of John Law of Lauriston*, Edinburgh, 1824, p. 51; and A. M. Sakolski, *The Great American Land Bubble*, New York, 1932, p. 249.)

These tales constitute the folklore of the financial markets, which, feeding on rumour, are particularly fertile grounds for their cultivation. Like the medieval *exempla*, the legends contain parables of the Seven Deadly Sins (pride, wrath, envy, lust, gluttony, avarice, and sloth) along with the folly that springs from human credulity. They reflect a popular distrust of the morally corrosive effects of speculation. Financial manias were seen as upsetting the social order (lackeys buying coaches), enfeebling the work ethic (hence the tale of the doctor's dereliction), and bringing ruin to the people. The bubble legends continue to serve an admonitory purpose, warning of the snare of speculation. The British journalist Christopher Fildes recently reminded readers of the *Spectator* (19 July 1996) that people who purchased houses at the top of the market in the late 1980s "have learned the hard way what a dangerous illusion a housing boom can be, and it seems rather soon to forget. Indeed, in any market, fallen favourites never quite come back. *Even today, in Holland, there is no great demand for black tulips*" (italics added). For speculators down the ages the message of the legends remains clear: Remember the Black Tulip! Remember the bodies lying beneath the skyscrapers! And beware!

AN AFFAIR OF FOOLS?

The presence of the tulip legends in a number of popular historical and financial books—including Thomas Babington Macaulay's *History of England*, Walter Bagehot's *Lombard Street*, and Charles Mackay's best-selling account of speculative manias, *Extraordinary Popular Delusions and the Madness of Crowds* (1841)—has led some to question whether a "mania" for tulips ever really existed.[43] Peter Garber, an American economist, has claimed that the falsity of the tulip legends undermines the credibility of the mania. He also argues that contemporary source material for the episode, including the *Dialogues of Waermondt and Gaergoedt*, should be seen as government propaganda and treated with scepticism. Instead of a mania, he claims, the tulip speculation was rational. In this view, the high prices for the more exotic flowers could be justified on the grounds that the mother bulb's offshoots would compensate for any subsequent decline in price. He also finds that the price changes for tulips conformed to a common pattern found for other precious flower bulbs: the first bulbs of a fashionable new variety sell for a premium price, but the price declines rapidly as the flower becomes more common, or as new varieties are introduced in competition. In eighteenth-century Holland, hyacinths also enjoyed a brief period of popularity when their prices soared. According to this thesis, the so-called mania for tulips reflected no more than a blip in demand for a modish commodity whose price was anyhow volatile.

This bold attempt at historical revisionism does not withstand scrutiny. Garber's aim is to lend support to the "efficient market" school of economic thought, which suggests that bubbles or manias cannot exist since market prices, whether of stocks or tulips, always reflect their intrinsic value.* Yet the *Dialogues* give the impression of being a balanced and analytical account of the tulip market in the 1630s. Their method of narration—a discourse between two fictional characters—was a conventional device for recording events. Although they carry a moralising antispeculative message, they do not contain any of the tulip legends which are related with such relish by Charles Mackay and others. Even if one were to accept that the *Dialogues* were issued for propaganda purposes, this presupposes a need for propaganda, namely a postspeculative crisis.

Nor can the high prices for tulip bulbs have reflected the "rational expectations" of investors, since it was not known until the twentieth century that the variegated tulip petals were the result of a virus which attacked the bulb. The bulbous offshoots of a Semper Augustus would neither flower nor produce further offshoots for several years and there was no guarantee that they would exhibit the special qualities of the mother bulb, since they were just as likely to revert to the plain breeder variety. Tulips did not even produce an annual cash yield (or "dividend"), because there was no trade in cut flowers at the time. Furthermore, the pattern of

*Garber had a special motive for revising the historical account of the Tulip Mania. His paper was published shortly after the October 1987 crash and was written with the intention of heading off proposed government regulation of the stock futures markets.

sharp price rises and declines that Garber finds for other flower types, such as hyacinths, does not disprove the existence of a tulip bubble. On the contrary, one might argue that the existence of later "bubbles" suggests that the Dutch flower market, like the stock market, was particularly susceptible to outbursts of speculative euphoria. Even Garber concedes that the prices of the common breeder bulbs—which increased twentyfold during the last phase of the boom—rose to "unexplainable" heights (he ascribes this to an outbreak of bubonic plague at the time which created an apocalyptic mentality and stimulated a brief spasm of speculation not justified by "market fundamentals"). We would go further and state that the purchase of any tulip bulb, whether variegated or plain, in the winter of 1636 could only be justified by the *hope*—not a rational expectation—that the bulb could be sold quickly at a higher price to some "greater fool." In short, the term "speculative mania" aptly describes conditions of the Dutch tulip market in the mid-1630s.

The trade in tulips was for many participants an alternative to speculation in company shares. In several ways the tulip and stock markets resembled each other. The great variety of tulip bulbs calls to mind the multitude of shares found in later stock markets, with the highly priced variegated bulbs playing the role of blue chips (like the so-called nifty fifty stocks of the early 1970s) and the common breeder bulbs resembling the penny stocks which attract speculators of limited means.* The *windhandel* in tulips was identical to the futures business at the Amsterdam Exchange (although Mackay's claims that tulips were traded on the Exchange is not accurate), and the style of trading at the tulip Colleges anticipated the share auctions in the New York stock market in the early nineteenth century.

The course of the Tulip Mania was similar to that of many later stock market manias. Just as the Tulip Mania was initially stimulated by a price rise for precious bulbs which attracted new entrants into the market, so stock market booms are commonly triggered by a sharp climb in the share prices of a particular sector—whether

*Incidentally, the term "blue chip" derives from the colour of the most expensive gambling chip at the Monte Carlo casinos.

railway stocks in the 1840s or motorcars in the 1920s—which entices outsiders to speculate. It is another common feature of bull markets that as a mania progresses, the quality of the stocks that attract speculation declines—a rising tide floats all ships, even the most unseaworthy. The *tulpenwoerde* was no different: speculation in the Semper Augustus bulbs gave way to a manic trade in breeder bulbs. Several other features of Tulip Mania are common to later stock market booms: rumours fuelling the boom, the rapid growth of leverage through the use of futures and paper credit, conspicuous consumption among speculators, sharply rising prices followed by sudden panic without cause, and initial government passivity followed by belated intervention.

The Austrian economist J. A. Schumpeter observed that speculative manias commonly occur at the inception of a new industry or technology when people overestimate the potential gains and too much capital is attracted to new ventures. Perhaps the speculators of the 1630s, entranced by the novelty of the tulip, were anticipating the development of the Dutch flower industry, now the largest in the world. If so, as with many later speculators, their foresight was not to be rewarded financially. As James Buchan observes, the vision of speculators is vitiated by their delusive conception of time: "The great stock market bull seeks to condense the future into a few days, to discount the long march of history, and capture the present value of all the future."[44] More often than not, the future turns out to be less tractable than the speculator would wish.

Perhaps the closest parallel to the Tulip Mania is provided by the Kuwaiti Souq Al-Manakh bubble of the early 1980s, which similarly demonstrates the effects of an excessive issue of paper credit in a speculative market. In the Kuwaiti stock market, speculation in the shares of local "Gulf companies" (whose interests ranged from property to poultry farming) was conducted by means of personal credit in the form of postdated cheques similar to the credit notes of the tulip speculators. In the first eight months of 1982, over 3,500 million shares changed hands with a market value of $6 billion (their book value was only $200 million). The outstanding value of deferred cheques exceeded $90 billion despite interest rates climbing to over 300 percent. Just as settlement for credit notes of the tulip speculators was delayed until spring, so the Kuwaiti cheques did not fall due until the end of the year. In the early spring of 1982, share prices commonly doubled by the hour and no price was considered too high to pay for a share. In August, however, a female speculator asked for her cheque to be cashed early. The spell was broken and the market crashed. The government was forced to step in to restore order at a cost of billions of dollars, contracts made during the boom were annulled, and the market was closed down.

THE CARNIVAL OF SPECULATION

An engraving entitled *Flora's Cap of Fools* by the Dutch artist Pieter Nolpe, published shortly after the demise of the Tulip Mania, depicts tulip dealers haggling inside a giant fool's coxcomb. During the American bull market of the 1990s, the most popular on-line investment forum has been *The Motley Fool*: its young founders wear coxcombs in public as they propose their "Foolery" as a path to stock market riches in place of the "wisdom" of Wall Street. This reappearance of the fool in the imagery of speculation is not fortuitous. Speculation grew out of the crowds and bustle of the Renaissance fairs and carnivals, and although by the seventeenth century the carnival was in decline and fairs had been replaced by permanent stock exchanges, the carnival spirit lingered in the markets.

Gambling was prevalent at carnivals and fairs. It was a typical carnival activity, both profane and antihierarchic: in the face of fortune, social distinction counts for nothing and everyone becomes equal. The carnival was accompanied by what the Russian literary critic Mikhail Bakhtin called a "grotesque realism," which involved the parodic degradation of values as everything spiritual was transferred to a material level. The *Liturgy of the Gamblers* was often found among the parodical texts. Carnival language was irreverent and obscene, it was the language of Billingsgate (the London fish market) which remains the vernacular of stock markets to this day. The carnival spirit of equality also suffused the exchanges. As Vega writes in *Confusion de Confusiones* (itself a parodic carnivalistic title), "a witty man, observing the business on the Exchange, the studied impoliteness there, remarked that the gamble on the Exchange was like death in that it made all people equal."[45]

While the spirit of carnivalism endures in the stock market, the speculative mania represents a continuation of the carnival proper.* Both carnival and mania produced "the world turned upside down." The carnival offered a moment of release from the rigidities and religious demands of the medieval world, when the traditional social hierarchy was inverted and the village idiot became carnival king. Although the modern market economy is far freer than its medieval antecedent, it has created new tensions. While the carnival deliberately undermined the authority of the Church, the speculative mania reverses the nostrums of capitalism such as devotion to a professional calling, honesty, thrift, and hard grind. Like the carnival, it provides only a temporary release since when the mania collapses these values are reinforced.

The medieval carnival was a cyclical event occurring in a special time divorced from daily realities—the French historian Emmanuel LeRoy Ladurie refers to what he calls the "orgasmic interim" of the carnival.[46] The time of the speculative mania is also both cyclical and abnormal—afterwards speculators recall it as unreal and dreamlike. For Bakhtin, the carnival is "linked to moments of crisis, of breaking points in the cycle of nature or in the life of society and man. Moments of death and revival, of change and renewal, always lead to a festive perception of the world."[47] This accords with Schumpeter's observation that speculative manias generally appear during periods of profound economic upheaval. The Dionysiac aspect of the carnival survives in the conspicuous consumption and revelry of speculators. Both carnival and speculative mania end in similar fashion. Order is restored after the carnival by the symbolic burning of the carnival king in effigy. After the mania, the leading speculators—from John Law of the Mississippi Company in 1720 to Michael Milken, the junk bond king, in 1990—are pilloried, stripped of their wealth, and imprisoned. Like the carnival king, they become scapegoats for the sins of the community and are sacrificed so that normality can return.

*The phrase "carnival of speculation" has been applied to both the New York gold market in the 1860s and the 1920s bull market on Wall Street. (See William Fowler, *Ten Years of Wall Street*, Hartford, 1870, p. 387; and Gordon Thomas and Max Morgan-Witts, *The Day the Bubble Burst*, London, 1979, p. 152.)

The spirit of speculation is anarchic, irreverent, and antihierarchic. It loves freedom, detests cant, and abhors restrictions. From the tulip Colleges of the seventeenth century to the Internet investment clubs of the late twentieth century, speculation has established itself as the most demotic of economic activities. Although profoundly secular, speculation is not simply about greed. The essence of speculation remains a Utopian yearning for freedom and equality which counterbalances the drab rationalistic materialism of the modern economic system with its inevitable inequalities of wealth. Throughout its many manifestations, the speculative mania has always been, and remains to this day, the Carnival of Capitalism, a "Feast of Fools."

CHAPTER 2

STOCKJOBBING IN 'CHANGE ALLEY: THE PROJECTING AGE OF THE 1690s

Nowhere does history indulge in repetitions so often or so uniformly as in Wall Street. When you read contemporary accounts of booms or panics, the one thing that strikes you most forcibly is how little either stock speculation or stock speculators today differ from yesterday. The game does not change and neither does human nature.

Edwin Lefèvre, *Reminiscences of a Stock Operator* (1923)

Take a contemporary investment banker, dress him in a wig, frock coat, breeches, stockings, and a pair of buckle shoes and send him back in time to Exchange Alley in the 1690s. It is a narrow street in the City of London winding between Cornhill and Lombard Street, where meat, fish, fruit, and vegetable vendors ply their wares. Their carts block our banker's progress and the stench of rotten vegetables forces him to seek refuge in one of a number of coffeehouses situated among the Alley's barbers, booksellers, and alehouses. After ordering a cup of tea, he acquaints himself with his new surroundings: he sees walls plastered with posters offering rewards for the return of diamonds and bills of exchange "dropt" in the vicinity, and gilt-framed notices advertising "Golden Elixirs, Popular Pills, Beautifying Waters, Drops and Lozenges, all as infallible as the Pope." In one corner of the coffeehouse, wine is being sold at auction by an "inch of candle" (when the candle burns out the bidding ceases); in another, men are wagering on the outcome of the siege of some Flemish town. Just as the time traveller is beginning to feel dazed and confused, a well-dressed man enters Jonathan's coffeehouse. "How go the stocks?" he inquires of a Jewish gentleman, who, extracting himself from a huddle of drab-looking men in Puritan garb, goes to greet him. "What stocks have you to dispose of? What price for Loftings or Blue Paper? How much an East India put?" The demoralised banker starts to cheer up, for he recognises at least some of the language of *interests, discounts, transfers, tallies, debentures, shares,* and *projects* which fills his ears. He beckons the stockjobber to his side for an explanation. The jobber tells the modern banker a familiar tale of a wave of exciting new technology companies coming to the market, of rising share prices and record stock turnover, or newfangled financial derivatives, of credit wildly extended, of stock market rumours and sharp practices, and of naive investors rushing to buy shares. Finally, the jobber speaks excitedly of the profits which he intends to make from this hullabaloo. The time traveller smiles knowingly, he is beginning to feel himself quite at home; the past is not a world *he* has lost.

The course and features of the 1690s stock market boom are clearly recognisable to any operator in the contemporary financial markets, even though the London stock market at that date was barely a decade old and remained fairly primitive—consisting of informal meetings of brokers and clients in the coffeehouses of 'Change Alley and the covered walks of the Royal Exchange. A few years earlier, the word *broker* had referred simply to a procurer or pimp and others such *stockjobber, director, subscription, underwriting, puts,* and *refusals* (i.e., call options) were unknown. All of a sudden, these words comprised a financial argot that spouted from every mouth. There had been no quiet evolution, no period of maturation, no learning process; like the goddess Athena, the stock market came into existence fully formed. Instead of wailing at its birth, the market boomed.

"CREDIT IS MONEY"

The emergence of the stock market in London was one of a number of innovations in late-seventeenth-century England—collectively termed the Financial Revolution—which coincided with the Glorious Revolution of 1688, when the Dutch Stadtholder William of Orange snatched the throne from his Catholic father-in-law, James II. They included the parliamentary guarantee for government loans (in 1693), which created what was later known as the "National Debt," the establishment of the Bank of England with permission to circulate a paper currency (in 1694), the introduction of Exchequer bills (1696), and the Promissory Notes Act of 1704, which made all debts negotiable, and hence transferable. These innovations, so heavily influenced by Dutch practice that they were sometimes known as "Dutch finance," were introduced to help the state tap the resources of the country for the costly war against Louis XIV's France.

Since the time of the Civil War (1642–51), English goldsmiths had taken on the functions of bankers, making loans and creating a market for merchants' bills of exchange (credit notes). By the 1690s, the total value of bills of exchange in circulation was believed to exceed the currency of the kingdom.* Several writers observed that through its circulation this new form of credit had many properties in common with money. Yet credit, unlike gold, could be created and destroyed. It had no utility and its value depended on an act of belief from which it derived its name (Latin: *credere, creditum,* to believe). Credit was in constant flux, elusive, independent, and uncontrollable. Contemporaries likened it to a flighty young maiden. It "is never to be forced," wrote the contemporary economist Charles Davenant, "it hangs upon opinion, it depends upon our passions of hope and fear; it comes many times unsought for, and often goes away without reason, and when once lost, is hardly to be quite recovered."[1] Credit was the Siamese twin of speculation; they were born at the same time and exhibited the same nature; inextricably linked, they could never be totally separated.

The 1690s spawned a breed of unprincipled and self-seeking characters—the so-called moneyed men—who turned the financial innovations of the day to their personal advantage. At their head

*By the end of the century, Charles Davenant estimated that assignable credit instruments in circulation totalled £15 million, exceeding the coinage by a quarter. See K. G. Davies, "Joint-Stock Investment in the later Seventeenth Century," *Economic History Review,* 2nd Ser., IV, No. 3 (1952), p. 287.

stood men such as Sir Josiah Child, the banker and East India stockholder, who argued that all men were "led by their profit," and James Brydges, Earl (later Duke) of Chandos, who made his fortune as paymaster general of the army. Less respectable were the dealers around the Exchange, such as the stationer Thomas Guy and the merchant John "Vulture" Hopkins, both of whose meanness was legendary. These men were the living embodiment of a new liberal ideology in which self-interest replaced noblesse oblige and the former vices of avarice and consumption were seen as having beneficial economic effects.* This development was most evident in the stock market, where jobbers and their clients pursued personal gain to the exclusion of any other consideration.

In *The True Picture of a Modern Whig* (1701) Charles Davenant satirised the new moneyed man: Tom Double, a denizen of Garraway's, one of the stock-dealing coffeehouses of Exchange Alley, is a model of amoral self-interest: "'Tis the principle of us Modern Whigs," he declares, "to get what we can, no matter how." He belongs to a group of men who, having raised themselves from poverty to great wealth, despise the advantages of birth.† Double flaunts his good fortune with all the pride of the parvenu: "I have my Country-House, where I keep my Whore as fine as an Empress . . . I have my *French* Cook, and Wax-Candles; I drink nothing but *Hermitage*, *Champagne* and Burgundy; Cahors Wine has

*According to the economic historian Joyce Appleby, the moneyed men of the late seventeenth century "introduced a theory of economic growth that endorsed competition and acclaimed vanity, ambition, and emulation as part of a new market dynamic." She cites the example of John Houghton, a contemporary journalist and merchant, who suggested that the traditionally anathematised vices of consumption—Prodigality, Pride, Vanity, and Luxury—were, in fact, a source of benefit to the nation. In this, Houghton anticipated the thesis of Bernard Mandeville in the *Fable of the Bees* (first published in 1714), which describes the consumption of luxuries as a stimulus to economic activity. See Joyce Appleby, *Economic Thought and Ideology in Seventeenth Century England* (Princeton, 1980).

†Tom Double boasts, "I have a good store of Mony in my Pocket; and he who has that shall be esteem'd and courted, let his Birth be never so mean, or his Life never so infamous . . . Thanks to my Industry I am now worth Fifty Thousand Pound, and 14 years ago I had not Shoes to my Feet . . . I can name fifty of our Friends who have got much better Fortunes since the Revolution, and from as poor Beginnings." (Charles Davenant, *The True Picture of a Modern Whig*, London, 1701, 6th ed., pp. 15–16.)

hardly admittance to my side-board; my very Footmen scorn French claret . . ." With his carriages, fine wine, and mistress, Double is the yuppie of his age, a "Master of the Universe" in the mould of the bond trader Sherman McCoy, Tom Wolfe's creation in *The Bonfire of the Vanities.* There is an affinity between the two periods; like the 1980s, the 1690s were a decade when "it rain'd Gold and Silver."*

DIVING AND FLOATING IN THE EARLY STOCK MARKET

Although joint-stock companies—business organisations whose capital was divided into shares—had existed in England since the sixteenth century, there was no regular market for trading in shares until the 1690s. Formerly, the East India Company shares had been sold at auction along with the company's wares. The necessary conditions for a "perfect market"—liquidity and the free transferability of shares—did not exist before this date. Foreigners were forbidden from holding shares, and share transfers required the approval of a special committee which had the right to levy "fines" on outsiders for admission to the company. Ownership of shares in the chartered companies—the East India, Royal African, and Hudson's Bay—was concentrated among a few wealthy persons, and stock turnover was so low that no continuous series of stock prices can be found from an earlier date. Before this period, speculation was confined to the commodities traded at the Royal Exchange, where it did not attract the interest of the public.

"The Nation was rich, Trade prodigiously great, Paper-Credit run high, and the Goldsmiths in Lombard-street, &c, commanded immense sums . . ." was how Daniel Defoe remembered the 1680s.[2] The Glorious Revolution is the only revolution in history to have occurred at a time of great prosperity; a prosperity fostered by a run

*A similarity between the two periods was observed by the modern English playwright Caryl Churchill, who used the scene of the stockjobbers in Shadwell's *The Volunteers* (1692) as a preface to her play *Serious Money* (1987), a satire on the money culture of Thatcherite Britain at the time of the "Big Bang" deregulation of financial services.

of good harvests, the profits from foreign trade, and the arrival of Dutch and Huguenot immigrants who brought with them new skills and capital. The chartered joint-stock companies shared in the general affluence. Between 1682 and 1692, the East India Company paid out dividends equal to four times its nominal capital. A "proprietor" who had bought into the company in 1660 and sold the stock in 1688 would have received a return on his investment of 1,200 percent above the prevailing rate of interest.[3] By the end of the decade, the chartered companies' shares were trading at a sizeable premium to their net asset value. When a regular market for stocks emerged in Exchange Alley turnover in shares increased dramatically, causing Sir Josiah Child to refer to a "kindly natural and continual changing Motion insomuch that the value of the whole stock [of the East India Company], once in Two Years, or thereabouts, changes Owners."[4]

According to the seventeenth-century statistician Gregory King, the economic surplus doubled in the quarter of a century to 1688. This provided the capital for a new breed of company promoters, or "projectors" as they were called, to draw upon. Even before the arrival of William of Orange, a vibrant spirit of enterprise was evident in the establishment of joint-stock companies, such as the Convex Lights Company founded in 1684 to manufacture a new type of street lighting. The rage for establishing new companies—what Defoe called the "projecting humour"—did not properly get underway until 1687. In that year, William Phipps, a New England sea captain, returned to England with thirty-two tons of silver and a quantity of jewels raised from a Spanish plate ship, sunk off the island of Hispaniola. After the King, Captain Phipps, and his sailors had received their portions, nearly £190,000 was left to distribute to the partners who had backed the expedition, in the form of a 10,000 percent dividend, "enriching them beyond expectation," as John Evelyn recorded in his diary.[5] The success of the expedition created a great stir across the country. Captain Phipps, a former shepherd boy, was knighted within three weeks of his return and a commemorative medal was struck. Others sought to emulate Phipps's success, yet instead of creating partnerships, as had been the case with the Phipps venture, the new treasure-hunting schemes were floated as joint-stock companies: the age of adventuring, a tradition going back to the Elizabethan privateers, suddenly gave way to an age of speculation.

Two types of "diving" company were launched in the wake of Phipps's success. The first kind acquired a "patent" from the government which gave it monopoly rights to "fish" for wrecks at specific locations. Thomas Neal, the Master of the Mint and the leading projector of the age, was involved in three patented salvage companies for operations off Jamaica, Bermuda, and Portugal. Captain John Poyntz of the Tobago Company applied for a patent for "taking up wrecks out of the sea and fishing for pearls and ambergris" in the West Indies.[6] The other kind of diving company was established with a technological patent for one of the recently invented diving engines. As "Engine begat Engine and Project begat Project" over a dozen new diving engine companies appeared. They included the Company for Raising Wrecks in England, secured on a patent for the "diving bell" of the Astronomer Royal, Edmund Halley (the company appeared in the early stock lists as "Diving Halley").* Daniel Foe (as the author of *Robinson Crusoe* then styled himself) was employed as the secretary-treasurer to another diving bell company, established by a Cornishman named Joseph Williams.

The diving company projectors set out to stimulate public interest in their shares. "The Wealth which was fetch'd out of the sea was trumpeted all over the World," public demonstrations of diving engines were given on the Thames, and free shares were given "to People of Note and Figure, to give Reputation to the Affair; and these doughty Names were subscrib'd to play the Part of a Shooing-Horn, and wheedle in the Easie; Treats and Money were given to the Necessitous and Sharp, to bring their Friends and Acquaintance to see the Engine . . ."[7] In its prospectus, the diving company of Captain Poyntz promised a return of 100 percent to investors. The hype sent shares to a great premium above their issue price. Defoe reported that he had "seen Shares in Joint-Stocks, Patents, Engines

*Halley's diving bell was a conical-shaped tub designed to lie on the sea floor. It was open at the bottom with a little bench fixed inside "for men to sitt on when they should be cold and whereon a man might sit with all his clouths at any depth drie." The diver was to be equipped in a suit of leather with a "Capp" attached by air pipes to the bell. Halley also invented a barometer to measure depth, an underwater lamp, and an "instrument for blowing up of ships under water." (*Correspondence and Papers of Edmund Halley*, Oxford, 1932, pp. 150–56.)

and Undertakings, *blown up by the air of great Words,*" with the shares of one diving company rising by 500 percent. However, the craze for diving machines and treasure-seeking companies soon died down after their failure to salvage anything more than "a few Iron-Guns, Chimney Backs, and Ship's Tackle." The share price of the same company that had increased fivefold began to "dwindle away, till it has been stock-jobb'd down to 12, 10, 9, 8 /. a Share and at last no buyer . . ."[8] Defoe was writing from unhappy experience, having lost £200 in Williams's diving company: years later he wrote, "I could give a very diverting history of a patent-monger whose cully [i.e., dupe] was nobody but myself."*

War had broken out with France in 1689, as Louis XIV sought to overturn William of Orange's usurpation of the English crown. Rather than causing a commercial crisis, however, the outbreak of war actually stimulated the nascent English stock market—as the French saying goes, *Achétez aux canons, vendez aux clairons* (buy at the cannons' roar, sell when the trumpets sound). The interruption of foreign trade obliged merchants to find another outlet for their capital, while Parliament passed an act forbidding French imports.† Promoters sponsored a crop of new companies to manufacture goods formerly brought over from France.‡ Typical of these ventures was the Royal Lustring Company, which in 1692 raised £62,000 from the sale of shares in order to manufacture a fashionable French cloth known as "alamode" or Lustring described as a "fine, light, glossy, black silk."[9]

*In the 1680s, Defoe operated as a merchant in Spain. In 1692, he bought seventy civet cats for perfume manufacture and invested £800 in the Africa Company. His losses on these and other speculations were so great that in 1694 he was declared bankrupt for the enormous sum of £17,000. From this date onwards he made his living from writing. (J. R. Moore, *Daniel Defoe*, Chicago, 1958, p. 284.)

†Reflecting on the rise of the stock market in June 1694, Houghton claimed that "Trade being obstructed at Sea, few that had Money were willing that it should lie idle . . ." As they did not want to tie up their money for long periods of time, they invested in stocks. (John Houghton, A *Collection for the Improvement of Husbandry and Trade*, 1694, issue 98.)

‡Among the manufactures covered by these new companies were "Dipping, Japanning, Glass-Bottles, *Venetian*-Metal, Leather, Linen . . . Paper White, Blue . . . Printed-Hangings, Pearl-Fishing, Salt-Petre, Sword Blades . . . Lifting-Engines, Drawing-Engines . . ." *Angliae Tutamen*, pp. 4–5.

Like the diving companies, these new flotations met with initial success in the stock market. Shares in the White Paper Company, floated in 1690 at 50, increased threefold over the following four years. Those in Nicholas Dupin's Linen Company rose from 10 in 1690 to 45 three years later (in June 1691, Dupin attempted a fashionable diversification, petitioning for the privilege to raise wrecks off the south coast of England "so that the linen industry should not sink for want of support during its minority").[10] Individual projectors hedged their bets by maintaining interests in a number of different schemes. Thomas Neale, for instance, was involved in thirty-nine companies with interests extending from diving patents to water, paper, steel, and mining companies. In several projects Neale was in partnership with John Tyzack, who besides owning the patent for a diving machine also received a patent for establishing a company to produce "imitation Russia leather." Nicholas Dupin managed three "White Paper" companies in England, Scotland, and Ireland, as well as a Scottish mining company.

Many of these new companies were floated with patents for inventions. Between June 1691 and October 1693, sixty-one patents were issued altogether (of which eleven were for diving engines). They included the Company for the Sucking-Worm Engines of Mr. John Loftingh, which held a patent for "an engine for quenching fire, the like whereof was never seen before in this kingdom." Another patent company, the Night Engine Company, manufactured a burglar alarm which it claimed could be "set in a convenient place of any house, to prevent thieves from breaking in."[11] From their first appearance the new companies were viewed with widespread scepticism. According to a contemporary author, most of them were "mere whims, and of little or no service to the World, though they [the projectors] proclaim loudly their Worth and Goodness, and employ Agents to magnifie their Inventions, and wheedle in innocent and ignorant People; who, being charm'd with the Novelty of Things, (though perhaps but reviv'd, or borrow'd from some Foreign Nation), purchase Shares, and so are cheated of their Money; which is worse than High-Way Robbing . . ."[12]

In his play *The Volunteers: or The Stock-Jobbers* (1692), the poet laureate Thomas Shadwell satirised the appearance of patent companies in the stock market. In one scene, a jobber tells of a new company to manufacture "a Mouse-Trap, that will invite all mice in, any rats too, whether they will or no; a whole share before the Patent is fifteen pound; after the Patent they will not take sixty: there is no family in England that will be without 'em." When the wife of a rich speculator expresses interest in a diving company, her husband gently chides her feminine naiveté: "Look thee Lamb, between us, it's no matter whether it turns to any use or not; the main end verily is to turn the penny in the way of Stock-Jobbing, that's all."[13] Although this was the "Scientific Age" of Sir Isaac Newton and the Royal Society, the patent companies of the 1690s were not genuine attempts to apply scientific advances for commercial purposes: patents were registered without examination of their efficacy and were used by promoters as a convenient device to launch companies in the stock market while avoiding the time and expense of incorporation.[14]

GAMBLING IN THE EARLY CAPITAL MARKETS

From 1692 onwards, the apothecary and coffee trader John Houghton provided regular lists of stock market prices in his twice-weekly commercial periodical, *A Collection for the Improvement of Husbandry and Trade*. As the boom progressed, the number of stocks named by Houghton increased from 10 to 57 (in May 1694), with the new companies listed by their market nicknames ("Night," "Lofting," "Diving W," et cetera). In order to facilitate the transfer of shares, standard sale contracts were printed. The sophisticated tools of speculation, including stock options and futures (then known as "time bargains"), were imported from Amsterdam.[15] Houghton even provided separate prices for East India Company futures, and described how "putting" (buying an option to sell a stock at a certain price) might be used by shareholders as a hedge or insurance against a drop in price. He also recognised that options could lead to straightforward speculation: "By this means many are incouraged to come into new stocks, the success whereof is very uncertain . . ."[16]

As stockjobbing became fashionable, Houghton endeavoured to inform his readers of its mysteries: "The manner of the Trade is this; the Monied Man goes among the *Brokers*, (which are chiefly upon the *Exchange*, and at *Jonathan's* Coffee-House, sometimes at *Garraway's*, and at some other Coffee Houses) and asks how *Stocks* go? and upon Information, bids the Broker buy or sell so many shares of such and such Stocks if he can, at such and such Prices: Then he tries what he can do among those that have Stocks, or the power to sell them, and if he can, makes a Bargain."[17] Houghton claimed that the shares of smaller companies were subject to manipulation "by the contrivances of a few Men in Confederacy . . . [who] strive to secure all the shares in a Stock" (what we would call "cornering" the stock). The dubious "contrivances" of financiers and the application of advanced speculative techniques—such as hedging with options and futures—reveal a remarkable sophistication in the early stock market.

While the stock market merrily bubbled along, the government of William of Orange decided to harness the nation's gambling propensity to raise funds for the war against France. Following Dutch precedent, in 1694 the ubiquitous Thomas Neale launched the first British government lottery. Enticingly styled "The Million Adventure," it offered a first prize of £1,000 a year for sixteen years for a £10 ticket (losing tickets or "blanks" received £1 a year for the same period). The hundred thousand tickets sold out quickly. A lottery fever ensued with a multitude of private lottery promotions advertised in the press. Eager to have a finger in every pie, Neale arranged three "Profitable Adventure to the Fortunate" lotteries for his own account. "Penny Lotteries" followed the larger promotions, and stockjobbers subdivided £10 tickets into smaller shares for the less well-off. By the middle of the decade, lottery tickets, like credit notes, were circulating as currency.*

Projectors in the stock market were not slow to capitalise on the lottery fever. The case of the Company of Mine Adventurers illustrates the curious fusion of lottery gambling and stock market speculation. Established in 1693 to mine for silver in Wales, the company was taken over the following year by an unscrupulous adventurer

*In modern Japan lottery tickets are still treated as negotiable securities (*yuuka shooken*), the legal equivalent of stocks and bonds, which must be handled by banks. (Grant, *Trouble with Prosperity*, p. 220 n.)

named Sir Humphrey Mackworth, who soon after announced the conversion of the £20 ordinary shares into interest-paying bonds. The incentive for conversion was that each bond also served as a lottery ticket: one in ten bonds would receive a prize, the top prize being a package of shares and bonds with a prospective income of £2,000 per annum. Seven hundred proprietors were involved in the conversion and more than four-fifths of the shares were converted in lottery bonds.* A slightly different use for lotteries, related by Macaulay, was found by the Royal Academies Company, whose directors advertised that they had "engaged the best masters in every branch of knowledge, and were about to issue twenty thousand tickets at twenty shillings each. There was to be a lottery: two thousand prizes were to be drawn; and the fortunate holders of the prizes were to be taught at the charge of the Company, Latin, Greek, Hebrew, French, Spanish, conic sections, trigonometry, heraldry, japanning, fortification, bookkeeping and the art of playing the theorbo."†

A recent historian of the Financial Revolution has found the late-seventeenth-century passion for gambling to be a "contradictory trend" running against the financial developments of the age.[18] It is contradictory only if one associates capitalism with the advance of rationalism in the modern world. The view of capitalism as a branch of the Enlightenment was put forward by the sociologist Max Weber, who argued in *The Protestant Ethic and the Spirit of Capitalism* that "the development of the spirit of capitalism is best understood as part of the development of rationalism as a whole, and could be deduced from the fundamental position of rationalism on the basic problems of life." For Weber, the advance of the capitalist system was not only a rational movement, it was also puritanical, combining

*The scheme was in fact "honeycombed with fraud" (W. Scott's phrase). Mackworth carefully cultivated good publicity for his company: the Duke of Leeds was elected governor, donations were made to charity, and pamphlets were commissioned to hype its prospects. Only later was it discovered that Mackworth had fiddled the accounts, issued false reports of the company's silver production, paid interest for the bonds with borrowed money, sold shares without authorisation, and retained the money for his own use. These frauds led to his eventual departure from the company. See Scott, *Joint-Stock Companies*, II, pp. 447–51.

†Macaulay, *History of England* (London, 1855) V, p. 321. Macaulay suggests the date of this offer was 1692, although it is doubtful that it could have preceded the Million Adventure. It is not mentioned by Scott.

frugality with the Calvinist notion of a professional calling.* The system was antithetical to the unlimited greed for gain: "Capitalism," he asserted, "*may* be identical with the restraint, or at least a rational tempering, of this irrational impulse."

The late seventeenth century did, in fact, produce several significant advances in the "rationalistic" quantification of risk. Alongside his work on the diving bell, Edmund Halley produced in 1693 the first mortality table based on statistics provided by the Prussian city of Breslau. This allowed Halley to estimate probabilities of death and provide a foundation for the development of actuarial science, upon which the life insurance industry is based. The contemporary passion for gambling also focused people's minds on the issue of probability. In 1693, Samuel Pepys and Isaac Newton engaged in a lengthy correspondence concerning dice throwing, probabilities, and wagers. John Law, the architect of the Mississippi bubble and the leading speculator of the next generation, earned his keep in the 1690s as a gambler and made a fortune by applying advanced probability theory to the game of hazard (a dice game similar to craps).† Law's subsequent transition from gambler to speculator was probably typical of the moneyed men of this era, since Davenant's fictional Tom Double also starts his ignoble career at the card tables of St. James's before progressing to Exchange Alley.

Betting on public and private events was common in the coffeehouses of Exchange Alley. According to Defoe, during the 1690s wagering ceased to be mere gambling and became instead "a Branch of Assurances," a trade found increasingly on the Royal Exchange

*Contemporaries considered Puritans to be appalling hypocrites for mixing business with piety. In *The Volunteers* (1792), Shadwell portrays a group of Puritan stockjobbers debating whether a scheme for bringing Chinese rope dancers to Britain was "lawful" according to their religion. They finally decide that if "we ourselves have no share in the vanity or wicked diversion thereof, by beholding of it, but only use it whereby we may turn the Penny, and employ it for Edification, always considered that it is like to take, and the said Shares will sell well; and then we shall not care, whether the aforesaid Dancers come over or no."

†One biographer claims that John Law's advanced calculations of the odds involved in the game of hazard anticipated the work on probabilities by Edmund Hoyle, whose *Essay towards making the Doctrine of Chances easy to those who understand Vulgar Arithmetick only* was first published in 1754. See H. Montgomery Hyde, *John Law: The History of an Honest Adventurer* (London, 1969), p. 21.

and in the coffeehouses, where it was taken over by stockjobbers.[19] Gambling fostered the growth of insurance. When Edward Lloyd moved his coffeehouse to Lombard Street in 1691 brokers were underwriting a variety of risks from highway robbery to the "assurance of female chastity."[20] The merchant who took a wager on the outbreak of war, the life expectancy of King William, or the outcome of a siege was more likely to be doing so because he wished to hedge a business risk than because he was consumed with a gaming lust.

The idea of reward offsetting risk was evident in the stock market. When contemporaries considered Phipps's treasure trove they discussed it in terms of probability: Defoe claimed the success of the expedition had been "a Lottery of a Hundred Thousand to One odds," while Aaron Hill stated that the odds against Phipps's backers had been over a million to one against "but they succeeded even against all Prospect of Probability and were enrich'd by Accident."* The constant analysis of risk and probability promoted by gambling and speculation may be seen as an extension of rationalism, although it has nothing to do with Weber's view of capitalism as an embodiment of Calvinist sobriety.

Despite its contribution to advances in probability theory, gambling retained its particular irrational qualities. As Sir Richard Steele observed in the choice of a lottery number, "Caprice very often acts in Place of Reason, and forms to itself some Groundless Imaginary Motive, where real and substantial ones are wanting."[21] Later, Adam Smith used the example of purchasers of lottery tickets to illustrate the "contempt of risk and presumptuous hope of success" that he considered a universal tendency in mankind.† This

---

*Hill's analysis is correct since the rewards of the project were 100 times the initial investment, but the odds against its success were far greater. Therefore, a rational, a priori assessment of Phipps's adventure would suggest it was a bad investment. Aaron Hill, *An Account of the Rise and Progress of the Beech-Oil Invention* (London, 1715), p. 13.

†Smith wrote in *The Wealth of Nations* that "the over-weening conceit which the greater part of men have of their own abilities, is an antient evil remarked by the philosophers and moralists of all ages. Their absurd presumption of their own good fortune, has been less taken notice of. It is, however, if possible, more universal. There is no man living who, when in tolerable health and spirits, has not some share of it. The chance of gain is by every man more or less overvalued, and the chance of loss is by most men under-valued, and by scarce any man, who is in tolerable health and spirits, valued more than it is worth."

observation might have been equally well applied to speculators investing in the patent companies of the 1690s. A gambling psychology infused every aspect of the new financial world, with the stockjobbers dealing in shares, lottery tickets, and wagers at the centre of this gambling maelstrom. The stock market did not emerge to finance the sober Calvinist capitalist, nor did it appeal to puritanical notions of thrift; rather, it took its cue from the fantastic lotterylike success of Phipps's adventure. In this context, the combination of stock market speculation and lottery gambling in a company such as the Mine Adventurers was an entirely natural development.

There was no contradiction between gambling and financial innovation, because gaming was the essence of the stock market, or as Defoe put it: "Stock-jobbing is play: a box and dice may be less dangerous, the nature of them are alike, a hazard."[22] Rather than being antithetical to capitalism as Weber suggested, greed and the irrational gambling impulse actually helped to advance its institutions. Keynes's claim that the game of investment is

> intolerably boring and over-exacting to any one who is entirely exempt from the gambling instinct; whilst he who has it must pay to this propensity the appropriate toll

is as valid for the seventeenth century as for the twentieth.[23] The successful establishment of the stock market and the joint-stock company over other forms of capital organisation lay in their incorporating within themselves elements of the gaming room. In the origins of financial capitalism, rationalism was very much a subsidiary element.

HEADDRESSES AND HEMLINES

Seventeenth-century investors were no less sophisticated than their counterparts in the modern world. The valuation of annuities and lottery tickets, both of which paid an income for a limited number of years but did not return the principal, involved the process of discounting future cash flows.* What is nowadays called the "time value of money" is clearly comprehended in John Law's remark that "anticipation is always at a *discount* . . . £100 to be paid now is of more value than £1,000 to be paid by £10 a year for 100 years."†

The concept of fundamental or "intrinsic" value was also understood by players in the early stock market, although misleading prospectuses, the manipulation of share prices, and the stock market boom made its discovery an even more difficult task than usual. After the 1690s boom, Defoe stated that many stocks had been raised above their "intrinsick value" and that shares in the East India Company had sold at between 300 and 400 percent above their nominal value "*without any material difference in Intrinsick value*" (my italics).[24] The contemporary land-bank projectors, who wanted to replace a gold-backed currency with one supported by the value of land, even realised that the notion of "intrinsic value" was an oxymoron, since "intrinsic" suggested an inward quality, while "value" was always external. For instance, Nicholas Barbon argued that "things have no Value in themselves, it is opinion and fashion which brings them into use and gives them a value."[25] John Law, who was also a land-bank projector, went even further and claimed that price was simply the result of the interaction of supply and demand. Applied to the stock market, Law's idea suggests that share prices are determined by liquidity (the supply of new funds to the market) rather than a reflection of inherent values.

The land-bankers' argument that value was an extrinsic quality—subject to changing "opinion and fashion"—was particularly relevant to the stock market, since from the launch of diving companies onwards the market had fallen for a succession of fads. The rise of the stock market in the early 1690s was accompanied by a

*Discounting works on the principle that "a bird in the hand is worth two in the bush." It involves calculating the value of future income by applying to it a discount rate, normally related to the prevailing rate of interest, which reduces the income to its present or current value. For more on discounting cash flows see Chapter 7.

†Law must have been aware that his calculation only holds true if a discount rate of more than 10 percent is applied to the future income in his example (from Law's *Essay on a Land Bank*, 1704, cited by Antoin Murphy, *John Law*, Oxford, 1997, p. 60).

fashion for increasingly extravagant ladies' headdresses, which climbed in height from the early 1690s until they peaked at over seven feet in 1695 (the year the stock market crashed). This prompted Sir Richard Steele to remark that "Stocks have risen and fallen in Proportion to Head-Dresses"—an observation which anticipates the connection made between women's rising hemlines and the stock market in the 1920s (what has become known as the "hemline theory of stock prices").* There are several possible interpretations of Steele's comment: A daring and extravagant fashion might indicate that stock market profits were being spent on gaudy display, a sign of the conspicuous consumption which accompanies every speculative episode. On the other hand, one might see in the rising headdress of the moneyed man's mistress (or later in the rising hemline of the 1920s flapper) an indication of the moral laxity of speculative periods, when the spirit of self-interest is dominant and more sober virtues are despised. It appears more likely, however, that Steele was suggesting that market values—evanescent, ephemeral, and extravagant—were as much a reflection of passing fashion as female modes of attire. A fashionable style, like a speculative movement, is subject to a popular consensus and follows a trend until it reaches a point of extravagance from which it can only retreat.†

A few years later, Steele articulated what is perhaps the earliest contrarian theory of investment (i.e., one that goes against the prevailing view):

---

*In *The Economics of Fashion*, Professor Paul H. Nystrom of the Columbia Business School showed that in 1919 the average level of the hem above the ground was 10 percent of a woman's height. In 1920, during the initial postwar recovery, the hemline rose to around 20 percent. In the recession of 1921, it fell back to around 10 percent. As the bull market took off in 1924, hemlines rose until they reached 25 percent in 1927, at which point they met the knee. They remained there until late 1929. After the Great Crash, hemlines fell until with the onset of the Great Depression they brushed the ground. See *The Spectator*, IV, p. 18; Frederick Lewis Allen, *Only Yesterday* (New York, 1957), pp. 103–4; and Burton Malkiel, *A Random Walk Down Wall Street* (New York, 1990), pp. 143–45.

†One might compare the activity of the fashion designer, leading changes in popular taste, to that of the speculator who attempts to anticipate shifts in market psychology. For a recent assessment of the relationship between stock prices and fashion, see the works of Professor Robert Shiller of Yale, especially his essay "Fashion, Fads, and Bubbles in Financial Markets" (published in *Knights, Raiders, and Targets*, eds. J. Coffee et al., New York, 1988).

> Is it possible that a young Man at present could pass his Time better, than in reading the History of Stocks, and knowing by what secret Springs they have such sudden Ascents and Falls in the same Day? Could he be better conducted on his Way to Wealth, which is the great Article of Life, than in a Treatise dated from Change-Alley by an able proficient there? *Nothing could be more useful, than to be well instructed in his Hope and Fears; to be diffident when others exalt, and with a secret Joy buy when others think it their interest to sell.*[26] [my italics].

Keynes argued that since the future could not be known with any degree of certainty values in the stock market ultimately depended on a state of confidence, itself the outcome of the "mass psychology of a large number of ignorant individuals."[27] Observing the undulations of the market and the constant flux of credit more than two centuries earlier, Steele anticipated what has been called the "Castles in the Air" theory of value.* In the pages of the *Spectator*, he describes entering the Palace of Vanity, whose dome "bore so far the resemblance of a Bubble," where Vanity sat attended by Ostentation, Self-Conceit, Flattery, Affectation, and Fashion. When Broken Credit appears alongside Folly (an allegory for speculative irrationality), there is consternation, and the visitor "plainly discern'd the Building to hang a little up in the Air without any real Foundation . . . But as they begun to sink lower in their own Minds, methought the Palace sunk along with us, till they arrived at the due point of esteem which they ought to have for themselves; then Part of the Building in which they stood touched the earth." In the new economic system brought into existence by the Financial

---

*The "Castles in the Air" theory of value suggests that shares have no intrinsic value and share prices are simply the product of investor psychology. One of the earliest associations of "castles in the air" with investment appears in Jonathan Swift's poem *The Bubble* (1720), written after the collapse of the South Sea Company. In this poem, Swift attacks the company's fraudulent directors and its credulous shareholders:

> *While some build Castles in the Air,*
> *Directors build'em in the Seas;*
> *Subscribers plainly see 'um there,*
> *For Fools will see as Wise men please.*

Revolution, there was no longer a substantial economic reality: values were the product of a skittish and trivial mass psychology, trade was dependent on a transient state of confidence, and companies "floated" on waves of speculative euphoria.

SCANDALS AND CORRUPTION

In the stock market of the 1690s, the line between commendable self-interest and arrant fraud was frequently crossed: sham companies were launched for the enrichment of projectors, share prices were manipulated, and false rumours were circulated. In *The Volunteers,* Thomas Shadwell described the stock market as a world of sharpers and cheats, where men "bubbled" each other for profit (at this date, "to bubble" meant to perpetrate a fraud).* Charles Davenant describes the moneyed men as practising a variety of "Cheats, Extortions, Frauds, Bribery and Corruption" in their pursuit of wealth. The term *stockjobbing*—synonymous with speculation as well as the trade in shares—also described the act of blowing up shares above their true value while simultaneously running down a company's real prospects.† In a world where credit notes and lottery tickets circulated as money, company shares became the currency of corruption. Gifts of stock were secretly made

*For instance, in *The Volunteers*, the "sharper" Nickum refers to a "Debt that's owing me by a Bubble in *England.*" However, Steele's reference to the "bubble" dome of the Palace of Vanity suggests a new connection was being made between speculation and the bubble allegory.

†The anonymous author of *Angliae Tutamen* described the "Tricks and Stratagems" used by mining company projectors to snare innocent investors. First, the projectors pretend to find a vein of gold, then they buy a lease for twenty-one years and "settle a Company under Articles, divide into Shares, usually 400, chuse a Committee, a Clerk, and Transfer-Book, and pretend to carry on this work to the Benefit of all the Proprietors; who, at the beginning, purchase shares at a low Rate, viz., Ten Shillings, Twenty, or a Guinea, then all of a sudden they whip up the Shares to Three, Five, Ten, nay; Fifteen Pounds a Share; then they fall to Stock-Jobbing which infallibly ruins these, and all other Projects; those principally concern'd, sell their Interest draw off, and wholly quit the Affair, which, by this and other means of underhand dealing, tricking and sharping one another, falls to the Ground, and is abandon'd by every Body."

to figures of note either to attract other investors or to silence their objections—as Shadwell's Colonel Hackwell boasts, "I have shares in some [companies] that cost me nothing, but were given me to prevent my Caveats."

Shares were also used to purchase political influence. In the great bribery scandal of the East India Company, age-old political venality came into contact with the new forces of financial speculation. The scandal had its origin in the failure of the East India Company, in March 1693, to pay a special tax on the value of its stock. As a result, the company's charters were technically forfeited at a time when a rival syndicate was attempting to snatch the Eastern trade monopoly from the old company. Both groups engaged in extensive bribery both at Court and in Parliament, with a view to securing a new charter. The contest ended in victory for the established company after the expenditure of over £200,000 of "secret service money." The application of options and shares in the bribery was relatively sophisticated. In one example, Sir Basil Firebras, a member of Parliament, contracted with the company an option to put (i.e., sell) £60,000 of East India stock to the company at a premium of 50 percent to the prevailing market price once the company had been granted a new charter. This deal brought him an eventual profit of £30,000. Many other parliamentarians received call options in the company, giving them the right to buy the stock at a fixed price. This allowed them to benefit from any gain in share price resulting from their ensuring the company's future. In 1695, the report of the parliamentary investigation into the scandal led to the expulsion of the Speaker of the Commons, the impeachment of the Lord President of the Council, and the imprisonment of the Governor of the East India Company. The scandal appeared to lend substance to John Pollexfen's celebrated contemporary remark that "companies have bodies, but it is said they have no souls; if no souls, no consciences." It revealed how contagious the mores of the moneyed men had become and showed how the stock market could become a dangerous snare for politicians whose self-interest was no less intense than that of the stockjobbers. All this foreshadowed the systematic corruption of politicians during later periods of speculation. As Defoe warned on the eve of the South Sea bubble, some two decades later, "when Statesmen turn jobbers, the state may be jobb'd."*

THE OLD LADY TAKES HER FIRST STEP

On 21 June 1694, the subscription lists opened for a venture incorporated as the Governor and Company of the Bank of England. This new establishment epitomised the financial marvels of the age. The Bank was granted a royal charter and banking monopoly on condition that it lent £1,200,000 to the government. However, it was allowed to provide this loan in the form of its own banknotes of no intrinsic value (i.e., they were not backed by gold), on which it nevertheless received an annual interest payment from the government of £100,000. Paper currency, the philosopher's stone of financial capitalism, had received the first tentative mark of government approval. The Bank of England's flotation was a great success: its subscription books were filled in a few days, with investors ranging from the Earl of Portland, King William's favourite, to a medley of apothecaries, carriers, cloth workers, embroiderers, farmers, mariners, and wharfingers.[28] Bank of England shares jumped to a 20 percent premium. The stock market boom entered its final phase. A variety of land-bank projects were brought forward but none got off the ground.[29] It was even suggested that the income from the City of London's Orphans' Fund should be pledged to provide the capital for an Orphans' Bank (an anonymous pamphleteer protested that "even at the bottom of this Charitable and Pious Project, Self-Interest and Private Profit lies securely entrench'd").[30]

The last great flotation of the period originated far from Exchange Alley, in Edinburgh. The Scotsman William Patterson, one of the founders of the Bank of England, established the Darien Company with the intention of settling the Isthmus of Panama,

*Defoe, *Anatomy*, p. 378. A link between the East India Company scandal of 1695 and the South Sea scandal of 1720 is provided by James Craggs, MP, who in 1695 was sent to the Tower for receiving bribes from the East India Company. A quarter of a century later, when he was Postmaster General, Craggs accepted free shares from the South Sea Company. He committed suicide after the bubble's collapse.

which he envisaged as a potential world entrepôt. The Darien Company's backers saw an opportunity to lay the foundations of a Scottish empire in competition with their Sassenach neighbour. Fuelled with nationalist sentiments, the Scots public showed great enthusiasm for the £300,000 subscription which opened in late June 1695. According to the Secretary of State in Scotland, Sir John Dalrymple, "'the frenzy of the Scots nation to sign the Solemn League and Covenant never exceeded the rapidity with which they ran to subscribe to the Darien company. . . . Young women threw their little fortunes into the stock, widows sold their jointures to command money for the same purpose."[31] The launch of the Darien Company exhibited certain novel features. As only half the capital was allocated to be raised in Scotland, Patterson attempted to sell the remaining shares first in London, then in Amsterdam, and finally in Hamburg, where £200,000 of stock was offered for sale in what was the first international flotation. A more dubious feature of the public offering was the decision by the Darien Company's directors to issue banknotes as loans to shareholders against the security of their stock. Patterson's example inspired his fellow Scot, John Law, who a couple of decades later issued millions of banknotes against the deposit of Mississippi Company shares.

While the Darien Company was being launched in a flurry of Scottish excitement (soon to be cruelly disappointed by the failure of the company), a financial crisis loomed south of the border. As with many later crises, its cause lay in a combination of monetary distress with speculative revulsion. Despite the many innovations of "Dutch finance," the costs of the war with France had exceeded public revenue and the government had turned to the age-old remedy of debasing the coinage. In accordance with "Gresham's Law" (named after Elizabeth I's finance minister, who observed that bad money drives out good money), people began hoarding the undebased coins. In the summer of 1696, John Evelyn recorded in his diary a "want of current money to carry on not only the smallest concerns, but for daily provisions in the Common Markets."[32] Riots broke out in the north of England. Credit, that nervous creature, took flight from the City. Government tallies (short-term public debt) fell to a 40 percent discount, and a lottery loan for £1,400,000 raised less than £18,000. Shares were badly affected.

The "bellwether" East India Company share price fell from 200 in 1692 to 37 in 1697. In the same period, shares in the Hudson's Bay Company and the Linen Company fell by 70 and 90 percent, respectively. Most of the new companies, including *all* the diving and patent companies, simply disappeared. Of 140 English and Scottish companies operating in 1693, only 40 survived the crisis to 1697—a failure rate of 70 percent.

Daniel Defoe, the projector's "cully," attributed the crisis to the activities of the stockjobbers in Exchange Alley:

> Anyone might have foreseen that the strife and contention of our two rival East-India Companies would produce some more than ordinary effect, and that *the raising of stock, of all sorts to a value so much above the Intrinsick, must have some fatal issue, and would fall somewhere at last so heavy as to be felt by the whole body of Trade.*[33] [my italics]

This was the first time an economic crisis had been linked to speculation. The anonymous author of a pamphlet, published in 1696 and entitled *Angliae Tutamen* (The Defence of England), hoped that "a fair and clear Discovery of many crafty Cheats, and villainous Knaveries, will be of vast Advantage to the Publick." He held opportunistic projectors to be responsible for the collapse of many worthy undertakings. This opinion was shared by the official trade commissioners, whose report on the crisis was published in late 1696.* The commissioners also attacked brokers who had "confederated themselves together" for the purpose of manipulating prices. In 1697, Parliament passed a law to "refrain the number and ill practices of brokers and stock-jobbers," restricting the total number of stockjobbers to one hundred, licensed by the Aldermen of the City of London. When the regulation was renewed in 1708 brokers were required to pay an annual subscription for registration and

*The commissioners accused projectors of establishing companies in order "to sell them with advantage to ignorant men, drawn in by reputation, falsely raised and artfully spread, concerning the thriving state of their stock." Having sold their stock for a profit, the projectors were said to have neglected the affairs of their companies until they fell into ruinous decline. *Journals of the House of Commons*, XI, p. 595.

the number of Jewish brokers was held to a maximum of twelve. Stockjobbers were also forbidden from dealing on their own account or charging a commission greater than an eighth of 1 percent.[34] As with the earlier Dutch attempts to regulate speculation, these provisions had little effect and most brokers continued their trade without official sanction.*

THE SPECULATIVE PARADIGM

Charles Kindleberger, in his book *Manias, Panics and Crashes,* suggests that speculative manias typically commence with a *displacement* which excites speculative interest. The displacement may come either from an entirely new object of investment or from the increased profitability of established investments. It is followed by *positive feedback* as rising share prices induce inexperienced investors to enter the stock market, and results in *euphoria*—a sign that investors' rationality is weakened. During the course of the mania, speculation becomes more diffuse and spreads to different classes of assets. New companies are floated to take advantage of the euphoria, investors leverage their gains using either financial derivatives or stock loans, credit becomes overextended, swindling and fraud proliferate, and the economy enters a period of financial distress which is the prelude to the onset of a crisis.

According to Kindleberger, although no two speculative manias are identical they develop along similar lines: "details proliferate; structure abides."[35] The same process was observed in the middle of the nineteenth century by John Stuart Mill in his *Principles of Economics:*

> Some accident which excites expectations of rising prices . . . sets speculators at work . . . In certain states of the public mind, such examples of rapid increase of fortune call forth

*The regulation of 1697 conforms to a pattern of antispeculator legislation in the aftermath of stock market crises, from the passing of Sir John Barnard's Act of 1734, intended to outlaw "the infamous practice of stock jobbing" after the collapse of the South Sea Bubble, to the establishment of the Securities and Exchange Commission after the Great Crash of 1929.

> numerous imitators, and speculation not only goes much beyond what is justified by the original grounds for expecting a rise of price, but extends itself to articles in which there never was any such ground; these, however, rise like the rest as soon as speculation sets in. At periods of this kind, a great extension of credit takes place.[36]

Although Britain remained a predominantly aristocratic and agrarian society in the late seventeenth century, the stock market boom of the 1690s appears to conform to this speculative paradigm.* The Projecting Age opened with several potential displacements, including the success of Captain Phipps's expedition, which inspired the diving engine companies, the extraordinary profitability of the East India Company and the other great trading companies in the 1680s, the innovations of the Financial Revolution and the war, which released surplus capital for stock market investment. Positive feedback in the market was also in evidence. According to the poet Aaron Hill, after Phipps's return the nation displayed "a general Byas towards enslaving Judgment to success." Thereafter, rising share prices attracted new investors from all social classes. The author of *Angliae Tutamen* observed:

> People have been drawn in and abus'd, of all Qualities, Gentle and Simple, Wise and Otherwise; and really some Men of incomparable Parts and great Qualifications were caught, being allur'd with the Hopes of gaining vast Riches by this means . . .[37]

Company promoters took advantage of investor "euphoria" to float new ventures, many of which were supposedly based on new technologies but in reality were little more than fraudulent undertakings, intended solely to profit the promoters and stock operators.

*Macaulay compared the 1690s boom with the speculative manias of 1720, 1825, and 1845: In each case, "an impatience to be rich, a contempt for those slow but sure gains which are the proper reward of industry, patience and thrift, spread through society." (*History of England*, 1855, IV, p. 322.)

Shares were given to great men to lend respectability to these ventures. Corruption was evident in the manipulation of share prices and attempts to bribe the legislature. Financial fraud and speculation became so intertwined that many found it difficult to discriminate between them. As with many later stock market booms (including that of the 1990s), the mania of the 1690s played itself out through a series of mini-bubbles, starting with diving schemes and finishing with banks. Shares were driven above their intrinsic values by speculators using financial derivatives (stock options and futures) as well as paper credit. The boom lost momentum after sanguine expectations were disappointed and doubtful enterprises failed. The collapse of share prices contributed to a severe economic crisis.

Speculative manias in Kindleberger's model are examined only from an economic viewpoint. Yet social and political attitudes are equally important in determining the course of a mania. According to the financial journalist Alexander Dana Noyes, the American stock market boom at the beginning of the twentieth century was "as much a social and psychological phenomenon as a financial episode."[38] The same words could be applied to any other period of speculative euphoria. We can supplement the economic model of speculation with two conditions, one social and the other political. The first being that self-interest should be the principal economic motivation since manias are less likely when society has other priorities. "The spirit of gain" was the guiding light of company projectors, stockjobbers (whom Defoe accused of "unbounded avarice"), and other moneyed men of the 1690s. In *Angliae Tutamen,* the outburst of speculation was attributed to the character of the English nation, which

> runs a madding after new Inventions, Whims and Projects: And this unhappy Ingredient my dear Country-men have in their Tempers, they are violent, and prosecute their Projects eagerly for a time, but, not meeting with Success, they give over, and abandon all Hopes of ever doing good . . .[39]

The same speculative temperament had been observed earlier in the Dutch Republic, and was found later in the United States.

Nations that exhibit an appetite for enterprise and risk-taking have a strong propensity to speculation.

The second condition is political, namely that speculation should be unchecked by government interference. In the economic thought of the 1690s, we find the early stirrings of a free-market ideology which both anticipated and influenced the later work of Adam Smith. Although William of Orange did not subscribe to this new liberal ideology, he was beholden to the moneyed men who espoused it. In any event, the war with France distracted the government from fulfilling its traditional role as an economic regulator. An economic historian of the period describes the British authorities as following the "negative *laissez-faire* policy of a disorderly political body."[40] The government's failure to regulate or supervise the new stock market and its stimulation of a lottery "fever" were key factors in the genesis and development of the 1690s boom. This was supplemented by the venality of members of Parliament who were more interested in profiting personally from the stock market than in opposing its excesses. As we shall see, a combination of laissez-faire and political corruption is a common feature of later manias—the most notable example being the Japanese "bubble economy" of the 1980s. When the boom ended and was followed by an economic crisis, the political situation changed. The selfish and shortsighted behaviour of stockjobbers and promoters suggested a limit to the economic role of self-interest, and laissez-faire was replaced by regulation of both trade and the stock market. Other manias have also been followed by a wave of popular, if rather hypocritical, revulsion against "greed." After the crisis of 1696, stockjobbers became a symbol for the avarice of society at large, just as the "moneylenders" (President Franklin D. Roosevelt's phrase) were castigated in the 1930s.

It is easier to observe the common traits of a speculative mania as they emerged in the 1690s than it is to explain why the pattern should have established itself so early in such an enduring form. While Kindleberger produces a convincing model for what he calls the "hardy perennial" of the speculative mania, he does not seek to explain why speculation has changed so little from its earliest appearance to the present day. Despite great trumpeting of the level of financial sophistication reached in the late twentieth century, there is really very little in our financial understanding that is actually new. Already in the seventeenth century, both in Amsterdam and in London, we find financial derivatives being used for both risk control and speculation. We also find sophisticated notions of value, together with the idea of "discounted" cash flows and present values. Wagering and probability theory provided contemporaries with an understanding that the risk-reward ratio could, in certain circumstances, be calculated. Defoe warned against buying shares above their intrinsic value, while Sir Richard Steele elaborated a contrarian investment strategy involving the suppression of hope and fear. Taken together, their advice more or less anticipates the "value investor" approach of Benjamin Graham, the twentieth century's so-called Father of Securities Analysis. If investor perceptions and behaviour have not changed significantly in three hundred years, it is natural that speculation should also retain its original qualities. The modern investor is just as liable to be whipped up into a frenzy over companies introducing a new technology as the diving engine "cullies" of the Projecting Age. According to the financial journalist and historian James Grant, "progress is cumulative in science and engineering but cyclical in finance."[41]

It is often said that speculation never changes because human nature remains the same. "Avarice, or desire of gain, is a universal passion which operates at all times, in all places, and upon all persons," wrote David Hume in the eighteenth century. To this we might add that the fear of loss, emulation of one's neighbour, the credulity of the crowd, and the psychology of gambling are equally universal. The early stock markets were moved by hopes and fears as much as their later counterparts. These emotions are unleashed during moments of speculative euphoria. They follow the path of least resistance, moulding each mania, regardless of its historical context, into a common form. This explains why all great speculative events seem to repeat themselves and why the experience of the 1690s seems so familiar.

CHAPTER 3

"THE NEVER-TO-BE-FORGOT OR FORGIVEN SOUTH-SEA SCHEME"*

There must certainly be a vast Fund of Stupidity in Human Nature, else Men would not be caught as they are, a thousand times over, by the same Snare; and while they yet remember their past Misfortunes, go on to court and encourage the Causes to which they were owing, and which will again produce them.

Cato's Letters, January 1721

All Europe as well as these Kingdoms, are on the point of being delivered . . . by the influence of British arms and counsels . . . so far as Prudence can foretell the Unanimity of this Session of Parliament must establish, with the Peace of all Europe, the Glory and Trade of these Kingdoms, on a lasting foundation. I think every Man may see the End of our Labours: all I have to ask of you is, that you will agree to be a great and flourishing People." Thus ran the King's Speech at the opening of Parliament on 23 November 1719. This hopeful rhetoric appeared well justified. The invasion force of the Old Pretender, son of James II, had recently been crushed at Glenshiel in the Highlands and the old Tory leadership was in exile in Paris, leaving George I and his Whig cronies to contemplate a future in which their power lay unchallenged. The accession of the Hanoverian dynasty in 1714

*Sir Robert Walpole's words.

and the peace with France that followed had given great satisfaction to the moneyed men, who recommenced trading with new vigour. Interest rates were low and the King's anticipation that his people would be "great and flourishing" seemed no idle boast. Only the author of *Robinson Crusoe*, published in 1719, failed to share in the widespread jubilation. In his *Anatomy of Exchange Alley*, Defoe warned of a "general visitation, where all distempers are swallowed up in the plague, like a common calamity, that makes enemies turn friends, and drowns lesser grievance in the general deluge."[1] But what did the rant of an undischarged bankrupt count for against the combined wisdom of the Court, Parliament, and City?

Within a year Defoe was vindicated. A calamity, popularly perceived as the biblical visitation anticipated by Defoe, had shaken the kingdom, root and branch. The prosperity, so recently in evidence, had disappeared, to be replaced by bankruptcies and suicides. The ministry was in disarray, Parliament unruly, and riotous crowds thronged Westminster, jeering at ministers and baying for blood. The new dynasty was shaken. A member of Parliament claimed that, had the Old Pretender chosen to invade at this moment, he could have ridden to Westminster unopposed. Such a dramatic revolution in political and commercial fortunes had never before been witnessed in the country, despite its history of civil wars and usurpations. The cause of this great *bouleversement* was known to all; it was described by the two monosyllables which resounded from every lip: the nation was submerged under the waves of the *South Sea*.

THE FIRST BUBBLES

Since the 1690s, the momentum of the Financial Revolution had continued with a number of important innovations. In 1710, there had been a brief boom following the successful flotation of Sun Fire, the first insurance company. A year later, the South Sea Company was established to take over £10 million of government debt, which it "converted" into its own shares. In exchange, the South Sea Company received an annual interest payment from the government and the monopoly of trade with the Spanish colonies in

South America. A couple of years later, the company received exclusive rights to sell slaves in South America. Although its trading activities always showed a loss, the South Sea Company succeeded as a financial institution. In early 1719, it took over a further £1,700,000 of government debt in the form of annuities, which it converted into South Sea stock.*

By this date, the ideology of self-interest had recovered from the battering it had received after the crisis of the mid-1690s. It was most famously articulated in Bernard Mandeville's *The Fable of the Bees* with its thesis that private vices—avarice, prodigality, pride, and luxury—produced public benefits.† The lust for gain remained most rampant in the coffeehouses of Exchange Alley. In her play *A Bold Stroke for a Wife* (1718), Susannah Centlivre, the dramatist spouse of the royal cook, portrayed the Alley as a place where "Bulls" contested with "Bears," brokers "bit" (i.e., cheated) their customers, and false rumours were deliberately circulated. A few years earlier, in January 1714, the notorious "Queen Anne is Dead" rumour had caused shares to slide (yet when the Queen actually died a few months later, the market took the news in its stride).

The year 1719 was one of general prosperity and confidence.‡ In France, the Scotsman John Law, perhaps the greatest financier of all time, was putting the finishing touches to his "System." His Mississippi Company controlled French Louisiana (including half the territory of the United States), the French East India and China

*These annuities had nearly 24 years to run and cost the government £135,000 a year to service. It was agreed to capitalise them at 11.5 years' revenue (i.e., the nominal value of South Sea stock to be exchanged for the annuities was to be 11.5 times the income the annuitants received), on which the government would pay 5 percent. As the South Sea's share price was above £100 nominal the annuitants received a capital gain on conversion. The company also agreed to lend the government £520,000 in cash, which it raised by selling shares in the market at £114. This raised £592,800, bringing the company a "profit" of over £76,000. The success of the whole venture as far as the company and annuitants were concerned had been dependent on the South Sea Company's shares trading above their par value of £100.

†On its first appearance this teasingly profane thesis produced little reaction, but when it was republished in 1723 (after the South Sea Bubble) it provoked a great furore.

‡P. G. M. Dickson writes that on the eve of the South Sea Bubble, England was "bolder and more confident than ever before." (*Financial Revolution*, p. 90.)

companies, the tobacco monopoly, the mint, the tax farms, the national bank (La Banque Royale), and, in August 1719, it took over the entire French national debt of 1,500 million livres. The System, which also involved substituting a paper currency for gold, was the most far-reaching economic experiment undertaken before the Russian Revolution. The son of an Edinburgh goldsmith, Law regarded money as a medium of exchange rather than a store of intrinsic value. His broad, indeed revolutionary, conception of money included paper currency, bonds, credit notes, and *company shares.* Following the example of the Darien Company in the 1690s, Law's bank issued increasing amounts of paper currency to provide loans for the purchase of shares. As the Mississippi shares rose in value, more money was printed, producing an inflationary spiral which pushed the share price from under 500 livres at the launch of the System to over 20,000 by late 1719.* The effect of Law's machinations was to produce an unprecedented outburst of speculation in France, where new fortunes brought the word *millionaire* into usage. Investors converged on the Parisian stock market in the rue Quincampoix from every corner of Europe; in Geneva house prices began to rise after its citizens cashed in their Mississippi profits; in Hamburg new insurance companies were floated; and, in Austria, an Eastern trading company was proposed. Europe was experiencing the first international bull market.[2]

By autumn, the speculative fever had reached London, where new companies were appearing in Exchange Alley. As speculative funds flowed from London to Paris, the Whig ministry agonised on the success of Law's project, fearing it would lead to French supremacy on the Continent and eventual war with Britain. Something needed to be done. If France's greatest company was named after a river, they already had a company named after an ocean: The South Sea Company would serve as an English Mississippi.

*Law's great error was his confusion of shares with money. Since rising share prices led to the printing of more money, which in turn was ploughed back into shares, there was no potential limit to the ensuing asset inflation. The same circularity existed during the Japanese "bubble economy" of the 1980s when rising asset prices caused Japanese banks' capital to rise, allowing them to make more loans (see chapter 9). Most pronounced in these two cases, this circularity is always present in modern financial systems where credit creation is dependent on asset values.

THE SOUTH SEA SCHEME

The scheme in its essentials was relatively modest in comparison to its French counterpart. The directors of the South Sea company proposed to take over—or *privatise*—the British national debt, comprising various annuities, which it agreed to convert into its own shares. In return, the company would receive from the government an interest payment on the debt. There were numerous precedents for the scheme. What was different was the scale of the operation, since the annuities were capitalised by the government at over £30 million.

Since the holders of government annuities could not be coerced into converting their assets into South Sea stock, the company had to make them an attractive offer. If it could inflate the value of its shares, which were already trading at a premium, it could offer a good price to the annuitants. The company was allowed to issue shares with a nominal value of £31.5 million (as the shares' nominal value was £100 this implied a maximum issue of 315,000 new shares). Those shares authorised for issue but not involved in the conversion could be sold in the market and the money raised used to pay the £7.5 million the company had agreed to give the government for the privilege of taking over its debt. Any proceeds that remained were considered a "profit" to the company.* The success of the scheme therefore depended on inflating the value of South Sea stock prior to the conversion so that fewer shares were actually exchanged for annuities.

These arrangements were as confusing to most contemporaries as they appear to the modern reader. It is possible to clarify them by explaining how the conversion would work at different levels of the South Sea share price. If the share price was at its £100 nominal value and all the annuitants accepted the conversion, then

*Modern accounting standards require that when new shares are issued at a premium to their nominal value, the surplus should be placed in an inviolable "share premium account" (i.e., it is considered part of the company's nondistributable capital reserve). In the early eighteenth century the position was quite different: the market premium for new shares was considered as so much "profit" that accrued to the company and could be distributed to its shareholders. This basic accounting error contributed greatly to the blowing up of the Mississippi and South Sea bubbles.

315,000 new South Sea shares would be created. The annuitants would receive a smaller income (since in its deal with the South Sea Company, the government had arranged to reduce the total interest payment on its debt by half a million pounds), but in exchange they would at least have a tradable security with a 5 percent yield. In this case, however, there would be no surplus for the company to pay the government its £7.5 million sweetener, nor would it have any shares remaining to sell for its own profit. Now, assume the share price was £200 and every annuitant accepted conversion. Only half the number of authorised shares need be offered for the conversion, leaving the remainder to be sold in the market for £31 million. This would cover the cost of the payment to the government and leave a large cash surplus for the company's shareholders. The principle of the scheme was essentially quite simple: the higher the share price, the greater the profit for the company.

What the company actually did was rather more complicated. It raised its share price and then offered the annuitants shares with a market value greater than the original terms of conversion (although the nominal value of the shares they received was actually smaller).This provided the annuitants with a quick capital profit if they accepted conversion. The details of the South Sea scheme are difficult to bear in mind and for the sake of simplicity it is well to remember two facts: (i) The *higher* the South Sea share price, the *fewer* shares were exchanged for annuities and the greater the profit to be divided between the company and the government. (ii) The higher the value of the South Sea shares, the greater the market value of the shares received by the annuitants upon conversion. All parties—annuitants, government, existing and prospective shareholders—had an interest in an inflated share price.

No sooner had the scheme been announced to Parliament by Sir John Aislabie, the Chancellor of the Exchequer, on 21 January 1720, than the price of the South Sea shares began to rise. By mid-February, it had reached 187, up from 128 at the start of the year. In *Mist's Journal,* Daniel Defoe reported that Exchange Alley was teeming with people from all over town. The South Sea had become the "English Mississippi." "Where must this fall at last," he asked with his customary prescience, "if new Shares are created to make this Purchase [of annuities], which Shares are vendible at double the intrinsick Value, where must it fall when the Price abates? and when what is bought for 200 may sell but at PAR?"[3] The public's avidity for South Sea stock had appeared *before* the company had received permission from Parliament to go ahead with the conversion and *before* it had announced the terms of the conversion to the annuitants.

The carefree spirit which characterised the South Sea speculator is revealed in a frank letter that the poet Alexander Pope sent to his stockbroker, James Eckersall, on 21 February:

> I daily hear such reports of advantages to be gaind by one project or other in the Stocks, that my Spirit is Up with double Zeal, in the desire of our trying to enrich ourselves. I assure you my own Keeping a Coach and Six is not more in my head than the pleasure I shall take in seeing Mrs Eckersall in her Equipage. To be serious, I hope you have sold the Lottery orders, that the want of ready mony may be no longer an Impediment to our buying in the Stock, which was very unlucky at that time. I hear the S. Sea fell since, & should be glad we were in: I also hear there is considerably to be got by Subscribing to the new African Stock, Pray let us do something or other, which you judge the fairest Prospect, I am equal to what Stock, so you do but like it. Let but Fortune favor us, & the World will be sure to admire our Prudence. If we fail, let's e'en keep the mishap to ourselves: But tis Ignominious (in this Age of Hope and Golden Mountains) not to Venture. I am very truly your Lady's and Sr Your most obligd humble Servant A. Pope.

A month later, with the South Sea stock at over 300, a debate took place in the House of Commons over the terms of the conversion. Several MPs, including Sir Robert Walpole, Sir Richard Steele, and Archebald Hutcheson, argued that the value of South Sea stock should be fixed in the terms for conversion. The ministry opposed this measure for reasons that were not public knowledge. Several members of the government and Court—including Chancellor Aislabie, Postmaster General James Craggs, Secretary to the Treasury Charles Stanhope, and the King's German mistresses—had been secretly provided with an allocation of shares in the South Sea Company by its directors. These shares were issued at a small premium to the prevailing market price for which no deposit was required. As the shares did not in fact exist, the bribe functioned similarly to a modern executive stock-options scheme: if the share price rose the recipients could redeem the shares and take their profits. After receiving their fictitious shares or options, these influential persons had a keen interest in seeing the South Sea share price rise, regardless of the cost to the nation. The grasping Aislabie, who had also bought South Sea stock in the market, argued forcefully against Walpole and his confederates. On 23 March 1720, the government's will prevailed and the company was left free to set the terms of the conversion.

The parliamentary debate on the conversion revealed a conundrum: all parties—government, company, annuitants, and existing shareholders—appeared to profit by the continuing rise in the South Sea stock. The circularity inherent in the scheme made a rational calculation of the shares' fair value difficult to compute. Some argued that the higher the shares rose, the more they were actually worth. This opinion was expressed by a correspondent in the *Flying Post* on 9 April who claimed that "the higher the Price is which is given for the South-Sea stock, the greater the Benefit will the Purchaser have thereby; And that at 300 / . per Cent. [i.e., £300] it is intrinsically Worth 448 /. and at 600 /. is worth 880 / ." This plausible, yet absurd, calculation so enraged the financially minded Archebald Hutcheson, MP, that he published the first in a series of anti–South Sea pamphlets. Hutcheson maintained that people who bought surplus South Sea stock at its elevated price must be "deprived of all common Sense and Understanding" since they would be giving their money away to the original stockholders and annuitants. "Was there ever such a Delusion from the beginning of the World to the 9th *April*, 1720, endeavour'd to be imposed on the British *Nation* . . . ," he asked, "according to this Way of Computing, no Person can Purchase at too high a Rate, since his Profit will increase in Proportion to the Price he gives." Hutcheson saw clearly that the scheme was dependent on gulling both the annuitants (into converting their securities into too few shares) and the purchasers of the money subscriptions (i.e., those who bought the surplus

South Sea shares from the company). After reminding his readers that Parliament was only committed to a 5 percent interest payment and that the trading prospects of the company were not good, he concluded "certain it is, that the Loss at last must rest some-where."[4] In his periodical *The Theatre*, Sir Richard Steele made a similar point, warning that if "this affair is not put upon the basis of trade, and that in a visible way of profit, with consideration of contingencies, a loss it will be; and is nothing but a great appearance, a bulky phantom."*

THE SECRET AND PUBLIC HISTORY OF THE SOUTH SEA

Within the South Sea Company itself there were no such qualms. The company was under the control of a cabal led by John Blunt, ably assisted by the company cashier, Robert Knight. Blunt was a founding director of the company and the leading figure behind the conversion scheme. The son of a shoemaker, a Baptist by religion, and a scrivener by trade, Blunt was a deeply unattractive character, described in a recent history of the South Sea Bubble as "burly and overbearing, glib, ingenious and determined to get on."[5] An insider account of his operations during 1720 is provided by an anonymous tract entitled *The Secret History of the South-Sea Scheme.*† According to its author, Blunt had one primary aim:

**The Theatre*, No. 20, March 8, 1720. On 19 March, Steele wrote that although he did not understand figures, "this much I know of numbers already, that they consist of cyphers and figures; and in this Project there is no more necessary to judge of it, but that the bubbles are the mere cyphers which are to make the sharpers significant figures." Steele estimated that the South Sea shares had an intrinsic value of around 140, while Hutcheson demanded that the stock be valued for conversion at 150.

†The *Secret History* was first printed in *A Collection of Several Pieces of Mr. Toland: With Some Memoirs of His Life and Writing* (London, 1726), having been discovered among the manuscripts of John Toland. It was possibly written by Toland's friend Sir Theodore Jannsen, one of the South Sea directors who did not belong to Blunt's inner circle. Jannsen assisted Toland in one of the money subscriptions of 1720, and later helped him during his final illness. After the collapse of the scheme, Toland wrote to Jannsen, "I have been urgent with you, ever since Parliament took this affair in hand, to clear yourself with the soonest, as believing you rather imprudent than criminal." The author of the *Secret History* confesses to being unused to writing books "outside his counting-house."

> 'Twas his avow'd Maxim, a thousand times repeated, That the advancing by all means of the price of stock, was the only way to promote the good of the company.*

He looked for a thousand ways to attain this end. Originally it had been planned that the company would sell any "surplus" shares after the conversion of annuities; instead Blunt decided to draw in the profit first. As soon as the South Sea Bill received Royal Assent on 7 April 1720, he offered a subscription of South Sea shares to the public—it was the first of the company's four "Money Subscriptions" during the year. On 14 April, £2 million of South Sea stock was offered to the public at 300 a share (i.e., three times nominal value). The public was enthusiastic, and the subscription sold out within an hour. The launch of the money subscription before the conversion of annuities caused confusion to anyone attempting to calculate the intrinsic value of the stock, as no one could know what profits would derive from the conversion. This was intentional. According to the *Secret History*, Blunt's second maxim was

> the more confusion the better; People must not know what they do, which will make them the more eager to come into our measures; the execution of the Scheme is our business; the Eyes of all Europe are upon us.[6]

In order to make the money subscription attractive, Blunt offered easy terms for subscribers, as John Law had done with the Mississippi Company's share issues (this imitation was deliberate). Only a 20 percent deposit was required, the remainder to be paid in eight instalments over the following sixteen months. Again following John Law's example, the South Sea Company started providing loans to shareholders against the deposit of South Sea stock.† Loans were made from proceeds of share sales—money coming in one

---

*Blunt told the General Court of the company on 21 April that "the profit of the Company . . . do's chiefly depend on the price of the Stock at the times of the execution of the Act." (Quoted by Dickson, *Financial Revolution*, p. 141; *Secret History*, p. 423.)

†£250 of credit was provided per share, with a maximum loan of £5,000 per shareholder (in fact, this limit was ignored by the company).

door and going out the other—and from a £1 million loan which the government had provided the company. Their effect was to bolster the share price by both increasing the demand for stock (since with credit speculators could buy more shares) and reducing the supply of stock to the market, as mortgaged shares were retained by the company. The latter effect was reinforced when Blunt delayed delivering South Sea shares to annuitants who accepted the conversion. On 30 April, following a further issue of shares at 300, the company announced an increased dividend of 10 percent. The venal Blunt must have long anticipated this raise since he had bought a call option on the midsummer dividend back in January.

On 28 April 1720, the company opened its books for the first class of annuitants (known as the "irredeemables"), who rushed to subscribe although the company had yet to provide them with the exact terms of conversion.[7] In July, the subscription was extended to the other holders of government debt (the "redeemables"), again without the terms being presented.* In the end, 80 percent of the irredeemables and 85 percent of the redeemables accepted the conversion. The holders of government debt who rushed blindly into the South Sea included such savvy professionals as the Bank of England and the Million Bank (an organisation which held a number of government and company securities and operated like a modern investment trust). In the end, of the £31 million worth of government annuities that the company had offered to take over, £26 million was tendered in exchange for South Sea stock with a nominal value of only £8.5 million.† This left the company with 175,000 surplus shares to sell to the public.

---

*In the words of Professor Dickson, the annuitants accepted the conversion offer of the company "with a blind enthusiasm reminiscent of the Gadarene swine." (*Financial Revolution*, p. 133.)

†The company offered 32 years' purchase for the long annuities rather than 20 years' purchase at which they had been capitalised by the government. However, over half was paid in stock (valued at 375) and the remainder in cash and bonds. The annuitants only profited from the deal if the stock remained above 146.5. The offer to the owners of short annuities was less good, as the South Sea share price had to be at 237.5 for them to break even. (Dickson, *Financial Revolution*, p. 136; Scott, *Joint-Stock Companies*, II, p.10.)

DEVIL TAKE THE HINDMOST

Not everyone was convinced by the rise in the South Sea share price. On 22 April 1720, the day after the company announced its willingness to make loans on stock, Thomas Guy, the miserly stationer who had amassed a fortune buying sailor's tickets (credit notes issued by the navy in lieu of pay) at steep discounts, began selling his holding of South Sea stock. Over the following six weeks he sold shares with a nominal value of £54,000 for £234,000 (repenting a life of avarice, he later used some of the profits to endow the London hospital that bears his name). At around the same time, Sir Isaac Newton, the Master of the Mint, began selling his £7,000 holding of South Sea shares (when asked about the direction of the market, he is reported to have replied, "I can calculate the motions of the heavenly bodies, but not the madness of the people").[8] Richard Cantillon, the banker and economist, saw clearly that the bubble could not last indefinitely. Writing on 29 April 1720 to his client Lady Mary Herbert, he foresaw that the stock could be kept up "for some time, perhaps some years . . . but a melancholy prospect for those who shall stay last."[9]

Adam Anderson, a former cashier of the South Sea Company, later claimed that many purchasers of shares in the South Sea and other promotions bought knowing that their long-term prospects were hopeless, since they aimed to get "rid of them in the crowded alley to others more credulous than themselves."[10] In May 1720, William King, the Archbishop of Dublin, also came to the conclusion "that most that go into the [South Sea] matter are well aware it will not [succeed], but hope to sell before the price falls."[11] An anonymous pamphleteer expressed the situation for investors with great clarity:

> The additional rise of this stock above the true capital will be only imaginary; one added to one, by any rules of vulgar arithmetic, will never make three and a half; consequently, all the fictitious value must be a loss to some persons or other, first or last. The only way to prevent it to oneself must be to sell out betimes, and so let the Devil take the hindmost.[12]

The South Sea year was not one of calm calculation by investors pursuing an optimal strategy under the guiding light of rational expectations. As Edward Ward observed in his poem "A South Sea Ballad":

Few Men, who follow Reason's Rules,
Grow fat with South-Sea Diet,
Young Rattles and unthinking Fools
Are those that flourish by it.

The inflated price of South Sea stock was not the most egregious example of investor irrationality. A number of new joint-stock promotions had preceded the announcement of the South Sea scheme in January. Known as the "bubble companies," these ventures appeared with increasing frequency during the summer months.* Their method of flotation was simple: A notice appeared in a newspaper advertising a company and offering to take subscriptions at one of a number of coffeehouses in the City. They served an extraordinary variety of purposes, ranging from financial services, such as Matthew West's "Company for buying and selling South Sea stock and all other public stocks," to overseas settlement, such as Captain Welbe's "Company of London Adventurers for the carrying on a trade to and settling colonies in Terra Australis"—this latter venture a true speculation since it was floated over half a century before Captain Cook discovered Australia![†] Several companies were founded on new technologies, including "Puckle's Machine Gun" and Sir Richard Steele's Fish-Pool company, which was launched on a patent design for boats to bring live fish to the London market.[‡]

*New "bubble" companies appeared as follows: 5 in January, 23 in February, 27 in April, 19 in May, and a massive 87 in June.

[†]Adam Anderson lists the following categories of new bubble companies: insurance (10), fisheries (12), salt production (4), land and building development (15), oil from rape, poppy, and sunflower (6), mines and metals (15), and over 80 categorised as "miscellaneous."

[‡]Steele had received a patent on 10 June 1718 for a "New way or Method of making a Shipp . . . for y[e] Conveying and Preserving of Fish (tho' caught in parts ever so remote) alive and in as healthy and thriving a Condition as they would be were they to be still in the Sea . . ." Unfortunately, the Fish-Pool scheme failed because in stormy seas the fish battered against each other and died.

For a while, the bubble companies flourished in the stock market. The two leading insurance bubbles, the Royal Exchange and the London Assurance, sold at their peak for twenty-five and sixty-four times paid-up capital respectively. Steele's Fish-Pool went to a premium of £160 before *any* call had been made on the shares. Globe Permits, giving the right to subscribe to a future sailcloth project, sold for £70 before the company had even been established.[13] Shares in the older corporations also soared in the bull market: the East India went from 100 to a high of 445, the Royal Africa from 23 to 200, and Million Bank rose from 100 to 440. The total capitalisation of the London stock market rose to over £500 million at its peak in the summer of 1720, roughly one hundred times the figure for 1695.[14]

"It is observed," wrote *The Weekly Packet* of 7 May 1720, "that many of these projects are so ridiculous and chimerical, that it is hard to tell which is most to be wondered at, the impudence of those that make the proposals, or the stupid folly of those that subscribe to them; yet many a gudgeon hath been caught in the net, though one would think that, with half an eye, he might discern the cheat." Several of the bubble companies served rather bizarre purposes: one company was established to garner saltpetre by emptying all the "necessary houses" (i.e., lavatories) in England; another promised to supply funerals across the country. The absurdity of these schemes and the credulity of investors produced tales of legendary companies that have subsequently found their way into the history books. *The Bubbler's Mirrour,* a fly sheet, playing on the themes of financial alchemy and investor irrationality, listed several real companies together with fabulous schemes for extracting silver from lead, for the transmutation of quicksilver, for building an Engine to Remove South Sea House to Moorfields (i.e., the mental hospital commonly known as Bedlam), and for an air pump for the brain.*

*W. R. Scott, who did not attempt to distinguish between the genuine bubble companies and the legendary satires, recorded one company "for extracting Gold and Silver from Lead and other sorts of ore," and another "for the transmutation of fluid mercury of quicksilver into a solid and malleable body . . . by a just calculation 'tis demonstrable that each subscriber will get 800 percent." (Scott, *Joint-Stock Companies,* III, pp. 457.)

Other schemes that most likely existed in legend rather than reality included companies "For better curing Venereal Disease," "For Trading in Human Hair," and "For a Wheel for Perpetual Motion, by means of a wheel moving by force of its own weight." The most famous of the legendary bubble companies was that "for carrying on an undertaking of great advantage but no one to know what it is."* The bubble legends—with their implied critique of corrupt projectors, financial alchemy, investor credulity, irrationality, and even madness—reveal in a parodic carnivalistic fashion the deep apprehensions that many contemporaries had about the speculative schemes. After the collapse of the bubble, they served as an admonition to future generations of speculators, taking their place alongside the earlier tulip legends.

A recent historian of the South Sea Bubble sympathetically interprets the bubble companies as attempts to realise a vision of material and technological progress ahead of their time.[15] For better or worse, the machine gun was eventually perfected and Australia discovered. It is true that certain bubble companies, such as Steele's Fish-Pool, were genuine, if flawed, promotions, but the great majority were fraudulent ventures designed to profit from the speculative euphoria. Their founders must have had little intention of creating legitimate enterprises. Only four of the 190 bubble companies founded in 1720 survived, although among them were two insurance companies, the Royal Exchange and London Assurance, which later flourished. Most bubble company projectors preyed on the credulity and cynicism of those who bought their shares. Speculators did not buy bubble company shares as long-term investments; they bought them with the intention of selling them on to greater

---

*This legendary company may relate to a spoof promotion recorded in *Mist's Journal* in early January 1720. J. P. Malcolm in *Anecdotes of the Manners and Customs of London during the Eighteenth Century* (London, 1808, p. 67) records a similar scheme, for "a joint co-partnership for carrying on a *thing* that will turn to the advantage of the concerned." John Carswell cites an advertisement in the *Daily Post* of 21 May 1720 for a "Proposal for raising the sum of Six Millions sterling to carry on a design of more general advantage . . . and of more certain profit . . . than any undertaking yet set on foot." (*South Sea Bubble*, p. 129.) James Grant has pointed out that this company might be seen as the first speculative "blind pool." (*Minding Mr. Market*, p. 113.)

fools. In a very short time, however, they were to discover that there were no greater fools in the market than themselves.

"DRIVEN AWAY FROM HIS ANCHORAGE"

On 15 June 1720, the South Sea Company launched its Third Money Subscription, with no limit on the amount to be issued. Three days earlier, Charles Stanhope, the Secretary to the Treasury, who had received Blunt's bribe of share options earlier in the year, secretly cashed in his shares for a profit of £249,000 (this fabulous sum was paid directly out of the South Sea Company's treasury and was nothing less than a fraud against the company's shareholders). On the very same day, Chancellor Aislabie attempted to persuade George I to sell his South Sea stock, but the King ignored this advice and sold only a few to raise cash to purchase more shares in the new subscription.

Where the King led, the nation followed. South Sea stock worth £50 million was subscribed in a few hours even though the price of the issue, at £1,000, was a third greater than the current market price of around £750. The incentive for subscribers was an easy payment scheme, which required only a 10 percent deposit with the next instalment due in one year and others payable over four years. The money paid into the company was immediately lent against the deposit of stock, with over £3 million worth of credit provided to shareholders in one day. By the date of the Fourth Money Subscription on 24 August, the South Sea Company had issued shares with an initial market value of more than £75 million and lent over £12 million against the deposit of stock.

These operations reveal an extraordinary recklessness on the part of Blunt and his fellow directors. Chancellor Aislabie later claimed that events had run away from the company and the government:

> It became difficult to govern it; and let those gentlemen that opened the floodgates wonder at the deluge that ensued as much as they please it was not in one man's power, or in the power of the whole administration to stop it, considering how the world was borne away by the torrent.

Yet Blunt and his fellow directors had deliberately opened the floodgates, and in the summer they displayed little desire to control the speculative torrent. Like the bubble itself, they had become inflated by the apparent success of the scheme and the glory that was showered upon them. According to the *Secret History*, Blunt, surrounded by universal flattery, had become untouchable:*

> He visibly affected a prophetic stile, delivering his words with an emphasis and extraordinary vehemence; and us'd to put himself into a commanding posture, rebuking those that durst in the least oppose anything he said, and endeavouring to inculcate, as if what he spoke was by impulse, uttering these and such like expressions: *Gentlemen, don't be dismayed: You must act with firmness, with resolution, with courage. I tell you, 'tis not a common matter you have before you. The greatest thing in the world is referred to you. All the mony of Europe will center amongst you. All the nations on the earth will bring you tribute.*[16]

Blunt's overblown messianic manner and his sense of boundless power—the *Secret History* describes him as "thinking himself no longer bound to keep any measures . . . he thought he had the world on a string"—is a common defect of leading financiers during a speculative mania. John Law during the Mississippi Bubble, George Hudson in the Railway Mania, Ivar Kreuger in the 1920s, and Michael Milken during the 1980s all displayed the same symptoms.[17] The plans of the great financier may act as a catalyst to a speculative mania, but the financier himself does not remain untouched by events. His ambition becomes limitless, a chasm opens up between the public appearance of success and universal adulation, on the one hand, and the private management of affairs which become increasingly confused and even fraudulent.

An insight into Blunt's behaviour is provided by Anthony Trollope, whose corrupt railroad financier Augustus Melmotte in his

*The author of the *Secret History* claimed that "he who shou'd dare oppose him [Blunt], or to exposes his artifices, wou'd have been generally decry'd as an envyer of his parts, an enemy to the Scheme . . . and 'tis doubtful, whether he could escape without ill treatment to his person, from more quarters than one." (*Secret History*, p. 415.)

novel *The Way We Live Now* was partly inspired by George Hudson, the Railway King of the 1840s. Describing Melmotte at the end of his career, Trollope claimed that "insane ambition had driven him away from his anchorage":

> It can hardly be said of him that he had intended to play so high a game, but the game that he had intended to play had become thus high of its own accord. A man cannot always restrain his own doings and keep them within the limits which he had himself planned for them. They will very often fall short of the magnitude to which his ambition has aspired. They will sometimes soar higher than his own imagination . . . He had contemplated great things; but the things which he was achieving were beyond his contemplation.

Blunt had projected the South Sea scheme with every intention of personal profit. He had bought options on the summer dividend which he planned to increase. Seeing the success of the early money subscriptions, he had secretly increased the issue of shares to himself and his friends. He had done everything in his power to force up the price of the shares. When the shares were at their height, he sold out and started to buy land with his profits. He even sold more shares than he owned, secure in the knowledge that the time would soon come when he could buy them back ("cover his shorts") at a cheaper price. When the fourth, and last, Money Subscription was called in mid-August, realising that the game did not have much longer to play, he instructed his fellow directors to purchase £3,000 worth of shares each but only subscribed for £500 himself.

If the South Sea scheme had been reasonably executed from the start with a fixed value for the conversion of annuities into shares, as Sir Richard Steele and others demanded, and if Blunt had striven for less, been content with a share price of £150 rather than £1,000, limited his desire for personal enrichment, and kept his head when he became the hero of the nation, then there is little reason to doubt that the conversion would have proved useful to all parties. But Blunt's restless ambition destroyed any chance of success the scheme might have had. He was greedy and vain, and conducted his affairs with no more circumspection than the wildest speculator. Operations of financial alchemy, as Sir Isaac Newton discovered, were more likely to damage the mind of the alchemist than to achieve any lasting transmutation of base metals into gold.

THE SOUTH SEA SPECULATORS

By summer, Alexander Pope had developed a rather confused attitude to the prevailing speculation: He was torn between a desire for personal profit and a disgust at the sordid money grubbing of the nation. On 24 June, he wrote to his friend William Fortescue, "I am really piqued at the stocks, which put a stop, at present, to all trade and all friendship, and I fear all honour too." A week later, he was less ill-humoured, writing to Fortescue that he and John Gay, the poet, intended to buy estates in Devonshire with their profits and entertained thoughts of representing the county in Parliament. Shortly after, he received a pair of letters from Robert Digby on the South Sea, to which he replied advising his friend to pay no attention to "this miserable mercenary Period; and turn yourself, in a just Contempt of these Sons of Mammon, to the Contemplation of Books, Gardens, and Marriage."[18] Yet on 22 August he wrote to Lady Mary Wortley Montagu warmly advising her to buy more stock.[19]

In his correspondence with Pope, Digby revealed how deeply the nation had immersed itself in the South Sea: "The London language and conversation is I find quite changed since I left it," wrote Digby, "tho' it is not above three to four months ago. No violent change in the natural world ever astonished a Philosopher so much as this does me." From The Hague, the *Mercure historique et politique* reported in July:

> The South Sea Company is continually a source of wonderment. The sole topic of conversation in England revolves around the shares of this Company, which have produced vast fortunes for many people in such a short space of time. Moreover it is to be noted that trade has completely slowed down, that more than one hundred ships moored along the river

Thames are for sale, and that the owners of capital prefer to speculate on shares than to work at their normal business.[20]

A few weeks earlier, Edward Harley, whose brother Robert, the former Tory minister, had established the South Sea Company, back in 1711, observed that "the demon stock jobbing is the genius of this place. This fills all hearts, tongues, and thoughts, and nothing is so like bedlam as the present humour which has seized all parties, Whigs, Tories, Jacobites, Papists, and all sects. No one is satisfied with even exorbitant gains, but everyone thirsts for more, and all this is founded upon a machine of paper credit supported only by imagination . . ."[21] The same month, Jonathan Swift, whose own investments were being handled by John Gay, wrote in a letter, "I have enquired of some that have come from London, what is the religion there? they tell me it is South Sea stock; what is the policy of England? the answer is the same; what is the trade? South Sea still; and what is the business? nothing but South Sea."[22]

The South Sea speculators came from every social class. At their head stood King George I, who had probably received an allocation of fictitious shares at the start of the scheme. His eldest son, the Prince of Wales, also held South Sea shares and was governor of the Welsh Copper Company (known commonly as "the Prince of Wales's bubble"). He was followed by an assortment of jobbing dukes, marquises, earls, and barons. Over a hundred peers and three hundred members of Parliament bought shares in the Third Money Subscription. The roads thronged with country gentlemen and rich farmers coming to London to buy stock.* City financiers were involved heavily in the early subscriptions, and foreign speculators, especially the Dutch, were prominent in Exchange Alley.† By the time of the Fourth Money Subscription, however, the domestic and international financiers suspected that the affair did not have much further to run. Many of the Dutch speculators sold up and

*_Mist's Journal_ (26 March 1720) reported an "abundance of our Country Gentlemen and rich Farmers are upon the Roads from several Parts of the Kingdom; all expecting no less than to ride home again, every Man, in his Coach and Six . . ."

†See C. Wilson, _Anglo-Dutch Commerce and Finance in the Eighteenth Century_ (Cambridge, 1941). Contact between London and Amsterdam was kept open by dozens of small fishing vessels (_pinkjes_) which brought the latest South Sea news to Kalverstraat.

repatriated their capital to invest in the booming Amsterdam stock market. The London bankers for their part simply refrained from partaking in the last subscription. The departure of the more experienced market operators at, or near, the peak of a bubble is a common feature of speculative booms. Blunt was well aware of this problem; in his insatiable desire to keep the share price rising he declared a preference for making loans on stock not to professionals but "to Ladies and young Gentlemen, who come from the other end of town, with a spirit of gaming: for such, according to him, were the most likely to advance the price of the stock."[23]

LADY SPECULATORS

Women have played an important part in the history of speculation. "Widows and Orphans" has long been the standard cry of those who seek to protect the innocent against the dangers of speculation. (Charles Kindleberger has found a protective allusion to them dating back to Mesopotamia in the third millennium B.C.)[24] The widow-investor is deemed to be financially naive and in need of protection against charlatans. Her antithesis is the female speculator who first emerged in France and Britain in the early eighteenth century.

In France, John Law was the object of relentless attention from ladies eager to receive shares in the Mississippi Company (the Regent's mother observed lewdly that if duchesses were prepared to kiss Law's hand, what parts of his body might not other ladies favour?). Chief among the aristocratic female speculators was the remarkable former nun Alexandrine de Tencin, mistress of the French chief minister Abbé Dubois and possibly lover of John Law (and later mother of the *philosophe* D'Alembert), who established her own *bureau d'agiotage*. Another "Mississippian," as they were called, was Lady Mary Herbert, daughter of the Earl of Carnarvon, who later bought South Sea stock against the advice of her banker, Richard Cantillon. The extent of female speculation in the South Sea is revealed by the presence of thirty-five ladies (out of the eighty-eight names) on Lord Sunderland's list for the Second Money Subscription.[25] Lady Mary Wortley Montagu, the celebrated traveller who introduced the smallpox vaccine to England, purchased South Sea stock in 1720, intending to use her profits to pay off a French blackmailer, called Rémond, to whom she had written some indiscreet letters. Many of the ladies at the Princess of Wales's court in Richmond were active speculators, including the Duchesses of Rutland and Marlborough. Female speculation was also strong at the other end of the social spectrum. At Billingsgate, the conversation of the market women was said to turn "to a merry Way of buying and selling *South-Sea* over a refreshing cup of *Gin.*"[26]

Ladies from the West End were reported to have rented a shop in the City, which they turned into a club for tea drinking and playing the stock market; "at leisure time, while their agents are abroad, they game for china."[27] The *Daily Post* of 20 April 1720, announced that a new company had been floated, involving "A proposal by several ladies and others to make, print and paint and stain calicoes in England and also fine linnen as fine as any Holland to be made of British flax . . . they are resolved as one man to admit no man but will themselves subscribe to a joint-stock to carry on the said trade. [Subscribers must be women dressed in calico.] Subscription taken at the China Shop in St. Martin's, near St. Paul's."* In his "South Sea Ballad," Edward Ward described the visitors to Exchange Alley:

Our greatest Ladies hither come,
And ply in Chariots daily,
Oft pawn their Jewels for a Sum,
To venture't in the Alley.

Young Harlots too, from Drury-Lane,
Approach the 'Change in Coaches,
To fool away the Gold they gain
By their obscene Debauches.

Women had various reasons to speculate. In eighteenth-century England, most landed estates were in male entail, but there were no

*Scott, *Joint-Stock Companies*, III, p. 450. This story is probably legend. Scott observes sardonically that calico was "a costume, one would imagine, somewhat light for April 19th."

such restrictions on the ownership of shares. As ladies could not be seen to work for a living, they were attracted to the world of the stock market, in which matters of sex, class, and race were treated with extreme indifference.* In *Ten Years on Wall Street* (1870), William Fowler claimed that the female character was perfectly fitted to a life of speculation that derived its food from excitement, came from fancy, and required both patience and fortitude.[28] Although speculation may have suited the feminine temperament, there is no reason to believe that lady speculators fared any better, or worse, than their male counterparts. The uncommonly astute Sarah, Duchess of Marlborough, sold her South Sea stock in late May, clearing a profit of nearly £100,000.† Others, such as Lady Mary Herbert and Lady Mary Wortley Montagu, were not so prescient. Successful speculation, however, could reverse the inequality between the sexes. In early August 1720, in a letter to *Applebee's Journal*, a lady speculator declared her intention of purchasing a "South Sea Husband . . . I am resolv'd to be even with the Money-Hunting Sex, and if I lay out my Money, to be sure of my Possession . . ."[29]

"ALL FOR THE BETTER, OR THE WORLD TURN'D UPSIDE DOWN"

> When these extraordinary Events are consider'd, and Women of the Town are become Dealers in the Stocks, Valets de Shambre [sic], Footmen and Porters (as well as Merchants, Tradesmen, and Pickpockets) walk on the Exchange, and ride in their Coaches, at the same time some good natur'd Gentlemen have

---

*As Gerry Tsai, a Chinese-American fund manager in the 1960s, remarked: "If you buy General Motors at forty and it goes to fifty, whether you are an Oriental, a Korean, or a Buddhist doesn't make any difference." (Quoted by John Brooks, *The Go-Go Years*, New York, 1973, p. 132.)

†The duchess wrote to a friend, "Every mortal that has common sense or that knows anything of figures sees that 'tis not possible by all the arts and tricks upon earth to carry £400,000,000 of paper credit with £15,000,000 of specie. This makes me think that this project must burst in a while and fall to nothing." Her descendant Winston Churchill referred to her "almost repellent common sense" in taking profits before the crash.

> quitted them; Projectors successfully Bubble the Publick in all their Schemes; Sharpers leave their Gaming-Tables in Covent-Garden, for more profitable Business in Jonathan's Coffee-House; and even Poets commence Stock-Jobbers, it is high time to pronounce Exchange-Alley truly a FARCE.[30]

Speculation penetrated the barriers between the social classes.* "We have seen," lamented Swift, "a great Part of the Nation's Money got into the Hands of those, who by their Birth, Education and Merit, could pretend no higher than to wear our liveries." The likes of Tom Double returned with a vengeance in the South Sea year. These "cyphering cits," as Steele called them, impudently flaunted their newfound wealth: buying houses, coaches, and embroidered coats for themselves and gold watches for their wives and mistresses. The rush to buy estates sent land prices soaring to fifty times their rental value. "Our South-Sea equipages increase every day," observed *Applebee's Journal* in August, "the City ladies buy South-Sea jewels; hire South-Sea maids; and take new country South-Sea houses; the gentlemen set up South-Sea coaches, and buy South-Sea estates . . ."[31]

Conspicuous consumption was accompanied by revelry. At St. James's in late May, the King's birthday was celebrated with over a hundred cases of claret and the Duchess of Kendal appeared in a dress embroidered with jewels worth £5,000.[32] In late July, great crowds of the nobility and gentry gathered at a house in Hampstead to divert themselves with nightly gambling and a weekly Masquerade.[33] The coffeehouses and taverns around the Exchange were packed with speculators indulging in bacchanalian excess.† On Monday, 22 August, when the subscription books for the Fourth (and last) Money Subscription were opened, huge crowds gathered around South Sea House and the entire issue of 10,000 shares,

*Anderson claimed the bubble's collapse brought "the ruin of many honourable and till then wealthy families, to the advancement of many low and obscure persons and families." (*Origin of Commerce*, III p. 92.)

†Anderson remembered the "taverns, coffee-houses, and even victualling houses, near the Exchange were constantly crowded, and became scenes of incredible extravagance." (*Origin of Commerce*, III p. 103.)

priced at £1,000 a share, was sold out by one o'clock. The historian John Carswell has described the atmosphere in the City: "The town was on the point of being given over to the great annual carnival of Bartholomew Fair . . . workmen were tearing up the paving-stones of Smithfield to drive in the stakes for the stalls and show-booths. The City was already full of freaks, fencers, play-actors, and mountebanks. As the week passed the streets were choked, day and night, with a roaring mob, drinking, gambling and gaping."[34] On Wednesday, 24 August, the wedding of "two vast rich Jews, both of the Name of Corney," was celebrated at the Leatherseller's Hall in Bishopsgate, attended by the Prince and Princess of Wales and "the greatest Concourse of the Nobility that was ever known upon such an Occasion."[35] Two hundred dishes were served at the entertainment and the public feasting continued for three days. Society, both high and low, was dancing to the frenetic beat of the stock market.

A RUDE AWAKENING

By midsummer, the directors of the South Sea Company were fearful that competition from "bubble companies," which were appearing almost daily in Exchange Alley, would damage their company's share price. In order to monopolise the speculative enthusiasm, Blunt persuaded his friends in the government to pass the "Bubble Act," which made illegal the establishment of companies without parliamentary permission and prevented existing companies from carrying on activities not specified by their charters. The act received Royal Assent on 9 June (the same day that John Blunt received a baronetcy), but it had little initial effect on the demand for bubble company shares, which remained strong. The South Sea directors were not to be outdone: They requested the Attorney General to issue a writ for prosecution, known as a *Scire Facias,* against three bubble companies which had diversified into areas not covered by their charters. Twelve days later, the South Sea Company announced a dividend of 30 percent for the year (i.e., £30 on a £100 nominal share) and a guaranteed 50 percent dividend for the next twelve years.

These three measures—the Bubble Act, the *Scire Facias* writ, and the enhanced dividend—were intended to sustain the flagging South Sea share price, which had peaked in late June at a price of 1,050 (an eightfold increase in under six months) but had fallen to 850 by August. To the horror of the directors, their machinations backfired. The publication of the *Scire Facias* brought panic to the stock market. Within a few weeks, York Buildings, a water company that had diversified outside its charter into property development, collapsed from 305 to 30. The leading insurance companies, the London Assurance and the Royal Exchange, fell by over 75 percent. Speculators who had purchased bubble company shares on credit were forced to sell their South Sea shares to make good their losses elsewhere. Even the company's announcement of a generous dividend failed to encourage investors, most of whom were more interested in capital gains. Besides no one really believed that the company could afford to pay a 50 percent dividend.

Other factors conspired to lower the South Sea share price. In June and July foreigners began disposing of their South Sea shareholdings to reinvest their profits in the new bubble companies appearing in the Hamburg and Amsterdam stock markets. The Canton of Berne, Switzerland, sold its South Sea stock and repatriated its profits. Speculation had also stretched domestic credit to its limits (interest rates rose to over 20 percent in the summer), and neither the South Sea Company nor City bankers had any funds left to lend against South Sea stock. None of these factors proved decisive. In fact, no trigger for the collapse was needed: by late summer the company had exhausted all available means of sustaining momentum in its share price, and without momentum, decline was inevitable.

The month of September opened with the South Sea stock below 800. The decline accelerated in the second week when the share price fell through a support level of 600, the price at which many bankers had provided loans against the deposit of stock. By the middle of the month, the South Sea directors gave up hope of staving off a collapse and started selling mortgaged stock with the intention of buying it back later at a lower price. A few days later, the Sword Blade Bank, which acted as banker to the South Sea Company and had made extensive loans against its stock, failed. By the end of September, the share price was below 200, a fall of around 75 percent in four weeks. At a meeting of the South Sea Company, a shareholder declared that with ruin so widespread it had "almost become unfashionable not to be bankrupt."[36] On 1 October, *Applebee's Journal* reported that "the sudden Fall of our Stocks, without visible reason, is the Surprize of the world." The author went on to describe how the decline had occurred: the initial fall had brought a "prodigious Number of Sellers to the Market, one Man selling alarms another, and makes him sell, and thus the Stock has run down insensibly, till all the People are put in a Fright; and such has been the panic Fear, that it has brought great Confusion along with it . . ."[37] In other words, the same feedback that had caused the bubble was working rapidly to deflate it.

The violence of the collapse took most people by surprise. "I owne I thought they would carry on their cheat somewhat longer . . ." wrote James Milner, MP. "I said, indeed, that ruin must soon come upon us, but I own it came two months sooner than I expected."[38] Alexander Pope, writing to Bishop Atterbury on 23 September, had finally decided where he stood on the subject of the South Sea. Gone was the ebullient speculator of the New Year to be replaced by the autumnal moralist, intoning in classical style against the vices of the age:

> The fate of the South-sea Scheme has much sooner than I expected verify'd what you told me. Most people thought it wou'd come, but no man prepar'd for it; no man consider'd it would come *like a Thief in the night,* exactly as it happens in the case of death. Methinks God has punish'd the avaritious as he often punishes sinners, in their own way, in the very sin itself: the thirst for gain was their crime, and that thirst continued became their punishment and ruin. As for the few who have the good fortune to remain with half of what they imagined they had, (among whom is your humble servant) I would have them sensible of their felicity . . . *They have dreamed out their dream, and awaking have found nothing in their hands.* Indeed the universal poverty, which is the consequence of universal avarice, and which will fall hardest upon the guiltless and industrious part of mankind, is lamentable. The universal deluge of the S. Sea, contrary to the old deluge, has drowned all except a few

> *Unrighteous* men: but it is some comfort to me that I am not one of them, even tho' I were to survive and rule the world by it.[39]

Pope's metaphorical characterisation of the speculative mania as a dream, in which people envisaged riches only to awaken and find them gone, was not unusual. Gibbon also called the South Sea a "golden dream," and similar references can be found relating to the Mississippi Bubble, the Railway Mania of 1845, the Souq Al-Manakh boom in 1982, and the junk bond market of the 1980s.* The dreaming speculator is seen as having surrendered both his reason and his wealth in the pursuit of phantom fortune.† On awakening and realising his losses, he is overcome with revulsion at his folly and avarice. "We know," wrote Freud in this commentary on dream legends, "that the gold the devil gives his paramours turns into excrement after his departure."[40]

The speculators' shame on awakening from their golden dreams was accompanied, as Pope suggests, by a sense that monetary losses were a sign of divine retribution, a punishment for the sin of Mammonism. "The Distemper," reported *Applebee*'s, "has been a Visitation; *South-Sea* had been a Judgement from Heaven; shall we not pity them whom God has smitten?"* In August, an outbreak of

---

*A few years after the collapse of the South Sea Bubble, the *Craftsman* wrote that "the People awoke from their Golden Dreams." Goethe's *Faust* describes the dreamlike quality of Law's scheme. Sir James Steuart calls the Mississippi Bubble "a golden dream, in which the French nation, and a part of Europe was plunged, for the short pace of 506 days." Washington Irving, also writing of the Mississippi Bubble, claimed that speculators "awoke as out of a dream, in their original poverty, now made more galling and humiliating by the transient elevation." John Francis in his description of the collapse of the Railway Mania observed, "the people awoke from their dream, and trembled." In Kuwait in 1982, the editor of a religious paper wrote that the "Souq-Al-Manakh was a nightmare, or a dream from the Arabian Nights; and the morning after, people awoke to realise the grand illusions they had lived through had been no more than a dream either." (Fida Darwiche, *The Gulf Stock Exchange Crash: The Rise and Fall of the Souq Al-Manakh*, London, 1986, p. 100.)

†Robert Heilbroner writes, "The speculator . . . plunges into a rising market with no thought but the affluence which will be effortlessly his. He operates as if he were pursuing a dream." (*The Quest for Wealth*, New York, 1956, p. 124.)

‡The paper (15 October 1720) reported a vicar's sermon on the "Sin of Stock-Jobbing" whose themes were that avarice was unlawful, the luxurious application of wealth had been unlawful, and the immoderate grief at its loss was equally unlawful.

bubonic plaque had occurred in Marseilles and slowly spread out across France, until it was feared that the plague would cross the Channel. The government ordered a Day of Humiliation to be observed "to beg of Almighty God to preserve these Kingdoms from the Infection."[41] It was unnecessary to state which sins in particular required atonement. To some it appeared as if the plague had already landed. According to Defoe, the crowds outside South Sea House resembled "walking ghosts [as if they] were all infected with the Plague; for never Men look'd so wretchedly . . . I shall remember a Man with a *S—— S— Face* as long as I live."*

Losses on South Sea stocks were deemed to have driven men mad—an unhappy extension of the joyous irrationality earlier in the year—and there were exaggerated reports of suicides (in fact, Charles Blunt, a nephew of the South Sea director, had committed suicide in early September after sustaining losses in the stock market).† Almost worse than suicide was the widespread destruction of business confidence. Defoe, who understood perfectly that trade (like credit and speculation) was dependent on confidence, penned an impassioned call for calm reminiscent of Roosevelt's famous inaugural address in 1933 ("the only thing we have to fear is fear

*From *Applebee's*, 1 October 1720. On 13 August, the paper reported: "The Plague in Exchange-Alley increases, and that at Marseilles Decreases; the former is real, but the latter, 'tis hoped is only Nominal." Speculative disaster has much in common with the plague: both generate fear and uncertainty, are contagious, spread panic, cause death (*viz.*, tales of speculators' suicides), are interpreted as a sign of divine disfavour, and lead to economic paralysis. The plague metaphor is found in later descriptions of speculative disasters. For instance, James Medbery, describing a stock market crash in New York in 1853, wrote, "Wall Street was as sombre as a plague-stricken city. Brokers flitted in and out like uneasy ghosts." (*Men and Mysteries of Wall Street*, New York, 1870, p. 308.) More recently, the financial "contagion" affecting the Asian economies following the collapse of the Thai stock market in August 1997 has been compared to the spread of the "bubonic plague." (See George Soros, *The Crisis of Global Capitalism*, New York, 1998, p. 145.)

†In late January 1721, *Applebee's* reported that "the Number of Distemper'd Heads is so strangely encreas'd for some Months pass'd, by the sudden rising and sudden falling of Men's Fortunes and Families, under the Operation of the South-Sea Vomits, and other Bubble Physick, that there is not room to be had among the private BEDLAMS, or Mad-Houses, as they are call'd, throughout the Town . . ." Madness could end in suicide, which according to the papers of the day was a common exit from the pain of speculative losses.

itself").* Writing in *Applebee's Journal* on 17 December 1720, he advised that the aftermath of the mania should be left to play itself out without interference:

> In a sick Body, when the Mass of Blood is corrupted, when the Constitution of the Body is subverted, and the Motion of the Spirits stop'd and stagnated, the Patient finds no Benefit by Medicine, he must be left to Nature, and to the Secret Operations of Nature either for Life or Death.
>
> The Body of South Sea People seem to be in just such a Crisis at this Time; the Distemper is strong upon them, they sink under it, and 'tis in vain to offer Reason or Arguments to them: the Patient must be left to Nature, and to the ordinary Operations of his own demented Understanding . . .†

Time would heal all wounds.

The wild popular fury at the collapse of the South Sea scheme was without parallel in English history. Anger was directed primarily at the directors of the company, who had misled the people and profited personally by selling out before the collapse. Next came the politicians, who had secretly profited from Blunt's distribution of share options in the South Sea Company and had subsequently allowed Blunt to "bubble" the people. A mob gathered at Westminster demanding retribution and restoration. A Secret Committee was established by the Commons to investigate the dealings of directors. Remarkable scenes took place in the Commons, where Lord Molesworth, an Irish member, declared: "Extraordinary crimes call aloud for extraordinary remedies. The Roman lawgivers had not

*"For God's Sake, and for our Country's Sake," wrote Defoe, "let us Consider what we are doing! 'Tis against Ourselves! 'Tis all setting the Knife to our own Throats! Setting Fire to our own Houses! Destroying our own Estates: Our own Commerce, and our own Hopes! We Hurt no Body but ourselves: Impoverish no Families but our Own; and Ruin no Families but our Own; and Ruin no Country but Great Britain."

†After the crash of October 1929, Treasury Secretary Andrew Mellon made the same suggestion using similar language. He argued that the crash would "purge the rottenness out of the system. High costs of living and high living will come down. People will work harder, live a more moral life. Values will be adjusted, and enterprising people will pick up the wrecks from less competent people." See Chapter 7.

foreseen the possible existence of a parricide. But as soon as the first monster appeared he was sewn in a sack and cast headlong in the river; and I shall be content to inflict the same treatment on the authors of our present ruin."[42] The Secretary of State, James Craggs, whose father had been a recipient of Blunt's bribe, rose furiously in the Commons to offer satisfaction to anyone who cast aspersions on his honour. The four MP directors found themselves expelled from the House, and Chancellor Aislabie, along with several South Sea directors, was sent to the Tower.

A bill was passed by Parliament to confiscate the profits that South Sea Company directors had made during 1720. It raised over £2 million, including £96,000 from the estate of Edward Gibbon, whose grandson, the historian, deplored this retroactive statute as a "pernicious violation of liberty."[43] By the rules of jurisprudence Gibbon was correct, but the public demanded a scapegoat more substantial than a carnival effigy. Legislation in the aftermath of the South Sea Bubble did not end with the South Sea Sufferers Act. In December 1720 a bill had been proposed "for the better Establishment of publick Credit by preventing, for the future, the infamous Practise of Stock-Jobbing." It was shelved. Fourteen years later, Parliament passed a measure, known after its sponsor as Sir John Barnard's Act, which made illegal short sales, and the trade in futures and options. It was to remain on the statute book until the middle of the nineteenth century.

A "RATIONAL BUBBLE"

Some speculators lost fabulous sums: Sir Justus Beck, a director of the Bank of England, went bankrupt for £347,000 and the Duke of Chandos surrendered £700,000 of his paper fortune. Sir Isaac Newton lost £20,000 by selling out too early and then reentering the market at its peak. He is said to have blanched at any mention of the South Sea for the remainder of his life. The men of letters who had dabbled in the stock market also suffered. Addison's nephew, Eustace Budgell, who a few years earlier had penned an article in the *Spectator* entitled "The Art of Growing Rich," suffered severe losses which led eventually to his suicide. Having followed the advice of her friend Alexander Pope, Lady Mary Wortley Montagu failed to sell out at the top of the market and continued to be blackmailed by Rémond for several years. A myth has grown up around the losses of John Gay, who had gambled away his advance for a book of poems and now bewailed his speculative foray in verse:

> *Why did 'Change Alley waste thy precious Hours,*
> *Among the Fools who gap'd for golden Show'rs?*
> *No wonder, if we found some Poets there,*
> *Who live on Fancy, and can feed on Air:*
> *No wonder, they were caught by South-Sea schemes,*
> *Who ne'er enjoyed a Guinea but in Dreams . . .**

Despite the loud lamentations of the losers, the depression which followed the collapse of the South Sea Bubble was neither long nor deep. Merchants' losses were limited, probably because as a group they had avoided the Fourth Money Subscription and sold out before the crash. Although South Sea stock fell to 15 percent of its peak (and Bank of England and East India shares fell by near two-thirds), the number of mercantile bankruptcies in 1721 did not increase significantly from the previous year and the economy recovered quickly.†

Adam Smith in his *Lectures on Jurisprudence* was rather dismissive of the whole South Sea episode as being of little consequence, a pale imitation of the Mississippi Bubble that "turned out at last a meer fraud."[44] This judgement is not quite fair. The South Sea scheme was not simply a copy of the Mississippi system. Imitation existed on both sides of the Channel: In his conversion of the

---

*Extract from "A Panegyrical Epistle to Mr. Thomas Snow." Dr. Johnson claimed that Gay had been "importuned to sell as much [South Sea stock] as would purchase an hundred pounds a year for life, which, says Fenton, will make you sure of a clean shirt and a shoulder of mutton every day. This counsel was rejected; the profit and principal were lost, and Gay sunk under the calamity so low that his life became in danger." Gay's recent biographer David Nokes maintains that Johnson exaggerated and that Gay lost only £600 from an initial investment of £1,000.

†See Julian Hoppit, "Financial Crises in 18th century England," *Economic History Review*, 39, No. 1 (1986). Hoppit concludes that "for the business community as a whole, through the length and breadth of England, the Bubble was not a catastrophe."

French national debt into company shares, John Law had borrowed from the example of existing English companies (including the South Sea Company). His initial success led the South Sea directors to attempt a more ambitious conversion than had ever been attempted in England. More important than imitation, the proximity of the two great bubbles showed how the contagion of speculation might pass from one country to another; in this case, not just from France to England, but throughout Europe to Amsterdam, Hamburg, and even Lisbon.[45]

There were more profound consequences to the events of 1720 than Adam Smith acknowledged. When he published *The Wealth of Nations* in 1776, the Bubble Act, which hindered the foundation of companies (by requiring that each receive its own act of Parliament), and Sir John Barnard's Act, which outlawed many of the techniques of speculation, were still on the statute book. As a result, the progress of financial capitalism in the eighteenth century was retarded and joint-stock companies contributed less than they might otherwise have done to Britain's Industrial Revolution (although other types of organisation, such as mutual companies, thrived in their place). The general revulsion against companies and speculation that followed the events of 1720 is evident in Smith's own work. He considered the joint-stock company to suffer fatally from the separation of management from ownership (what modern economists refer to as the "agency problem"): "Negligence and profusion," he concluded, "must always prevail, more or less, in the management of the affairs of such a company."* As a result, Smith did not develop a theory of speculation.†

*Smith claimed that given the "immense number of proprietors [of the South Sea Company] . . . It was naturally to be expected, therefore, that folly, negligence, and profusion should prevail in the whole management of their affairs. The knavery and extravagance of their stock-jobbing projects are sufficiently known, and the explication of them would be foreign to the present subject." Adam Smith, *The Wealth of Nations* (eds. R. H. Campbell et al., Oxford, 1976), p. 741.

†The speculator's trade, according to Smith, was irregular in its results: "A bold adventurer may sometimes acquire a considerable fortune by two or three successful speculations; but he is just as likely to lose one by two or three unsuccessful ones." As befitted a man of Scottish Presbyterian upbringing, Smith concluded that "great fortunes" were normally the "consequence of a long life of industry, frugality, and attention."

Any interpretation of the bubble of 1720 which neglects the role of the government is severely limited. The South Sea Company systematically bribed both the Court and Parliament. Part of this bribe was overt (the £7.5 million for converting the annuities) and part covert (in the form of illegal share options granted to courtiers and ministers).* Later, Blunt gave parliamentarians the first opportunity to get their names on the lists of the Money Subscriptions and many invested heavily for themselves and their friends. Because they stood to profit twice from the rising share price, few politicians heeded the eminently sensible demand for fixing the rate of conversion of annuities into South Sea stock. Instead, Chancellor Aislabie—a man described by another MP as "dark, and of a cunning that rendered him suspected and low in all men's opinions . . . [and] much set upon increasing his fortune"—persuaded Parliament to allow the company to set its own terms for the conversion. There is no reason to doubt that Aislabie and others in the executive knew that the company would do everything possible to inflate the share price, even at the expense of the annuitants. Archebald Hutcheson asked Parliament whether it was "not the Duty of a British Senate to take all necessary Precautions, to prevent the Ruin of many Thousands of families?" His question fell on ears that were not disinterested, and it was therefore ignored.

The British government in 1720 not only abdicated its responsibility to protect its existing creditors; its support for the scheme sent out the message to speculators that South Sea shares were a sure thing. If the King was prepared to invest in the Third Money Subscription at a price of £1,000, it appeared safe for his subjects

*Blunt's distribution of share options in the South Sea Company anticipates the behaviour of U.S. companies in the 1990s which have distributed options like confetti at a wedding party. There are reasons to believe that the excessive distribution of stock options contributed significantly to the inflation of a speculative bubble: companies did not report the cost of options in their profit and loss accounts, they took on debt to repurchase shares for options schemes and used accounting tricks to smooth their earnings growth. At times, buybacks for share options have resembled a Ponzi scheme. For instance, Gateway 2000, a computer manufacturer, announced in June 1997 that it was repurchasing shares at $35 which it had issued twenty months earlier for $14.50. Executive stock options were particularly lavish at Sunbeam, a consumer appliances manufacturer, and Cendant, a marketing company, both of which fraudulently overstated their profits for 1997. Sir John Blunt was a man before his time. Were he to return today, he would be hailed as a champion of "shareholder value."

to do likewise. The belief that the government would support the share price above its intrinsic value was not a singular occurrence. As we shall see, it recurred in Japan in the 1980s when it was argued that the Ministry of Finance would not allow share prices to fall. The government's failure to protect the nation from the pitfalls of speculation was the single most important lesson to come out of the calamitous events of the South Sea. Adam Anderson, a former cashier of the South Sea Company, hoped that the year 1720 "may serve for a perpetual memento to the legislators and ministers of our own nation, never to leave it in the power of any, hereafter, to hoodwink mankind into so shameful and baneful an imposition on the credulity of the people, thereby diverted from their lawful industry."[46]

Joseph Schumpeter identified the events of 1720 with the financial innovations over the previous thirty years: "The mania of 1719–20 . . . was, exactly as were later manias of this kind, induced by a preceding period of innovation which transformed the economic structure and upset the preexisting state of things."[47] Recently, this interpretation has been refined by an American economist, Larry Neal, in whose view the bubble was "less a tale about the perpetual folly of mankind and more one about financial markets' difficulties in adjusting to an array of innovations."[48] The essence of the South Sea scheme was the offer to convert illiquid government annuities into marketable joint-stock shares. For Neal, it was this conversion process that produced the bubble: "The South Sea Bubble should be viewed not simply as a wild mania or as a massive swindle," he concludes. "These played a role, but the driving force in the bubble was the technical problem of converting government war debts into easy-to-exchange, low-interest, long-term securities."* Neal argues that the rise of the South Sea share price during the early phases of the scheme reflected the fact that

*Neal sees three stages to the bubble: (i) Up to the middle of May, South Sea stock rose on improved fundamentals. (ii) From mid-May to 22 June, when the company's books for the transfer of shares were closed, and speculators realised that the South Sea stock was a one-way bet. (iii) From late June to late August, when the transfer books were closed and all dealing was for forward delivery of stock. According to Neal, the great prices for forward delivery reflected a tightening in the credit market.

investors were prepared to pay a premium for converting annuities, which were expensive and difficult to transfer, into the more "liquid" South Sea stock. By late May 1720, according to Neal, a "rational bubble" set in as investors realised that the directors were manipulating the stock upwards and they had nothing to lose by following the trend.* The bubble finally came crashing down because the directors overreached themselves and the company could not meet its commitments.

There are several reasons for rejecting this thesis. The liquidity premium for the conversion of annuities into joint-stock shares cannot have been that great, as investors who wanted marketable securities before 1720 were not obliged to hold annuities; they could buy stock in the Bank of England, the Million Bank, or any of the other chartered companies. The South Sea conversion of 1720 was not the first time that government debt had been converted into corporate stock. The Bank of England had engrafted government debt into its own shares in 1697, and the South Sea Company had done the same on two previous occasions, in 1711 and 1719. In the first two of the three South Sea conversions, the engraftment had actually led to a *fall* in the price of shares below their nominal level.

Despite its grandiose title, the South Sea Company had no genuine prospects of a profitable trade with South America. The value of its shares was derived entirely from the income the company received from the government. It is therefore possible to calculate with an unusual degree of precision how much the South Sea shares were "intrinsically" worth (as is not the case with most companies whose future earnings are to a great extent indeterminate). In the spring of 1720, Archebald Hutcheson and Richard Steele argued that, given the fixed income the company received from the government, the fair value of South Sea stock was around £150. They

*The concept of the "rational bubble" was first elaborated by Oliver J. Blanchard and Mark W. Watson. They argue that, given the immediate prospect of capital gains, investors may be acting rationally when they purchase shares above their fundamental value. More tendentiously, Blanchard and Watson are attracted to the concept of the "rational bubble" because from a methodological standpoint it is easier to deal with: "It is hard to analyze rational bubbles. It would be much harder to deal with irrational bubbles." (See "Bubbles, Rational Expectations, and Financial Markets," in *Crises in the Economic and Financial Structure*, ed. P. Wachtel, Toronto, 1982, p. 196.)

concluded that any rise above this level would lead to a loss for both the annuitants and subscribers of South Sea stock. As the South Sea stock fell back to its fair value in the autumn of 1720, their opinion was vindicated. If investors chose not to heed the warnings of Hutcheson and Steele and preferred to convince themselves that there was no limit to the potential price for South Sea stock, it was because they chose to act irrationally in pursuit of short-term gains. A vast amount of contemporary documentation relates to the "irrationality" of investors in the South Sea year. According to the Dutch banker Crellius, Exchange Alley in April 1720 resembled "nothing so much as if all the Lunatics had escaped out of the Madhouse at once."*

Neal's account of the South Sea Bubble, like Garber's version of the Tulip Mania, is intended to bolster the modern theory of efficient markets and rational investors.† In its most extreme form, this theory denies the possibility of irrationality in speculative bubbles, and claims that investors are acting rationally even when they purchase shares above fair market value in the expectation that the price will continue to rise, at least in the short run. A rational investor is one who seeks to optimise his wealth by offsetting risk with reward and using all publicly available information. Was the investor who bought South Sea stock at £1,000 behaving rationally? The answer is no. First, there was sufficient public information to suggest that the share price was severely overvalued. Second, by entering the bubble at an advanced state the investor faced a poor ratio of risk to reward: he was chasing a small potential gain and risking a larger and more certain loss. Third, the "fundamentals" (i.e., the long-term prospects of the company) did not change significantly in the year; as its future income remained fixed, there was no reasonable cause for its share price to exhibit such extreme volatility.

*Several years later, the *Craftsman* recalled reason's flight during the bubble: "here are many people . . . who appear, in other particulars, to be Men of *Reason*, and yet, on the first mention of these syllables *South Sea Stock*, lost at once all reflection and comparison . . ." (27 May 1727).

†Peter Garber claims that the South Sea Bubble "is easily understandable as a case of speculators working on the best economic analysis available and pushing prices along by their changing view of market fundamentals." P. Garber and R. P. Flood, *Speculative Bubbles, Speculative Attacks, and Policy Switching* (Cambridge, Mass., 1994), p. 50.

The theory of the "rational bubble" appears to be nothing more than an elaborate restatement of the "greater fool" investment strategy, whereby the speculator knowingly buys shares above their intrinsic value hoping that a "greater fool" will pay more for them later. The exponents of the "rational bubble" appear to overlook the fact that the success of this strategy is dependent on liquidity (i.e., the constant presence of both buyers and sellers in the market) and that in a panic buyers vanish at the very moment when "rational bubble" speculators are seeking to unload their shares. The "greater fool" method of investment has enjoyed great popularity in the 1990s American bull market where it has been renamed "momentum investing." Speculators look to buy shares that are rising faster than the market and sell quickly when the rise begins to peter out.* The fate of the London banker John Martin in 1720 illustrates the dangers of this frivolous approach to investment. Early in the summer, he had gleefully argued that "when the rest of the world is mad, we must imitate them in some measure," but he failed to sell out before the crash, lost a fortune, and ended up complaining pathetically of being "blinded by other people's advice."[49]

---

*Momentum investors helped push the share price of Ascend Communications, a computer networking firm, from its issue price of $1.40 in 1995 to over $80 a year later. Nicknamed "Ass-end" by the traders, the company's descent was equally rapid. When sales growth slowed marginally in early 1997, the momentum traders turned bearish and hammered the stock down to $40 on a daily turnover exceeding twenty million shares.

CHAPTER 4

•

FOOL'S GOLD: THE EMERGING MARKETS OF THE 1820s

•

". . . Her husband broke his heart in—how did you say her husband broke his heart, my dear?"

"In pumping water out of the Peruvian Mines," replied Miss Tox.

"Not being a Pumper himself, of course," said Mrs. Chick, glancing at her brother; and it really did seem necessary to offer the explanation for Miss Tox had spoken of him as if he had died at the handle; "but having invested money in the speculation, which failed."

Charles Dickens,
Dombey and Son (1846)

In late 1821, His Highness Gregor, Cacique of Poyais, a small territory on the border of present-day Nicaragua, arrived in London. His intention was to sell land rights, military commissions, and titles of nobility to British subjects and encourage emigration to his country. Finding a growing appetite for foreign loans in the City, the Cacique arranged to float a £600,000 Poyaisian loan, with a 6 percent dividend, through the offices of Sir John Perring, a former Lord Mayor of London. The issue was a tremendous success, and the bonds soared to an early premium in the market (although some suggested this was mainly the result of dubious manipulation on the Exchange). Early in 1823, two hundred colonists—including a bank manager, a jeweller, a cabinetmaker, and a gentleman's servant—were sent out to the Poyaisian capital, St. Joseph. Instead of the opulent baroque city promised by the Cacique, they found a collection of mud huts surrounded by swamps and threatening Indians. Suffering from heat, starvation, and fever, several of the colonists drowned while attempting to flee to neighbouring Belize. A Scottish cobbler, who had been appointed Official Shoemaker to the Princess of Poyais, shot himself. Of the two hundred colonists, only fifty succeeded in returning to Britain. By this time, the Cacique—whose real name was Sir Gregor Macgregor, a Scottish adventurer and renegade general from Simón Bolívar's army who laid claim to his "kingdom" after a drunken deal with the chief of the Miskito Indians—had fled to France with his family, taking with him the proceeds of the bond issue. Hope springs eternal in the financial markets, and half a century later Poyaisian land grants and debt certificates were still to be found in the bulging wallets of the "Alley-men" of the Stock Exchange, along with the bonds and shares of busted companies. To this day, the Poyais loan remains the only loan for a fictitious country to be floated on the London Stock Exchange.[1]

SPECULATION AND GOVERNMENT LOANS

British government bonds, known as Consols (named after the "consolidation" of government loans in the 1750s), replaced shares as the primary object of speculation after the events of 1720. As the speculative spirit abhors government regulations, various ways were found to get round the restrictions on futures and options enshrined in Sir John Barnard's Act of 1734. Settlement for a distant account day became an alternative to an illegal futures transaction. Quarterly settlement became regular in the 1730s, replaced by six-week account periods in the 1780s. Bull operators could sell on settlement days (when they were due to pay for their stock) and repurchase almost simultaneously for the new account period—a process known as "backwardation." Loans for speculators in government stock were also commonly available. Often the law was simply ignored. On the Stock Exchange, dealing in options continued unabated. Although options contracts were unenforceable at law, the broker's pledge—"my word is my bond"—was deemed sufficient. In 1821, a broker complained that the options trade was "now so frequent as to constitute the greater part of the business done in the House," but a Committee of the Stock Exchange backed away from banning the business after several brokers threatened to establish a rival exchange.[2]

During the Napoleonic Wars, the British government issued over £400 million of bonds. Fortunes were made speculating in these issues; the broker David Ricardo amassed over half a million pounds before retiring early to pursue a second career as an economist and member of Parliament. (Ricardo is credited with formulating the "golden rules" of speculation: "Cut short your losses" and "Let your profits run on.") The decline of British government borrowing after peace with France forced investors to look abroad for opportunities. The French reparation loan of 1817, arranged by Baring Brothers, produced a quick capital gain for British investors and whetted their appetite for more foreign loans. The next year, Nathan Rothschild launched a £5 million loan for Prussia, the first foreign bond denominated in sterling (and an antecedent of the modern Eurobond market). Soon after, Rothschild was asked by a Commons Committee whether the "growing passion" for foreign stocks was a sign of investment or speculation; half and half, he replied, but when a price rise took place all purchases became speculative.[3]

Among the foreign loans offered to the British public, a more romantic object appeared—the South American bond. For several years, various provinces of South America had been fighting for independence under the inspirational leadership of Simón Bolívar. British support for the liberation movement was strong, stemming from ancient prejudices against Spain, the old Catholic enemy, and a more modern liberal enthusiasm for independence. After the expulsion of the Spaniards, rapid economic progress was anticipated for the continent: "We may indulge the brightest hopes of these Southern Republics," proclaimed the *New Times*. "They have entered upon a career of endless improvement. And . . . will soon attain the knowledge and freedom and civilisation of the happiest states of Europe."[4] British technology and arts would assist this process of modernisation. The proposition was enticing, and with a declining supply of Consols available, the investing public became ensnared in the first "emerging market" boom.

In March 1822, Bolívar's envoy for the new Republic of Colombia arranged a £2 million loan with the City merchants Herring,

Graham, and Powles. A prospectus was issued alluding to Colombia's "unbounded" resources and plentiful mines, intricate bond certificates were engraved by London's leading printer, and their interest payments were set at over 7 percent, double the return on Consols. Other Latin American states were quick to exploit the opportunity. Two months later, a subscription for a Chilean loan was launched which entitled the bearer to purchase five £100 bonds for only 10 percent down. These loans met with immediate success. By the middle of October, the value of the Chilean bonds had risen over a quarter, a profit of more than 150 percent to the purchasers of "scrip" (short for "subscription," this was the name given to partly paid shares or bonds). The demand for a Peruvian loan was so great that a near-riot broke out at the Royal Exchange. "If the very respectable Mr. Lemuel Gulliver were to appear on stage again," remarked the *New Times*, "and to issue proposals for a loan to the Republic of *Laputa*, he would run hazard of being suffocated by the pressure of subscribers to set down their names."* The paper proved remarkably prescient, as shortly after the Poyais loan came to the market.

Euphoria for foreign loans was not confined to South America. The public's enthusiasm for the Greek struggle against Turkey was even stronger. In late February 1824, a banquet was hosted by the Lord Mayor of London at the Guildhall to launch a Greek loan. A shady City character, named Herman Hendriks, was appointed agent for the rebel Greek government. The heavily oversubscribed loan—£800,000 at 6 percent—was issued amid great excitement and the proceeds were sent to a committee of English Philhellenes in Greece, of which Lord Byron was a member.† A few months earlier

*More seriously, the paper warned that Peru "is a country on the other side of the globe, of which we know absolutely nothing, but that it is or has lately been the scene of a desperate conflict between two contending parties." At this date, the Stock Exchange decided that foreign loans should be issued in its own building in the rooms of a newly created Foreign Stock Exchange. (Dawson, *Debt Crisis*, p. 38.)

†In 1825, a second Greek loan was launched for a nominal £2 million. Of this sum only £257,000 was even sent to Greece. The rest of the money was either purloined by the Greek commissioners or used to prop up the loan stock in a falling market and make good the losses of leading Philhellenes. (See L. H. Jenks, *The Migration of British Capital*, London, 1938, p. 51.)

a prospectus had circulated in the City to raise funds for the Order of St. John of Jerusalem in order to expel the Turks from the island of Rhodes. However, this curious attempt to launch a medieval crusade with modern finance attracted insufficient interest from investors and the loan was withdrawn.

As well as appealing to liberal sentiments, the foreign loans were designed to be attractive to investors. Their interest payments were set so high that the South American bonds had to be contracted in Paris to avoid British usury laws which limited interest charges to a maximum of 5 percent (an early example of "offshore" finance being used to evade government regulations). The market yield of the bonds was even higher since they were issued at steep discounts to their nominal value. Moreover, only small initial deposits were required, with further payments stretched over a lengthy period. Thus, a small percentage rise in the market value of the bonds brought far greater returns to the holders of scrip. A large percentage of the money raised by the loans was retained by British contractors to pay dividends, while the proceeds from later loan issues were used to repay earlier debts. The payment of interest from capital, otherwise known as "Ponzi finance," created the illusion of viability although no money was ever actually sent from South America to service the loans (to which it must be added that the borrowing countries received only a tiny fraction of the total sums for which they contracted).

THE SOUTH AMERICAN MINING MANIA

Investors were not prepared to accept this state of affairs indefinitely. They expected the South American states to find the money to service the loans once their economies had recovered from the turmoil of the independence wars. The prospectuses asserted that the loans were backed by the abundant gold resources of the continent.* The output of the Latin American gold mines had been severely disrupted by the wars. In early 1822, J. D. Powles, one of

*The prospectus of the first Colombian loan promised that "the revenue from the mines is considerable when they are in full work which it is expected they will shortly be." (Dawson, *Debt Crisis*, p. 29.)

the Colombian loan contractors, established a joint-stock mining company to restore gold production. In no time, new South American mining companies replaced foreign loans as the favoured object of speculation. British capital and modern mining techniques, it was hoped, would exploit the mineral resources of South America with greater efficiency than the backward Spanish had ever attained: "will not the probability be," inquired a jingoistic shareholder in a letter to *John Bull*, "that these things may be much better performed by Englishmen, who so well understand the use of machinery, than by Spaniards, who are comparatively ignorant of its application?"[5] Posed to the inhabitants of the world's greatest industrial power, the question required no answer.

The promoters of the South American mining companies larded their prospectuses with fabulous tales. One prospectus declared that "lumps of pure gold, weighing from two to fifty pounds, were totally neglected" and that the company's mines would yield "considerably more than the quantity necessary for the supply of the whole world."[6] The prospectus of the Rio Plata Mining Association claimed that within the area of the company's concession grains of gold "appear in sight when the rain washes away the dust which covers the surface. After a very heavy rain a woman stepping forth from her hut, a few yards from the door, found a *piece of gold weighing twenty ounces*. . . . These instances happen so frequently that it would require much time to detail them."[7] The claim that the mines would produce more gold than Europe required was taken seriously. It was feared that the great inflation brought by South American gold in the sixteenth century would return, and some people, according to the Russia merchant Thomas Tooke in his *History of Prices*, "believed and acted upon the belief of a diminished value of gold and silver, in consequence of the vast additional quantity which was speedily thus about to be raised."*

The mining euphoria, which took off in 1824, coincided with a period of domestic prosperity in Britain. "The trade and manufactures of the country," reflected Tooke, "had never been in a more

*Thomas Tooke, *History of Prices* (London, 1838), II, p. 145. Another writer claimed "the earth was to yield in such quantities of the precious metals, that fears began to be entertained of their becoming almost valueless." (Francis, *Bank of England*, II. p. 2.)

regular, sound, and satisfactory state than in the interval from 1821 to 1824."[8] The national sense of well-being was so great, according to the *Annual Register*, that "even the country gentleman, the most querulous of all classes . . . could no longer complain." Speculation flared up in the commodity markets: first, the price of cotton and silk rose, which encouraged outsiders to enter the market; then other commodities including indigo, rice, gum, nutmegs, coffee, and pepper followed suit. By the end of the year, according to Tooke, "the example of early successful speculation had become infectious."[9]

Demand for commodities was rising because the inventories of manufacturers and merchants had remained low after the severe postwar depression of 1817 and now needed replenishing as prosperity returned. In particular, the anticipation of exports to the liberated countries provoked fears of raw material shortages. This "emerging market" story revived an old dream that went back to the establishment of the South Sea Company (in 1711) when exporters had prepared a variety of articles ranging from silk handkerchiefs to Cheshire cheeses for export to South America. In 1824, British goods were sent out to South America in such quantities that they outstripped both local demand and warehousing facilities, and were left to rot on the beaches of Rio de Janeiro. "It is positively declared," wrote Harriet Martineau, "that warming-pans from Birmingham were among the articles exposed under the burning sun of that sky; and that skates from Sheffield were offered for sale to a people who had never heard of ice."[10] Stranger still was the dispatch to Buenos Aires of British dairy maids to milk the cows of the River Plate and supply butter to the city. This venture proved fruitless after it was discovered that locals preferred oil in their cooking and the butter soon turned rancid in the fierce tropical climate.[11]

On New Year's Eve of 1825, the foreign secretary George Canning, in response to the invasion of Spain by a French army, unexpectedly announced the official British recognition of South American independence—in Canning's famous phrase, he "called the New World into existence, to redress the balance of the Old." The effect of this declaration on the South American mining market was electrifying. The Anglo-Mexican shares (on which £10 had been paid) rose from 33 in December to over 150 a month later.

Shares in the Real del Monte—a Mexican mine that had first produced silver in 1525—climbed from £550 to £1,350. As only £70 had been paid on these shares, speculators who had bought them at their issue were sitting on a paper profit of more than 2,000 percent.

The excitement in the stock market was too much for one young man, who, reversing his previously negative stance on mining shares, turned bullish. Benjamin Disraeli, still only a teenager in 1824, combined youthful impetuosity with a deep and restless ambition. Born the son of a distinguished literary critic of Jewish birth (his grandfather had been one of the select group of "Jew brokers"), the young Disraeli was profoundly conscious that lack of riches excluded him from influence.* He had been placed by his father in a solicitor's office in Gray's Inn, but the prospect of a legal career appalled him. "To succeed as an advocate," he wrote, "I must be a great lawyer, and, to be a great lawyer, I must give up my chance of being a great man." Financial speculation offered a speedier and less demoralising route to wealth and power. "It immediately struck me," he wrote, recalling the fervid atmosphere of late 1824, "that if fortunes were ever to be made this was the moment and I accordingly paid great attention to American affairs."[12]

Disraeli was commissioned by J. D. Powles, the mining company promoter, to write in support of the South American mining companies.† He set about the task with great gusto and soon produced a hundred-page pamphlet in which he reiterated the familiar arguments of the mining bull: South America was on the verge of a great increase in wealth; gold, extracted from the mines, would revive the South American continent; and Britain, with its investments and

---

*These traits are found in the hero of his first novel, *Vivian Grey*, composed in 1826. Disraeli writes, "Were I a Millionaire, or a noble, I might have *all.* Curse on my lot that the want of a few rascal counters, and the possession of a little rascal blood, should mar my fortunes." He reaches the conclusion that the way forward is to blend with the crowd: "Yes we must mix with the herd; we must enter into their feelings; we must humour their weaknesses; we must sympathise with sorrows we do not feel; and share the merriment of fools. Oh, yes! to *rule* men we must be men . . . Mankind then is my great game."

†Powles was a client of Disraeli's employers, the solicitors Swain, Maples & Co., who had drafted the prospectuses for Powles's Anglo-Mexican Mining Association and the Colombian Mining Association.

manufactured exports, would be the main beneficiary of this economic revolution.[13] Although Disraeli falsely portrayed himself in the pamphlet as "one whose opinions are unbiased by self-interest and uncontrolled by party influence," he did, at least, follow his own advice. Financed with a loan of over £2,000 from Robert Messer, the son of a wealthy stockbroker, Disraeli began buying mining shares in November 1824. His speculations continued into the following year. On April Fools' Day, 1825, he wrote to his publisher and fellow speculator, John Murray, that "an immense and permanent rise is to be looked to" in the mining market.[14] The same month, he boasted to Messer:

> All the information which is now received from America passes thro' my hands . . . I have perused secret reports which have not even been seen by many of the Directors themselves. I have read every book upon the subject and conversed with some secret agents of the Companies in which I am interested and I have come to the conviction that the 100£ shares in the Mexican mining Companies will in a very few years be worth upwards of 1000£ a piece.[15]

Exhausted by speculation and pamphlet writing, his head spinning with ambition, he told Messer, "I feel actually dizzy. It is truly work for life . . . On the Mexican mines I rest my sheet anchor."[16] Dizzy indeed!

DOMESTIC VENTURES

For those unable or unwilling to gamble on the South American mines, new domestic joint-stock companies appeared of a number not seen since the days of the South Sea. In March 1824, Nathan Rothschild founded the Alliance Fire and Insurance Company, allegedly after his cousin had been refused a position at an established company because of his faith. Following the successful flotation of the Alliance (which later prospered), less substantial companies were floated, several of which appealed to contemporary urban fashions. The Metropolitan Bath Company was established to pipe seawater from the coast to London, offering the benefits of seawater bathing to those who could not afford the expense of the resorts. Another venture, the London Umbrella Company, promised to free the public from the "inconvenience of carrying an umbrella when the weather was fine, and of being without one when it is wet," by establishing a number of "stations" in the City and West End from which umbrellas could be rented for a small charge.

Several of the new companies purported a philanthropic concern for their future customers. The Metropolitan Fish Company promised to supply fish at low cost to the poor of the capital, who until then could only afford to feed on "sprats and herrings." The London Pawnbroking Company claimed it would assist the poor by undercutting usurious pawnbrokers and "employ Capital profitably, without the slightest Risk of Loss." The London Cemetery Association for the Security of the Dead was established to end the activities of body snatchers, and assure "perfect security for the repose of the Dead, effectively remedying various other evils long complained of, and yielding a very handsome return for the investment." Profits were to be derived from burial fees and the sale of vaults, which "considering the number of deaths, will almost exceed the powers of calculation."[17]

As in 1720, humorous fable pursued investor credulity. A prospectus was circulated on the Stock Exchange to raise money for a company "to drain the Red Sea, in search of the gold and jewels left by the Egyptians, in their passage after the Israelites."[18] A newspaper reported that the high price of iron had induced several merchants and bankers to form the Resurrection Metal Company to raise tons of cannonballs that lay on the seabed near Trafalgar and other scenes of British naval victories. The government, reported the paper, had no claims on the balls, for "by cannon law, the act of firing guns under proper authority was an authorized surrender of all property in the balls on the part of the Crown."[19]

The South American mines were to be rendered profitable by the application of British technology. Writing in early 1825, an anonymous pamphleteer observed "a vague, indefinite and feverish expectation of magnificent results to be produced by the advance of science, and the acuteness of modern research."[20] In England, the railways made their first appearance. "Nothing now is heard of but railroads," complained one journal, "the daily papers teem with notices of new lines of them in every direction; and pamphlets and paragraphs are thrown before the public eye recommending nothing short of making them general throughout the kingdom . . ."[21] In Parliament, the President of the Board of Trade, William Huskisson, argued in favour of the bill for the London and Birmingham (at the opening of the line five years later, Huskisson became the first railway fatality when he was run over by George Stephenson's locomotive, the Rocket).

As in earlier speculative periods, most companies were established for no purpose other than to benefit their promoters.* "All we have to do," claimed the fictional promoter in a contemporary novel, "is to puff up shares to a premium, humbug the public into buying them, and then let the whole concern go to ruin."[22] A variety of means were employed to advance this "humbug": Only a small deposit was required on new issues; rumours of speculators' fortunes were circulated in order to entice new players into the market; brokers were employed to manipulate share prices; and journalists were paid to puff companies in the "money market" columns that had recently appeared in the papers. The editor of the *Morning Chronicle* accused his fellow editors of undermining their journalistic integrity by taking shares in many of the new schemes (editorial indifference to the exposure of fraud was also influenced by a court case involving the *Chronicle* itself, which had concluded with the trial judge opining that "the conductors of newspapers had no recognised vocation to enlighten the public with regard to abuses").[23]

PARLIAMENT AND THE MANIA

The most common practice of projectors seeking to promote their companies was to employ members of Parliament and peers as "guinea pig" or "decoy" directors. In the first "Directory of Directory," published by the *Times* in February 1825, the names of nearly thirty MPs appeared. Members of Parliament proliferated

*Henry English, a contemporary stockbroker, claimed that the typical company projector was "either an attorney . . . or some unprincipled person actuated solely with a view to pecuniary profit." (*A Complete View of the Joint Stock Companies formed During the Years 1824 and 1825*, London, 1827).

on the boards of the South American mining companies.* Two earls and one member of Parliament sat on the board of the Colombian Pearl Fishery Association, which was established to dive for oysters in the Pacific.[24] The Duke of Wellington, who privately expressed fears about the mania, nevertheless sat with the Duke of York on the board of the American Colonial Steam Navigation Company.[25] The prime minister, Lord Liverpool, together with three members of his cabinet, accepted directorships in an ill-fated scheme that proposed to invest £1 million for the cultivation of mulberry trees and the propagation of the silkworm in Great Britain and Ireland.[26]

The MPs and peers who sold their names to flaky enterprises did not escape public censure. The *Times* complained of "the leprous infection of avarice" which led them to become directors.[27] Later, Harriet Martineau blamed the speculative mania on the "decline of the character of the House of Commons, too many of whose members acted, in regard to these bills [for joint-stock companies], with a recklessness which subjected them to a suspicion that they, like others, had forgotten themselves, and had sacrificed their legislative conscience to the interests of themselves and their friends."[28] Parliament, so far from acting as a counterweight to the excesses of speculation, appeared to be actively stimulating it. After a hundred and five years, the lesson of the South Sea year had been forgotten.

Gross complacency, even contemptuous arrogance, was evident among the ruling classes. At the opening of Parliament in early February 1825, politicians basked in the economic prosperity of the nation. The King's Speech, delivered by the Lord Chancellor, boasted: "There was never a period in the history of this country, when all the great interests of the nation were at the same time in so thriving a condition, or when a feeling of content and satisfaction was more widely diffused through all the classes of the British people."[29] In his budget speech, the Chancellor of the Exchequer, Frederick "Prosperity" Robinson, congratulated the House on the circumstances of the period: "We may safely venture to contemplate

*J. D. Powles employed four MPs as directors of the Anglo-Mexican. The Peruvian Mining and Trading Association, formed in March 1825, had on its board a peer, an MP, and an admiral. In the Commons, Alexander Baring denounced the company's bill as seeming "to be rather a specimen of parliamentary mining than of fair commerce." (Dawson, *Debt Crisis*, p. 102.)

with instructive admiration the harmony of its proportion and the *solidity of its basis.*"

Despite these declamations, some members of Parliament expressed a concern that speculation had gone too far. In the middle of March, John Cam Hobhouse, Byron's former travelling companion, complained to the Commons that projectors were manipulating stock prices and "evidently proceeded upon the supposition, that there was an infinite fund of gullibility in the dupes to whom they addressed themselves." Alexander Baring, a member of the banking family, announced that he "saw no difference between the gambling of the nobleman in the hells of St. James's Street, and the gambling of the merchant on the Royal Exchange; except that the latter kept earlier hours and more respectable company than the former." Baring told the Commons that he believed that all the mining speculations would turn out to be delusions, and that many innocent persons would lose thereby. The great error of the mining speculations, in his view, was the belief that the mines could be exploited more efficiently with British capital, labour, and technology.[30]

A few days later, Lord Liverpool rose in the House of Lords to issue a stern warning to speculators. He could, he said, accept that in a commercial country a great deal of speculation was unavoidable and this spirit of speculation, if kept within certain limits, was attended with much advantage. He understood also that in a time of peace, when interest rates were low, speculation would be prevalent: "He wished it, however, to be clearly understood, that those who now engaged in Joint-Stock Companies, or other enterprises, entered on those speculations at their peril and risk. He thought it his duty to declare, that he never would advise the introduction of any bill for their relief; on the contrary, if such a measure were proposed, he would oppose it, and he hoped that Parliament would resist any measure of the kind."[31] Behind this admonition lurked an uncertainty on the part of government as to how to deal with the phenomenon of overspeculation. The cabinet was strongly, if not dogmatically, influenced by the emergent free-trade movement, and free trade was linked inextricably with the free movement of capital, which was seen both as a civil right and as the begetter of Britain's manufacturing and trading supremacy. As Lord Liverpool acknowledged, speculation was inevitable in a modern commercial society and an attempt to control it would restrain the "invisible hand" that directed economic affairs with an almost divine omniscience. The government also recognised that joint-stock companies had an increasingly important role to play in providing funds for capital-intensive businesses such as banks, insurance companies, canals, railways, gasworks, and waterworks.

Yet there was an acute awareness of speculation as an "evil," both corrupting and—in its etymological sense—overbearing and excessive. Speculation threatened to induce a general crisis in which the innocent would suffer along with the guilty. Initially, the government promised new legislation to halt speculation, and even threatened prosecutions under the old Bubble Act of 1720. Disraeli was hastily commissioned to write a pamphlet against the threatened regulation: "We fear," he wrote with characteristic flippancy and a great deal of truth, "that the folly of man is not subject matter for legislation."[32] The government eventually reached the same conclusion. In the middle of March, Huskisson told the House of Commons that there would be no legislation. He was sure that "the high-raised hopes of many who embarked in such speculations would, in the end, vanish into thin air, and leave those who entertained them nothing but regret and disappointment. At the same time . . . he did not see how the parliament could at present interfere."[33] In June, the Bubble Act of 1720, for many years a dead letter, was finally repealed.

The government failed to find a balance between its economically liberal instincts and its moral repugnance to speculation. The speculative mania raised important questions that it was unable to answer. What was the difference between "overspeculation" and "legitimate commerce"? How could the former be controlled without hindering the latter? The dilemma was expressed succinctly by Alexander Baring:

> The evil [of speculation] was certainly one which deserved to be checked; though he hardly knew how the check could be applied. The remedy would be worse than the disease, if, in putting a stop to this evil, they put a stop to the spirit of enterprise. That spirit was productive of so much benefit to the community, that he should be sorry to see any person drawing

a line, discriminating between fair enterprise and extravagant speculation.*

There was to be no legislative remedy. Instead, the evil was left to produce its own cure.

"A TORRENT OF DISTRUST"

In January 1825, nearly seventy companies (including five railways) were floated. Speculation in commodities, loans, and shares continued strongly for several months, but in the spring the euphoria began to wane. South American bond prices went into decline, and continued falling throughout the summer. In late August, a small loan for the United Provinces of Central America was floated, but it failed to attract any support and its scrip fell to an immediate discount.[34] In the same month, Brazilian scrip also dropped despite an announcement of continuing interest payments. Investors had tired of receiving their dividends out of capital. As a summer torpor set in, trading on the stock market was thin. Investors began ignoring calls on partly paid shares, which led several companies to petition for dissolution.† The leading stock of the mining mania, the Real del Monte, fell from a high of 1,550 to under 200.

A crisis beckoned. During the mania, banks had recklessly extended credit, discounting bills for merchants who were speculating in commodities and lending against the inflated collateral of bonds and shares. In late August, the Bank of England became alarmed by the decline of its gold reserves: it had over £19 million of banknotes in circulation, but less than £4 million in gold specie with which to support this paper credit. In order to avoid its

*Canning later told the Commons, "I really do not know, Sir, what legislative interference could possibly effect in such a case. I do not know how a measure could be framed to deal with those speculations of unreasoning avarice which would not, at the same time, have borne so hard on honest industry and rational enterprise, that it would have been likely to do more harm than good." (*Parliamentary Debates*, XII, 1063.)

†After deductions had been made for the expenses of directors, lawyers, and various friends in Parliament and the press, shareholders received only a fraction of their initial capital outlay.

potential failure, the Bank rapidly contracted its operations, and even refused to discount (provide credit against) the notes of Barings and Rothschilds. Against the strong opposition of William Huskisson, the Bank continued building up its hoard of bullion throughout the autumn.

The tightening of credit by the Bank of England had a knock-on effect throughout the financial system. Worst affected were the country banks. These institutions were unregulated and unprofessional (as Lord Liverpool remarked, "Any petty tradesman, any grocer or cheese-monger, however destitute of property, might set up a bank in any place"). Although Britain had officially returned to the gold standard in 1819, the country banks had been permitted to issue paper notes, unbacked by specie, until 1832. During the boom, they had stimulated the asset inflation by doubling their issues of paper currency, lending to stock market speculators and discounting notes for long periods. When confidence evaporated and credit dried up, their weaknesses were exposed. Across the nation, local panics or "runs" afflicted the country banks. In early October there were two failures in the West Country, followed soon after by the collapse of the Plymouth Bank. As the crisis deepened, the *Morning Chronicle* warned that "the Bank [of England] has to choose between its own insolvency, and the insolvency of these imprudent speculations, and as *it is impossible*, in the present state of things, for the Bank, with *any regard for its own safety, to stretch out a friendly hand to them*, the consequences may easily be foreseen."[35] In other words, the Bank of England was not in the position to act as lender of the last resort.

By December, the City was in a state of commotion. Early that month, a run appeared on the London bank of Pole & Co. The Bank of England agreed to an emergency loan to stave off its collapse, but the failure of Wentworth & Co., a leading Yorkshire bank, heightened the tension. On 14 December, Pole's stopped payment, dragging down over forty of its correspondent country banks. On the same day, City merchants gathered at the Mansion House in an attempt to boost public confidence, declaring that they had "the firmest confidence in the stability of the public credit of the country." The private opinion of a Bank of England director was more frank: "Never were such times, if this state of things continues, we must ask not who is gone, but who stands? For unless something is done to relieve the pressure, and to restore confidence, few can resist so overwhelming a torrent of distrust."[36] On the stock market, share prices fell by up to 80 percent while some stocks went unquoted. Troops were called to Threadneedle Street after a mob gathered at the doors of a faltering Bank of England, whose gold reserves had dwindled to under a million pounds. In the midst of unprecedented prosperity, economic activity ground to a halt. Although the shops were overflowing with goods and food was abundant, credit had taken flight. Only gold remained acceptable and, in spite of the South American fables, there was not enough of it to go round. The country, Huskisson remarked, was only forty-eight hours away from barter.

"All confidence was lost," Alexander Baring later told the Commons. "Scarcely one man could be found to trust his neighbor, every one endeavouring to husband his own resources for himself. Such a state of panic had hardly ever before existed amongst us."[37] It was imperative that the Bank of England resume its discounting operations. In emergency session, the cabinet decided to permit the Bank of England to circulate notes of small denomination (it was previously forbidden from issuing notes with a value of less than £5). A box of unissued £1 notes was discovered in the Bank's vaults and hastily distributed.[38] The Mint was set to work coining sovereigns at the rate of 150,000 a day. Nathan Rothschild brought over from France 300,000 gold sovereigns, which he paid into the Bank. These emergency measures saved the day. By Christmas Eve, despite the failure of around seventy banks, the Bank of England was no longer threatened with failure and was able to resume discounting the bills of the more creditworthy banks and merchants.

The stock market *panic* was over, but the period of economic *crisis* was just beginning. Among the casualties of the crisis was Sir Walter Scott, whose publisher, Constable, and manager, James Ballantyne, were brought down by the failure of their London bank, which had engaged in commodities speculation. Linked by partnership, Scott became legally responsible for £46,000 worth of Ballantyne's debts. At the age of fifty-five, the author decided to face his creditors:

> I will be their vassal for life, and dig into the mine of my imagination to find diamonds . . . to make good my engagements, not to enrich myself.[39]

This mine provided richer lodes than those in South America, and Scott eventually discharged his debts. In February 1826, the banking firm of B. A. Goldschmidt & Co., which a few years earlier had earned over a quarter of a million pounds contracting a Mexican loan, failed. Its principal partner, L. A. Goldschmidt, died shortly afterwards of a broken blood vessel in his head induced by anxiety.[40] The same month, the London merchants requested an issue of Exchequer notes to be provided against the collateral of their inventories, as had occurred during the financial crisis of 1793.*

Lord Liverpool, however, remained deaf to these pleas, and reminded Parliament of his earlier warnings to speculators. He invoked the principle of moral hazard which dictates that the rash and foolhardy should suffer, since any relief would only stimulate the revival of speculation and provoke another crisis in the future. As Huskisson explained in the Commons, if parties "might always expect to obtain asylum in government, it was as much calculated to encourage speculation as the poor-laws were to encourage vagrancy, and to discourage honest industry."[41] Suffering for the evil of speculation was deemed purgative: "The inordinate appetite for gain, if left to itself, could not fail to work its own cure, through its own certain disappointment," declared Canning, the foreign secretary. "It is most unfair," he added defensively, "to infer from any hesitation on the part of Government to adopt any particular remedy, under such circumstances, that there exists, therefore, on their part, an insensibility to the extent or nature of the existing evil."[42]

Unfortunately, the existing evil, as Canning so delicately called the economic crisis, was not visited upon sinful speculators alone. Throughout the greater part of 1826 the country remained in severe depression. Bankruptcies for the first half of the year tripled.

*Alexander Baring supported their petition, claiming that "if all the cases of distress that had ever, in any former time, occurred in this country, were summed together, they would fall far short of equalling the mass of distress and suffering which at present oppressed the nation." (Quoted in Smart, *Economic Annals of the Nineteenth Century*, II, p. 327.)

Manufacturers curtailed their output, and worker unrest fanned out across the country. In Norwich, weavers rioted throughout the early part of the year. The unemployment situation became so bad that a colonial secretary suggested an inquiry "into the expediency of encouraging Emigration from the United Kingdom."[43] He was supported by a group of unemployed Scottish weavers, who entreated the government to cast them into exile.[44]

SOUTH AMERICAN BLUES

Towards the end of 1826, the *Morning Chronicle* reported the death of a ham merchant of St. Nicholas Lane who had "destroyed himself in a fit of temporary derangement caused by the depreciation in value . . . of some Spanish bonds."[45] Earlier in the summer, the market value of South American loans, issued with a face value of £25 million, had declined to less than £12 million. These bonds had initially paid dividends from reserves set aside at the time of their issue, but these reserves had run out, and every South American state defaulted on its debt, with the sole exception of Brazil. It was not only the bondholders who lost out; the South American people also suffered. The small sums which had actually been remitted to the states by the loan contractors were expended on military equipment for war against neighbouring states or used to suppress internal opposition to the regimes.* The loan mania also created what has aptly been called "The First Latin American Debt Crisis." Interest due on loans became an obstacle to trade between Britain and South America, and for over half a century the loans went through a tortuous process of rescheduling and default.

"As for shares," wrote the *Morning Chronicle's* money market columnist in February 1826, "no person thinks of mentioning their names, and thousands wish they had never had a name to mention."[46] Over a hundred companies floated during the mania were

*According to the financial historian L. H. Jenks, "the violence, the corruption, the instability, [and] the financial recklessness which characterised most of the South American republics during a large part of the [nineteenth] century are in no small way attributable to the early laxity of the London money market." (*Migration*, p. 63.)

abandoned during the course of the year. The *Monthly Review* dismissed them as "a great shoal of monstrous abortions—begotten by fraud upon credulity!" The Real del Monte, on which £400 had been paid, sunk to 115, and the Bolivar Mining Association, organised to extract copper from the Liberator's Venezuelan family property, fell from 28 to 1. The crash of the mining market shattered Disraeli's youthful dreams. Saddled with debts of several thousand pounds, which were not finally discharged for a quarter of a century, the future prime minister now turned his abundant energy to writing fiction, and drew on his personal experience to produce his first novel, *Vivian Grey*. Exhausted by events, he subsequently suffered a nervous breakdown and was sent abroad to recover.*

The collapse of the mining stocks was largely the result of an account of the South American mines, published in early 1826, by Captain F. B. Head, chief engineer of the Rio Plata Mining Association. Head had travelled more than three thousand miles across the South American continent, earning himself the nickname "Galloping Head." His company's prospectus had claimed that gold was so abundant in its concessionary area that it need only be washed from the mud. The reality, according to Head, was rather different. The company's mining concessions were either disputed or worked bare by slave labour, which British miners could not emulate. In extremely inhospitable mining conditions, British technology turned out to be useless. Nor was the Spanish legacy so easily dispensed with: Captain Head found the South American people to be "perfectly destitute of the idea of a contract, of punctuality, or of the value of time."[47]

The universal failure of the mining companies, wrote Head, "proceeded from one cause—our Ignorance of the country which was to be the field of speculation."[48] The same was true of the South American loans, most especially the Poyais loan. Creditors displayed a total ignorance of the incapacity of the disorganised,

*Having opened his career with a disastrous foreign speculation, Disraeli closed it with a more successful overseas purchase. In 1875, he negotiated on behalf of the British government the purchase of a half-share in the Suez Canal. Bought for £4 million, half a century later the Suez shares were worth £40 million. "As an investment," wrote L. H. Kenks, "the purchase of the [Suez] shares may be regarded as one of the most fortunate that Englishmen ever made." (*Migration* p. 324.)

unstable, and poverty-stricken Latin American countries to service their loans. The lack of knowledge about the mining companies was so general that, it was said, the less known of the place where a mine was to be sunk, the higher the premium its shares reached.[49]

Instead of acting on sound information, speculators were driven by fantasy. Since the time of Drake's circumnavigation and his return in 1580 with Spanish booty, South America had retained a special allure for the English people. Yet they were not solely motivated by greed. Their investment had a romantic and political aspect to it. They were purchasing the freedom of a continent that, in English eyes, had suffered long enough from Spanish exploitation, intolerance, and backwardness. The mining speculators were doing something far grander than simply engaging in seedy operations for personal gain; they were, in Disraeli's words, "patronising infant liberty and liberal principles."* In short, the South American mania represented the triumph of a soaring imagination over rational financial calculation. As Harriet Martineau later recalled:

> the charm was in the excitement—in the pleasure of sympathy in large enterprises—in the rousing of the faculties of imagination and conception, when their field of commerce extended over the Pampas and Andes, and beyond the farthest seas, and among the ice-rocks of the poles. When the grey-haired merchant grew eloquent by his fireside about the clefts of the Cordillera, where the precious metals glitter to the miner's torch, it was not his expected gains alone that fired the eye, and quickened his utterance; but that gratification of his conceptive faculty to which his ordinary life had ministered too little.[50]

The events of 1822–25 were only the first in a long succession of "emerging market" booms. For much of the nineteenth century, the

---

*Disraeli wrote that mining shares were considered less seedy than other speculations: "there was nothing *ungenteel* in watching the turn of a *mine* market; it was compared to purchasing an estate, and . . . there was something gorgeous and aristocratical in the idea of succeeding to the possessions of the Valencianas and the Reglars . . ." (Disraeli, *Inquiry*, p. 99.)

United States was an emerging market for British investors, who poured capital into state bonds and railroad companies and experienced frequent losses. Towards the end of the century, South America attracted a fresh bout of speculation which ended with the collapse of Alexander Baring's family bank after it was left holding a pile of Argentine utility bonds. The U.S. bull market of the 1920s, like the British boom a century earlier, was preceded by a spate of speculative lending to South American countries, all of which defaulted in the depression years. The contraction of American foreign lending in the early 1930s served to deepen the international depression.

More recently, the American bull market of the 1990s has been accompanied by speculative loans and investments in the emerging markets of South America, the Far East, and the countries of the former Soviet Union.* The motivation behind these foreign investments has been similar to that which inspired British investors in the 1820s. Whereas British goods, capital, and skills were to modernise the South American states after their liberation from the dead hand of the Spaniard, in the 1990s it was to be American goods and capital that replaced the sclerosis of state socialism. In their euphoria, modern investors in emerging markets ignored the profound differences between their own political and economic cultures and those of the countries in which they invested, just as their British predecessors had done in the 1820s.†

The 1990s has witnessed an unprecedented number of stock market bubbles in far-flung places, from Chile to Bangladesh. According to one investment strategist, "The challenge to investors

*The term "emerging market" was first coined in 1986 by a bureaucrat at the International Finance Corporation, a World Bank affiliate. It sounded a more appealing place in which to invest than the "third world" or a "less developed country." Between 1991 and 1995, U.S. pension and mutual fund emerging market investments rose from under $200 billion to over $500 billion.

†Echoing the comments of Captain Head, a recent article in the *Financial Times* claims that emerging markets are not suitable for Western investors, as, in many cases, they lack the necessary institutions, the rule of law, proper bankruptcy procedures, reliable accountancy, non-corrupt administrations, predictable taxation, monetary stability, deposit insurance, adequate financial regulation, and independent central banks capable of acting as lenders of the last resort. Its author concludes: "In finance, ignorance is only briefly bliss." (6 October 1998.)

[in emerging markets] is to time the surfing of the bubble correctly—stay in long enough to benefit, but get out before the bubble bursts." Investors sought a high return on their foreign stock investments and loans but took fright at the first signs of distress. Fears of a "domino effect," as speculators fleeing one country destroy confidence in its neighbours, have produced a new era of international instability with competitive currency devaluations reminiscent of the 1930s. As a bear market developed in emerging market debt in the middle of 1998, the fallout looked depressingly similar to earlier periods.* The stock markets of the "submerging markets," as they were quickly renamed, have fared equally miserably, sinking back to their levels at the beginning of the decade. Just as in the 1820s, the effect of this speculative boom will most likely be to sour relations between the developing nations and the West and to discredit the free-market model in the eyes of those who have seen piles of money thrust through their front door only to witness it leaving twice as speedily out the back door.

THE TRADE AND SPECULATIVE CYCLES

Emerging market speculation tends to appear at a juncture in the economic cycle when declining yields on domestic bonds combine with an excess of capital to make foreign investments particularly attractive. The mania of 1822–25 marks the beginning of a close connection between speculation and the business cycle. Sir William Petty had first observed the trade cycle (which he described as successions of "dearth and plenty") back in the seventeenth century. Originally this cycle was associated with crises brought on by poor harvests, war, and problems of public finance, rather than speculative excess. (For instance, the original Black Friday of 6 December 1745 was caused by the Jacobite invasion and the Young Pretender's

*For instance, Venezuelan bonds issued at 93 in September 1997 were trading at 45 a year later. The average yield on emerging market debt above the rate on U.S. Treasury bonds (i.e., the risk premium for lending to emerging markets) went from less than 4 percent in July 1998 to over 16 percent six weeks later. This represents a relative decline for emerging market bonds against U.S. Treasury bonds of around 75 percent.

progress to Derby.) As the economy became more advanced in the second half of the eighteenth century, the agricultural and fiscal nature of the economic cycle gave way to a new cycle based upon the expansion and contraction of credit.* "Within the last sixty years," wrote Samuel Taylor Coleridge in his *Lay Sermon* of 1817,

> . . . there have occurred at intervals of about 12 or 13 years each, certain periodical Revolutions of Credit . . . for a short time this Icarian Credit, or rather this illegitimate offspring of CONFIDENCE . . . seems to lie stunned by the fall . . . Alarm and suspicion gradually diminish into a judicious circumspectness; but by little and little, circumspection gives way to the desire and emulous ambition of *doing business*; till Impatience and Incaution on the one side, tempting and encouraging headlong Adventure, Want of principle, and Confederacies of false credit on the other, the movements of Trade become yearly gayer and giddier, and end at length in a vortex of hopes and hazards, of blinding passions and blind practices.[51]

These thoughts were articulated in the midst of the severe depression that followed the end of the Napoleonic Wars. Within a few years, credit and confidence had revived and the economic cycle developed along the lines predicted by Coleridge, until it erupted in a full-blown speculative mania. The boom of 1822–25 can be understood as the product of easy credit conditions. The bonds of the South American states were attractive to British investors because the supply of Consols was drying up and their yield was shrinking. The country banks contributed to the boom by deluging the nation with paper notes ("This fictitious surplus," according to Alexander Baring, "was the fuel by which the fire was fed").[52] During the boom, the unrestricted growth of credit caused

*The financial crisis of 1772 was preceded by widespread speculation in canals and turnpikes (private toll roads) and the excessive issue of bills of exchange. Its immediate cause was the collapse of the Ayr Bank, which was brought down by the failure of the banking firm of Alexander Fordyce, a former hosier of Scottish extraction who had speculated unsuccessfully in the stock of the East India Company. A similar crisis occurred in 1793 after speculation in canals and exorbitant issues of credit.

asset prices to rise, stimulating yet further credit creation. The situation reached a turning point in the spring of 1825, after which declining asset prices undermined confidence, caused a contraction of credit, and eventually brought on a crisis.*

After the crisis of 1825, the banker and bullionist S. J. Loyd (later Lord Overstone) described a cycle very much like Coleridge's:

> First we find it in a state of quiescence,—next improvement,—growing confidence,—prosperity,—excitement,—overtrading,—convulsions,—pressure,—stagnation,—distress,—ending again in quiescence.[53]

In Overstone's description, the cycles of trade, credit, and speculation are all connected. During the mania of 1822–25, speculation in stocks, bonds, and commodities was matched by a keen anticipation of exports to South America and hazardous lending by banks against the collateral of stocks and shares. Overstone's psychological interpretation of the economic cycle was taken up and elaborated by Walter Bagehot, the editor of the *Economist.* Bagehot explained "hazardous" speculation as the result of "an excess of accumulation over tested investment" which recurred in periods of prosperity:

> The fact is, that the owners of savings not finding, in adequate quantities, their usual kind of investments, rush into anything that promises speciously, and when they find that these specious investments can be disposed of at a high profit, they rush into them more and more. The first taste is for high interest, but that taste soon becomes secondary. There is a second appetite for large gains to be made by selling the principal which is to yield the interest. So long as such sales can be effected the mania continues; when it ceases to be possible to effect them, ruin begins.[54]

*Tooke claims that the losses sustained in stock speculation "entered into the causes of the banking and commercial crisis which followed." (*History of Prices,* II, p. 159.)

During the upturn of the cycle, Bagehot argued, people become convinced the prosperity will last forever and mercantile houses engage in excessive speculations. At the same time, an increasing number of frauds are perpetrated on investors, which only come to light after a crisis: "All people are most credulous when they are most happy."

After 1825, there was a succession of booms and crises at roughly ten-year intervals. At the end of the nineteenth century, they were analysed by the French economist Clément Juglar, who gave his name to the decennial "Juglar cycle."* The ten-year cycle was related by nineteenth-century economists to various factors, such as the expansion and contraction of credit, the rise and fall of manufacturers' inventories, and even the periodic appearance of sunspots.† According to John Stuart Mill, the seeds of each boom are sown during the preceding crisis, when the liquidation of credit causes asset prices to decline so severely that they become genuine bargains. Their subsequent sharp rise from a low level leads to a revival of speculation.[55] After each crisis, the financial markets invariably shrug off past follies and losses to confront the future with bright optimism and fresh credulity. Capital becomes "blind," to use Bagehot's term. Unable to remember the past, investors are condemned to repeat it.

*Juglar's analysis of crises is essentially a monetary one: protracted periods of inflation and expansion are brought to an end when the banking system initiates a contraction in the face of unacceptable pressures on its specie reserves.

†The sunspot theory was first suggested by W. S. Jevons.

CHAPTER 5

"A READY COMMUNICATION": THE RAILWAY MANIA OF 1845

Men have an indistinct notion that if they keep up this activity of joint stocks and spades long enough all will at length ride somewhere, in next to no time, and for nothing; but though a crowd rushes to the depot, and the conductor shouts "All aboard!" when the smoke is blown away and the vapor condensed, it will be perceived that a few are riding, but the rest are run over,—and it will be called, and will be, "A melancholy accident."

Henry David Thoreau, *Walden* (1854)

Innovation," wrote Joseph Schumpeter, "is the outstanding fact in the economic history of capitalist society."[1] Speculators are in the vanguard of the capitalist process. Once an innovation has been successfully established and produces steady returns, speculation gives way to investment, which is more concerned with safety of principal and regularity of income than with capital gains. Unlike the speculator, the investor is primarily interested in the current state of affairs; insofar as he anticipates the future at all, he hopes that it will be a seamless continuation of the present.

Inventions and novelties have always excited speculators. The diving machine, fire engine, and burglar alarm companies in the 1690s, and the machine gun and "wheel for perpetual motion" in 1720, are early examples of speculators' enthusiasm for technological advances. Until the Industrial Revolution, however, the innovations which attracted the attention of speculators were either of limited application or mere frauds thrown up during boom times.

From the late eighteenth century, however, there have occurred a number of genuine innovations in the field of communications which have had very far-reaching effects on society. First came the canals, followed in succession by railways, motorcars, radio, aircraft, computers, and, most recently, the Internet. Each of these advances in communications attracted the fervent attention of speculators who contributed greatly to their successful establishment.

THE CANAL MANIA

The canal age in Britain commenced with the completion, in 1767, of the Duke of Bridgewater's canal, which ran some thirty miles from the coal mines on the Duke's estate at Worsley, northwest of Manchester, to Runcorn in the southwest, where the new textile factories were situated. Over the following two decades more than a thousand miles of canals were constructed. The first canals produced tremendous returns on capital, paid large dividends, and enjoyed soaring share prices. They also generated great popular excitement, as the benefits they provided—in the form of cheaper transport costs for coal, manufactures, and agricultural produce—appeared to have the potential of transforming the old world.[2] In the early 1790s, popular speculation in canals appeared for the first time. During this period, over fifty parliamentary acts for new canals were passed—more than double the number of the preceding fifty years. Meetings of subscribers were held in fields, inns, and even churches. Local dealers, often the clerks of canal companies, solicitors, or innkeepers, set up "Navigation Offices" reminiscent of the tulip Colleges of the 1630s.[3]

Canal speculation reached a climax in the winter of 1792–93. The newspapers in the Midlands—where the majority of schemes were projected—were filled with advertisements for stockbrokers, reports of crowded shareholders' meetings, and spectacular prices for canal stock.[4] The subscribers to the Leicester Navigation Canal adopted as a motto for their company some lines from Horace: *Liquidus Fortuna Rivus Inauret* (May the liquid stream of fortune cover you with gold).[5] It was wishful thinking. The canal mania came to an abrupt end with the commercial crisis of 1793, brought on by the outbreak of the French revolutionary wars. Canal share prices collapsed. The investment returns of the new canals turned out to be miserable in comparison with their predecessors, which had been built by local landowners and merchants with a clear idea of their advantages.* By the turn of the century, the overall return on capital invested in canals had fallen from a pre-mania level of 50 percent to around 5 percent.[6] Even a quarter of a century later, one in five canals was still unable to pay a dividend, and aggregate dividends as a percentage of capital invested produced a return similar to those of risk-free government bonds.[7]

Although the opening of new canals linking towns and cities, manufacturers and markets, aroused local enthusiasm, the technology itself was not new—after all, the Romans had built aqueducts. Canals simply extended the benefits of water transportation to areas which had not previously enjoyed it. The advent of the railways, on the other hand, represented a far more significant change in the life of man. So profound was this change that when the first steam engines appeared in the 1820s, they were greeted with a mixture of scepticism and trepidation. It was anticipated that locomotives would prevent cows from grazing and hens from laying eggs, that their poisonous fumes would kill birds and blacken the fleeces of sheep, and that their speeds of up to fifteen miles an hour would blow passengers to atoms.[8] Railways also faced opposition from canal owners, coaching establishments, and landlords who feared for the tranquillity of their estates and the ruin of their fox hunting. When the Great Western Railway was proposed to connect London with the west of England, both the University of Oxford and Eton College initially refused a connection.

Despite widespread hostility, the early history of the railways was marked by two outbreaks of speculative enthusiasm. The first "railway fever" appeared in 1825 with the opening of the first steam railway, the Stockton and Darlington. Soon after, six railway acts were passed by Parliament. This brief outbreak of railway euphoria was extinguished in the economic crisis at the end of the year. Six years later, the opening of the Liverpool and Manchester Railway finally

*The costs of building the canals had risen substantially and the prime routes had already been taken. Moreover, many of the second-generation canals took a long time to complete (forty-six years in the case of the Leeds and Liverpool).

established the superiority of locomotive power over fixed steam engines and horse traction, which until then had seemed viable alternatives. The Liverpool and Manchester soon paid a dividend of 10 percent, and the market value of its shares doubled. Its success sparked a second "railway fever," which appeared amidst a general bout of speculation (a cyclical revival after the crisis of 1825), ranging from Spanish bonds to joint-stock banks. When the boom progressed to bust in 1837, the crisis extended to the railways.* Few new railways were projected over the next five years. By the early 1840s, shares in the majority of railway companies sold at a discount to their issue price. With nearly two thousand miles of track in operation, many believed that the national railway system was already complete.†

It was around this date, however, that reflection on the profound changes wrought by the railways began to grip the public mind. In the summer of 1842, the young Queen Victoria was persuaded by Prince Albert to make her first railway trip. (She is reported to have found the short journey from Slough to Paddington pleasantly free from dust, heat, and crowds.) The opposition of landlords diminished as they discovered that land lying adjacent to railway lines tended to rise in value. Throughout the country, journals and pamphlets proclaimed the railways as a revolutionary advance unparalleled in the history of the world. They not only focused on the economic benefits of railway transport, but concerned themselves with its more widespread effects on human civilisation. "Railway time," it was said, would change forever the pace of human existence: "Our very language begins to be affected by it," wrote a contemporary, "men talk of 'getting up the steam,' of 'railway speed,' and reckon distances by hours and minutes."[9] A railway director announced to a meeting of shareholders that "nothing, *next to*

*The Great Western's cheques were dishonoured, and the partly paid shares of one railway company actually sold at a premium to the buyer (the shares were considered a liability because the shareholder was legally bound to make further payments or "calls" on them).

†The journey from London to Glasgow by rail and steamer had been cut to twenty-four hours. "'What more can any reasonable man want?'" asked the *Railway Times*. (Cited by Sir John H. Clapham, *An Economic History of Modern Britain: The Early Railway Age*, Cambridge, 1930, I, p. 390.)

religion, is of so much importance as a ready communication."[10] One paper jubilantly declared that

> the length of our lives, so far as regards the power of acquiring information and disseminating power, will be doubled, and we may be justified in looking for the arrival of a time when the whole world will have become one great family, speaking one language, governed in unity by like laws, and adoring one God.[11]

There was no limit to the imagined effects of this revolution. It was even anticipated that the railways would produce "a gradual thawing of that reserve, for which the people of Great Britain are celebrated."* From an investment point of view, it was argued that railway shares would remain "safe in midst of panic."[12]

The public was gripped by a railway vogue. In *Dombey and Son* (1846), Dickens lampooned the contemporary fashion for "railway hotels, office-houses, lodging-houses, boarding houses; railway plans, maps, views, wrappers, bottles, sandwich-boxes, and time-tables; railway hackney-coach and cab-stands; railway omnibuses, railway streets and buildings . . ." A rapidly expanding railway press contributed to the development of the popular enthusiasm. In the early 1840s, there were three railway journals, led by the authoritative *Railway Times*, and during the "mania" year of 1845, new railway papers appeared nearly every week. They included fourteen weekly papers (which were issued twice weekly at the height of the fever), two daily papers, and both a morning and an evening paper.†

---

*The author further speculated: "The prejudices and mistaken interests which separate one district of the same nation from another, are broken down by such noble inventions as these; and the same spirit of civilisation which results from that increase of our reason, which bestowed by a beneficent Providence, will eventually render all men as brethren, and children of one great Father . . . and will, there is no possible doubt, above all, spread knowledge and diffuse intelligence over towns and cities, and finally tend to 'universal good.'" (H. Wilson, *Hints to Railway Speculators*, London, 1845, p. 12.)

†Their titles included the *Iron Times*, the *Railway Express*, the *Railway World*, the *Railway Examiner*, the *Railway Globe*, the *Railway Standard*, the *Railway Mail*, the *Railway Engine*, the *Railway Telegraph*, the *Shareholders Advocate*, the *Railway Director*, the *Railway Register*, and the *Railway Review*. The railway papers which survived the mania included the *Railway Times*, the *Railway Chronicle*, the *Railway Record*, *John Herapath's Railway Journal*, and the *Railway Gazette*.

THE RAILWAY KING

One man understood best how to direct the public enthusiasm for railways to his own ends. George Hudson, the chairman of the York and North Midland Railway, was an energetic, overweight, and abrasive Yorkshireman. The son of a farmer in the East Riding, he had started his professional life as a linen draper and risen—thanks to a sizeable inheritance from a great-uncle—to become mayor of York. Hudson's interest in railways dated to 1834, when he first met the engineer George Stephenson, the "Father of the Railways." According to legend, Stephenson was persuaded by Hudson to make York the centre for a northeastern system of lines and branches; or, as Hudson put it in his gruff Yorkshire brogue, to "mak all t'railways cum t'York."[13]

After the York and North Midland opened in 1842, Hudson set about planning new lines and branches, and purchasing or leasing existing companies. He projected new lines to join York with Edinburgh. Through a series of mergers (or "amalgamations" as they were called), he extended his railway system to reach Birmingham, Bristol, and eventually London. By 1844, he controlled over a thousand miles of railway, more than a third of the total track in operation at the time. It was in this year that Hudson acquired the sobriquet of "Railway King"—allegedly conferred by the Reverend Sydney Smith, the greatest wit of his day. He was also known as the "Yorkshire Balloon" owing to his gluttonous appetite and wide girth. Perhaps he was most accurately described by another title, the "Railway Napoleon," for Hudson succeeded in linking his own destiny to that of the railway era.

Hudson contrived to associate himself with the advance of the railways and deliberately fanned the public's growing ardor. He carefully stage-managed the opening ceremonies of new lines to extract maximum excitement: "All railways are yet in their infancy, and day after day, week after week, and month after month, they will go on increasing their resources," he announced at the opening of a new line in early 1841. When he was elected member of Parliament for Sunderland in August 1845, he arranged for an express train to bring an early edition of the *Times* from London to Sunderland announcing his election victory before the voters themselves knew of it: "See the march of the intellect! See the power of steam!" He shouted at the crowd as he distributed free copies of the newspaper.[14] A few days later, at a celebratory dinner, Hudson extolled the virtues of fantasy: "Gentlemen, there is something in imagination. I don't say it ought to govern us; but having formed our judgement, let imagination have a little play . . ."[15]

Hudson's management of railways was marked by a combination of ostentation, rule-bending, and penny-pinching. Red tape, he announced, was a commodity he had formerly sold by the yard in his shop but which had no place in his railway empire. As the chairman of several railway companies, he acted in secrecy and kept his fellow directors in the dark. The companies' accounts were his own special preserve and he refused to hold meetings of finance committees. When he joined the board of the Midland in 1842, he immediately changed the company's accounting methods, announcing, "I will have no statistics on my railway!"[16] (On another occasion, Hudson is said to have declared, "We don't mind principle in matters of business!") Although given to personal extravagance and display, Hudson maintained a tight control of costs and charged the highest tariffs on his lines. In November 1840, a fatal accident on the York and North Midland line occurred after Hudson had employed an elderly train driver with defective eyesight in order to save on wages. Similar accidents became frequent on his railways and Hudson's critics accused him of sacrificing public safety to profitability. But lower costs enabled Hudson to pay higher prices when taking over rival railway companies and distribute greater dividends to his shareholders.

Even while still under construction, the York and North Midland Railway under Hudson's management had announced an improbably generous dividend of 9 percent. Large dividends, in turn, purchased the support of shareholders. When Hudson freely admitted that the York and North Midland was paying its dividend out of capital, there was no murmur of disapproval from shareholders. Nor did they object when the share price of companies amalgamated by Hudson rose prior to a takeover announcement—a sure sign of insider trading. In October 1844, he was able to raise £2.5 million from the shareholders of the Midland Railway without telling them his plans: "Well," he boasted, "I have carried my point, I have got my money, and I have not told a soul what I am going to do with it!"[17] An atmosphere of elation and ecstasy characterised the shareholders' meetings: the railway was their new religion and Hudson their Messiah.

THE RAILWAY ACT OF 1844

During the railway fever of 1836 some had argued that a government survey of the country should be made so the best routes were chosen for development. However, the absence of political agreement combined with the prevailing doctrine of laissez-faire to ensure that the British railway system would develop piecemeal. The process of establishing a railway was uncomplicated: it required only a few local dignitaries to organise themselves into a committee, for them to register the company provisionally (the organisers were known as provisional committeemen), raise money from the public by advertising subscriptions for shares, employ an engineer to survey the route, and apply to Parliament for a railway bill. Once a company was provisionally registered, the subscription certificates for its shares (scrip), on which only a tenth of the capital had been paid (the rest would be "called" later when construction was underway), could be traded in the market. The only check to the process was the examination by Parliament.

In the early days of the railways it was believed that on payment of a certain toll to the proprietor anyone might run a train on a railway track and that the railways would produce their own competition.* By the early 1840s, however, it had become clear that railways formed natural monopolies. With the further extension of the railway system imminent (sixty-six applications for railway bills arrived before Parliament in early 1844), there was a need for fresh public direction in a field almost devoid of government regulation. In early 1844, the talk of framing new railway legislation fell to William Ewart Gladstone, the recently appointed President of the Board of Trade.

*In practice, railway companies were unable to run services on lines other than their own, as they did not have access to either railway stations or watering places. During the early history of the railways, there were no restrictions on the charges rail companies could levy for carrying passengers or goods in their own trains.

When he consulted the railway interest about regulation, Gladstone encountered differing opinions. George Carr Glyn, the London banker and chairman of the mighty London and Birmingham Railway, foresaw a depreciation in railway property unless measures were taken to systematise railway legislation. George Hudson, on the other hand, argued fiercely against regulation as an undue interference with private property. Hudson got his way. Under pressure from the prime minister, Sir Robert Peel, Gladstone was obliged to water down his initial proposals. Although the Railway Act, which became law in the summer of 1844, created a Railway Department to examine new lines, its recommendations were not binding on Parliament and it lacked the facilities to investigate the mountain of schemes about to arrive at its door. "I do not believe that the precautions taken by [the Railway Act] will have the effect of impeding or preventing the application of private capital [to the railways]," asserted the laissez-faire prime minister.[18] Fearing this would indeed be the case, in the autumn of 1844 Gladstone raised the deposit on new railway schemes from 5 to 10 percent, in the hope of deterring the more speculative promotions. Shortly after, he resigned his post at the Board of Trade, citing a conflict between his official position and his family's own railway interests. In private, he anticipated a return of speculation: "I have a feeling," he wrote before his resignation, "that . . . circumstances connected with the state of the commercial world will undoubtedly subject present legislation to a very severe and early trial."[19]

THE BEGINNING OF THE MANIA

By late 1844, the economic situation was benign: interest rates were at their lowest point in almost a century and, after a series of excellent harvests, corn was cheap and plentiful. Railway construction costs had fallen, and railway revenues were rising rapidly. The three largest railway companies were paying dividends of 10 percent (four times the prevailing rate of interest), and public interest in the "railway revolution" was growing. Sensing a groundswell of speculative interest, Hudson purchased large quantities of railway iron for his own account in the winter of 1844. His judgement was shrewd; within three months its price had tripled.

In January 1845, sixteen new railway schemes were projected. By April, with rail receipts continuing to grow rapidly, over fifty new companies had been registered. Advertisements for railway prospectuses, soliciting subscriptions from the public, flooded the newspapers. The standard notice contained a list of provisional committeemen, a paragraph extolling the benefits of the proposed line, and in most cases the promise of a final dividend of at least 10 percent. If the subscription was successful, the committeemen retained a large allocation of stock for themselves and their friends and released only a few shares in the market, thus creating a scarcity which threatened to snare speculators who had sold shares short in anticipation of buying them back at a lower price.* The new railway company was then hyped by friends in the railway press and its stock bid up by agents in the stock market. Once the shares were trading at a premium, the promoters would off-load their retained shares at a vast profit.† Some companies even employed special "share committees" to oversee the success of these operations.

Many of the promoters of the new railways appeared interested only in their own personal profit. The same individuals were found on the committees of numerous new railways, in some cases representing rival schemes. Public figures offered their services as committeemen in exchange for shares at a discount. Other committeemen were penniless impostors who fabricated respectability with false titles and postions.‡ Occasionally the name of a local bigwig was

---

*The *Morning Chronicle* (24 October 1845) claimed that often less than a quarter of the shares in new schemes were distributed, with the remainder reserved to exchange for property on the line or kept by the committee.

†In late October, it was reported that promoters had launched a new railway company, made £25,000 from selling shares at a premium, and subsequently liquidated the company, returning deposits, less expenses, but retaining the premium for themselves (*Times*, 31 October 1845).

‡A letter to the *Times* complained that many of the people who advertised themselves in railway prospectuses as Fellows of the Royal Society had no connection with that institution. Another letter described the majority of committeemen as "the most notorious scamps, alias swindlers, who never possessed a penny in the world, and never could or would possess one save what may arise from their trafficking as 'stags,' in getting up and carrying out their infamous designs to fleece the public." (*Times*, 24 and 17 October 1845).

included among the published lists of directors without his knowledge or permission. Although committeemen were liable in law for the debts of their companies, many discreetly failed to sign the deeds and thus avoided liability. "If one black sheep can taint a whole flock," proclaimed an editorial in the *Times*, "there is scarcely one of the speculative lines that does not contain the element of contamination among the number of its provisional committee-men."[20]

Naturally, the railway journals were enthusiastic and uncritical supporters of the railway schemes. They "puffed" dubious new railways in their editorial pages, and received, in return, some of the hundreds of thousands of pounds spent weekly on advertising the prospectuses. "Such has been the mania for railway advertising," declared the *Times*, "that papers have been started which were never intended to be sold or read, but only to catch some of the money that was daily being thrown away in preliminary announcements and prospectuses."[21] The most reprehensible creature of the railway mania, concluded the paper, was "the Stag of the Press."[22]

The government remained impassive in the face of the growing public involvement in new railway schemes. In April, Alexander Baring, by now Lord Ashburton, declared in the House of Lords that "nothing more important could occupy the attention of Parliament than the present feverish state of gambling events connected with railways. In this case, as in many others, it was easier to point out the difficulty than to suggest the remedy." Some argued that the government should control speculation by outlawing the trade in railway scrip before companies had received their parliamentary bills. But the government ignored this advice, and allowed railway companies unhindered access to the legislature. By the close of the first session of Parliament in August over a hundred railway acts had been passed, authorising the construction of around three thousand miles of railway track.

The prime minister, Sir Robert Peel, embroiled in arguments within his party over the repeal of the Corn Laws, showed no initial anxiety about the potential dangers arising from the mania and stuck to his laissez-faire position. The previous year, Peel had secured the passing of the Bank Act, which prevented the Bank of England from increasing its note issue above a specified limit. Its aim had been to end the periodic sequence of boom and bust by preventing the explosion of credit during a cyclical upturn.* In the early summer of 1845, Peel expressed his satisfaction that the Bank Act had prevented "all undue speculation."[23] By late August, however, the prime minister was more concerned, writing to Henry Goulburn, the Chancellor of the Exchequer, "Direct interference on our part with the mania of railway speculation seems impracticable. The only question is whether public attention might not be called to the impending danger, through the public press."[24] Peel was reluctant to go further than soliciting an unofficial warning, and deferred to the Bank of England's opinion that raising interest rates in order to dampen railway speculation would only produce a panic. This policy was supported by the *Economist*, which argued that the mania would not be checked by a small rate rise: "It would be the greatest folly of the Bank Directors to disturb their otherwise legitimate routine of business for any such vain hope as deterring or checking such a mania."[25]

The only positive action of the government was to disband the ineffective Railway Department in early July. In the first half of the year, the decisions of the department on new schemes had been eagerly anticipated, and fluctuations in share prices prior to the publication of official notices suggested that insider trading was prevalent.[26] After the dissolution of the Railway Department, the plans for new railways were laid directly before select committees of the Commons for consideration. So many members of Parliament, however, were committeemen or railway shareholders that Lord Salisbury complained it was impossible to find sufficient disinterested parties to examine the new schemes. One railway company boasted of commanding a hundred votes in the Commons, and members of Parliament were said to go from one railway office to another hawking their votes in support of fresh railway bills.

The mania was particularly strong in the provinces. This reflected the extension of the railway network away from the metropolitan centres. London had long been connected by rail with the other

*Under the terms of the Bank Act (also known as Peel's Act after the prime minister), the Bank of England's discretionary ability to issue notes was restricted to a statutory £14 million above its holdings of bullion. A currency tied firmly to gold, argued the bullionists, would prevent overspeculation by defining the limit of credit and offering no escape for the reckless during a crisis. The belief that the government had legislated away financial crises provided many with a false security in the year ahead.

major trading and manufacturing towns and failed to share in the railway euphoria. In his journal, the poet Wordsworth observed the spread of the railway mania north of the border:

> From Edinburgh to Inverness, the whole people are mad about railways. The country is an asylum of railway lunatics. The Inverness patients, not content with a railway to their hospital from Aberdeen, insist on having one by the Highland road from Perth. They admit that there are no towns, or villages, no population, and no chance of many passengers. But then they will despatch such flocks of sheep, and such droves of nowt![27]

Northern speculation was facilitated by the establishment of Exchange Banks, which provided loans against the collateral of railway shares.* In Glasgow, Edinburgh, Bristol, Birmingham, and a number of smaller towns, new stock exchanges were established for the trade in railway shares.† Leeds had three competing exchanges where half a million transactions were processed daily by some three thousand stockbrokers.[28] In late July, the *Leeds Mercury* described the intensity of the market:

> Never was anything like the amount of business done in this town . . . the streets which are blessed with the presence of our three Stock Exchanges resembled a fair on the mornings of those days. Crowds of anxious brokers and speculators thronged them, and the rushing to and fro of brokers, eager to save the precious moments, was worthy of the promoters of rapid locomotion.[29]

In neighbouring Wakefield, nine stockbrokers plied their trade and two express trains travelled twice daily to Leeds bringing back information on the latest movement in share prices.[30]

---

*Originating in Glasgow in May 1845, Exchange Banks soon spread throughout the north, providing loans of up to 80 percent of the value of railway shares. They suffered in the crisis of 1847 and not one survived the decade. (See Tooke, *History of Prices*, V, p. 368.)

†Stock markets also opened in Leicester, Wakefield, Bradford, Halifax, and Macclesfield. (See M.C. Reed, *Railways in the Victorian Economy*, Newton Abbot, 1969, p. 180.)

THE RAILWAY STAGS

A parliamentary report published in June 1845 revealed the identity of twenty thousand speculators who had each subscribed for more than £2,000 worth of railway shares. Heading the list was a Francis Mills of New Street, Spring Gardens, with commitments of over £670,000. Hudson's name appeared in eleventh place with subscriptions of just under £320,000. Alongside the names of 157 members of Parliament (one of whom had signed for £157,000) and 257 clergymen, appeared "40 Browns and 28 Jones and 2½ pages of Smiths."[31] Observing the broad social base of the railway speculators, the *Times* announced, "We are a nation of plethoric capitalists."[32]

Naturally, many of those whose names appeared on the list had contracted obligations beyond their means. Two brothers, who together subscribed for £37,500 worth of shares, were discovered to be the sons of a charwoman living in a garret off a guinea a week.* Such people had no intention of meeting the subsequent "calls" on railway shares; they signed the subscription documents in the hope of selling "scrip" at a premium in the market (an act of dubious legality since full transferability of shares came only after a company had received its parliamentary bill). Known as "railway stags," they joined a burgeoning stock market menagerie:

> Bulls and bears, and lame ducks [reported the *British and Foreign Railway Review*] have long flourished there; but of late, a whole herd of stags have invaded the place, of whom there exists at this moment an extraordinary amount of somewhat indefinite terror. The stag, in a state of nature, is a harmless timid, graminivorous animal, whose appetite is small, and easily satisfied; whereas there is no end to the voracity of the carnivorous railway stag; who is always in search of these premiums which constitute the very flesh and blood of railway speculators. The railway stag has only one characteristic in common with his antlered namesake; he is very shy of being seen, and the most experienced

*In the House of Lords, Lord Clanricarde complained that a gentleman of Finsbury Square had subscribed for £25,000, though he was reliably informed that no one lived at that address. (Francis, *Railways*, II, p. 169.)

hunters find great difficulty in tracing him to his lair. He is, in fact, more cunning than a fox, by which cognomen he would have been more appropriately designated.[33]

In the first half of the year all the new railway schemes yielded profits (or "premiums") for the stags, even those projected to uninhabited wildernesses and those whose bills had been rejected by Parliament.[34] The *Economist* denounced the irrationality of this situation:

> The market value [of railway scrip] . . . depends, not on the opinion as to the ultimate success of the undertaking, but rather how far circumstances will tend to sustain or increase the public appetite for speculation. Nothing can show this more powerfully than the fact that we see nine or ten proposals for nearly the same line, all at a premium, when it is well known that only one CAN succeed, and that all the rest must, in all probability, be minus their expenses.[35]

A letter in the *Times* stressed the cynicism of the speculators: "There is not a single dabbler in scrip who does not steadfastly believe—first, that a crash sooner or later, is inevitable; and, secondly, that he himself will escape it. When the luck turns, and the crack play is *sauve qui peut*, or devil take the hindmost, no one fancies that the last mail train from Panic station will leave him behind. In this, as in other respects, 'Men deem all men mortal but themselves.' "[36] In an editorial, the *Times* itself suggested that the speculators were more naive than cynical: "It is only the play of children, trying to lift up one another in the air at the same time . . . It is the simpler part of the public which is deceived."[37] All commentators agreed none of the speculators was interested in the long-term future of the railways: "To a man [wrote the *Times*], all live upon the present moment, or look at most but a fortnight before them, from one settling-day to another."[38]

Although both the *Times* and the *Economist*—which published a "permanent" sixteen-page supplement, entitled "The Railway Monitor," in early October—accepted railway advertisements, neither was swayed from its duty to inform the public of the corruption of the mania and the inevitability of a crash. Never before had foreboding of a crisis been more strongly and frequently articulated by the leading journals of the land. In particular, the newspapers attempted to draw the public's attention to the insupportable amount of capital that was required to finance the reckless extension of the railway system. By June 1845, plans for over eight thousand miles of new railway—four times the size of the existing railway system and nearly twenty times the length of England—were under consideration by the Board of Trade. In the following month, new schemes appeared at the rate of over a dozen a week.

In a supplement published in early November, entitled "The Railway Interest of the United Kingdom," the *Times* provided a definitive picture of the current state of railway speculation and the unbearable demands it was making on the country's economy. To the end of October, the paper reported, over twelve hundred railways were being projected at an estimated cost of over £560 million. The total amount of outstanding railway liabilities was nearly £600 million. This figure exceeded the national income, estimated at around £550 million, of which perhaps £20 million a year could be spent safely on the railways without starving the rest of the economy of capital.[39]

Where, asked the newspapers, was the capital required for railways to come from? They answered that it could only come from a forced conversion of the nation's "floating capital" (i.e., the capital used to support the normal operations of business) into the temporarily unremunerative fixed capital of uncompleted railways, "which for the time," observed the *Globe*, "is as much sunk as if it were expended in an attempt to drain the ocean. It is palpably possible even for such a country as this to sink too much in this manner within a given time."[40] A pamphlet published in Manchester during the summer warned of an impending crisis as money was drawn from the legitimate channels of commerce by tradesmen expending their capital on railway calls.[41] Once again the old cry was raised that speculation was distracting people from their lawful occupations.* The *Economist* feared that the real consequences

*David Morier Evans claimed that by late summer, "the neglect of all business has been unprecedented; for many months no tradesman has been found at his counter, or merchant at his office, east, west, south or north. If you called upon business you were sure to be answered with 'Gone to the City.'" (*Commercial Crisis 1847–1848*, p. 167.)

of railway speculation would not be felt immediately, but in later years when construction was underway and railway calls would consume the nation's capital resources: "To think or dream that the present mania will subsist without a crisis the most severe ever experienced in this country," wrote the paper in the middle of August, "would be to shut our eyes to all past experience."[42]

Throughout the hectic summer months, Hudson was at the height of his glory. Although he disapproved of the reckless extension of the railway system which threatened the profitability of his own lines, new schemes rumoured to be connected with the Railway King attracted a ready premium in the stock market. (In fact, Hudson was involved with only one new scheme during this period.) When he became chairman of the failing Eastern Counties Railway in the summer of 1845, its shares soared. Hudson retained the highest public profile in the railway world: "In the journals of the day, men read of [Hudson's] wonderful doings," recalled John Francis in his *History of the Railways* (1850). "The press recorded his whereabouts; the draughtsmen penciled his features . . . He wielded an influence in England unparalleled and unprecedented. Peers flattered the dispenser of scrip, and peeresses fawned on the allotter of premiums."*

As long as the mania continued, Hudson remained a hero to the people. The former linen draper, who literally had gone from "rags to riches," became a living symbol of the get-rich-quick mentality that enthralled the nation. He celebrated his success at the Sunderland election in August by purchasing a twelve-thousand-acre estate from the Duke of Devonshire for nearly half a million pounds. For his London residence, he acquired the five-story Albert Gate mansion in South Kensington, one of the largest private houses in the capital, for £15,000 and spent an equal amount on decorating it. Shareholders at one of his railway companies proposed building a statue of the portly Hudson as a public testimonial to his achievements. Twenty

*Francis, *History of the Railways*, ii, pp. 218–19. Hudson did receive some criticism. For instance, a correspondent to the *Times* (on 24 October, 1845) observed: "One 10 per cent good line [i.e. the York and North Midland] has been the nucleus or basis on which are centered new projects, with a view to delude the public. The great abettor of this system is Mr. George Hudson, whose name has been considered a guarantee of everything good." The author also accused Hudson of buying up worthless lines at high premiums: "Amalgamation with good names has created a fictitious value which will find its level when the railway fever has abated."

thousand pounds were soon raised. Among the subscribers were Emily and Anne Brontë, who had invested in the York and North Midland back in 1842 and contributed a grateful pound from their paper profits (against the wishes of Charlotte, who, expecting the bubble would soon burst, advised her sisters to sell their shares).[43]

By late summer, speculation was reaching a climax. Certain railway scrip showed a 500 percent profit, and interest on loans against railway stock was being charged at rates of up to 80 percent. "Direct" routes between towns served only by branch lines became the craze. Foreign railways were projected around the globe, from British Guyana to Bengal. Over a hundred railways were planned for Ireland. A Railway Club was established in the West End, where "gentlemen of all ranks, connected with railway projects, may daily meet for the interchange of information."[44] In September, over four hundred and fifty new schemes were registered, and a single issue of the *Railway Times* contained over eighty pages of prospectus advertisements. In just ten days in early October, over forty new schemes with a capital requirement of £50 million were announced.

Overshadowed by the euphoria was growing evidence of the corruption and fraud begot by the mania. According to a contemporary financial journalist, "All rule and order are upset by the general epidemic [of speculation], as in the Plague of London, when all ties of blood, honour, or friendship, were cast away."[45] At the Board of Ordinance, which inspected new railway schemes, two members were forced to resign after they were discovered to have speculated in scrip. In August, share deals were repudiated at Leeds after it was revealed that the number of shares sold in one recently amalgamated company was ten times greater than had actually been issued. Forged scrip for several companies was in circulation, including the Kentish Coast Railway, whose shares continued to trade at a premium despite the fact that its proposed scheme had been rejected by the Board of Trade and the directors had voted to wind up the company.*

*In December 1845, a court case was brought by a speculator who had purchased forged scrip in the Kentish Coast line. It was later discovered that the fraud had been perpetrated by the company solicitor but judgement was given against the selling broker (for selling faulty goods). During 1846, forged scrip was uncovered in several other railway companies, and the *Railway Times* ran a column entitled "The Progress of Exposure."

As construction got underway, railway companies raised funds by "calling" some of the remaining capital on their shares. By early October, shares were sliding as speculators were forced to reduce their shareholdings in order to meet the costs of railway calls. The *Times* reported that early on the morning of Tuesday, 14 October, a Mr. Elliott of Bayswater had shot himself in Hyde Park. A search of the dead man's pockets revealed papers connected with a number of railways throughout the country.[46] Two days after this tragic episode, the directors of the Bank of England, worried by a slight decline in their reserves, decided to raise interest rates by half a percent (to 3 percent). Although the rise was small, it signalled the end of the railway fiesta. In the stock market, there was talk of a railway "avalanche" as the premiums on scrip evaporated. From London, the bad news travelled rapidly by rail to the provincial exchanges, bringing paralysis to these markets. "The transition," declared the *Newcastle Journal*, "has been from unexampled buoyancy to almost hopeless depression—from an unnatural and unstable elevation to the lowest depths of suspicion and distrust."[47] In the general revulsion, even the market for the established dividend-paying railways dried up. By the end of October, Great Western shares were down 40 percent from their August peak. "A mighty bubble of wealth is blown before our eyes," announced the *Times* with a certain satisfaction, "as empty, as transient, as contradictory to the laws of solid material, as confuted by every circumstance of actual condition, as any other bubble which man or child ever blew before."[48]

A RUNAWAY TRAIN

Although the period of intense activity in the provincial stock markets was over, the Railway Mania had set in motion events that were to lead directly to the great financial crisis of 1847. After the crash, provisional committeemen found their interests diverged from those of the shareholders. If a railway project was aborted without a public subscription, the committeemen were legally responsible for all its costs. As a result, when speculators attempted to withdraw their applications for shares, they were refused by the committeemen and held to their contractual obligation to pay the subsequent share calls. Earlier in the year, when premiums were high, speculators had obtained only a small fraction of the shares they applied for, but after the panic, when scrip was at a discount, they received a full allocation of shares and were ordered to pay up sharply.

"The lust of gain which animated all speculators," reported the *Glasgow National Advertiser*, "is now changing into the cruelty of a reign of terror, and the ferocity of a revenge . . . the world of speculation is transforming into a world of litigation."* The growth of litigation led the government to pass an act, in May 1846, enabling the dissolution of railway companies with the assent of three-quarters of the shareholders. The Direct Western, which in January 1845 had received nearly a million and a half applications for 120,000 shares, became the first company to put an end to itself under the new law. By July 1846, eight companies had already advertised dissolution meetings under the act.

Despite the Dissolution Act and declining share prices, railway activity continued at a frenetic pace. During the course of 1846, there were over a hundred mergers of railway companies and 270 parliamentary railway acts were passed, authorising the building of nearly five thousand miles of railway with a capital requirement of over £130 million—more than double the number of acts and two thousand more miles of railway than had been authorised in the previous year. This has led some commentators to suggest that the mania continued past the October panic of 1845. In fact, most of the railway companies which received their bills in 1846 had been launched the previous year (the most important of them, the Great Northern, was first proposed in early 1844), and the majority of railway bills were for branch extensions of established concerns that were expanding rapidly in order to fend off competition from the new railways. In three hectic days in May, Hudson secured permission from shareholders in three of his railway companies to apply for forty bills, involving an expenditure of over £10 million.[49]

The inevitable consequence of this continuing railway activity was to build up even further the burden of railway calls, which

*"Some of the bubble companies, we have heard," reported the *Railway Times*, "sold the whole number of their letters of applications to speculative attorneys who have at once proceeded to issue threatening notices, and who, in some instances, have reaped a rich harvest."

exceeded £40 million in 1846. As construction got under way, money was diverted from the normal channels of business to pay for land, iron, timber, and, above all, labour. In July 1846, a parliamentary committee reported that around 200,000 men, mostly of Irish origin, would be employed in railway construction for several years to come. (The railway labourers were named "navvies" after the "navigators" who had built the canals in the previous century.) These costs had to be shouldered by railway speculators, who were forced to reduce their employment of domestic servants, consumption of wine, and sporting activities in order to meet their ongoing railway calls.[50]

After a harvest failure in the summer of 1846, economic conditions deteriorated. The rapid switch to railway transport, which allowed for smaller inventories to be kept by businesses and caused a one-time reduction in demand, worsened the situation. The *Economist* blamed the unsettled climate on "the enormous private losses which the wild speculations of the autumn of 1845 have entailed upon the community."[51] In October 1846, Thomas Carlyle, the historian, observed that railway scrip had declined by more than £60 million in value over the past year, and that the losses of the inhabitants of Exeter alone were estimated at more than £8 million.[52] The schedules of the bankruptcy courts were filled with accounts of "losses by railway shares."[53] "It is the conviction of those who are best informed," wrote John Francis a few years later,

> that no other panic was ever so fatal to the middle class. It reached every hearth, it saddened every heart in the metropolis. Entire families were ruined. There was scarcely an important town in England but what beheld some wretched suicide. Daughters delicately nurtured went out to seek their bread. Sons were recalled from academies. Households were separated: homes were desecrated by the emissaries of the law. There was a disruption of every social tie. The debtor's jails were peopled with promoters; Whitecross-street was filled with speculators; and the Queen's Bench was full to overflowing.[54]

In January 1847, the Bank of England raised interest rates to 4 percent after a decline in its reserves. Throughout the early part of the year, railway calls continued to average around £5 million a month. In early summer, wheat prices fell sharply after early signs of an abundant harvest. This was followed, in August, by the failure of thirteen corn merchants, including the firm of W. R. Robinson, the Governor of the Bank of England. Nearly forty leading mercantile houses failed the following month. Disraeli later recalled a "commercial distress of unprecedented severity—private credit was paralysed, trade was more than dull, it was almost dead—and there was scarcely a private individual in this kingdom, from the richest and noblest in the land down to the most humble among the middle classes, who was not smarting under the circumstances of commercial distress . . ."[55]

By early October 1847, dangerously low levels of bullion led the Bank of England to announce it would no longer make advances on public securities. On Monday, 17 October, the "week of terror" commenced in the City. Consols fell sharply as everyone sought safety in gold. On Tuesday, the Royal Bank of Liverpool failed, followed shortly after by three other joint-stock banks. "Everyone seemed afraid of his neighbour," remembered George Norman at the Bank of England. The Stock Exchange was in a tumult, creditors were distressed, and the best short bills changed hands at 10 percent.[56] By the end of the week, the Bank of England held less than half a million of gold and one and a half million of notes in its reserves. Any further run and the Bank would be forced to close its doors. On Saturday, 23 October, a deputation of leading City bankers went to Downing Street for a meeting with Lord John Russell, the prime minister, and Sir Charles Wood, the Chancellor of the Exchequer. They requested a suspension of the Bank Act. Two days later, a letter arrived at the Bank of England from Downing Street, authorising the Bank to ignore the terms of the Bank Act and continue its discounting operations. Only three years earlier, the act had been passed with the promise that it would put an end to speculative excesses and financial crises by making them too painful to endure. Now it was suspended in order to save Britain from economic collapse.

The suspension brought the financial crisis to an end. In the ensuing debate on the causes of the crisis, contemporary commentators were unanimous. Although Lord Overstone blamed the Bank of England for decreasing its reserves in the face of a continuing drain of bullion, he thought the deeper cause of the crisis was want of capital caused by the "extraordinary diversion of capital from trading purposes to the construction of railways." Likewise, Lord Ashburton blamed the Bank for mismanagement but attributed the crisis to "the extravagant circulation of railroad paper by which much of our present difficulties has been caused."* The *Economist* also ascribed the economic crisis to excessive railway expenditure that had consumed the credit available to normal trade and forced up the rate of interest from 2½ percent in 1845 to around 10 percent in October 1847.[57] It had taken nearly two years for the full impact of the reckless railway speculations to be felt in the economy at large.

DETHRONING THE RAILWAY KING

The final act of the Railway Mania was still to come. During the revolutionary year of 1848, Hudson became markedly less sanguine about railway prospects. He was frequently observed drunk in the House of Commons and lost his temper when another member suggested he "join a temperance society."[58] In August 1848, a pamphlet appeared entitled *The Bubble of the Age; or, the Fallacies of Railway Investments*, whose author, one Arthur Smith, accused railway directors of manipulating their accounts and paying dividends out of capital.[59] Two of Hudson's companies, the York and North Midland and the Eastern Counties, were specifically mentioned. Smith also attacked the practice, pioneered by Hudson, of leasing railway lines with the promise of dividends of more than 50 percent on paid-up capital, which had inflated share prices and encouraged insider trading by directors.

Shortly after the publication of Smith's pamphlet, railway share prices went into sharp decline. Despite an increase in passenger traffic, lower fares and more lines had brought a decline in average

*Lord Ashburton, *The Financial and Commercial Crisis Considered*, London, 1847, p. 24. Carlyle wrote to Ashburton: "I must say further that the diagnosis of the malady (railway speculation, pp. 24, 30 &c) agrees with all that poor Common-Sense could ever teach me on the matter: if you waste your substance, of course your lose your 'credit,' you have in fact nothing to be 'credited,' or believed in, for the present!" (26 May 1847, in *Collected Letters*, XXI, p. 220.)

receipts per mile of track from £3,500 in 1845 to £2,500 in 1848. As a result, dividends were cut on all the major lines. By August 1848, it was estimated that the total decline in railway stocks was £230 million (a figure equivalent to almost half the national income).[60] The share price of the York and North Midland had fallen two-thirds from its 1845 peak and was trading at a discount to its paid-up capital. The Great Western, whose price had risen to 236 during the Railway Mania, was also trading below par at 65.[61] The railways had lost their appeal: it was time to dethrone the railway king.

Long before Arthur Smith accused railway directors of false accounting, there had been private suspicions that Hudson's business practices lacked probity. In August 1845, Richard Cobden, the free-trade activist and member of Parliament, had remarked on Hudson's "*undetectable* corruption." While Hudson's activities remained outwardly successful, such criticisms were muted; but as the dividends of his companies were cut and their shares fell to a discount, the attacks became more open. In the first few months of 1849, Hudson's rule over the railway world came to an abrupt end. At a shareholders' meeting in February, Hudson was accused of profiting from the sale of shares in one of his companies to another (of which he was chairman) at above market prices. Shortly after, he failed to attend a meeting of shareholders of the Eastern Counties. "A day of reckoning will come," crowed the *Yorkshireman*, a longtime enemy of Hudson, when "peculation, and jobbing, and grave injustice, will meet with retributive punishment."[62]

In April 1849, a committee investigating Hudson's management of the Eastern Counties concluded that Hudson had exaggerated revenues and paid over £200,000 of dividends out of capital. A similar inquiry at the York and North Midland found he had paid out £800,000 from capital. On 8 May, Richard Nicholson, Hudson's brother-in-law and fellow railway director, committed suicide by leaping into the river Ouse in York, only yards away from the railway station which Hudson had built. During the following months a variety of accusations dogged Hudson: insider trading before takeovers, personally profiting from the sale of iron to one of his companies, holding back funds which had been allocated for land purchases, secretly issuing shares to himself and selling them in the market at a premium, and managing a "secret service" fund to bribe Parliament.

It was even said that Hudson had purloined the money raised from the public for his testimonial and used it to purchase his London mansion. In total, Hudson was estimated to have embezzled just under £600,000, excluding the payments made to all shareholders of dividends from capital.

In his defence, Hudson claimed that his private affairs and those of his companies had become unfortunately intertwined (on several occasions he had offered personal surety for the liabilities of his railway companies). The practice of charging certain expenses to the capital account was common at the time and had been accepted when the railways were successful. The *Times* maintained that the fault did not lie with Hudson alone: "The system is to blame. It was a system without rule, without order, without even a definite morality."[63] Yet Hudson had taken advantage of the absence of regulation: acting in secrecy, bullying fellow directors to bow to his will, and opposing any outside supervision of the accounts or any general regulation of the railways. His false accounting and generous dividends had misled speculators into believing that the railways were more profitable than they actually were.

Several contemporaries felt that Hudson was simply a scapegoat for the failed speculations. According to Richard Monckton Milnes, the Tory politician, the Railway Mania had been "mere gambling; and the shareholders, having lost, are now kicking over the table and knocking down the croupier."[64] For Carlyle, however, the failure of the speculations and the fall of Hudson represented the restoration of a divine order: "What a world this ever is!" he wrote in his journal in May 1849, "full of Nemesis, rule by the Supernal, rebelled in by the Infernal, with prophetic tragedies of old."[65] The historian had long been incensed by the Hudson testimonial. In an essay on Hudson's statue, published in the summer of 1850, he imagined Hudson as a scapegoat swinging from a gibbet,

> as a tragic pendulum, admonitory to Earth in the name of Heaven,—not some insignificant, abject, necessitous outcast, who had violently, in his extreme misery and darkness, stolen a leg of mutton,—but veritably the Supreme Scoundrel of the Commonwealth, who in his insatiable greed and bottomless atrocity had long, hoodwinking the poor world, gone himself,

> and led multitudes to go, in the ways of gilded human baseness; seeking temporary profit (scrip, first-class claret, social honour, and the like small ware), where only eternal loss was possible; and who now, stripped of his gildings and cunningly-devised speciosities, swung there an ignominious detected scoundrel; testifying aloud to all the earth: "Be not scoundrels, not even gilt scoundrels, any one of you; for God, and not the Devil is verily king, and this is where it ends, if even this be the end of it!"

Although Hudson was never charged with criminal wrongdoing, his exposure revealed to all the general corruption engendered by the Railway Mania. When a manager at the Hudson-controlled York Union Bank was discovered to have stolen and subsequently lost £20,000 in railway speculations, the *Yorkshireman* declared that Hudson was "not only corrupt in himself, but corrupted everyone around him."[66] Seven years later, in February 1856, the poisoned corpse of John Sadleir was discovered on Hampstead Heath. Sadleir, a former Irish MP, banker, and railway promoter, had issued forged shares with a nominal value of £150,000 in the Royal Swedish Railway (of which he was chairman) and had misappropriated £400,000 from an Irish bank. These frauds had been perpetrated in order to cover his stock market losses. Dickens drew on the histories of Hudson and Sadleir for his portrait of the swindling banker Merdle in *Little Dorrit*. Dickens's epitaph for Merdle (who, like Sadleir, commits suicide after his exposure) is an astute analysis of the relationship between the corrupt financier and the public during times of speculative euphoria.

> The next man who has as large a capacity for swindling will succeed as well. Pardon me, but I think you have really no idea how the human bees will swarm to the beating of any old tin kettle; in that fact lies the whole manual of governing them. When they can be got to believe that the kettle is made of precious metals, in that power lies the whole power of men like our late lamented.

Once the talisman of the mania, Hudson became its longest-suffering victim. Having paid back the money taken from his companies, he spent much of his time on the Continent to escape his creditors. He lost his parliamentary seat in 1859 and was arrested for debt six years later. When he died in the winter of 1871, he left an estate, once estimated in millions, of only two hundred pounds.

THE ROAD AHEAD

Railway legislation during the mania had been a wild scramble, with no directing principle.* A pamphlet, published in 1847, regretted the

> grand error of abandoning a national work to what is called "private enterprise," but which, as matters turned out, should be rather termed individual caprice and cupidity. Had the state fortunately taken up the work itself *ab initio*, it would not only have been executed more conveniently and economically for the country, but a vast revenue must have accrued to the nation at large.[67]

Other countries had taken steps to avoid the dangers of uncontrolled railway speculation. When a railway mania had suddenly appeared in Prussia in early 1844, the government reacted quickly by condemning speculation, banning the sale of options and settlement for differences (or futures), and refusing to sanction new lines.[68] In France, military engineers decided on railway routes, before construction was put out to tender by private companies. The most extreme example of government intervention was provided by the Belgian state, which undertook responsibility for the construction and management of the nation's railway system. In Britain, on the other hand, the spirit of laissez-faire dictated that the development of the railways should be left entirely to private

---

*In March 1846 the *Circular to Bankers* had criticised the government for "the laisser-faire principle applied to the new element of national strength and economic power, the system of railways; a system which obviously required the interposition and regulation of Government as imperatively as the police system or the Post Office." (Quoted by Hunt, *Business Corporation*, p. 105.)

enterprise. The uncontrolled expansion of the railway system, in the hands of semi-criminal entrepreneurs, produced a haphazard network. For instance, by the 1850s there were three independent routes from Liverpool to Leeds and three alternative routes from London to Peterborough. In many cases the optimal lines had not been chosen. "We now have to pay for the waste of capital in fruitless Parliamentary contests, uneconomic branch lines, and futile competition," wrote the railway historian T. H. Lewin in the 1930s.*

By January 1850, railway shares had declined from their peak by an average of over 85 percent, and the total value of all railway shares was less than half the capital expended on them. Owing to overconstruction of railroads and increased competition, the average receipts per mile of rail track were a third less than those before the mania. Railway dividends averaged less than 2 percent of capital expended. Even five years later, more than a quarter of the rail companies could not afford to pay dividends and the great majority paid less than 5 percent. Many railroads built in the 1840s produced only poor returns, until they were eventually killed off by the arrival of the automobile.

The results of the mania, however, were not entirely negative. With over 8,000 miles of track in operation by 1855, Britain possessed the highest density of railways in the world, seven times greater than that of France or Germany.[69] This brought great benefits to the Victorian economy in terms of faster and cheaper transportation for passengers, raw materials, and finished goods. During the period of construction in the late 1840s, over half a million people—a figure equal to those employed in British factories—were dependent on the railways for employment at a time when the country was experiencing a severe economic crisis (albeit one induced by the mania). Tens of thousands of Irish navvies were provided with work throughout the famine years. Viewed from this perspective, the Railway Mania represented a transfer of income

*T. H. Lewin, *The Railway Mania and Its Aftermath* (London, 1936), p. 19. More recently, another railway historian has claimed that the mania led to competing lines, uneconomic routes, and a waste of capital: "The consequences of all this affect the railway map adversely to the present day." (P. J. G. Ranson, *The Victorian Railway and How It Evolved*, London, 1990, p. 85.)

from middle-class speculators to needy labourers, while simultaneously providing the country with the infrastructure for a modern industrial economy.

Although the advent of the automobile produced great excitement among British speculators in the 1890s and their American counterparts in the 1920s, the closest parallel to the Railway Mania is provided by the more recent expansion of the Internet in the mid-1990s. The changes to be wrought by the latest "Information Revolution" were described in language strikingly similar to descriptions of the "Railway Revolution" of the 1840s. In 1995, Nicholas Negroponte, an American academic and author of *Being Digital*, claimed that "digital living" would reduce man's dependence on time and place, close the generation gap, and contribute to "world unification."[70] In *The Road Ahead*, Microsoft chief Bill Gates wrote that "the information superhighway will change our culture as dramatically as Gutenberg's press did the Middle Ages."[71] Another proselytiser of the Information Revolution, George Gilder, described the Internet emerging as the "central nervous system of capitalism."[72] By early 1996, America was consumed with a craze for Internet books, Internet films, Internet exhibitions, and even children's Internet swap cards. Just as the Railway Mania stimulated the growth of a specialist press, so the Internet spawned dozens of national magazines, some of which specialised in Internet investment.

Unlike the railways, new Internet companies required little capital investment. Their speculative potential was first realised in the summer of 1995 after the successful flotation of Netscape Communications, an Internet software company. By the spring of 1996, new Internet stocks were flooding the U.S. stock market. In April, three providers of Internet browser services were floated on the Nasdaq Stock Exchange. The most successful of these, Yahoo!, a company founded a year earlier, which boasted meagre quarterly sales of $1 million, soared to a 153 percent premium on its first day (the third-greatest rise in history), giving it a market capitalisation of $850 million. When Zenith, a loss-making television manufacturer, announced in early May that it would begin producing televisions with Internet connections, its shares rose threefold. "Breathe the word

'Internet' around a stock," announced an analyst, "and anything can happen."*

Whereas in the 1840s the speculative fervour was sustained by the crowds around the provincial exchanges, a century and a half later it was nourished on the Internet itself. Discount brokerages thrived by offering cheap Internet share-dealing services, and on-line investment forums, such as the "Waaco Kid Hot Stocks Forum" and the "Motley Fool," became some of the most popular destinations on the Internet. Just as the railway boom spawned new stock exchanges, the Internet itself became a stock market enabling companies to float their shares in cyberspace. The medium was no longer just the message, it was both the source and object of speculation. "Gold rushes," wrote Bill Gates in a prophetic conclusion to his book, "tend to encourage impetuous investments. A few will pay off, but when the frenzy is behind us, we will look back incredulously at the wreckage of failed ventures and wonder, 'Who funded those companies? What was going on in their minds? Was that just mania at work?' "[73]

---

*The boom in Internet stocks strengthened in 1998. By the end of the year, the market values of leading Internet companies competed with those of America's largest corporations; the market capitalisation of Charles Schwab, the discount broker with on-line trading facilities, overtook that of Merrill Lynch; eBay, a recently founded on-line auction house, outstripped Sotheby's; and AOL, the Internet service provider, became more valuable than the Disney Corporation. The market capitalisation of Yahoo! was over 800 times its earnings and over 180 times its sales revenue, or $35 million per employee. The share price of Amazon.com, an on-line bookstore, multiplied 18 times during 1998 (despite the company's escalating losses). One fund manager described it as "the most outrageously priced equity in the world," but advised buying the stock nevertheless. The market's response to initial public offerings was particularly feverish: When theglobe.com, an Internet chat service, was floated in mid-November, its shares rose a record-breaking 866 percent on the first day of trading. On 15 January 1999, Marketwatch.com was floated: Offered to investors at $17, the shares closed at $97.50. Internet stocks were boosted by a shortage of shares available for trading, stock splits, and euphoria surrounding the potential for "e-commerce."

Fred Hickey, editor of the *High-Tech Strategist*, called this upsurge "the greatest investment mania since Tulip Bulbs." In late January 1999, Alan Greenspan, Chairman of the Federal Reserve, observed that Internet valuations were "pie in the sky" and that investors were indulging in a lottery, since most Internet companies were doomed to failure and their shares would become worthless.

CHAPTER 6

"BEFOOLED, BEWITCHED AND BEDEVILED": SPECULATION IN THE GILDED AGE

Speculation, at first a sentiment, or if you please, a taste, passes next into a habit, then it grows into a passion, a master passion, which like Aaron's serpent, swallows up and strengthens itself with other passions. It becomes at last more fierce than anger, more gnawing than jealousy, more greedy than avarice, more absorbing than love. The stock-market may be likened to a withered old harridan, enameled, painted, and decked in the latest mode, which leers on the speculator, and points to golden prizes, that like the desert mirage, fades away and leaves him to his ruin.

William Fowler, *Ten Years on Wall Street* (1870)

The colonial movement was in the nature of a speculation. Columbus himself was a speculator, and North America the greatest speculative prize of all. The first American colonies were established as joint-stock ventures. When Sir Walter Ralegh's Virginia Company was reorganised in the early seventeenth century, it promised investors a return of 20 percent and incorporated a subsidiary company "for Transporting 100 Maids to Virginia to be made wives."[1] A few years later, the settlement of New Amsterdam (later New York) was undertaken by the Dutch East India Company, whose shares at the time were the main object of speculation on the Amsterdam bourse. In the middle of the seventeenth century, the "wall" of Wall Street was constructed on the orders of Governor Stuyvesant of the Dutch West India Company.* Towards

*The original purpose of the wall was to keep out bears and marauding Indians and keep in bulls and other livestock. In its subsequent history, Wall Street has penned in its bulls and bears together.

the end of the century, shares in the New Jersey and Pennsylvania "companies" were traded in Exchange Alley, alongside the diving bell and fire engine ventures. Among other things, John Law's Mississippi Company comprised a speculation in half the territory of the modern United States.

The speculative character of the American people derives in great measure from the colonial venture. The American dream is posited on the vision of a beneficent, ever-improving future. "The difference between an American and any other person is that the American lives in anticipation of the future because he knows what a great place it will be," said Ronald Reagan with his characteristic mixture of folksy sentimentality and insight. The American settlers had forsaken their historic lands for a nation whose boundaries were limited only by their dreams. As the nineteenth-century financial writer William Fowler observed, "Imagination, in this country, lives in the future rather than the past."[2] Only in America could a man declare that history was bunk.

America is a democratic nation where social status is up for grabs, and wealth, not birth, provides the ultimate measure of distinction. During his American travels in the early 1830s, the French aristocrat Alexis de Tocqueville observed a vibrant spirit of materialism. "I never met in America," he wrote, "any citizen so poor as not to cast a glance of hope and envy on the enjoyments of the rich or whose imagination did not possess itself by anticipation of those good things which fate still obstinately withheld from him. . . . The love of well-being has now become the predominant taste of the nation; the great current of human passions runs in that channel and sweeps everything along its course."*

*Alexis de Tocqueville, *Democracy in America*, Henry Reeves text, ed. Philip Bradley, New York, 1948, II, pp. 128–30. Tocqueville's view may have been influenced by the fact that his travels in the United States coincided with the beginning of a speculative mania. In 1834, Michael Chevalier noted, "Everybody is speculating and everything has become an object of speculation. The most daring enterprises find encouragement; all projects find subscribers. From Maine to the Red River, the whole country is an immense rue Quincampoix [i.e., the French stock market at the time of the Mississippi Bubble]. Thus far, everyone has made money as is always the case when speculation is in the ascendant. . . . The principal objects of speculation are those subjects which chiefly occupy the calculating minds of the Americans, that is to say, cotton, land, city and town lots, banks and railroads." (*Society, Manners and Politics in the United States*, New York, 1839, p. 305.)

The American is equipped with more than just a hopeful vision of the future and a drive for self-improvement. He is prepared to take enormous risks to attain his ends. To emigrate to America was, in itself, a great risk. Settlement of the frontier involved even greater risks, such as fending off Indians and wild animals (many of the great nineteenth-century speculators came from the frontier regions). This appetite for risk—so great that one might say it was imprinted in American genes—has not diminished with time but remains a continuing source of the nation's vitality. Even rich Americans found themselves dissatisfied with their lot and were prepared to gamble to improve it. After a stock market panic in the late nineteenth century, the London *Spectator* commented bemusedly:

> The millionaires of America make corners as if they had nothing to lose. Let some amuse themselves financing as if it were only an expensive game. The English, however speculative, fear poverty. The Frenchman shoots himself to avoid it. The American with a million speculates to win ten, and if he loses takes a clerkship with equanimity. This freedom from sordidness is commendable, but it makes a nation of the most degenerate gamesters in the world.[3]

Risk is, of course, the essence of speculation. The textbook economic function of speculation is the assumption of risk. And no one is prepared to assume more risk than the American speculator. At times, the transfer of risk in the stock market goes beyond the inevitable risks of business and becomes an end in itself. Under such circumstances, speculation becomes purely ludic, a national sport played with the ferocity of war and offering the rewards of a lottery.*

It may appear paradoxical that Americans love equality, having enshrined it as a founding principle in the Declaration of Independence, and yet they strive ceaselessly to create material inequality amongst themselves. "They have swept away the privileges of their

*According to Max Weber, in the United States "the pursuit of wealth, stripped of its religious and ethical meaning, tends to become associated with purely mundane passions, which often actually give it the character of sport."

fellow creatures," wrote Tocqueville, "which stood in their way, but they have opened the door to universal competition; the barrier has changed its shape rather than position." In a democratic society, such as the United States, where wealth is the ultimate determinant of status, there lingers a constant fear of being left behind materially. We may say that the guiding principle of American society is not to grow richer in absolute terms, but to avoid becoming poorer in relative terms. And nothing makes a man feel poorer than being a passive bystander during a bull market. Therefore, the fiercest struggle for the preservation and restitution of economic equality in the United States takes place in the stock market, where everyone is seeking to discover what others are doing and anticipate what they intend to do. As Keynes observed with all the cultured disdain of the Old World for the New: "Even outside the field of finance, Americans are apt to be unduly interested in discovering what average opinion believes average opinion to be; and this national weakness finds its nemesis in the stock market."[4]

THE EARLY HISTORY OF SPECULATION IN AMERICA

America's vast wilderness invited speculation. Many of the country's founding fathers were land speculators: George Washington started his own Mississippi Company to purchase lands in the West; Benjamin Franklin was involved in an Illinois land speculation of sixty-three million acres; Patrick Henry, the fiery revolutionary, was among the investors in the "Yazoo Company," which attempted to purchase ten million acres in Georgia; even Thomas Jefferson and Alexander Hamilton were occasional "land-jobbers." For a century after independence, the country was in a constant ferment of land speculation. In the late eighteenth century, millions of acres in large blocks were exchanged in Maine, Georgia, and New York State. The developing towns and cities were also the objects of speculation. Fittingly, the capital city, Washington, D.C., was founded by land speculators. Forty years later, Chicago was the new boomtown. Later still, the railroads opened up the western part of the country to the national pastime (the railroads themselves, established with federal land grants that exceeded 170 million acres, were primarily vehicles for land speculation). "Were I to characterise the United States," wrote the English traveller William Priest in the late eighteenth century, "it would be by the appellation of the land of speculations."[5]

The stock market did not appear in New York until after American independence. In the 1790s, a speculative mania in government loans and bank stocks developed not unlike that found in Exchange Alley a century earlier. There was, however, a significant difference. From its very inception, the American market was dominated by stock operators whose activities were on a scale unsurpassed in the Old World. In late 1791, William Duer, an Eton-educated former colonel in Washington's army, organised a "pool" with the intention of driving up the share price of the Bank of the United States. He financed this speculation with personal notes of credit for a reported $30 million. Duer's subsequent failure brought the first U.S. stock market crash and led to his eventual death in prison.

Although "corners" were as old as the stock markets themselves, it was only in America in the nineteenth century that they became a hallmark of speculation. The aim of the corner was to acquire a sufficient number of shares to force up the price and catch out the bears who had sold stock short in anticipation of buying it back cheaper at a later date. When a stock was effectively cornered, the operator could demand any price he wished from the short-sellers, who were legally obliged to cover their positions. As the great stock operator Daniel Drew mused:

He who sells what isn't his'n,
Must buy it back or go to pris'n.

Corners were normally undertaken by informal speculative partnerships, known as "pools," and accompanied by devious market manipulation. It was a tense game and often failed. The stock market operator, who arranged corners and manipulated the market, became a familiar figure. The typical operator was described by a mid-century commentator as "an individual of Bonapartean capacity, who has risen with the velocity of a comet, for a while carries everything before him, and raises and depresses any particular stock or stocks at his sovereign will and pleasure."[6] The favoured stocks of operators became known as "footballs" because they were so frequently kicked around between the bulls and the bears (they were also called "fancies"). Often broken-down companies of little intrinsic value, they served the function of gambling chips (like certain "penny stocks" in the over-the-counter market in America today).

Around the middle of the nineteenth century, the "call loan" system emerged.* Although loans against the collateral of stock—known to Americans as "call" or "margin" loans—had been available in Amsterdam since the early seventeenth century, they came to dominate the New York stock market to an unprecedented degree. Stock loans were supplied by New York banks to brokers who lodged their customers' securities as collateral. The credit was termed "call" because the banks could demand or "call" it back at any moment. They were also called "margin loans" since there was a margin of safety between the size of the loan and the securities' market value. This margin varied from a relatively conservative 20 percent to 5 percent or less. Thus, a share trading at $100 was good for a loan of between $80 and $95. If the market was particularly volatile, or if the shares used as collateral were speculative "footballs," then a higher margin was normally demanded.† When the shares held on margin declined in value, the broker demanded more cash from his customer (known as a "margin call"), and if this was not forthcoming, he would sell the stocks in the market. The regular supply of margin loans to the stock market was a great boon to brokers, as it enabled small-time speculators to make bigger purchases than they could otherwise afford and stimulated market turnover. "The word *margins*," wrote William Fowler in *Ten Years on Wall Street*, "contains the essence of *stock-speculation*."[7]

Although stock market loans had been available since the 1830s, for the next decade options and futures (known as time transactions) remained more common.[8] In the 1850s, however, people

*The authors of a recent history of Wall Street claim that call loans stimulated the financial district and "were crucial to New York's growth. . . . The vitality of Wall Street helped fuel New York's rise to become the financial capital of the United States." (Walter Werner and Steven T. Smith, *Wall Street*, New York, 1991, pp. 43–46.)

†In this way, margin loans resemble stock options, whose price is also determined by volatility, interest rates, and time.

started to complain that the growth of call loans was squeezing out legitimate commercial borrowers.* After the crash of 1857, known as the "Western Blizzard," time transactions began to fade away. At around this time, a stock market commentator described speculators using call loans to pyramid their investments, selling existing holdings after a rise and doubling up. The abundant supply of short-term credit to speculators made the stock market more than usually sensitive to monetary conditions.† Bankers' balances in New York, from which call loans were supplied, varied with the agricultural cycle; when wheat was due to be shipped east, money would flow to the interior of the country, leading to a tightness in the New York money market and the "calling" of loans from the stock market. This tendency was strongest in October, traditionally a black-letter month for American speculators.‡ Money flowed back to New York at the beginning of the year, making it a good season for speculation.

Call loans increased the volatility of a stock market already subject to constant manipulation and corners. During a stock market crisis, call rates rose sharply and loans were withdrawn, but because liquidity in the stock market dried up and borrowers were unable to sell securities, banks often experienced difficulty in retrieving their loans. The effect of the call loan system was therefore to make American banks especially vulnerable to panics when customers would protect themselves by withdrawing bank deposits

---

*In November 1872, the *Bankers' Magazine* complained that "the pernicious practice of allowing interest on current deposits impels their employment in the kindred evil of call loans; and these made to stock speculators, too often reckless and unprincipled, subject our money market to violent disturbances, deprive the business community of accommodations justly their due, [and] increase largely the lists of failures . . ." (Cited by O. M. W. Sprague, *History of Crises Under the National Banking System*, Washington, 1910, p. 21.)

†After the Civil War, federal law demanded that country banks keep a quarter of their deposits with certified National Banks, which were based mainly in New York. The New York banks had to pay interest on these deposits which might be recalled at any moment, and therefore they needed a short-term and profitable place to lend funds. The New York stock market offered a seemingly perfect solution; rates were high, the collateral was good on a daily basis, and call loans were the very definition of liquidity (except during stock market crises).

‡As Mark Twain wrote, "October. This is one of the peculiarly dangerous months to speculate in stocks. The others are July, January, September, April, November, May, March, June, December, August, and February." (From *Pudd'nhead Wilson*.)

and hoarding money.* Brokers made matters worse by selling their customers' margin stocks during a panic in order to protect themselves.† "A margin," wrote William Fowler, "may be called a device contrived to create crisis and panics, and to keep the market in a ferment, so that brokers may make, and their customers lose, money."[9]

WAR AND SPECULATION

The outbreak of the American Civil War in 1861 ushered in a new era of speculation. Initially, the stock market was apprehensive about war, and leading stocks declined sharply after the attack on Fort Sumter. Conditions changed in early 1862, after Congress passed the Legal Tender Act, authorising the issue of $150 million worth of a new paper currency, the "greenback." Gradually speculators realised that industry and agriculture would be stimulated by the need to equip, clothe, and feed the Union forces, and that the greenbacks would bring inflation into the system. A few months after the passing of the act, the stock market began to rise as the greenbacks worked their effect on the economy, "like the kiss of the prince on the cheek of a sleep-enchanted lady in the fairy tale."[10]

The uncertainty of war produced an ideal climate for speculation. As the stock operator Daniel Drew said, "Along with ordinary happenings, we fellows in Wall Street had the fortunes of war to speculate about and that makes great doings on a stock exchange. It's good fishing in troubled waters."[11] The price of gold became the barometer of military fortunes. It crashed whenever the Union was victorious, for fear that the supply of greenbacks would dry up, and climbed on news of defeat as the market anticipated further note

*See Sprague, *History of Crises*, passim. Sprague's work, which highlights the instability that margin loans produced in the banking system, was influential in leading to the establishment of the Federal Reserve System.

†Because they encouraged speculators to buy when the market was rising and forced sales when the market declined, the effect of margin loans on the U.S. stock market from the 1840s to 1929 was similar to that of portfolio insurance in the 1980s. (See Chapter 8.)

issues. The gold bulls whistled "Dixie," and the bears sang "John Brown."* With bold forward movements and subtle feints, grand strategy and clever tactics, and endless skirmishing between bulls and bears, events on Wall Street mimicked the war itself.†

Despite a great disparity in their moral ends, war and speculation have much in common. Clausewitz's description of war as "the province of uncertainty" subject to unforeseen accidents or "friction," applies just as well to stock market speculation. What George Soros has called "reflexivity," the influence of subjective factors on outcomes, has its place on the battlefield as well as in the stock market. Morale could determine the outcome of both military and speculative battles, where daring and brilliance might snatch an unexpected victory and panic and disorder bring defeat. The Lees, Grants, and Shermans had their counterparts in the great stock operators who bribed soldiers, sutlers, politicians, and telegraph operators, in order to get the latest information from the front.‡ The mercenary corps of Wall Street were fickle alliances, and the speculative history of the period is marked by constant betrayals and double-dealings. Yet occasionally, for brief periods, the forces of speculation marshalled by the stock operators displayed the cohesion and discipline of a professional army.

Like the generals of the Civil War, the leading operators attracted public adulation. As Matthew Josephson wrote in *The Robber Barons*, "If the doctrine of the nation favored an ideal of

---

*By the end of 1862 the first manipulations in the gold market appeared. Lincoln, disgusted by the antics of gold speculators at a time of national self-sacrifice, decided to act. In June 1863, Congress passed a law forbidding the trade in gold futures, but the market only interpreted this regulation as a sign of weakness on the part of the administration and the price of gold shot up by over a third. The government backed down and the law was repealed. No official attempt to restrict speculation was ever more futile or short-lived.

†Medbery uses military metaphors in his description of activity on the stock market; he writes of "surging masses of attack and defence, rumors which start panics, stratagems,—all the forces of speculative warfare in fullest play." (*Men and Mysteries*, p. 153.) Fowler notes another parallel between warfare and the speculative bouts in the stock market. After each battle the names of the fallen were printed in the newspapers; after each decline in the stock market, the page of the Gazette appeared "in which the names of the losers, and of the financially dead, are recorded." (*Ten Years*, p. 415.)

‡Pierpont Morgan is reputed to have had the first telegraph installed in Wall Street so that he could be the earliest to hear news from the front.

free and equal opportunity for all, so its current folklore glorified the freebooting citizen who by his own efforts, by whatever method feasible, had wrested for himself a power that flung its shadow upon the liberties and privileges of others."[12] James Fisk, Jay Gould, and Cornelius Vanderbilt were the heroes of the Gilded Age; their operations brought them national fame and their fortunes were the object of envious admiration. In times of panic, however, these men were vilified for their lack of scruple and the walls of the Long Room, where the share dealings of the Open Board took place, were covered with graffiti cursing their names.[13]

The most renowned and feared stock operator in the early 1860s was Daniel Drew, known variously as the "Great Bear," the "Old Bear," and "Ursa Major" due to his preference for selling stocks short, the "Sphinx of Wall Street" for his inscrutability, the "Old Man of the Street" for his age, and more familiarly as "Uncle Daniel." He was born the son of a poor farmer from Putnam County, New York, in 1797. After deserting from the army to join the circus, he worked as cattle drover, before eventually settling in Wall Street. Although Drew was a devout Baptist, who endowed churches and even a ladies' seminary, he had no difficulty in reconciling his religion with the amorality of the stock market, where his own treachery was notorious.* Charles Francis Adams described him as "shrewd, unscrupulous, and very illiterate,—a strange combination of superstition and faithlessness, of daring and timidity,—often good-natured and sometimes generous."[14]

In the early 1850s, Drew had joined the board of the Erie Railroad. He became notorious for his operations in Erie stock, which earned him the sobriquet of the "Speculative Director" and the railroad that of the "Scarlet Woman of Wall Street." He manipulated the Erie share price with such facility that it became a saying on Wall Street that "when Daniel says 'up'—Erie goes up. Daniel says 'down'—Erie goes down. Daniel says 'wiggle-waggle'—it bobs both ways."[15] He liked nothing better than to mislead his "boys," as

*One paper said of Drew that "when he has been unusually lucky in his trade of fleecing other men, he settles accounts with his conscience by subscribing towards a new chapel or attending a prayer meeting." The stockbroker Henry Clews said that Drew made religion the "handmaid of speculation." (Bouck White, *The Book of Daniel Drew*, New York, 1910. p. 399.)

he called the younger speculators, about his intentions, and revelled in "taking a slice out of them."* As a young drover, Drew had fed his cattle with salt before bringing them to market so that they would drink and put on weight. In later years, he introduced to Wall Street the practice of "watering stock." This involved using his position as a director to issue vast unauthorised quantities of new stock, in order to depress the share price and thwart attempted corners.† A disgruntled speculator accused Drew of treating his "stocks just as he used to treat cattle. He pens'em, drives'em up and down the market, corners'em; in fact, Daniel Drew calls stocks his critters and abuses them accordingly. He waters'em and plasters'em all over with dirt till they are not worth shucks."[16]

The other leading operator of the day, Cornelius Vanderbilt, struck a sharp contrast to his rival Drew.‡ The old drover was unkempt, wizened, and sinewy, whereas "Commodore" Vanderbilt was tall, handsome, and finely dressed, with "a face like a Roman senator." Drew had a henlike cackle; Vanderbilt a booming laugh. Drew cared nothing for the management of railroads and concentrated exclusively on his stock market speculations; Vanderbilt succeeded in building a great network of railroads (it was said that "Vander built and Dan drew"). Drew was sly and gave out false tips; Vanderbilt was mostly open in his dealings and never informed anyone of his intentions. In a crisis, Drew became flustered and lost his nerve; Vanderbilt's will was unbreakable and his purpose always firm. But for all their differences, the two men had much in common. They were both illiterate, ruthless, grasping men. Vanderbilt was said to raise men up in the Street only to break them, to have fleeced his son-in-law, Horace Clark, of hundreds of thousands of dollars, and even to have misled his son William into selling a stock which he was buying.[17] On one occasion, Vanderbilt sent a brief note to associates who had betrayed him: "Gentlemen, You have undertaken to cheat me. I will not sue you, for the law takes too long. I will ruin you." He kept his promise.[18]

---

*Drew's favourite ploy was to lend money against the collateral of stock which he would then dump on the market to drive down the price, reaping profits from his short sales.

†It was by "watering" stock that Drew escaped the Erie corner of 1866, when his adversary was Cornelius Vanderbilt.

‡Vanderbilt was born three years after Drew. Their rivalry dated back to the 1830s, when they both operated steamboats on the Hudson.

Beneath the titanic figures of Drew and Vanderbilt stood a host of lesser operators, who experienced fleeting moments of success before they disappeared into obscurity. In 1863, Addison Jerome enjoyed a brief reign as the "Napoleon of the Public Board," when he organised several successful corners. After only a few months, however, he was bankrupted by a failed corner in the Michigan and Southern Railroad. A year later, he died from a heart attack induced by the pressures of work. His brother, Leonard Jerome, first rose to prominence in the 1850s, when he made a fortune anticipating the stock market crisis of 1857. His operations were characterised by great boldness and animal spirits, and even when disaster threatened he always maintained his good humour. Unlike his brother, Leonard did not overstay his welcome on Wall Street, but departed for Europe with his fortune intact. His beautiful daughter, Jennie, married Lord Randolph Churchill, a descendant of that shrewd South Sea speculator, Sarah, Duchess of Marlborough. Their son, Winston, exhibited the same indomitable spirit and sangfroid that had marked his grandfather's operations in the stock market.

Henry Keep, born in a poorhouse and a former bootblack, was another leading operator of the early 1860s. It was Keep who broke Addison Jerome's attempted corner in Old Southern, by issuing new shares. Known as "Henry the Silent," Keep had a reputation for discretion and probity rare among his fellow operators. He set up the first "blind pool," in which a number of speculators combined their resources without being informed by Keep of what he intended to do with their money. They were kept "blind" to prevent news of the pool's operations from leaking into the market. The most dashing operator of the Civil War era was Anthony Morse, known as the "English Jew" for his hooked nose and financial acumen (he was also nicknamed "the lightning calculator"). Morse came to prominence with a blind pool organised in Rock Island in late 1863. Early the following year, he became the leader of the bull faction, bidding openly for stocks in blocks of five or ten million shares. At the height of his fame, crowds surrounded Morse's brokerage office and he was mobbed by strangers who thrust their wallets into his hands and begged for tips.[19] His failure in the spring of 1864 caused a panic on the Exchange. Ostracised, Morse haunted Broadway for a year and died penniless in a seedy boardinghouse, where his landlady refused to release the corpse until his bills were paid. A contemporary considered Morse a brilliant mathematician and a shrewd financier, "but like most great speculators he got at last to believe in his star. Then he attempted impossibilities."[20]

The "Gilded Age," as Mark Twain and his co-author, Charles Dudley Warner, observed in the novel which gave its name to the period, was a time when everybody nursed a speculation and people pursued the acquisition of wealth by fair means or foul. The rags-to-riches tales of Horatio Alger that appeared after the Civil War, with titles such as *Fame and Fortune* and *Strive and Succeed*, presented an idealised version of the same fierce material ambition. Gustavus Myers, in his *History of the Great American Fortunes*, describes the era as "the period of periods when there was a kind of adoration of the capitalist taught in the press, college, and pulpit."* Egregious displays of wealth characterised the age, inspiring Thorstein Veblen's ideas on conspicuous consumption expounded in his *Theory of the Leisure Class*† At society parties, cigarettes were rolled in hundred-dollar bills, black pearls were stuffed into the guests' oysters, and dogs were adorned with diamond-studded collars. Gold, the source of many speculative fortunes, was also "the most desirable thing to have," according to Elisabeth Lehr (in *King Lehr and the Gilded Age*), "because it cost money, and money was the outward and visible sign of success." Throughout the 1860s fortunes were gained and expended with equal rapidity. It was alleged that the speculators' vicious extravagance was motivated by a desire to take revenge on the money that had cost them so much anxiety to gain.[21] No speculator was more extravagant and

---

*Elsewhere Myers states, "Society had made money its god and property its yardstick. . . . Every section of the trading class was permeated with a profound admiration, often tangibly expressed, for the craft that got away with a pile of loot." This apotheosis of businessmen has occurred in other speculative periods, most notably in the 1920s and 1980s. (Gustavus Myers, *History of the Great American Fortunes*, New York, 1937, p. 293.)

†Veblen claimed that in a modern industrial society "relative success, tested by an invidious pecuniary comparison with other men, becomes the conventional end of action." Esteem is only awarded on evidence of wealth and this is the source of conspicuous consumption. For Veblen, "emulation is probably the strongest and most alert and persistent of economic motives proper." The motive of emulation links speculation—"keeping up with the Dow Jones," as a *New York Times* headline recently put it—to Veblen's notion of conspicuous consumption.

high-living than Leonard Jerome, who drove through Central Park with a team of dazzling Thoroughbreds, purchased a magnificent steam yacht, built a racecourse and a private theatre, and distributed diamond bracelets as gifts to the ladies at his sumptuous dinner parties. Some contemporary commentators were disgusted by such vulgar displays of wealth. The journalist E. L. Godkin, founder of the *Nation*, described America in 1866 as a "gaudy stream of bespangled, belaced, and beruffled barbarians."[22] When Georges Clemenceau, the future French prime minister, visited the United States after the Civil War, he concluded that the country had passed from a state of barbarism to one of decadence without an intermediate period of civilisation.

"The civil war in America, with its enormous issue of depreciating currency, and its reckless waste of money and credit by the government, created a speculative mania such as the United States, with all its experience in this respect, had never before known," wrote Henry Adams. "Not only in Broad Street, the center of New York speculation, but far and wide throughout the Northern States, almost every man who had money at all employed a part of his capital in the purchase of stocks or of gold, of copper, of petroleum, or of domestic produce, in the hope of a raise in prices, or staked money on the expectation of a fall."* The expansion of the rail system and the advent of the telegraph fostered speculation by bringing far-flung places into daily contact with the financial centre.† In

*This seems to have been a general opinion. William Fowler claimed that in 1862 there "began the greatest era of speculation the world has ever seen." James Medbery wrote, "Flushed with greenbacks, and influenced by the varying fortunes of our armies, the whole population of the North gave itself up to a speculative frenzy." He claimed that "the war, which made us a great people, made us also a nation in whom speculative ideas are predominant." (Henry Adams, "The New York Gold Conspiracy," in *Chapters of Erie and Other Essays*, Boston, 1871, p. 100; Fowler, *Ten Years*, p. 36; and Medbery, *Men and Mysteries* pp.10–11.)

†According to Medbery, "Villages whose names are scarcely known beyond the boundary of their counties have their rustic Fisks and Vanderbilts . . . Sparks of electricity fly up from the marshes of the Mississippi Valley, from the golden desolation of Nevada, from factory hamlets in Connecticut, from the pastoral seclusions of Vermont; bearing emergent orders to sell Hudson short, to buy 500 Fort Wayne, to take a put on Rock Island or a call on Tennessee sixes." (*Men and Mysteries*, p. 196.)

1867, the "ticker" was introduced, flashing the latest stock prices around the country and linking provincial brokerage offices to Wall Street. By the end of the century, it was estimated that nearly half of all messages transmitted by telegraph involved speculative transactions.[23] The ticker also gave birth to the bucket shop, which was a cross between a betting shop and a brokerage where people could gamble on share price movements without actually buying the stocks (i.e., the same effect as buying futures). Bucket shops were shady places whose owners were often engaged in manipulating stocks and had a reputation for disappearing into the night when faced with a large payout. Nevertheless, they provided many with their first taste of speculation, and remained popular until the 1930s, when they were outlawed by the Securities and Exchange Commission.

Although the total number of speculators during the Civil War is uncertain, contemporaries believed the figure to be far larger than the 200,000 holders of stocks and bonds in the previous decade.They came from all classes and backgrounds. On the sidewalks of the financial district, young dandy speculators from Broadway jostled with farmers, store owners, lawyers, doctors, clergymen, mechanics, and penniless "gutter-snipes."* Clerks formed small clubs in order to pool their limited resources, and shady brokers offered to finance them with the slimmest of margin cover, ensuring that the slightest setback would see them wiped out.[24]

Outside brokerage offices, lady speculators waited in their carriages for news of the latest stock prices. In Saratoga, upstate New York, three young ladies set up a pool in Harlem stock and bought two thousand shares. Vanderbilt's former mistress, Mrs. Tennessee Claflin, and her sister, Mrs. Victoria Woodhull, established their own brokerage in Broad Street in 1870, and became known as the "bewitching brokers." Hetty Green, the Quaker heiress, dressed from head to foot in black crêpe with black-gloved hands resembling

---

*Fowler records that in early 1864 "the whole street was lined with rustics. . . . Lank, sunburned men, stout men, with husky voices, tall short and middle-sized men, with country-cut coats, entered the city in the morning with nothing but a paper collar and a comb in their carpet bag and a small check on some city bank, and left town the next day with a bundle of greenbacks larger than a small sized-encyclopaedia." (*Ten Years*, p. 291.)

talons, was a familiar figure on Wall Street. She bought shrewdly during panics, succeeded in cornering the noted operator Addison Cammack, once threatened the railroad baron Collis Huntington with a revolver, and even brought about a minor stock market panic when the withdrawal of her account caused her brokers to fail. Vindictive, garrulous, and neurotically fearful of poverty (when staying in hotels, she was said to save money by washing her own underwear), Hetty Green was a cautious operator who believed in getting in at the bottom and selling out at the top: "All you have to do is buy cheap and sell dear, act with thrift and shrewdness and be persistent" was her advice to other speculators.[25] "Wall Street is not the place for a lady to find either fortune or character," claimed the stockbroker Henry Clews. Yet Hetty Green became the richest woman in America and died with a fortune estimated at over $100 million. As for character, the "Witch of Wall Street" was as feared and disliked as any of her male counterparts.

Male or female, rich or poor, healthy or infirm, the vast majority of speculators were necessarily outsiders, mere fodder for the great operators. It was a saying of the drover Drew that "anybody who plays the stock market not as an insider is like a man buying cows in the moonlight." So efficient were the operators at fleecing outsiders that Henry Adams feared speculation would eventually consume itself as "the largest combination of capital was destined to swallow every weaker combination which ventured to show itself in the market."[26] Even if the speculator evaded the operators' snares, he was likely to fall prey to his own weaknesses. Fowler depicted the amateur speculator as the "opium-eater of finance," a man torn by conflicting passions, beset by uncertainty and fears, prone to buying high and selling low: "befooled, bewitched and bedeviled by what he hears in the market."*

James Medbery claimed that outsiders were prey to "suspicion, overconfidence, timidity and vacillation" when they entered the stock market. "You will find confidence," he wrote, "where the registry shows there should have been distrust, hesitation which ought

*According to Fowler, "It is an adage in the stock market, that the outside public, as it is called, buys stocks when they are high, and sells them when they are low." (Fowler, *Ten Years*, p. 249.)

to have been daring, doubts where faith would have been wealth. This weakness of humanity is the life of speculation."* Not all outsiders, however, were unsuccessful. Some speculators, known as "panic birds," came to the market only once prices had crashed and money was scarce; they bought carefully, locked up their investments, and kept away from Wall Street until the next calamity struck. But they were a rare breed, and most who ventured into the financial district in the turbulent years of the 1860s became entranced by the carnival atmosphere and remained there until the last penny had been picked from their pockets.

NEW EXCHANGES, OLD BUBBLES

A number of new exchanges were established to accommodate the growing fever. The most important of them, the Open Board, founded in 1862 to compete with the older exchange, operated initially from a subterranean "coal hole" in William Street. When the new exchange prospered, the tiny basements around William Street were turned into offices for fly-by-night operators offering brokerage services at reduced commission rates. At its peak, the Open Board was said to transact ten times as much business as the regular Board (the two markets merged in 1869 to form the New York Stock Exchange). In February 1864, an Evening Exchange was set up in the basement of the Fifth Avenue Hotel. Speculators paid 50 cents to enter, and trading lasted until nine o'clock at night, after which business continued in the hotel's bar. Curbstone brokers also traded in William Street, between Exchange Place and Beaver Street, where "gutter-snipes" enticed bystanders by brandishing their arms and vociferating loudly. These new markets had none of the exclusivity and pretension to rectitude of the old exchange, outsiders were

*In language that anticipates Keynes's description of speculative psychology in the *General Theory*, Medbery saw "animal spirits" at work in the stock market: "The atmosphere is so fickle, there are such swarms of rumors, the whole market is so subject to evanescent unreasonable transitions that a man who buys or sells, unless on accidental certainties, uses such prevision as is granted him, and trusts to luck for the sequel." (Medbery, *Men and Mysteries*, pp. 209, 211.)

encouraged to mingle in the crowd, and brokers provided credit on small margins to finance their speculations.

With the price of gold floating after the advent of greenbacks, the Gold Room became the venue for some of the most daring and celebrated speculative feats of the period. Situated at Gilpin's reading room on the corner of William Street and Exchange Place, the room itself was modest and undistinguished, a dingy hall full of nooks where speculators lurked. In its centre stood a cast-iron Cupid, splashing water into a bowl, "tinkling and clinking like coin of gold," around which gathered brokers shouting out their offers and bids. In the background the telegraph clattered noisily and on one wall was placed a large dial, whose arm swung to and fro, indicating the latest price (a similar dial on an exterior wall signaled the price to crowds of speculators on the street). Speculation in the Gold Room was said to be purer and more intense than in the stock market. According to the journalist Horace White, the room resembled a "rat-pit in full blast." For James Medbery, the Gold Room was a "human maelstrom," where "men battle for gold, gold, gold, with a naked greed and fury that satirizes life beyond all imaginings."[27]

Gold speculation reached a climax in early 1864 when a new Gold Exchange opened. Since the prices of gold and other metals were rising faster than wages, it was natural that the attention of speculators should turn to mining. A Mining Board was established in March, and nearly two hundred mining companies, with a capital of over $300 million, were floated in the following month. These new companies were ventures in distant territories. Exotic names adorned them, such as the Arizona Metaliferous and Scalping Ledge Gold and Silver Mining Company, the Mount St. Elias Silver Lode and Gold Vein Mining Company, the Aligator Bayou Salt Company, and the Angels' Rest Quicksilver Company.[28] Brokers, eager to attract custom, affected a knowledge of "fissure veins," "faults," "spurs," "lodes," "pyrites," and other mining terms, and filled their offices with cabinets containing assays of gold and specimens of other metals and minerals.

The promoters of the mining companies harnessed the mood of the day with age-old ploys. First, a claim in some unknown place was purchased for a pittance in cash or a quantity of shares and specimens of ore were submitted to an assay and certificated by a mineralogist. Then, a wealthy and respectable merchant, joined by other notables, was brought onto the board in return for a free distribution of shares. The capital of the company would be inflated to many times its value. For instance, the property of the Titan Ledge and Black Mountain Gold, Silver and Copper Company was bought for a thousand dollars and later capitalised at a million dollars. A broker was hired and advertisements placed in the papers announcing a "limited" subscription. On street corners, boys were employed to hand out prospectuses with lavish descriptions of the company's prospects. Scouts, known as "bubble-blowers," were hired to lure the bigger investors. Several companies were brought under the control of the same directors, who used the capital raised for one company to pay the unearned dividends of another. The mining mania took place against the background of rising gold prices and a bull market led exuberantly by Anthony Morse. When Morse failed on 18 April 1864, there was a panic in the stock market in which mining company stocks declined by an average of more than 90 percent. Eventually, speculators came to heed Mark Twain's warning that "a mine is a hole in the ground with a liar standing next to it."*

Although the market was quiet for a few months after the collapse of the mining mania, by late summer exuberance had returned. In early 1865, a new bubble was blown, this time tinged with the translucent colours of petroleum, a new wonder product hailed as a "disinfectant, a vermin killer, hair oil, boot grease, and a cure for kidney stones."[29] During this boom, which was linked to the discovery of oil in Pennsylvania, the price of crude oil increased ninefold within a few months, reaching a level that in real terms has never been equalled. The brokers cleared their offices of mineral samples and certificates of assay, and in their place installed models of oil

*Twain himself prospected for gold in California in the early 1860s. He was the originator of several witty epigrams on investment and speculation, the most famous appearing in *Pudd'nhead Wilson* (1894): "Behold, the fool saith, 'Put not all thine eggs in the one basket'—which is but a manner of saying, 'Scatter your money and your attention'; but the wise man saith, 'Put all your eggs in the one basket and WATCH THAT BASKET.' " He warned against speculation ("There are two times in a man's life when he should not speculate: when he can't afford it, and when he can"), and rued his own failure as an investor ("I was seldom able to see an opportunity until it had ceased to be one").

barrels, phials of petroleum, and framed property deeds. A Petroleum Board was inaugurated in October 1865, and thirty-five companies were floated. In a rerun of the mining mania, new companies were formed at little or no cost, fraudulent claims to oil-rich land were incorporated into companies with inflated capitalisations, and petroleum stocks were heavily manipulated. Shares were run up to a great height before the petroleum bubble evaporated into thin air.

"MILKING THE STREET"

The great stock operators did not trifle with the transient mining and petroleum bubbles. Their attention was focused almost exclusively on the market for railroad stocks, where manipulation was a fine art and consequently the investment returns more certain. The great aim of the operator was to achieve one of the railroad corners which recurred with unprecedented frequency throughout the period. Among the most notorious corners were those in Harlem (1863 and 1864), Michigan Southern (1863 and 1866), Prairie du Chien (1865), Erie (1866, 1867, and 1868) and Chicago and Northwestern (1867 and 1872). The profits could be enormous: Henry Keep's pool in the Chicago and Northwestern Railroad in 1867 netted over $2 million.[30] These operations were not without danger, as corners could be broken by "watering" existing stock with new issues or by repatriating stock held in Europe. Therein lay the excitement of the game.

A pool operator would start by simulating weakness in a particular stock in order to shake out those holders on small margins and entice others to sell the stock short (this was known as the "partridge trick"). The pool even lent from its own stockholding to facilitate short sales. Disreputable brokers provided "wash sales," which set misleading prices. In a market hungry for "points" or tips, false rumours were rife. Broken speculators, known as "pointers," "singed cats," or "ropers-in," were commissioned to put out specious stories and solicit short sales. False rumours became so common that many acted contrary to what they were advised in the market, a practice known as "coppering." Once the stock had been oversold, the operator would catch out the short-sellers and force up the price (this was known as the "scoop game"). A corrupt press was a useful tool in the hands of a stock manipulator. The notorious operator Jay Gould (of whom more later) controlled several newspaper editors, who in exchange for share tips would print whatever story he told them. After his death, the *New York Times* remarked:

> Mr. Gould's editors were known to the public as stool pigeons. It was their function to entice the incautious investor or speculator within reach of his ammunition; to "hammer" securities that he wished to acquire, and to exalt by artful misrepresentation the quotations of those he desired to "unload."[31]

Away from the stock exchange, other ways were found to manipulate securities. Influence over the board of directors was the most common and effective method, as Daniel Drew had shown with the Erie Railroad. Drew was frequently a bear, even in the stock of his own company, since his ability to issue new Erie shares made it almost impossible for other operators to corner him. "Railway directors," wrote James Medbery, "are the heavy artillery of the stock market, and no corner can attain Napoleonic victory without them."* Directors manipulated dividends to suit their speculative activities (sometimes paying them out of capital), broadcast false rumours (in 1869, the directors of the Pacific Mail circulated stories of an impending dividend increase in order to unload their shares), passed expected dividends, and issued unauthorised stock. Occasionally, speculating directors went even further. When Jim Fisk was a director of the Erie Railroad, he sold short the stock of the United States Express Company, which had a contract with the Erie, and then cancelled the contract. Once the express company's share price had fallen, Fisk covered his shorts, bought more shares, and then reinstated the contract.[32] This technique was refined later in the century by the notorious gambler and speculator John "Bet-a-Million" Gates, who shut down his Chicago steel plant during a

*Medbery describes how a corner in the Milwaukee and St. Paul Railroad was attempted without the cooperation of directors. After the share price had risen from 47 to 111, the directors issued new shares and broke the stock. (Medbery, *Men and Mysteries*, p. 99.)

period of prosperity and put thousands out of work, claiming that the business was not making money. Like Fisk beforehand, Gates had sold the stock short and after making a killing in market, he reopened his factories.[33]

The behaviour of speculating directors corrupted the relationship between directors and shareholders (especially the British shareholders, who, on the other side of the Atlantic, were unable to influence events and were led like lambs to the slaughter). It appeared to justify Adam Smith's claim that joint-stock companies were beset by "negligence and profusion" since the personal interests of directors differed from those of their shareholders. In his *Theory of Business Enterprise*, Thorstein Veblen contended that it was the custom of American directors to mislead the stock market in order to profit from successive over- and undervaluations of stock.* Jay Gould, who once described the Erie Railroad as his "plaything," was accused by Matthew Josephson of pursuing

> a deliberate policy of mismanagement, "as a matter of principle," deriving his gains from the discrepancies between the real value of the affair and its supposed or transient value in the securities markets. In good times, he would give an appearance of gauntness and misery to his enterprises; in bad times he would pretend affluence.†

The example of Gould and many contemporary directors perhaps explains why ordinary stocks in nineteenth-century America provided a higher yield than fixed-interest bonds, despite the growing wealth of the nation. Directorial depredations and speculations

---

*According to Veblen, "the certainty of gain, though perhaps not the relative amount of it, seems rather more assured in the large-scale manipulation of vendible capital [i.e., shares] than in business management with a view to a vendible product [i.e., ordinary business activities] . . . Indeed, so secure and lucrative is this class of business that it is chiefly out of gains accruing, directly and indirectly, from such traffic in vendible capital that the great modern fortunes are being accumulated." (Thorstein Veblen, *Theory of Business Enterprise* [1904], New York, 1965, pp. 82–83.)

†A recent revisionist biography of Gould (Maury Klein's *The Life and Legend of Jay Gould*) seeks to show that Gould did not run his companies solely for purposes of speculation. It fails, however, to dispel Gould's deserved reputation as a notorious manipulator of stocks.

meant that the ownership of shares carried an added uncertainty, justifying (what one might call) an "agency risk premium."*

Even the federal government was entangled in the national web of speculation. The process of milking the state came very close to that of "milking the Street." In Twain and Warner's *The Gilded Age*, Congress resembles a caricature of the stock market, where votes are traded, lobbyists assume the role of stock operators whom they match in guile and intrigue, members of Congress take the part of brokers, and battles between opposing factions for federal grants and appropriations are engaged with a passion and excitement similar to the contests between the bulls and the bears on Wall Street.† Like broken speculators on the curb, the shabby old claimants who loiter around the Capitol are sustained by nothing save eternal hope. When he arrives in Washington, Colonel Sellers, an irrepressible speculator, is in his native element. Philip Sterling, the novel's hero, on the other hand, finds Washington "the maddest Vanity Fair one could conceive. It seemed to him a feverish, unhealthy atmosphere in which lunacy could be easily developed."[34] Throughout the Civil War, Washington swarmed with war contractors eager to make a fast buck: Cornelius Vanderbilt furnished the navy with unseaworthy vessels, the young Pierpont Morgan sold faulty carbines to the army, and other contractors supplied goods to the government that were equally "shoddy" (the word derived from a material made from shredded rags used for Union soldiers' coats). This "Vanity Fair" on the Potomac—where

*Another reason shares yielded less than bonds in nineteenth-century America is that when earnings grew the stock would be watered, while the dividends remained the same. Although Drew may have initiated watering stock, it was also practised by Vanderbilt on his railroads and later by Pierpont Morgan when he set up the great trusts, such as U.S. Steel. Men who controlled companies issued new stock (the "water") to themselves, thus purloining any increase in intrinsic value of the shares. Nowadays, the situation is replicated by the (often) excessive issue of company stock options to senior executives.

†Describing the contest for the "Knobs Industrial University Bill," Twain writes: "This was war in earnest. The excitement was furious. The galleries were in commotion in an instant, the reporters swarmed to their places, idling members of the House flocked to their seats, nervous gentlemen sprang to their feet, pages flew hither and thither, life and animation were visible everywhere, all the long ranks of faces in the building were kindled." With minor changes this description could be applied to a lively day's trading in the New York stock market.

everything was for sale—took its place alongside the "Carnival of speculation" (William Fowler's phrase) on the banks of the Hudson.[35]

The satire of *The Gilded Age* was directed against the venality of Washington politicians exposed by the Crédit Mobilier scandal in 1872. A decade earlier, the Union Pacific Railroad (parodied in the novel as the "Salt Lick Pacific Extension") had been established, with the aid of vast federal land grants and loans, to provide the first transcontinental rail connection.* After the Civil War, the railroad fell into the hands of a businessman named Oakes Ames, who was also a member of Congress. Ames created a holding company, the Crédit Mobilier, through which all the railroad's construction contracts were placed. This presented a perfect opportunity for graft: construction costs were inflated, for which the Crédit Mobilier received Union Pacific shares in payment (that is to say, the shareholders of the Union Pacific were "milked" to provide profits for the shareholders of Crédit Mobilier). In December 1867, the Crédit Mobilier declared a dividend equal to its entire capital and its stock soared to $260 a share. In order to maintain support in Washington, Ames distributed Crédit Mobilier shares freely to a number of poiticians, including the future President James Garfield, the future Vice President Schuyler Colfax, the leading Republican James Blaine, and many other senators and "Railway Congressmen." By the time the scandal was uncovered, it was estimated that Ames and his group had plundered nearly $44 million from the Union Pacific. Crédit Mobilier was the most prominent of many examples of political corruption involving railroads and federal grants going back to the 1850s. After the election of President Grant in 1868, the unsavoury intimacy between the federal government and business interests deepened, providing an ideal breeding ground for speculation and corruption.

At the lower levels of government, the fusion of political venality and financial speculation was laid bare by the two celebrated Harlem corners of 1863 and 1864. Since the beginning of the war,

*The Union Pacific received 12 million acres of land and $27 million in government bonds. The Central Pacific, which formed the western part of the transcontinental rail link, received 9 million acres and $24 million in government bonds. In all 158 million acres of federal land was granted to the railroads.

Vanderbilt had been buying up Harlem Railroad stock in an attempt to gain control of Wall Street's favourite "football." In late April 1863, the New York City authorities gave the railroad permission to run streetcars down Broadway. Not long after, the stock market surged, with Harlem, whose share price more than doubled, leading the way.* Once Harlem had peaked at 75, the city's aldermen colluded to sell Harlem short before rescinding permission to build the Broadway line. Unfortunately for them, Vanderbilt had picked up so much stock that its price kept on rising, reaching a peak of nearly 180 in August, when the city's representatives found themselves cornered. Unable to cover their shorts because Vanderbilt already owned all the available shares, they were obliged to settle with him. History repeated itself the following April, when the New York legislators in Albany, coaxed on by Daniel Drew, refused permission for the Harlem extension. On this occasion, Vanderbilt and his ally John M. Tobin succeeded in buying up 27,000 more Harlem shares than were in circulation. In early July, the price of Harlem shot to over a thousand dollars and the legislators were forced to treat with the Commodore to his enormous profit and pleasure: "We busted the whole Legislature, and scores of the honourable members had to go home without paying their bills," he boasted.[36]

Having burnt their fingers at direct speculation, the New York legislators reverted to the more certain profits of bribery. Four years later, in 1868, they opened their pockets wide to receive the largesse distributed during the so-called Erie War. This event, recorded by Charles Francis Adams, Jr., in *Chapters of Erie*, concerned Vanderbilt's attempted takeover of the Erie Railroad, which was thwarted by Daniel Drew and his younger confederates, Jay Gould and Jim Fisk. Defying court injunctions and hiring a judge of their own, the "Erie gang," as they became known, dropped millions of dollars' worth of new Erie shares on the market. Afterwards, they repaired with their spoils to Jersey City, beyond the

*The bull movement in May 1863 was known as the "Chancellorsville rise" after the Confederate victory at the battle of Chancellorsville, Virginia, in which more than 17,000 Union soldiers lost their lives. The market rose because it anticipated a prolongation of the war and the further issue of inflationary greenbacks.

reach of New York's jurisdiction. Gould subsequently travelled to Albany with half a million dollars in cash—needless to say, the money technically belonged to Erie shareholders—in order to bribe the legislators to validate retrospectively the new issue of shares. Vanderbilt played the same game but was defeated by Gould at (what Adams called) the "legislative broker's board, where votes are daily counted."* The total expenditure on bribes in Albany during the summer of 1868 was estimated to exceed a million dollars.

JAY GOULD'S BLACK FRIDAY

The victory of the Erie gang marked the sudden ascendancy of Jay Gould and James Fisk among the leading group of stock market operators. Together they comprised the oddest couple ever to enter Wall Street. James Fisk was the son of a Vermont peddler who had worked first in the circus, then as a dry goods merchant in Boston, and subsequently as a cotton smuggler during the war. In the early 1860s he came to Wall Street, where he was taken up as Drew's protégé. He was a tubby, expansive extrovert with a large walrus moustache on a face framed by fair "kiss curls," who loved dressing up in absurd uniforms (in the summer of 1869, Fisk entertained President Grant on his pleasure boat dressed "in a blue uniform, with a gilt cap-band, three silver stars on his coat sleeve, lavender gloves, and a diamond breastpin as large as a cherry . . .").[37] His operatic attire was not out of place in Pike's Grand Opera House, which Fisk purchased as the headquarters for the Erie Railroad. Inside this marble palace, "Prince Erie Jim Jubilee Admiral James Fisk, Jr.," was enthroned, surrounded by a harem drawn from a troupe of ballet dancers. Jim Fisk was, in Henry Adams's description, "coarse, noisy, boastful, ignorant; the type of a young butcher in appearance and mind" who considered his Wall Street operations as a "gigantic side-splitting farce." Yet for all his faults, he was charismatic and loveable even to his enemies.

*Of the legislature, Adams wrote, "probably no representative body were ever more thoroughly venal, more shamelessly corrupt, or more hopelessly beyond the reach of public opinion, than are certain of those bodies which legislate for republican America in this latter half of the nineteenth century." (Charles Adams, *Chapter of Erie*, p. 59.)

Fisk's partner, Jay Gould, created an altogether different impression. Gould was slight, consumptive, dark, secretive, scheming, and loathed passionately by all except his family and Russell Sage, the skinflint millionaire usurer and speculator. The son of a poor farmer from Delaware Country, New York, Gould worked his way from New York's leather market, "the Swamp"—his partner in the leather business shot himself after being ruined by Gould—to Wall Street. He became one of the most vilified figures in nineteenth-century America. "His touch is death," said Daniel Drew from personal experience. "He was not a builder, he was a destroyer," wrote the financial journalist Alexander Dana Noyes. His sometime partner, the legendary speculator James R. Keene, known as the "Silver Fox," called him "the worst man on earth since the beginning of the Christian era. He is treacherous, false, cowardly, and a despicable worm incapable of generous nature." To Joseph Pulitzer, he was "one of the most sinister figures that ever flitted batlike across the vision of the American people." In his *History of Great American Fortunes*, Gustavus Myers described Gould as

> a freebooter who, if he could not appropriate millions, would filch thousands; a pitiless human carnivore, glutting on the blood of his numberless victims; a gambler destitute of the usual gambler's code of fairness in abiding by the rules; an incarnate fiend of a Machiavelli in his calculations, his schemes and ambushes, his plots and counterplots.*

In short, Gould was the epitome of a robber baron.

After the Erie War, Fisk and Gould made peace with Vanderbilt at a cost of nearly $5 million paid from the Erie treasury (the sum included half a million paid to the Commodore's associates as compensation for their "failed speculation"). They soon forced Drew off the Erie board, before breaking him in a corner later in the year. "The survival of the fittest," Herbert Spencer's axiom of social Darwinism

*Myers also denounced Gould as "the most cold-blooded corruptionist, spoliator and financial pirate of his time . . . For nearly half a century the very name of Jay Gould was a persisting jeer and byword, an object of popular contumely and hatred, the signification of every foul and base crime by which greed triumphs." (*American Fortunes*, p. 398)

then popular in the United States, was nowhere in greater evidence than in the stock market. In autumn, Gould flooded the market with new Erie shares and effected a "lock-up" of greenbacks (i.e., a credit squeeze) which caused railway stocks to crash. After ousting Drew, Gould brought the notorious Tammany boss Bill Tweed onto the Erie board so as to increase his sway over the city and its judiciary. In less than six months Gould and Fisk had, according to Henry Adams,

> created a combination more powerful than any that had been controlled by mere private citizens in America or in Europe since society for self-protection established the supreme authority of the judicial name. They exercised the legislative and judicial powers of the state; they possessed almost unlimited credit, and society was at their mercy.[38]

By the end of 1868, Gould was ready to attempt the most audacious speculative feat in history. In his secretive mind he harboured plans to corner the supreme object of speculation and emblem of the age: gold.

A man of few words and a supreme cynic, Jay Gould understood well enough the uses of cant. During the Erie War, he had posed as the people's champion, raising the cry against Vanderbilt's creeping railroad monopoly. With the gold scheme in mind, Gould became the farmer's friend. Since the end of the Civil War in 1865, agricultural prices had been falling, mainly as a result of extensions to the railroad system. At the same time, the federal government was withdrawing greenbacks from circulation, which caused gold to fall from nearly 300 (i.e., the number of greenbacks required to buy $100 in gold specie) in 1864 to around 130 in early 1869. As U.S. exports were paid for in gold, the decline in the gold price made American grain more expensive in Europe. This had a knock-on effect on the Erie Railroad, which derived much of its earnings from shipping grain to the East for export. Gould realised that if the price of gold were to rise, this predicament would be resolved. By posing as a monetary inflationist, he gave his planned gold corner a legitimate political gloss. As the corrupt Senator Dilsworthy declares in *The Gilded Age*, "I never push a private interest if it is not justified and ennobled by some larger public good."

Since the federal gold reserves were over a hundred million dollars, compared to a mere fifteen million dollars' worth in circulation, the success of Gould's plans depended on control of government policy. In early 1869, Gould recruited as an ally in his scheme an ageing political lobbyist and speculator named Abel Corbin, who had recently married President Grant's sister-in-law. Through Corbin, Gould gained access to the President, whom he entertained at the Opera House and on Fisk's steamboat in June, occasions which he used to extol the political benefits of allowing the gold price to rise and to impress upon Grant the necessity of halting further federal gold sales. In July, Corbin secured the appointment of Gould's man, General Daniel Butterfield, as Assistant Treasurer in New York. Gould's next move was to improve his access to credit by taking control of the Tenth National Bank. So far everything was going well, and in late summer Corbin and Butterfield were rewarded with an allocation of $3 million worth of gold bullion at the price of 133.

Early in September 1869, Corbin arranged a further meeting with Grant, at which Gould became convinced that the President was prepared to pursue an inflationist policy in order to assist the western farmers. Gould started buying more gold, although he suffered a setback at the end of the first week in September when his two partners cashed in their profits and withdrew from the pool. As a result, Gould felt obliged to bring in Fisk, who so far had stood aloof from the scheme (perhaps Gould felt that Fisk's boisterousness was ill-suited to the fine political manoeuvring required by the situation). It was at this stage, as the game became deeper, that the gold ring started to overplay its hand. They attempted to bribe Grant's private secretary, General Horace Porter, with a half million allocation of gold, but Porter indignantly turned it down. In the middle of September, Corbin was pressured into writing to Grant, who was then on holiday in western Pennsylvania, imploring him to stand firm against further gold sales. The letter was delivered by an Erie employee, who telegraphed to Fisk the brief reply: "Delivered all; right." This was intended to signify merely the successful conveyance of the letter, but was interpreted by the ring as meaning that the President was in agreement with the letter's contents.* In fact, Grant was far from pleased with the letter and in his obtuse way perceived that Corbin was involved in a scheme to put up gold. The President instructed his wife to write to Mrs. Corbin, expressing his unease and advising Corbin to have nothing to do with the gold speculators.

Grant received Corbin's letter on Sunday, 19 September. The following day gold opened at just under 138 and, despite heavy buying by the clique, it remained around that level for the next couple of days. On Wednesday, Fisk boldly entered the Gold Room, buying heavily and offering bets of $50,000 that gold would reach 145. That evening after the exchange closed, Gould paid a visit to Corbin only to find him in a desperate state, his wife having received Mrs. Grant's letter. Corbin begged for permission to sell his gold and take his profits, but Gould demurred and ordered Corbin to keep silent about the letter's contents. Gould now realised that Grant could not be relied upon to restrict further federal gold sales and that his own situation was perilous. As a result, he decided to unwind his gold position in secret. What followed next is subject to dispute. It is has been suggested that Gould did not inform Fisk of his reversal, although this seems unlikely given that the partners did not fall out afterwards (when, in later years, Gould double-crossed his brokerage partner Harry Smith and the speculator James R. Keene, all Wall Street heard about it). What appears more credible, given Gould's lack of scruples, is that he decided to sell his gold holdings under the cover of Fisk's continuing purchases. Presumably, Fisk knew that the gold scheme was doomed, since he placed all his orders through a broker intermediary, William Belden, and wrote nothing down that would make him liable for the debts. Gould was careful to make no sales of gold to Belden or his associates, as the hapless broker's ruin was carefully prepared.

On Thursday, 23 September 1869, the Gold Exchange opened in pandemonium with gold at just under 142. Throughout the day,

*This is the version given by Henry Adams and taken up by later historians. However, it is difficult to believe that Gould could have expected the President of the United States to communicate his response to a private letter from his brother-in-law to a lowly railroad employee who could have no legitimate interest in the matter.

the smaller bear speculators, operating on tiny margins, were wiped out as the price edged upwards despite Gould's sales, on a turnover exceeding $325 million. That evening Belden reported that his brokers held $110 million worth of gold on Fisk's behalf. Early the next day, a day remembered thereafter as "Jay Gould's Black Friday," a massive crowd gathered in New Street outside the Gold Room in anticipation of the climax that everyone knew was coming. Not daring to appear directly on the exchange, Gould and Fisk directed operations from the broker Heath's offices in Broad Street. When the market opened at ten o'clock, three hundred brokers gathered nervously around the cupid statue in the centre of the room. Albert Speyers, Fisk's broker, opened the bidding at 150. At eleven o'clock, it was observed that General Butterfield's broker was selling, which suggested that government gold sales were about to commence. Fisk ordered Speyers to put the price up to 160, while Gould, employing a dozen brokers, continued his sales. Less than an hour later, word reached the room that Treasury Secretary George S. Boutwell had ordered the sale of $4 million worth of gold. Speyers, "crazy as a loon" (in Fisk's words), carried on bidding at 160 even as the price crashed to 135 and the market descended into chaos. Brokers became

> quite crazy, or at least, irresponsible, and ran hatless to and fro, gesticulating and making incoherent bids and offers among others who hardly saw them or realized where they were. Then the rumours grew wilder and wilder—true and false mixed up together.[39]

According to Fisk, the atmosphere was not so much *sauve qui peut* as "each man drag out his own corpse." The rapid fluctuations bankrupted thousands of margin holders, mobs formed in Broad Street and outside Gould's brokerage office, and troops were put on alert to enter the financial district. Mindful for their own skins, Gould and Fisk slipped out of Heath's offices by a side entrance and retreated to the "Erie Castle," where they were protected by an armed corps of railroad employees.

Scores of brokers failed on Black Friday; one of them, named Solomon Mahler, shot himself the next day. Fisk cheerfully repudiated his contracts—as he said after the Erie War, "nothing is lost, save honour." But his brokers Speyers and Belden failed with debts nearing $100 million (Speyers was reportedly driven mad by the experience). The Gold Exchange Bank, which operated as the clearing house for the Gold Room, was swamped by over $500 million worth of transactions and gave up attempting to sort them out. The daily rate charged on margin loans (the "call rate") rose to over 1,400 percent and railroad stocks crashed, Vanderbilt's New York Central falling by nearly three-quarters from its peak. The chaos continued into the following week. One man on Wall Street remained safe. Huddled with his pet judge, Jay Gould shielded himself from his creditors with twelve injunctions. When the wreckage was cleared, his own brokerage firm, almost alone, stood strong. It was rumoured that Gould had even made $11 million from the debacle. On the subject of profit and loss, however, the "Mephistopheles of Wall Street" was grimly silent.

JAY COOKE'S BLACK THURSDAY

The panic of Black Friday did not bring the era of speculation to a close. The railroads, in particular, continued to attract huge capital investment. Between 1865 and 1873, the addition of over 30,000 miles of new track, at a cost of nearly one and a half billion dollars, almost doubled the size of the rail system. This massive investment was fuelled by the anticipation that new railroads would produce a rapid settlement of the uninhabited western territories, which in turn would make the railroads' huge landholdings rise dramatically in value. When the Union Pacific advertised the sale of its plots in Columbus, Nebraska, it lured potential purchasers with the prospect that "a fifty-dollar lot may prove a $5,000 investment," and asked of them, "Would you make money easy? Find, then, the site of a city and buy the farm it is built on! How many regret the non-purchase of that lot in New York; that block in Buffalo; that acre in Chicago; that quarter section in Omaha."[40]

In 1869, Jay Cooke, the banker who had made his name and fortune distributing federal bonds during the war, took over the Northern Pacific Railroad, whose land grant of nearly fifty million acres in the Northwest was larger than the entire territory of New England. Cooke set about hyping the land through a network of agents. His chief publicist, a journalist named Sam Wilkerson, described the railroad's property as a "vast wilderness waiting like a rich heiress to be appropriated and enjoyed." Duluth, where the Northern Pacific had a terminus, was promoted as the "Zenith City of the Unsalted Seas."[41] Unfortunately, the agents and publicists could not stir up sufficient popular enthusiasm for what became known derisively as "Jay Cooke's Banana Belt." Cooke's bank was saddled with the responsibility for distributing $100 million of Northern Pacific bonds, a task made substantially more difficult by the outbreak of the Franco-Prussian War in July 1870, which halted the flow of European capital to America.

By the spring of 1873, fears of an imminent financial crisis were mounting. Conditions in the New York money market were tight and speculators were forced to pay half a percent a day on their margin loans. Apparently, these high rates were not sufficient to put them off their game, since in May the *Bankers' Magazine* complained that the excessive demand for margin loans was depriving legitimate business of credit and fostering a "growing mania for gambling which is one of the worst features of the day."[42] The atmosphere was further soured by the continuing revelations of the Crédit Mobilier scandal, which undermined investor confidence in the railroads.

Nevertheless, intense speculation continued. In the summer, share turnover on the New York Stock Exchange reached 100,000 a day for the first time and the *Nation* warned of increased bucket shop activity. Uncertainty increased in August when several railroads experienced trouble refinancing their outstanding loans and newspapers carried stories of forged railroad bonds and shares in circulation. At the end of the first week in September, the New York Warehouse and Security Company announced its insolvency after making imprudent loans to certain western railroads.

On Thursday, 18 September 1873, Jay Cooke was entertaining President Grant at Ogontz, his lavish mansion in Pennsylvania. That afternoon, at half past two, it was announced on the New York Stock Exchange that Jay Cooke & Co. had failed (unable to sell its railroad bonds, the bank had lost the confidence of its creditors).

The initial reaction to the collapse of America's leading bank was disbelief: in Pittsburgh a paper boy was arrested for shouting out the news. Incredulity soon gave way to panic, as the stock market collapsed and daily call rates rose to 5 percent. The next day, crowds thronged the financial district to witness the unravelling of the speculative drama that had entranced the nation for the past decade and a half. Jim Fisk was no longer on the scene, having been murdered by his mistress's lover two years earlier (although Vanderbilt continued to contact him through a medium for stock tips), but other characters emerged to play their accustomed roles: Jay Gould viciously shorted stocks, Hetty Green bargain-hunted among distressed stocks, while Cornelius Vanderbilt drove his carriage furiously down Broad Street with the intention of dispersing the crowd and with it the atmosphere of panic. Vanderbilt's son-in-law, Horace Clark, was found dead after the failure of the Union Trust Bank, from which he had borrowed heavily to finance his margin speculations. Daniel Drew, the "Old Man of the Street," took his final curtain call as his brokerage, Kenyon, Cox & Co., was swept away in the panic. Declared bankrupt, Drew retreated to his bed, where he covered himself with blankets and fought off the demons born of over half a century's speculation. He died a year later.

When the panic continued into Saturday, the president of the New York Stock Exchange announced that, for the first time in its history, the exchange would close until further notice.

> Anyone who stood on Wall Street [reported the *Nation*] or in the gallery of the Stock Exchange last Thursday, or Friday, and Saturday, and saw the mad terror, we might almost say brute terror (like that by which a horse is devoured by a pair of broken shafts hanging to his heels, or a dog flying from a tin saucepan attached to his tail) with which great crowds of men rushed to and fro trying to get rid of their property, almost begging people to take it from them at any price, could hardly avoid feeling that a new plague had been sent among men, that there was an impalpable, invisible force in the air, robbing them of their wits, of which philosophy had not yet dreamt.

The plague metaphor, first applied to describe a financial crisis by Daniel Defoe in 1720, was revived by a Wall Street broker who described the events of Black Thursday as "the worst disaster since the Black Death."[43]

The Stock Exchange reopened after ten days. This time, however, the nation did not escape the consequences of over a decade of speculative excess and overinvestment. Throughout the following winter factories closed down, railroads discharged employees, banks failed, wages were cut, and money was hoarded. By the end of 1873, over five thousand commercial failures had been announced, among them the Northern Pacific Railroad and nearly fifty New York brokerages. In January, a crowd of unemployed protesters rioted in Tompkins Square, New York, and were charged by mounted police armed with billy clubs. The depression continued for the remainder of the decade. By 1877, it was estimated that only a fifth of the labour force was in regular employment. Strikes and unrest became frequent. The conflict between capital and labour escalated into violence with the terrorist activities of the Molly Maguires in the Pennsylvania coalfields and the riots in Pittsburgh during the Great Railroad Strike of 1877. In New York, a religious revival movement thrived in response to the apparent endlessness of the depression. The evangelist Dwight L. Moody together with the gospel singer Ira Sankey filled huge halls in the city, where attendance was noticeably drawn from the Wall Street and Fifth Avenue crowd, driven perhaps by a desire to atone for their sins, which had brought the nation to its parlous state.[44]

PECULATION, SPECULATION, AND MANIPULATION

After the advent of the ticker machine it became a saying on Wall Street: "Don't argue with the tape. Don't buck the market." It was also said that "there is no such thing as a free lunch," which meant that easy profits are not to be found in the stock market.* Such adages suggest a market acting efficiently where risk is offset by

*This at least is the interpretation of the saying given by Professor Paul Samuelson. (Peter Bernstein, *Capital Ideas*, New York, 1992, p. 115.)

reward and market price is a reflection of true or fair value. Market operators were happy to promote a view of speculation that fitted this benign picture. When the stockbroker Henry Clews gave testimony to a legislative committee in 1881, he argued that "speculation is a method for adjusting differences of opinion as to future values, whether of products or of stocks. It regulates production by instantly advancing prices when there is scarcity, thereby stimulating production, and by depressing prices when there is overproduction." Speculation, Clews added impudently, was also "one of the most beneficial agents in the business world for the prevention of panics."[45] While Clews's depiction of speculation might have come straight from the pages of a modern economics textbook, it does not adequately, or even honestly, describe the nature of American speculation in the second half of the nineteenth century. The role of speculation was not limited to regulating the distribution of capital and the forces of production. In reality, its influence was far broader and more sinister.

Periods of speculation had always fostered dishonesty, but in the nineteenth-century American stock market this tendency was even more pronounced. The corruption of speculation was not limited to company promoters and stock operators; it infected the entire political class in the 1860s (even three decades later, the "reforming" President Grover Cleveland was implicated in a stock market pool arranged by James Keene).[46] The "rogue trader," much in evidence in the 1990s, was a common figure in nineteenth-century Wall Street. According to James Medbery writing in 1870, "the story of financial 'irregularities,' caused by unsuccessful stock speculations, is one of the sombrest chapters of our recent history." Throughout the second half of the nineteenth century, there were many infamous cases of financial fraud in the United States: Robert Schuyler's railroad stock forgery in 1854, E. B. Ketchum's gold certificate forgery in 1865, and forgeries of railroad stock at the brokerage White & Company in 1868, which caused losses estimated at $10 million. In 1884, massive frauds were discovered at the brokerage house of Grant & Ward (where General Grant was a partner, albeit of the sleeping variety), which according to Alexander Dana Noyes were accompanied by "individual wrongdoing, of a kind and on a scale for which even the lax financial morality of those days provided no precedent."[47] During the Gilded Age, frauds by speculating employees of brokers were so common that Medbery claimed "every day clerks are discharged for dishonesty. There is hardly a house in the whole money-quarter that has not suffered from peculation."[48] Trustees and guardians also speculated with their charges' property. In February 1869, it was discovered that the Metropolitan Church trustees were using $2 million of church funds in personal stock transactions.[49] It is difficult to ascertain whether the prevalence of speculation actually lowered moral standards, or whether the moral decay of the era simply manifested itself through speculation. It is clear, however, that speculation and financial fraud were frequent bedfellows.

Far more serious than the lone activities of "rogue traders" was the persistence of manipulation by operators in the stock market. This undoubtedly undermined the beneficial aspects of speculation claimed by Clews and made speculation the cause of frequent panics and depressions. As Matthew Smith noted towards the end of the century, "men who 'corner' stocks in Wall Street . . . can produce a panic in an instant, that will be felt like an earthquake . . . A Wall Street panic comes suddenly like thunder from a blue sky. No shrewdness can foresee and no talent avert it."[50] Speculative manipulation both soured the relationship between directors and shareholders, leading to serious mismanagement, and drove share prices away from their "intrinsic" or fair value. Charles Dow, the founder of the *Wall Street Journal*, divided stock market movements into three classes: the result of changes in intrinsic value, the product of manipulation, and the outcome of daily trading. Stock speculators, he suggested, focused on the movements caused by manipulation. The vagaries of manipulation, according to Medbery, "gives even to irrefragable values the quality of quicksilver."[51] When Jay Gould as president of the Erie was asked about the railroad's actual value, he replied brazenly, "There is no intrinsic value to it probably; it is speculated in here and in London and it has that value."* In other

*According to Henry Adams, the Erie "stock was almost exclusively held for speculation, not for investment; and in the morals of Wall Street speculation means, or had almost come to mean, disregard of intrinsic value. In this case society at large was the injured party, and society knew its risk." (Josephson, *Robber Barons*, p. 136; and Adams, "Gold Conspiracy," p. 108.)

words, the value of one of the world's great railroads derived solely from its attraction as a Wall Street "fancy."

Although the markets are far better regulated today than in the nineteenth century, the speculator's propensity for manipulation has not diminished with time. In May 1991, a bond trader at Salomon Brothers was discovered attempting to corner the market in two-year U.S. Treasury notes. Attracted by rising stock prices during the 1990s bull market, the American Mafia became involved in several "pump & dump" schemes for penny stocks. In the on-line investment world, manipulation and false rumours abound. One of the most spectacular examples of stock ramping in history occurred in the spring of 1996, when the share price of Comparator (a failed manufacturer of fingerprint identification technology with net assets of less than $2 million and cumulative trading losses of around $20 million) soared from 3 cents to $1.75—at which price the company's market capitalisation exceeded a billion dollars. On 9 May 1996, 177 million Comparator shares were traded on the Nasdaq Exchange, a record figure for an individual company. Belatedly, the Securities and Exchange Commission intervened and suspended trading in the stock.

Less than a year later, in the early spring of 1997, the share price of Bre-X, a Canadian gold mining operation quoted on the Vancouver Exchange, soared from a few cents to C$280, valuing the company at nearly seven billion Canadian dollars. The company purported to have discovered two hundred million ounces of gold on its Indonesian mining concession. Tragically in late March, the company's deputy geologist fell to his death from a helicopter over the Borneo jungle. Bre-X's own demise followed shortly after when its auditors released a report condemning what they called a "fraud without precedent in the history of mining anywhere in the world." By this date, however, the company's chief executive had cashed in his profits and was enjoying an extended holiday on some sunny island beyond the reach of the law. Such are the tales of a modern Gilded Age.

Believers in efficient markets claim that speculators help to "discover" values and that stock prices move randomly because they reflect all information relevant to their value. In the nineteenth-century American market, however, intrinsic values were actually hidden by the operations of speculators. Under such conditions, the outsider could only trust to luck in making an investment decision. This suggests a "random walk" of a different nature; not the randomness of efficiency where every share price reflects its current inherent value and future changes in price come about only on the receipt of new information, but the randomness of manipulation where a stock might be bulled, beared, trapped, gunned, or cornered at the whim of a small clique of operators. As one stock market commentator advised in the middle of the century, "the most rational mode of deciding, in our opinion, with regard to the expediency of being a Bull or a Bear, is to close one's eyes, toss up a penny, and abide by the result."[52] What were known as the three M's—*mystery*, *manipulation*, and (thin) *margins*—hindered the stock market from fulfilling its theoretical function of allocating capital efficiently. Instead, railroads were placed where they were not needed, companies were crippled that might have prospered had they kept away from the stock market, and stock market panics caused unnecessary bank failures.

At the end of the nineteenth century, the American economist H. C. Emery wrote that "whereas gambling consists in placing money on artificially created risks of some fortuitous event, speculation consists in assuming the inevitable economic risks of changes in value."[53] In the American stock market, however, the greatest risks were neither inevitable nor strictly economic, since they were mostly the creation of market operators. Samuel Johnson defined gambling as the redistribution of wealth without an intermediate good. The speculation of the Gilded Age conformed to Dr. Johnson's definition: it brought more harm than good and transferred property from the hands of the many into the pockets of the few.

CHAPTER 7

THE END OF A NEW ERA: THE CRASH OF 1929 AND ITS AFTERMATH

The four most expensive words in the English language are "this time it's different."

Attributed to Sir John Templeton

"Stock prices have reached what looks like a permanently high plateau," declared the eminent Yale economist Irving Fisher in the autumn of 1929. A few weeks after this oracular pronouncement, the Dow Jones Industrial Average had declined by more than a third. The worst was still to come. On 8 July 1932, the Dow Jones closed at 41.88, a drop of nearly 90 percent from its 1929 peak. The stock market chart of these years resembles a precipice rather than a plateau. Why did Professor Fisher get things so wrong? The answer is that he had fallen for the decade's most alluring idea, a thesis which underpinned the great bull market of the late 1920s: He believed that America had entered a *new* era of limitless prosperity.

In fact, the notion of the dawning of a new age of capitalism had appeared in several former speculative periods. Disraeli had asserted that the boom of 1825 would not turn to bust because the period was distinguished from previous ages by superior commercial knowledge.

The nineteenth-century journalist Walter Bagehot claimed that during each speculative revival merchants and bankers "fancy the prosperity they see will last always, that it is only the beginning of a greater prosperity."[1] Alexander Dana Noyes, the financial editor of the *New York Times* during the 1920s, remembered the stock market boom at the beginning of the century associated with the creation of the great "trust" companies, such as U.S. Steel, as "the first of such speculative demonstrations in history which based its ideas and conduct on the assumption that we were living in a New Era; that old rules and principles and precedents of finance were obsolete; that things could safely be done to-day which had been dangerous and impossible in the past."[2]

This new era came to an end in the panic caused by the Northern Pacific corner in May 1901. It was soon forgotten, only to be replaced by a far more powerful and persuasive "new era" argument that came to the fore in the second half of the 1920s. The first premise of the "new economics," as it was otherwise called, was that the business cycle—the periodic undulations of trade first observed in Sir William Petty's successions of "dearth and plenty" back in the seventeenth century—had been effectively abolished by the establishment of the Federal Reserve System in 1913. Before this date, financial crises in the United States had been exacerbated by the absence of a central bank to provide funds to the banking sector during periods of instability. The Federal Reserve, with its ability to control interest rates and conduct "open market operations"—buying and selling government bonds in order to affect the supply of money available to banks—was hailed in the 1920s as "the remedy to the whole problem of booms, slumps, and panics."[3] As a result, bankers and speculators alike were lulled into a false security which led them to operate irresponsibly, exacerbating the severity of the ensuing crisis.

Alongside the belief in the omnipotence of the Federal Reserve, a variety of additional explanations were offered for the endurance of the "Coolidge prosperity" which had commenced with the election of President Calvin Coolidge in 1924, and promised to continue into the administration of his successor, Herbert Hoover. They included the extension of free trade, the decline of inflation, and a more "scientific" style of corporate management, associated with the alumni of the recently established Harvard School of Business Administration and the automated car production lines of Detroit (known in the managerial technospeak of the day as "Fordism"). Better management brought improvements in productivity and lower levels of inventory stocks (the excessive buildup of inventory was believed to be the most common cause of the economic cycle). Professor Fisher argued that modern production "is managed by 'captains of industry.' These men are specially fitted at once to forecast and to mould the future, within the realms in which they operate. The industries of transportation and manufactures, particularly, are under the lead of an educated and trained speculative class."[4]

Fisher found other reasons to be optimistic. The relaxation of the antitrust laws during Coolidge's presidency allowed for a series of mergers of banking, railroad, and utility companies that promised greater economies of scale and more efficient production. Gains in productivity, which rose by over 50 percent between 1919 and 1927, were ascribed to increasing investment in research and development. American Telephone & Telegraph employed over four thousand scientists, and over a hundred thousand applications were lodged with the Commissioner of Patents at the end of 1928.[5] Fisher also celebrated the compliant attitude of labour after the "Great Red Scare" and strikes of the early 1920s. His most singular "new era" argument, however, lay in the benefits he saw flowing from prohibition, which had begun in 1920. Fisher cited the work of Professor Paul Nystrom of the Columbia Business School, who concluded that a "dry" nation would increase the efficiency of workers and switch demand from liquor to "home furnishings, automobiles, musical instruments, radio, travel, amusements, insurance, education, books and magazines."[6]

Fisher was not the only proponent of the new era. In 1927, John Moody, founder of the credit ratings agency, declared that "no one can examine the panorama of business and finance in America during the past half-dozen years without realizing that we are living in a new era."[7] In April of that year *Barron's*, the investment weekly, envisaged a "new era without depressions."[8] Bernard Baruch, the patrician Wall Street financier who later excoriated the "New Economics," argued in 1929 that the prospects of peace and free trade, improved statistical information, better understanding of economics among businessmen, and cooperation among the world's central bankers were producing an "industrial renaissance" in the United States.[9] Even Herbert Hoover's presidential nomination acceptance speech in the summer of 1928, when he declared the end of poverty to be in sight, was marked by the prevailing "new era" optimism.

If the economic fundamentals of the country had changed and panics along with cyclical fluctuations were consigned to history, then it followed that these changes should be reflected in the stock market. If corporate earnings were both stable and growing, then a higher value should be attached to them. In 1924, the year of Coolidge's election and the beginning of the great bull market, Edgar Lawrence Smith published a little book entitled *Common Stocks as Long Term Investments.* In this work, Smith attempted to overthrow the conventional wisdom that common stocks were solely a medium for speculation. Given the history of American stock markets, such an attitude was understandable, argued Smith, but it had led investors to exaggerate the dangers of stocks to those who bought them as long-term investments.* Applying a statistical analysis to the investment returns of bonds and stocks from the middle of the nineteenth century onwards, Smith showed that stocks had outperformed bonds, especially during the inflationary period of the first two decades of the twentieth century. Smith's conclusion was axiomatic. Even when stocks were bought at a market peak, "there is definitely to be expected a period in which we may recover as many dollars as we have invested."[10] Translated into statistical terms, he found that in any fifteen-year period there was only a 1 percent chance of a stock market investor suffering a loss of principal. Smith concluded the case for stocks with a few more "new era" arguments: management was becoming more responsive to shareholders' interests and investment research was improving. The result, he forecast, would be improved returns for common stocks in the near future.

*E. L. Smith, *Common Stocks as Long Term Investments,* New York, 1924, p. 4. Keynes reviewed Smith's book favourably in the *Nation and Athenaeum* (2 May 1925). According to Keynes, the outperformance of stocks over bonds was mainly explained by the retention of earnings and the element of compounding that takes place, which over the years is of "startling magnitude."

For Smith, the chief attraction of stocks derived from the compound growth of retained earnings (i.e., the earnings of companies that were not paid out in dividends). Another contemporary investment writer, Kenneth van Sturm, supplemented this argument with the observation that bonds, unlike stocks, lost "purchasing power" during inflationary periods. The writings of Smith and van Sturm brought about a profound change in the public's attitude to stock market investment. They provided an intellectual framework for what was soon called "the cult of the common stock."

Old yardsticks of valuation, which priced stocks at roughly ten times earnings and expected dividend yields to be greater than bond yields, were replaced by the discounting of future earnings. By this method, future receipts were reduced to their present value by applying a discount rate: so that $100 paid in one year's time, discounted at 10 percent, is valued today at $90. The discount method of valuation is the most speculative method of valuing stocks since it relies entirely on estimates of future earnings which remain uncertain. As Keynes wrote in the *General Theory*, "The outstanding fact is the extreme precariousness of the basis of knowledge on which our estimates of the prospective yield have to be made. Our knowledge of the factors which will govern the yield of an investment some years hence is usually very slight and often negligible." Some years later, Benjamin Graham (who commenced his own career as an investor in the 1920s) attacked the methodology of discounting profits:

> . . . the concept of future prospects, and particularly of continued growth in the future, invites the application of formulas out of higher mathematics to establish the present value of the favored issues. But the combination of precise formulas with highly imprecise assumptions can be used to establish, or rather to justify, practically any value one wishes, however high, for a really outstanding issue . . . The more important the good will or future earning-power factor the more uncertain becomes the true value of the enterprise and therefore the more speculative inherently the company stock . . . Mathematics is ordinarily considered as producing precise and dependable results: but in the stock market the more elaborate and

> abstruse the mathematics the more uncertain and speculative are the conclusions we draw from them. Calculus . . . [gives] speculation the deceptive guise of investment.[11]

Contemporaries were aware of this problem: in 1929, it was commonly said that the market was "discounting not only the future, but the hereafter."

Several commentators warned against these new era developments in the pricing of stocks. "To forego a fair normal current return for the sake of hoped-for enhancement of principal," wrote Lewis H. Haney in the *North American Review* (August 1929), "is speculation pure and simple. It is not investment, for it takes a chance on the future at the expense of safety in the present."[12] In the same journal, Alan Temple analysed the state of the speculative psychology as the market approached its peak:

> As stocks cannot be purchased upon the basis of what they are intrinsically worth now these [new era] buyers pay what they hope the shares will be worth in a year from now, accepting the handicap of a year's start in the race ahead, perhaps a lifetime. Over such a period, they say, a few points more or less difference in the price of a stock will be insignificant. Nor does the possibility of a recession worry them very much, so strong is their belief in stability, in the new era, in the destiny of large corporations.

He concluded with an attack on E. L. Smith's thesis: "The policy of buying stocks at prices which have already discounted the future to a considerable extent constitutes an amendment to the theory of common stock investment as originally outlined, and the amendment conceivably may destroy its validity."[13] It is an irony, not uncommon in the looking-glass world of the financial markets where "proven" investment theses tend to lose their validity when acted upon, that the great stock market boom of the 1920s was induced by the statistically reasoned proposition that stocks were neither speculative nor even particularly risky investments.

Aside from new era arguments, there were strong reasons to be bullish on stocks in the second half of the 1920s. The indolent

President Coolidge, given to catnapping in the Oval Office, followed a personal and economic philosophy of *laissez-faire, laissez-dormir.* In the absence of an ideology for purposeful government, business was venerated. As Coolidge famously expressed it, "the business of America is business." His Treasury Secretary, the wealthy Philadelphia banker Andrew Mellon, agreed. In his opinion, government existed mainly to facilitate business, indeed it was no more than a business itself. Mellon set about improving the conditions for business by reducing the top rate of income tax from 65 to 32 percent, cutting corporation taxes to 2½ percent, and slashing capital gains taxes. As a result of these tax cuts the rich had more money to invest in stocks, companies reported higher after-tax earnings, and more of the profits of speculation could be retained by the players.

MORTGAGING THE FUTURE

While the rich became richer during the 1920s, unions were weak and workers were unable to enjoy the benefits of their improved productivity. At his Baton Rouge plant, Henry Ford employed armed thugs to terrorise his employees against collective action. Unable to maintain their share of the economic surplus, workers experienced a decline in real wages during the decade and corporate profits rose as a percentage of national income. Capitalism, however, requires consumers as much as savers and demand was maintained by the massive expansion of consumer credit, then called "instalment purchases." Radios, fridges, cars, and clothes could all be purchased on credit. By the end of the decade, when outstanding instalment debt had risen to $6 billion, it was estimated that around an eighth of all retail sales were made on credit.* There was a decidedly speculative element in the growth of instalment credit: present consumption was being financed with anticipated earnings. Put another way, in their appetite for immediate gratification, the

*Frederick Lewis Allen, *Only Yesterday* (New York, 1957), p. 168. By 1926, 65 percent of motorcars were purchased on instalment credit. Department stores sold over 40 percent of goods on credit.

consumers of the 1920s were devouring their future. When the future eventually arrived, they found the cupboard bare. At the time, however, instalment purchases were seen as yet another beneficial new era development. Credit and consumption, it was argued, formed a virtuous circle since from the immediate increase in prosperity would come the ability to pay off debt.

Margin loans comprised another popular source of personal credit during the 1920s. When the stock market rose investors could cash in some of their profits by increasing their margin loans and use the money to make good any shortfall in their earnings. Margin loans climbed in tandem with the stock market in the second half of the 1920s.* By October 1929, brokers' loans and bank loans to investors had reached a total of nearly $16 billion. At this level, they represented roughly 18 percent of the total capitalisation of all listed stocks.[14] As we have seen, margin loans had long been considered a source of instability in the American financial system. President Coolidge, however, viewed the escalation of stock market credit without concern. In January 1928, he announced that margin loans were no cause for concern; they were, he claimed, merely rising in line with bank deposits and stocks.

As the bull market continued, others became less sanguine. The Federal Reserve in Washington—the institution that had supposedly abolished panics—had inadvertently ignited the stock market boom by lowering interest rates in 1925. This policy was intended to accommodate the Bank of England, which was suffering from an outflow of gold after a disastrous return to the gold standard at the prewar exchange rate. In the summer of 1927, the Fed bowed once more to British demands (backed by the French and Germans) and lowered the discount rate to a record low of 3½ percent. Faced with the growth of speculation, the Fed changed tack and from February 1928 successively raised the discount rate until it reached 6 percent in August 1929. Yet the profits from buying shares on margin were simply too enticing. As long as the market continued rising, speculators were prepared to pay more for their margin

*During 1927 outstanding margin loans increased by $800 million to $3.6 billion—a rise in percentage terms that nearly matched the 28.75 percent registered by the Dow Jones Industrials.

loans. While interest rates remained too low to restrain speculation, they became too high for the economy as a whole (or what in the nineteenth century used to be called "legitimate commerce"). In February 1929, the Federal Reserve warned its member banks that it did not consider brokers' loans a suitable use for funds, but this attempt to restrain speculation through "moral suasion" was equally ineffective.

One reason margin loans proved intractable was that they were increasingly supplied by American corporations and foreign banks, neither of which were responsive to the Federal Reserve.* Companies boosted their profits by raising funds in the stock market (which cost around 4 percent in dividends) and lending their surplus cash in the call loan market at rates of up to 15 percent. Stock prices, in turn, were propelled forward by speculators buying shares on margin. The effect of call loans on the stock market, in the words of one contemporary, was "truly, a vicious circle."[15]

SELLING STOCKS

Brokerage houses expanded rapidly in the second half of the decade, with nearly six hundred branch offices opening in 1928 and 1929, an increase of over 80 percent. In the summer of 1929, Mike Meehan, the broker-cum-pool operator, opened the first brokerage office on a transatlantic liner using new wireless technology supplied by the Radio Corporation of America. Equipped with the new era ideology of common stock investment and a limitless supply of brokers' loans, American financial institutions began applying new hard-sell methods in their dealings with retail investors.

Although American commercial banks were forbidden to deal in securities, they circumvented the law by using fully owned affiliates to handle their stock and bond sales. This practice was pioneered after the First World War by Charles E. Mitchell, the president of

*Barrie Wigmore estimates that over 60 percent of brokers' loans were supplied directly by corporations. Corporate lenders to the call loan market included U.S. Steel, General Motors, AT&T, and Standard Oil Company of New Jersey. (*Crash and Its Aftermath*, p. 94.)

the National City Bank, who established the National City Company to sell securities to the public. Mitchell, a former electrical goods salesman, ran the business in an aggressively commercial fashion: securities were first "manufactured," then distributed (in Mitchell's words) "like so many pounds of coffee." Potential clients were viewed as "prospects," and sales staff were urged to lie in wait and pounce on them outside nightclubs, railway stations, and bucket shops. Other clients were drawn from the parent bank's customers—a practice now known as "cross-selling." Quotas were instituted and sales contests organised in order to keep the salesmen on their toes.

After the Great War, the United States emerged as the world's leading creditor nation and the stock market boom was accompanied by an explosion of speculative lending to foreign countries. The National City Company became a prominent distributor of high-yielding bonds from South American and Central European states to American investors. In 1928, it sold bonds for Minas Gerais, a Brazilian state, despite an internal company report highlighting "the inefficiency and ineptitude . . . [and] complete ignorance, carelessness and negligence of the former state officials in respect to external long-term borrowing."* The term "Mitchellism" came to describe the peddling of second-rate securities to the public.

Charles Mitchell became the most prominent cheerleader of the bull market. As an advocate of the new era ideology, he informed the public that stocks were as safe as bonds. Throughout the summer and early autumn of 1929 he remained indefatigably bullish. In August, he cabled Bernard Baruch from the grouse moors of Scotland with the message that the stock market was "like a weather-vane pointing into a gale of prosperity." In Germany a few weeks later, he declared that "the industrial condition of the United States is absolutely sound . . . nothing can arrest the upward movement." On the eve of the Crash, he assured investors that stocks

---

*In a repeat of the British experience a century earlier, the "emerging market" loans of the 1920s turned sour soon after the Crash. The bonds issued by the National City Company on behalf of Peru, a country notorious for its broken pledges, fell from an issue price of 96½ to a low of under 5 after the country defaulted in 1931. (Ferdinand Pecora, *Wall Street Under Oath*, London, 1939, pp. 98–102.)

had already declined too far and that he knew "of nothing fundamentally wrong with the stock market or the underlying business or credit structure . . . The public," he added, "is suffering from 'brokers' loanitis'"[16] When the Crash came, he personally borrowed and lost millions of dollars in a failed attempt to support his bank's share price. Mitchell resembled a snake-oil peddler who had come to believe in his own pitch.

POOLS OF SPECULATORS

In a nation where a twentieth of the population controlled nine-tenths of all wealth, the stock market was naturally dominated by the wealthier class of speculator. Among the rich speculators two groups stood out. The first comprised businessmen who had made their first fortunes in the automobile industry and later turned to the stock market for their entertainment. According to Professor Charles Amos Dice of Ohio State University, these men were particularly well-suited to speculative activities since "they did not come into the market hampered by the heavy armour of tradition."[17] The "Detroit crowd," as they were known, included Walter Chrysler, the car manufacturer, the Fisher brothers, whose family firm produced car bodies, and John J. Raskob, a director of General Motors. The most flamboyant member of this group was William Crapo Durant, the founder of General Motors. He had resigned from the company in 1920 after losing a fortune speculating in its stock, and thereafter dedicated his professional energies to stock operations, which he conducted on a grand scale. In 1929, Durant's investment pool was rumoured to control more than $4 billion worth of stocks (roughly $38 billion at today's prices) and his profits from speculation were estimated at over $100 million. Although in his private life Durant displayed certain eccentricities—he travelled everywhere with a folding barber's chair and had all his meals prepared at home and driven in to work—his speculations were straightforward and always on the bull side.

Irish-Americans comprised another leading clique of speculators. They included Charles Mitchell, raised in the immigrant Boston suburb of Chelsea; Mike Meehan, another Irish Bostonian, who had earned his living as a Broadway ticket tout before turning broker and organised two famous pools in the stock of the Radio Corporation of America; Bernard "Sell'em Ben" Smith, the trader who managed the Radio pool for Meehan; Joseph P. Kennedy, the father of the future President, who famously sold out before the collapse; and J. J. Riordan, the president of the Country Trust Bank and another member of Meehan's Radio pool, who lost his fortune in the Crash and committed suicide a few days later. Born mostly into poverty and excluded by their religion from the East Coast financial elite, which was dominated by Wasps and German Jews, these men were prepared to take great risks in order to establish themselves. As outsiders, their speculations conformed to the observation of the eighteenth-century financial writer Thomas Mortimer: "He who values not his neck, because he is conscious it is worth nothing, may take the boldest leap."[18]

Whereas in the nineteenth century the vulnerability of the stock market to manipulation had tended to frighten away the public, the operations of the major players in the 1920s served as an enticement to outsiders who hoped to share in the good fortune of a Durant by hanging on to his coattails. Rumours that pool operators were taking a stock "in hand" were eagerly received. Taking advantage of the public's weakness, one pool operator bribed journalists on several newspapers to plant stories. Mike Meehan's first pool in the stock of Radio Corporation of America, which propelled RCA's share price from 95½ to 160 in only ten days in March 1928, was credited with reviving bullish sentiment in the market. Mitchell's National City Company left nothing to chance. In late 1928 it joined a pool in Anaconda Copper, whose shares it sold on, at inflated prices, to its own clientele. In two months the company off-loaded a million and a quarter Anaconda shares to the public, making a profit of more than $20 million at a time when the price of copper actually declined by over 25 percent. (Anaconda shares subsequently fell from $125 to less than $4.)[19]

Company directors were also frequent pool members. Both the chairman and president of Anaconda were involved in the pool in their company's stock, along with Percy Rockefeller and James Stillman, who were directors of the National City Bank. Walter Chrysler operated a pool in the stock of his own company, while Mrs. David Sarnoff, the wife of the founder and chairman of Radio

Corporation of America, was a member of Meehan's Radio pool. In late 1928, Harry T. Sinclair, the oilman implicated earlier in the decade in the Teapot Dome scandal (involving the corrupt distribution of Naval Oil Reserve leases during President Harding's administration), hired the speculator Arthur Cutten along with Chase Securities Corporation, an affiliate of Chase National Bank, and Blair & Company, an investment bank, to drive up the share price of Sinclair Consolidated Oil Corporation. The successful operation netted the syndicate a profit of $12 million. In this case, both the presidents of Blair & Company and Chase National were also directors of Sinclair Oil. It was estimated that during 1929 the stocks of over a hundred companies listed on the New York Stock Exchange were subject to similar pool manipulations.[20]

A BALLYHOO FOR STOCKS

Although the total number of stock market players in the late 1920s is variously estimated at between one and two million out of a population of over a hundred and twenty million, the bull market attracted a public interest far exceeding these numbers. As J. K. Galbraith observed, "the striking thing about the stock market speculation of 1929 was not the massiveness of the participation. Rather it was the way it became central to the culture."[21] The stock market lured the leading celebrities and entertainers of the age, including Groucho Marx, Irving Berlin, and Eddie Cantor, the Ziegfeld Follies comedian, who all speculated on margin and eventually lost fortunes. (Charlie Chaplin was more fortunate; he sold his stocks in 1928 and remained in cash thereafter).

In the stock market of the Roaring Twenties, Americans found a secular religion whose ludic qualities, cynicism, and materialism reflected the zeitgeist of the Jazz Age. F. Scott Fitzgerald's *The Great Gatsby* (published in 1925), a tale of hope and disillusionment, is a parable for the era. Its hero, Jay Gatsby, is a self-made man with deluded social ambitions. Born in the Midwest (the breeding ground for many of the great nineteenth-century speculators), he has risen from poverty to great wealth by mysterious means involving bootlegging and forged bonds. His romantic dream is rooted in materialism: the wellborn Daisy Buchanan, the object of his love, is described in his own words as having a "voice full of money" and can only be attained with riches. Gatsby's decadent parties are compared to Trimalchio's feast in Petronius' *Satyricon:* "We are meaner than flies; flies have their virtues, we are nothing but bubbles," says one of Trimalchio's guests, an observation that links the vanities of ancient Rome and its Forum to those of Long Island and Wall Street. For the evanescent Gatsby—the epitome of the *homo bulla* of humanist discourse—the price for living a single dream too long is death. A similar fate lay in store for the nation's speculators.

The 1920s were an age of women's emancipation. Employed in ever-greater numbers since the war and granted the vote in 1920, women enjoyed greater social freedom: they smoked, danced to the music on the radio, and, in the face of the law, drank cocktails. The motorcar provided them with the freedom to enjoy illicit sexual encounters (and was denounced by one preacher as "the house of prostitution on wheels"). More than ever before, women came to exercise their economic franchise in the stock market. In an article entitled "Ladies of the Ticker," published in the *North American Review* in the spring of 1929, Eunice Fuller Barnard reported that Wall Street had finally arrived in Fifth Avenue. In the hotels of upper Broadway, special brokers' rooms were set aside for women, where according to Barnard:

> Day in and day out through a long five hours, aggressive and guttural dowagers, gum-chewing blondes, shrinking spinsters who look as if they belonged in a missionary-society meeting, watch, pencil in hand, from the opening of the market till the belated ticker drones its last in the middle of the afternoon.[22]

It was estimated that women possessed over 40 percent of the nation's wealth and accounted for 35 percent of stock market turnover. Their presence was heavy in the shareholder registers of America's largest companies: they owned over 30 percent of the shares in U.S. Steel and General Motors, and more than 50 percent of the shares in American Telephone & Telegraph and the Pennsylvania Railroad (which became known as the "Petticoat Line"). It was a sign of the times that J. J. Raskob of General Motors chose the *Ladies' Home Journal* to publish his essay entitled "Everybody Ought to Be Rich," where he suggested that, through a judicious selection of stocks and the application of debt, a small regular investment would inevitably turn into a large fortune.

Women were said to provide the main impetus behind the bull market. "In the past year," wrote Eunice Barnard, "the growth of the woman investor and the woman speculator has been amazing and it is getting larger almost weekly." They came from all classes: heiresses, stenographers, businesswomen, housewives, farmers' wives, cleaning ladies, waitresses, telephone girls, cooks, and washerwomen. Rumours circulated of great fortunes attained by the "lady bulls." It was argued that as women spent the household money, they knew better than their husbands which retailing and manufacturing stocks to invest in. They were said to be good losers. A lady speculator told the financial journalist Edwin Lefèvre that she had lost a million dollars: "I had a perfectly stunning time while it lasted. I never knew what fun it was to make money."[23] Yet some brokers found their female customers to be "hard losers, naggers, stubborn as mules, [and] suspicious as servants."[24] As in earlier periods, there was a feminist angle to women's involvement in the stock market:

> Women are at last taking a hand in man's most exciting capitalist game [wrote Eunice Barnard]. For the first time they have the interest, the self-assurance, and the entrance fee. If they become intelligent players, and if to any extent they should win financial power, they would probably in our economic society, as a matter of pragmatic fact, do more to raise the level of common respect for women as a class than all the hard-fought suffrage campaigns.[25]

THE PICK OF THE STOCKS

The speculator's fancy for new technologies was well served by the bull market. The motorcar replaced the railroads as both the engine of economic prosperity and the favoured object of speculation. It transformed the culture and geography of the nation; roads were surfaced, highways built, and garages erected to accommodate the increasing number of passenger cars, which rose from seven million to twenty-three million during the 1920s. Over a million visitors flocked to view the new Model A at Ford's New York headquarters. The excitement was reflected in the stock market, where General Motors' share price increased over tenfold between 1925 and 1928, an advance so rapid that it put the stock market on the front page of the newspapers. When J. J. Raskob made his proposal for universal wealth in August 1929, he pointed out that $10,000 invested a decade earlier in General Motors would have grown to more than $1.5 million.*

The public interest generated by the motorcar was exceeded only by that for the radio, first launched by Westinghouse in 1920. The wireless became the purveyor of fashions across the nation. Sales of radio sets rose from $60 million in 1922 to $843 million six years later. The new industry was dominated by Radio Corporation of America (often referred to simply as "Radio"), which was both the largest manufacturer of radios and the leading broadcaster. The company's earnings increased from $2.5 million in 1925 to nearly $20 million in 1928, and its stock climbed from a low of 1½ in 1921 to 85½ in early 1928. From there it was propelled by Meehan's pool operations to a high of 114 in 1929, seventy-three times its earnings and nearly seventeen times book value. RCA was highly leveraged, paid no dividends, and expanded rapidly through acquisitions. In 1929 it was the most heavily traded stock on the New York Stock Exchange, where it was known as the "General Motors of the Air."

The national euphoria following Charles Lindbergh's solo crossing of the Atlantic in 1927 propelled the speculative appeal of the young aircraft industry. Wright Aeronautical, Curtiss, and Boeing Airplane (renamed United Aircraft and Transport in 1929) became favourites in the stock market. The motion picture industry was also attractive to speculators. As Hollywood made the transition from silent films to talkies, the large studios were consolidating their positions and profits expanded rapidly. In October 1928, Joseph Kennedy merged his

*The top management of General Motors were solicitous of a rising share price, as they were rewarded by the Du Pont family (which controlled the company) with shares in the company. By 1930, eighty top executives owned an average of over $3 million worth of GM stock.

movie interests to form the giant RKO, and the following year the Fox Film Corporation paid $72 million for Loew's chain of movie theatres. The debt taken on by this deal caused Fox's share price to collapse from 106 to 19 after the Crash. Contrary to public perception, movie stocks performed badly during the Depression.

THE APPEAL OF LEVERAGE

The dominant feature of the 1920s stock market was not the wild pursuit of speculative innovations but the use of debt to pyramid investments and enhance gains. With margin loans speculators could afford to "buy AOT"—Any Old Thing. As Groucho Marx, who personally borrowed over a quarter of a million dollars to play the stock market, recalled in his memoirs, during the bull market there was no need to employ a financial advisor to select your stocks: "You could close your eyes, stick your finger any place on the big board and the stock you bought would start rising."[26]

Leverage was not confined to individual speculators' margin holdings; it became built into the financial structure of corporate America. Utility and railway companies were consolidated into giant holding companies, called "systems" (an unconscious echo of John Law's Mississippi System), which were constructed upon multiple layers of debt. Samuel Insull, a former secretary to Thomas Edison, constructed a giant utility network in the Midwest which diversified into tyre manufacturing, shoe factories, and real estate. Insull Utility Investments, an investment trust, owned cross-shareholdings in a number of utility companies, each of which was highly leveraged with debt, so that a small rise in the earnings of the operating businesses had a disproportionately large effect on the profitability of the holding company.* Profits were also manufactured by subsidiaries selling assets to each other at inflated prices. As the structure of

*Corporate leverage operates in a similar manner to the speculator's margin loan. For example, if a company has earnings before interest of $100 million and interest payments of $90 million, then its net profits before tax are $10 million. A 10 percent increase in earnings to $110 million will produce a 100 percent rise in pre-tax profits to $20 million. Insull and other holding company operators in the 1920s enhanced the effects of corporate leverage by creating a pyramid of cross-shareholdings between heavily indebted companies.

Insull's business empire was too complex for even the sophisticated investor to understand, Insull arranged to sell his companies' shares directly to their customers.

A frenzy for utility holding companies dominated the last phase of the bull market, their shares reaching a 1929 peak of more than four times book value and dividend yields falling to less than 1 percent.[27] In January 1929, J. P. Morgan, the investment bank, acted as the promoter for the United Corporation, a holding company that produced a fifth of the nation's electricity. It was later revealed that Morgan had retained for itself nearly two million warrants, providing the right to subscribe to new shares in the company at a fixed price, and had distributed United's shares at below market prices to its "preferred" clients, who included Charles Mitchell of the National City Bank, J. J. Raskob of General Motors, and former President Calvin Coolidge.*

The fashion for holding companies extended far beyond the utilities. The van Sweringen brothers, two property developers from Cleveland, Ohio, used a complicated structure of holding companies to merge a number of railroads in the Midwest. Their Alleghany Corporation, sitting atop a mountain of debt, was also sponsored by J. P. Morgan. Ivar Kreuger, the Swedish "Match King," built an international chain of monopolies which controlled around three-quarters of the world's match production. His heavily-indebted holding company, Kreuger & Toll, financed its operations by issuing bonds in New York. Banks also clustered themselves together. The Transamerica Corporation merged the banking interests of A. P. Giannini, which included the California-based Bank of Italy and the Bank of America in New York. In Detroit, two holding companies, the Guardian Detroit Union Group and the Detroit Bankers Company, had a monopoly on local banking.†

The holding company concept found its widest application in the field of investment trusts. The purpose of the investment trust

*The combination of retained warrants and the preferential distribution of securities is reminiscent of Michael Milken's junk bond operations in the 1980s. (See Chapter 8.)

†Following the lead of the National City Bank, the Detroit holding company banks engaged in the securities business. The subsequent decline of the stock market caused their failure, which in turn brought on a crisis of confidence in the banking system, leading to Roosevelt's declaration of a national bank holiday in early 1933.

(which originated in Scotland in the late nineteenth century) was to hold the securities of other companies, providing the small private investor with the benefits of professional management and investment diversification at a low cost. They thrived in the bull market. In 1928, over two hundred new investment trusts were launched with combined assets of over a billion dollars. Three years earlier, the combined capital of American investment trusts had been less than half a million dollars. During the first nine months of 1929, a new investment trust appeared for every working day and the industry issued over two and a half billion dollars' worth of securities to the public.

Investment trusts were sold to the public with all the puffed-up rhetoric of the new era. In an article published in the summer of 1929, Professor Irving Fisher asserted that "the influence of investment trusts . . . is largely toward cutting the speculative fluctuations at top and bottom, thus acting as a force to stabilise the market. Investment trusts buy when there is a real anticipation of a rise, due to underlying causes, and sell when there is a real anticipation of fall," thus ensuring that stocks sold more nearly to their true value.[28] The high turnover of shares in the investment trust portfolios was hailed as sound management. It was even argued that investment trust purchases were providing stocks with a new "scarcity value."

In reality, the effect of investment trusts on the stock market was highly destabilising. Their managers invested heavily in blue chip stocks and lent their surplus cash to the call loan market, thus serving both to increase the demand for shares and to stimulate speculation. They borrowed heavily against their assets in order to leverage profits, thereby increasing stock market volatility. The high stock turnover in the trusts' portfolios reflected baneful trend-following rather than the sober pursuit of intrinsic value. The investment banks, which sponsored the new trusts, frequently dumped stocks into their portfolios that they found difficult to sell elsewhere—as a result the investors were diversified in junk. Worst of all, several investment trusts invested in the shares of affiliated trusts. The history of the Goldman Sachs Trading Corporation is exemplary. Launched in December 1928 with a capital of $100 million, the company first "invested" $57 million in its own shares, then in July 1929 it launched the Shenandoah Corporation, in which it retained a sizeable stake. A month later another investment trust, called Blue Ridge, issued forth from Shenandoah. As with the "systems" of Insull and others, the returns of these investment companies were enhanced with leverage. The public was initially enthused by this exercise in what Professor Galbraith has called "fiscal incest," and shares in Goldman Sachs Trading rose to nearly three times book value.

Not all contemporaries were sanguine. In the summer of 1929, the chairman of the New York State Assembly's Committee on Banks feared that if a crash were to happen "the investors who own investment trust shares would be worth little or nothing after the banks took up the stocks that are given as security for loans."[29] Paul M. Warburg, a prominent banker and a leading figure behind the establishment of the Federal Reserve System, dismissed the investment trusts as "incorporated stock pools." Warburg's fears were not confined to the vogue for investment trusts. In March 1929, he alerted readers of the *Commercial and Financial Chronicle* that

> History, which has a painful way of repeating itself, has taught mankind that speculative overexpansion invariably ends in overcontraction and distress . . . If orgies of speculation are permitted to spread too far, however, the ultimate collapse is certain not only to affect the speculators themselves, but also to bring about a general depression involving the entire country.[30]

Warburg was not alone in harbouring fears of the possible outcome of the speculative mania. Herbert Hoover, Commerce Secretary under Coolidge, had warned privately since early 1926 that excessive speculation and the overextension of instalment credit were threatening the long-term prosperity of the nation. When he assumed the presidency early in 1929, Hoover attempted to address the issue of speculation. Since he did not feel it was constitutionally proper for him to dictate the level of stock prices, he urged newspaper editors to warn their readers about stock prices. Treasury Secretary Mellon, who until this date had been decidedly bullish, was asked to exhort the public to purchase bonds rather than shares. Yet Hoover's admonitions were as ineffective as those of Prime Minister Robert Peel during the Railway Mania of 1845. The bankers with whom Hoover consulted politely informed him of the tenets of the new era philosophy, while less eminent Cassandras were told to stop "sandbagging America."

THE MADNESS OF CROWDS

The arguments against the new era revaluation of stocks, which had sent shares trading to thirty times income, were compelling. Since 1924, share prices had risen three times faster than corporate earnings. High interest rates were beginning to throttle economic activity. Instalment loans had reached the limits of their expansion since wages were not rising. Gold was flowing to New York from London and Berlin, forcing up European interest rates and weakening their economies with negative consequences for American exports. In the United States, declining agricultural commodity prices brought a reduction in the purchasing power of American farmers, who then comprised a sizeable proportion of the population. In August 1929, the *North American Review* noted:

> Over against the mergers, increased exports, growing population, and multiplication of new products, which the prophets of the new era visualize, we must set the possibility of anti-trust law enforcement, increased European competition, retaliation to tariff measures, declining price levels and limited purchasing power.[31]

Yet none of these points carried much weight against the prospect of continuing profits from stock speculation. In his introduction to the 1932 edition of Mackay's *Extraordinary Popular Delusions and the Madness of Crowds*, Bernard Baruch suggested that American speculators in 1929 displayed the attributes of a crowd psychology. He cited the German playwright Schiller's dictum that "anyone taken as an individual is tolerably sensible and reasonable—as a member of a crowd, he at once becomes a blockhead."[32] Although they were not directly concerned with financial markets, the early studies of crowd (or herd) mentality conducted by Freud and the nineteenth-century psychologist Gustave Le Bon identified certain features also commonly found in a bull market *mentalité.* According to Freud and Le Bon, the defining characteristics of a crowd are invincibility, irresponsibility, impetuosity, contagion, changeability, suggestibility, collective hallucination, and intellectual inferiority.[33]

The crowd and the stock market have other features in common. They both thrive on uncertainty and rumour. While crowds generally seek out a leader (whom Freud termed the "dreaded primal father"), this figurehead may be substituted by a "common tendency, a wish in which a number of people can have a share."[34] In *Crowds and Power,* Elias Canetti claimed that money was capable of creating the focus of interest and purpose necessary for a crowd mentality to form. Like the forces behind a bull market, the crowd is inherently unstable; it has no stasis, no point of equilibrium, and is driven by a dynamic either to grow or to shrink. At the moment of its dispersal, a crowd frequently succumbs to panic: "It is of the very essence of a panic," wrote Freud, "that it bears no relation to the danger that threatens it, and often breaks out on trivial occasions."[35]

The intellectual inferiority of the crowd is a sign that people are filtering and manipulating new information to make it accord with their existing beliefs. Psychologists call this behaviour "cognitive dissonance." Dissonant information, which contradicts the collective fantasy, is uncomfortable and people seek to avoid it. They may do this either by shooting the messenger or by proselytising and seeking fresh converts to their fold. In his *Theory of Cognitive Dissonance,* Leon Festinger argued that people will tolerate increasing degrees of dissonance if they are motivated by a sufficiently enticing reward. In financial markets, one might say they are prepared to ignore bad news because they still hunger after the immediate profits of speculation. A description of the speculators in William Fowler's circle during the 1860s provides an illustration of this behaviour. They were engaged, wrote Fowler, "in bolstering each other up, not for money, for we thought ourselves impregnable in that respect, but by argument in favour of another rise. We knew we were wrong, but tried to convince ourselves that we were right."[36]

Baruch's assertion that, as a group, the stock market speculators of 1929 displayed a crowd mentality fits well with the analysis of Freud and others. The "crowd" mentality may be seen to have its source on the floor of the New York Stock Exchange. Like the war drum of the African tribes, the ticker, excitedly clattering out the latest stock prices to brokers' offices, spread the spirit of the crowd from further afield. During the normally torpid summer months, an actual crowd, estimated at ten thousand persons, filled New York's financial district, lending a carnivalistic atmosphere to the last days of the bull market. Informal speculative groups congregated everywhere, while the radio joined those living in isolated communities to the bull crowd. This crowd, led by men such as Charles Mitchell and Mike Meehan, gained cohesion from the new era ideology and a collective faith in rising stock prices. In the face of minor stock market panics—in June and December 1928 and later in March 1929—the bull forces succeeded in regrouping. They came out stronger for their trials, until the point was reached when speculators became deaf to warnings they did not wish to hear and developed a belief in their own invincibility. Instead of reasoning, they thrived on the countless rumours of fabulous wealth gained in the stock market by valets, chauffeurs, cattlemen, actresses, farmers' wives, and so on. In *Only Yesterday*, Frederick Lewis Allen described the trance into which the average American had fallen by the summer of 1929:

> He visioned an America set free from poverty and toil. He saw a magical order built on the new science and the new prosperity: roads swarming with millions upon millions of automobiles, airplanes darkening the skies, lines of high-tension wire carrying from hilltop to hilltop the power to give life to a thousand labor-saving machines, skyscrapers thrusting above onetime villages, vast cities rising in great geometrical masses of stone and concrete and roaring with perfectly mechanized traffic—and smartly dressed men and women spending, spending with the money they had won by being far-sighted enough to foresee, way back in 1929, what was going to happen.[37]

NEMESIS

According to Festinger, a group will maintain a state of cognitive dissonance until the pain exceeds the rewards. In stock market terms this might be seen as the moment when the fear of loss outweighs the greed for gain. That point was reached on 3 September 1929, when the Dow Jones reached its year high. The following day, at the annual National Business Conference, an investment adviser named Roger Babson forecast an imminent stock market crash. He predicted that "factories will shut down . . . men will be thrown out of work . . . the vicious circle will get in full swing and the result will be a serious business depression."[38] The pronouncement elicited a savage response from the apostles of the new era. No pun was too corny. One paper dubbed Babson "the prophet of loss." Another suggested that he was suffering from "an attack of Babsonmindedness." Stockbrokers pointed out that Babson had made the same forecast in the two previous years. Professor Irving Fisher emerged from his ivory tower to justify the current stock price levels and deny the likelihood of a crash. Yet on this occasion the market appeared to heed Babson's warnings and weakened sharply. The new era invocations had suddenly lost their potency.

Although investment trusts issued a record $600 million worth of new securities in September, the stock market remained weak throughout the month. It became increasingly receptive to bad news. In the middle of September, the information was received from London that the business empire of Clarence Hatry had collapsed amidst revelations of fraud. The Bank of England reacted by raising interest rates, causing British investors to start selling their American investments and repatriating their capital. On 4 October, Alfred Sloan, the head of General Motors, observing a sudden dip in car sales, announced that the "end of expansion" was at hand. A week later, the Massachusetts Department of Public Utilities denied the request of the Boston Edison Company to split its stock, four shares for one, on the grounds that speculators had already driven its share price above intrinsic value. Rumours surfaced that bear pools, led by the renowned speculator Jesse Livermore, were preparing to drive the market down with short sales.

Livermore received a mailbag of death threats and issued a public statement denying the rumour.

At the beginning of September, Winston Churchill had arrived in the United States on a lecture tour. The former Chancellor of the Exchequer was not only the descendant of speculators (Sarah, Duchess of Marlborough, and Leonard Jerome), he was also connected with the leading players in the current bull market. In New York, he stayed with Percy Rockefeller, a member of numerous stock pools, and dined with Bernard Baruch. Churchill enlivened his visit by purchasing shares on margin, using as capital £20,000 he had recently earned from journalism and lecture fees. On Thursday, 24 October, Churchill was walking down Wall Street when a stranger invited him to enter the visitors' gallery of the New York Stock Exchange. Two months earlier, James Walker, the mayor of New York, had visited the same place to witness what he called "the eighth wonder of the world—the continuing bull market on the Big Board."[39] A rather different spectacle confronted Churchill that day—a day known thereafter as Black Thursday.

The panic that unfolded before his eyes had no palpable cause. Unlike former stock market panics, it was not preceded by tightness in the money market. No banking, brokerage, or industrial failures served as a trigger—and yet panic there was. Within half an hour of opening, many stocks were dropping ten points between trades. Several stocks hit "air pockets" when no bid was offered. By one o'clock, the ticker was running an hour and a half late. There was a surreal quality to events. Churchill had expected to see pandemonium, but the rules of the Exchange precluded members from running or shouting:

> So there they were, walking to and fro like a slow-motion picture of a disturbed ant heap, offering each other enormous blocks of securities at a third of their old prices and half their present value, and for many minutes together finding no one strong enough to pick up the sure fortunes they were compelled to offer.[40]

A measure of calm was restored after leading bankers met at the offices of J. P. Morgan and supplied funds to buy shares and stabilise the market. Although the stock averages had not fallen greatly by the close of trading (the Dow Jones closed down only 6 points at 299), nearly thirteen million shares had changed hands on the New York Stock Exchange, triple the normal daily turnover and more than double the previous record.

Black Thursday marked only the beginning of the disorderly liquidation of financial assets inflated by the preceding bubble. The following two trading days were relatively quiet. Over the weekend staff at the brokerage houses remained at their desks, clearing up the backlog of paperwork and calculating the margin calls to be sent out by telegram to their clients. On Monday, 28 October, disaster struck. The Dow Jones Industrial Average fell 38 points to 260, the largest drop on record. The ticker ran three hours late at closing. Throughout the day, foreign and corporate lenders to the call market scrambled to withdraw their loans.

From the moment it opened on Tuesday, 29 October, the stock market was deluged by a further wave of sale orders as margin calls forced speculators to dispose of their stocks. Gone was the composure witnessed by Churchill a few days earlier. On the floor of the Exchange, a broker grabbed a messenger by his hair, another fled the floor screaming like a madman, jackets were torn, collars dislodged, and clerks in their frenzy lashed out at each other. The panic worsened after the technology upon which the market had become dependent collapsed: the transatlantic cable broke, the ticker stopped running, telephone lines became clogged with enquiries, and the telegraph system was unable to cope with the volume of brokers' margin calls sent out across the nation. In New York, Western Union was forced to hire a fleet of taxis to deliver its telegrams. When the market closed, the ticker carried on clattering its dismal message for two hours. The Dow Jones Industrials were down 30 points at 230, on a massive turnover of sixteen and a half million shares. They called it the "day of the millionaires' slaughter."

On Black Tuesday, the glamour stocks of the bull market suffered the worst damage. Radio Corporation of America, which on Monday had shed $19, collapsed from 40.25 to 26 in the first two hours of trading (at which point it was down over 75 percent from its peak); the Goldman Sachs Trading Corporation opened at 60 and closed at 35; Blue Ridge, its affiliated investment trust, which a few weeks earlier was selling for 24, dropped from 10 to 3; and the United Corporation, J. P. Morgan's giant utility, went from 26 to 19.30. Bank stocks were slaughtered. The First National Bank of New York declined from $5,200 to $1,600, while National City sank from 455 to 300, despite a rearguard action from Charles Mitchell, who personally borrowed $12 million to support the stock. The Hollywood favourites—Paramount, Fox, and Warner Brothers—were also hit hard. For many stocks there was simply no bid. A messenger boy was reported to have picked up a parcel of White Sewing Machine Company, which had traded earlier in the year at 48 and closed the previous day at 11⅛, for a dollar a share.[41]

THE SLIDE INTO DEPRESSION

America faced its stock market ordeal with a sense of humour. The market steadied the day after Black Tuesday when John D. Rockefeller, Sr., announced that he and his son were purchasing "sound common stocks." "Sure," replied Eddie Cantor from the Broadway footlights, himself down a reported million dollars, "who else had any money left?"[42] It was Cantor who gave publicity to the suicide legends of two speculators leaping from a bridge holding hands because they shared a joint account, and of hotel reception clerks asking new arrivals whether they came to sleep or to jump.* He also observed that since the Crash women's hemlines had come down. The Jazz Age, according to Scott Fitzgerald, had "leapt to a spectacular death." More austere times were around the corner.

Although stocks continued to slide until the middle of November, Hoover's administration acted promptly to mitigate the fallout from the Crash. The President's public pronouncements were consistently upbeat. He convened business leaders and urged them to maintain wages in order to sustain demand; private and public organisations were asked to bring forward their construction plans;

*Galbraith asserts that the stories of suicide associated with the Crash are myths. Yet the day after Black Thursday, Churchill wrote, "Under my window a gentleman cast himself down fifteen storeys and was dashed to pieces, causing a wild commotion and the arrival of the fire brigade." (Gilbert, *Churchill*, V, p. 350.)

and Treasury Secretary Mellon announced a small tax cut in November. The banking authorities also acted speedily. On 31 October, the Federal Reserve reduced the discount rate to 5 percent (followed by a further reduction of half a percent two weeks later). The New York Federal Reserve Bank oversaw a massive shift in the call loan market, as outstanding margin loans dropped by 50 percent between September and November. Foreign and corporate lenders continued to withdraw their funds from the call loan market, and were replaced by the New York banks which maintained low rates on loans and reduced margin requirements to 25 percent. There were no significant banking or brokerage failures in the immediate aftermath of the Crash, apart from the Industrial Bank of Flint, Michigan, which was forced to close its doors after it was discovered that a cabal of employees had stolen $3.5 million and lost it in the stock market. American corporations also did their best to steady nerves. The day after Black Tuesday, U.S. Steel and several other companies announced increased dividends. Samuel Rosenwald of Sears, Roebuck and Samuel Insull declared they would guarantee their employees' margin accounts. When General Motors announced an extra dividend on 14 November, the news was greeted jubilantly and the Dow Jones stepped off its low of 198 and rose by nearly 25 percent over the next few days.

Optimism was quick to resurface. On the day the market turned, Bernard Baruch cabled Churchill to inform him that the financial crisis was over, although this was of little comfort to the future prime minister, who lost more than £10,000—roughly £300,000 at today's values—in the Crash and was obliged to live frugally for the next few years. Baruch's was a conventional opinion shared by many of the smaller market players who believed the Crash presented them with yet another buying opportunity. The news was mostly positive. Turnover in the stock market was lively at five to six million shares a day; many corporations announced record profits for the previous year; and mergers in banking and utilities continued, as did the property boom. People took comfort in the fact that the major banks appeared well capitalised. In New York, J. J. Raskob continued with his plans for the hundred-storey Empire State Building, which he described as a symbol for "a land which reached for the sky with its feet on the ground."[43] In his ambition to build the world's tallest building Raskob faced competition from his fellow speculator, Walter Chrysler, who was building his own 1,146-foot-high skyscraper.* Meanwhile, William Crapo Durant busied himself with new stock pools. In March 1930, President Hoover announced that "the worst effects of the crash upon employment will have passed during the next sixty days."[44] The following month the Dow Jones broke through the 300 barrier, up nearly 50 percent from its post-Crash low.

Yet the "suckers' rally," as it was later called, came to an end in the spring of 1930 and the market resumed its downward course until the summer of 1932, when the Dow reached a low of 41.88 on a turnover of under 400,000 shares. In the intervening period, the country's gross national product had fallen by 60 percent from its 1929 level, and unemployment had risen to twelve and a half million. Over a third of the nonagricultural workforce was unemployed.

As the nation sank into depression, the apotheosis of the businessman came to an end. In March 1932, Ivar Kreuger, the Swedish Match King, committed suicide in a Paris hotel after his business empire collapsed under the weight of debts and the discovery of Kreuger's own frauds. The following month, Samuel Insull's Middle West Utilities went into bankruptcy, and Insull fled the country (he later returned to face trial and was acquitted of fraud). The directors of the Goldman Sachs Trading Corporation were put on trial for wasting the company's assets. Charles Mitchell was forced to resign from the National City Bank, whose share price fell to 4 percent of its 1929 peak, and in 1934 he was tried for income tax evasion. William Crapo Durant was sold out by his brokers in late 1930 and declared bankrupt in 1936 with debts of nearly a million dollars. He found temporary employment washing dishes in a New Jersey restaurant. Jesse Livermore, who had made his first fortune in Wall Street during the 1907 panic, lost an estimated $32 million

*The Chrysler Building provides the classic example of what economists half jokingly call the "erection index." This predicts that the top of a bull market can be called when the height of a new building exceeds all previous records. The erection index has recently proved a reliable indicator, since the world's tallest building, the Petronas Towers in Malaysia, was completed a few months before the onset of the Asian crisis of 1997.

before being declared bankrupt in March 1934. Six years later, Livermore blew his brains out in the washroom of the Sherry-Netherland Hotel in New York. When the market touched bottom in 1932, Radio Corporation of America was selling for $2.50 a share, down from $114 three years earlier. Mike Meehan, the Radio specialist on the New York Stock Exchange, was reported to have lost $40 million in the Crash. His seats on the Exchange were put up for sale and his brokerage offices on the transatlantic liners were closed down. In 1936, Meehan entered a lunatic asylum.

Popular history holds these men, along with their countless followers, responsible for the Great Depression. At his inauguration in March 1933, Franklin Delano Roosevelt addressed the nation:

> . . . Plenty is at our doorstep, but a generous use of it languishes in the very sight of the supply. Primarily this is because rulers of the exchange of mankind's goods have failed through their own stubbornness and their own incompetence, have admitted their failure, and have abdicated. Practices of the unscrupulous money changers stand indicted in the court of public opinion, rejected by the hearts and minds of men.
>
> True they have tried, but their efforts have been cast in the pattern of an outworn tradition. Faced by the failure of credit they have proposed only lending of more money. Stripped of the lure of profit by which to induce our people to follow false leadership, they have resorted to exhortations, pleading tearfully to restore confidence. They know only the rules of a generation of self-seekers. They have no vision, and when there is no vision the people perish.
>
> The money changers have fled from their high seats in the temple of our civilisation. We may now restore that temple to the ancient truths. The measure of the restoration lies in the extent to which we apply social values more noble than mere monetary profit.

Had Roosevelt referred to "speculators" rather than "money changers" his meaning might have been clearer, but as it was a time for divine retribution, with the new President playing the role of a wrathful Christ, the biblical "money changers" had a more suitable ring. Less than a year earlier, in the summer of 1932, Roosevelt had staked his claim to presidential office on the failure of economic individualism and the responsibility of Wall Street for the Depression. Hoover was stigmatised as an unfeeling, laissez-faire, new era Republican (an attack that unfairly overlooked Hoover's unceasing, if futile, attempts to revive the economy). In the spring of 1932, the Senate Committee on Banking and Currency opened its investigation into the operations of Wall Street during the 1920s. Ferdinand Pecora, the Sicilian-born head counsel for the investigation, interrogated the prominent financiers of the 1920s and mercilessly exposed their shortcomings. Tales of pools, market manipulation, preferential treatment for insiders, shoddy treatment of outsiders, tax evasion, and excessive remuneration were revealed to the public at the moment of its greatest distress. It was Pecora's conclusion that the Exchange had become "a glorified casino where the odds were heavily weighted against the eager outsiders."[45]

During Roosevelt's first administration a series of measures were initiated to restrict the freedom under which speculators had formerly operated. Investment and commercial banking were separated by the Glass-Steagall Act of 1933. In future, the capital of commercial banks and their ability to lend would no longer fluctuate with the rise and fall of the stock market, and their customers would no longer be pushed second-rate securities. A year later, the Securities Exchange Act became law. Stock market pools, insider trading, and market manipulation were proscribed. The Federal Reserve was given the power to restrict margin loans, which were limited to a maximum of 50 percent of the collateral value of shares. The Securities and Exchange Commission was established to police the capital markets and prevent "unnecessary, unwise and destructive speculation" (in a controversial move, Roosevelt appointed Joseph Kennedy, a member of numerous stock pools, as its first chairman). Bear speculators, whose short selling was blamed by nearly everyone, including Hoover, for the collapse in market confidence, were restricted by the introduction of the "uptick" rule, which permitted short sales only after a stock had risen on its last trade.

The politics of Roosevelt's New Deal rejected the freewheeling individualism of the 1920s and replaced it with governmental direction in economic affairs. In place of market forces came federal welfare, housing and work programmes, bank deposit insurance, prices and incomes policies, minimum wage legislation, and a number of other measures. Speculation, whether in stocks, bonds, land, or commodities, was no longer to play such a key role in economic life. These largely ad hoc measures were provided with an intellectual framework by the publication of Keynes's *The General Theory of Employment, Interest and Money* in 1936. Keynes attacked the earlier prominence given to speculators and the stock market in the allocation of capital resources. He asserted that "there is no clear evidence from [recent] experience that the investment policy which is socially advantageous coincides with that which is most profitable." In perhaps the most quoted passage from the book, Keynes wrote:

> Speculators may do no harm as bubbles on a steady stream of enterprise. But the position is serious when enterprise becomes a bubble on a whirlpool of speculation. When the capital development of a country becomes a by-product of the activities of a casino, the job is likely to be ill done.[46]

In support of this statement, Keynes drew his readers' attention to the recent history of Wall Street, whose success in directing new investment towards the most profitable channels "cannot be claimed as one of the outstanding triumphs of *laissez-faire* capitalism." As a cure for the evil of speculation, he suggested a punitive capital gains tax on stock market transactions in order to force investors to take a long-term view. For the state, a body free from the "animal spirits" that characterised the speculator and thus able to consider social advantages rather than mere profit, he foresaw a greater role as an investor. In Europe, at least, the age of nationalisation beckoned.

Not all economists and historians have been convinced by this scapegoating of speculators in the wake of the Crash. Milton Friedman, the monetarist economist, has claimed that "the stock market crash in 1929 was a momentous event, but it did not produce the Great Depression and it was not a major factor in the Depression's severity."[47] Instead, Friedman (and his co-author Anna Schwartz in their *Monetary History of the United States*) blamed the Federal

Reserve for following an overly restrictive monetary policy which caused the stock of money to decline by a third between August 1929 and March 1933. According to Friedman and Schwartz, the Depression deepened after the first banking crisis in the autumn of 1930 when the Bank of the United States was (in their view) unnecessarily allowed to fail. This analysis appears to play down the degree to which the early major banking failures—of both the Detroit banks and the Bank of the United States—were largely due to their exposure to declining property prices and stock market losses at their securities affiliates. It was these failures which, in turn, triggered the general banking crisis. The experience of the Japanese banks after the bubble economy of the 1980s (considered in Chapter 9) reinforces the impression that the banking crisis of 1932 was the direct result of the preceding era of speculation.

Charles Kindleberger, viewing events from a more international perspective, saw the Depression as the result of declining commodity prices (due to endemic overproduction since the First World War) and the failure of the United States to adopt the role as international lender of the last resort to European nations. In place of loans, the Hoover administration introduced tariffs which led swiftly to retaliation, followed by competitive currency devaluations across the world. Other economic historians have blamed the Depression on the rigidities caused by the gold exchange standard which operated during the 1920s and early 1930s.[48]

Murray Rothbard, an American economist, has argued that the policies of Herbert Hoover were to blame for the Great Depression, not for being too laissez-faire as Roosevelt asserted, but because they were insufficiently so. Hoover's essential failure, Rothbard claimed, was to ignore Treasury Secretary Mellon's advice that the Crash would be beneficial if it were allowed, in his oft-quoted phrase, to "liquidate labor, liquidate stocks, liquidate the farmers, liquidate real estate."[49] In other words, Mellon suggested that the market should be left to fall until it found its own clearing level when demand would return and the economy revive. Instead, Hoover's policies prevented wages from falling at a time when asset and commodity prices were declining. This served to increase unemployment and reduce the returns on capital, thus preventing reinvestment. Rothbard concluded that the "guilt of the Great Depression must be lifted from the shoulders of the free market economy, and placed where it properly belongs: at the doors of politicians, bureaucrats, and the mass of 'enlightened' economists."[50]

As if this were not enough, Herbert Hoover blamed Franklin Roosevelt and the Democrats for deepening the public's fear and distrust throughout the election campaign of 1932 and for failing to cooperate with the outgoing administration's relief measures. Hoover has received recent support from Barrie Wigmore (in *The Crash and Its Aftermath*), who claimed that Roosevelt's speeches in 1932 and his refusal to guarantee the gold standard precipitated the public's hoarding of money and brought on the banking crisis of early 1933. Wigmore concludes that Roosevelt "as much as anyone, raised the Crash to its symbolic position as the cause of the Depression."[51]

The relationship between the Crash and the Great Depression is one of the most keenly debated issues in economic history. Because the debate is politically charged, concerning whether markets should ultimately be controlled by governments or left to their own devices, it will never be resolved to the satisfaction of all parties. As Roosevelt showed, political capital could be earned by insinuating a causal link between the Crash and the economic crisis. Subsequently, that link was used to justify the policies of the New Deal. A generation later, Professor Friedman's assertion that the stock market collapse did not cause the banking crisis or lead to the Great Depression was taken up fervidly by the Reagan Republicans who wished to overturn Roosevelt's legacy.

We find from the record of contemporaries that the Crash and the subsequent decline in asset values had a profound effect on people's expectations. In an essay entitled "Echoes from the Jazz Age" (first published in *Scribner's Magazine* in November 1931), Scott Fitzgerald claimed that the Jazz Age ended with the Crash. The "most expensive orgy in history" was over

> because the utter confidence which was its essential prop received an enormous jolt, and it didn't take long for the flimsy structure to settle earthward . . . It was borrowed time anyhow—the whole upper tenth of the nation living with the insouciance of grand ducs and the casualness of call girls.[52]

As the market crashed, the happy vision of the future dispelled, leaving the American people uncertain and unprepared for the difficult economic conditions of the early 1930s. In *Only Yesterday*, Frederick Lewis Allen saw the Depression as a "profound psychological reaction from the exuberance of 1929":

> Prosperity is more than an economic condition; it is a state of mind. The Big Bull Market had been more than the climax of a cycle in American mass thinking and mass emotion. There was hardly a man or woman in the country whose attitude toward life had not been affected by it in some degree and was not now affected by the sudden and brutal shattering of hope. With the Big Bull Market gone and prosperity going, Americans were soon to find themselves living in an altered world which called for new adjustments, new ideas, new habits of thought, and a new order of values.[53]

During the late 1920s, American economic reality had become dependent on a precarious vision of the future. After the Crash, when every tenet of the new era philosophy was shown to be false, Americans lost that confidence in the future which is necessary for the successful operation of the economic system. As George Orwell observed, "poverty annihilates the future." When asset values declined, causing havoc in the banking system, a psychology of fear replaced the optimism of the previous decade. Perhaps, as some claimed, the Roaring Twenties were morally degenerate years deserving of a biblical visitation; but they were also a period when people exhibited a capacity for dreaming, a faith in the future, an entrepreneurial appetite for risk, and a belief in individual freedom. These profoundly American traits took a severe knocking in October 1929 and appeared to be extinguished during the Great Depression. They would return.

POSTSCRIPT: THE NEW PARADIGM, A 1920S REVIVAL ON WALL STREET

During the 1990s, the United States experienced a bull market remarkably similar to that of the 1920s. The Dow Jones Industrial

Average rose from a low of 2,365 in 1990 to reach 10,000 in March 1999, a gain of more than 320 percent. As in the 1920s, the recent rise in speculation was initially stimulated by low interest rates set by the Federal Reserve during the early 1990s.* The rapid expansion of information technology provided the stimulus to economic growth in the 1990s, just as the motorcar did in the 1920s. The profitability of American corporations was similarly enhanced by the inability of unions to push through real wage increases. Once again workers maintained their consumption by purchasing goods on credit—an indulgence which led a million Americans to declare themselves bankrupt in 1997.

Although the presidency was held by a Democrat throughout the 1990s bull market, the Republican control of Congress and the shift of the "New Democrats" to the political centre have meant that the policies emanating from the White House resembled more closely those of Calvin Coolidge than those of Franklin Roosevelt. Lax enforcement of antitrust laws has facilitated a series of corporate mergers on a far greater scale than that experienced in the 1920s. During the same period, the separation of investment and commercial banking enshrined in the Glass-Steagall Act of 1933 was under siege.

By the middle of the 1990s, the "cult of equity" a slight rephrasing of the 1920s "cult of common stocks," was clearly in evidence. Approximately fifty million Americans held shares, and the stock market was being discussed everywhere: in bars, golf courses, clubs, gyms, beauty salons, and on television chat shows. Mutual funds were featured on the front cover of *Playboy* magazine. A primary school in Florida launched a new course entitled "Material Wealth and the Stock Market." Within six months the children's model portfolios were up by a third and they all dreamed of becoming stockbrokers. An investment seminar held in Las Vegas by Louis Rukeyser, the presenter of *Wall Street Week* on public television,

*James Grant calls the Fed's lowering of interest rates in the early 1990s "the miracle cure of American credit." He argues that "the bull market [from 1991 onwards] became the most important financial fact in America, more important than the federal funds rate or the Federal Reserve Board's forecast of the gross domestic product." (See Grant, *Trouble with Prosperity*, p. 193.)

attracted nearly ten thousand people (on his show Rukeyser hailed investors who maintained "the Faith"). The business channel, CNBC, drew the fastest-growing audience in America. By 1998, there were over 37,000 investment clubs (up from 6,000 at the beginning of the decade) where amateur stock market players gathered to exchange ideas and swap tips.

The explosion of investment trusts during the 1920s was exceeded by the rapid growth of mutual funds in the 1990s. Between 1990 and the first quarter of 1998, equity mutual funds attracted over a trillion dollars from American investors. In 1990, there were 1,100 mutual funds in operation. Seven years later, nearly 6,000 mutual funds competed to attract investors' capital. Inflows into mutual funds became the mainstay of the bull market. During 1996, a total of $221.6 billion was invested in U.S. equity funds, with a further $231 billion invested the following year. By the end of 1997, the total assets of U.S. mutual funds had risen to $4.2 trillion, a sum roughly equal to the assets of the banking system. Just as in the 1920s, it was argued that private investment in shares by people saving for retirement would provide a long-term support for the stock market.

The revival of faith in the stock market was accompanied by the observation that shares had provided superior investment returns compared to bonds since the 1950s. In April 1996, on the occasion of the hundredth anniversary of the establishment of the Dow Jones Industrial Average, the *Wall Street Journal* reported that in 98 percent of all twenty-year periods since 1925 shares had outperformed bonds. This was, of course, exactly the same message that E. L. Smith popularised in the 1920s. One fund manager described the stock market as "a very nice casino in which everyone can get to go home with a return of 10 percent *after* the house take."[54] Such a sentiment appeared to echo the claim of Will Payne, who argued, in the January 1929 issue of *World's Work,* that the difference between gambling and investment was that while a gambler could only profit at the expense of someone else, with stock market investment everyone was a winner.[55]

The belief that the stock market would invariably produce the greatest returns led investors to purchase shares regardless of price (the market's price-earnings ratio rose to a historic high of more than 28 times earnings in the spring of 1998). The only financial risk in the 1990s bull market was to leave money idle in a bank account while the stock market notched up gains of over 20 percent, year after year.* The rising market inflated investors' expectations to irrational levels. On the eve of the market correction in October 1997, a broker's poll found mutual fund investors expecting an average 34 percent annual return over the next ten years, an expectation which if realised would send the Dow Jones to 151,000 and the total U.S. stock market capitalisation to 1,500 percent of national income.

The American investor of the 1990s had many qualities in common with his 1920s predecessor. Although the use of leverage was less conspicuous than in the 1920s, margin debt increased from around $30 billion in 1990 to $154 billion in July 1998. A number of ploys were used to skirt the Federal Reserve's restriction on margin loans to 50 percent of the collateral value of the shares: speculators slowed down the repayments of their mortgages or took out home equity loans to finance stock purchases; they bought shares on credit cards and availed themselves of the futures markets where no margin regulations were applied (the Chicago Mercantile Exchange obligingly created a "mini S&P" contract that required a deposit of only $3,000). Several finance companies used the futures markets to hedge loans they made to private investors. James Grant, editor of *Grant's Interest Rate Observer*, discovered one company, First Security Capital of San Diego, providing 90 percent loan-to-value margin loans with a minimum loan of $100,000 (since First Security was neither a bank nor a broker-dealer, its margin loans were not controlled by the Federal Reserve).[56]

The 1990s American investor, just like his earlier counterpart, convinced himself that he was buying shares for the long term rather than speculating for quick profits. "'Buy and hold,'" observed James Grant, "have replaced 'I love you' as the most popular three words in

*This notion was succinctly expressed by Ian Rushbrook, a British fund manager: "It is always dangerous to be out of equities, because in the longer term equities always rise. In equity investing, the perceived risk is that your equities will fall. The real risk is being out of equities."

the English language."[57] In both periods, investors saw each market decline as an opportunity to "buy into the dip." As a result, every downturn was quickly reversed, supplying the bull market with an aura of invincibility. This tendency reached its apogee on Monday, 27 October 1997, when the Dow Jones fell by over 7 percent on fears generated by the collapse of the Asian economies a couple of months earlier. Employing the same language as Herbert Hoover used after the 1929 crash, U.S. Treasury Secretary Robert Rubin reassured investors that the fundamentals of the American economy were sound. On Tuesday, long lines were seen outside New York brokers' offices; however, they were queuing to *buy* more shares rather than sell. That day the market rose by more than 5 percent on a record New York Stock Exchange turnover of 1.2 billion shares. Within six months the Dow had climbed by over a quarter from its low of 27 October and the S&P 500 index was up over 50 percent on the last twelve months.

The 1990s bull market was accompanied by the reappearance of a new era ideology similar to that of the 1920s. Known as the "new paradigm," or the "Goldilocks economy" (like the porridge in the fairy tale it was neither too hot nor too cold), the theory suggested that the control of inflation by the Federal Reserve, the decline in the federal deficit, the opening of global markets, the restructuring of corporate America, and the widespread use of information technology to control inventory stock levels had combined to do away with the business cycle. Point for point, this was a reiteration of the new era philosophy of Irving Fisher's day.

The new paradigm made its first appearance in the middle of the decade. In late 1995, a Salomon Brothers analyst named David Shulman produced a report entitled "1996: Stock Market Bubble or Paradigm Shift?" in which he argued that the decline in inflation had caused "the third fundamental shift in stock market valuation in forty years." Abby Joseph Cohen, chief investment strategist for Goldman Sachs, became the best-known advocate of the new paradigm, the Irving Fisher of her day. Appearing frequently on television shows, on magazine covers, and in the newspapers, she was hailed as the "guru" who had first identified the outlines of the latest new era. Ralph Acampora, chief technician of Prudential Securities, was another prominent spokesman for the new paradigm. "It makes all the sense in the world that our stock market should go up, because we have more confidence in our way of life," he told *Fortune* magazine in August 1997.

As the rising stock market served as a palliative to the scandals that dogged Clinton's presidency, the new paradigm was warmly received in Washington.* In February 1997, a member of the Clinton administration was quoted in the *Herald Tribune* as saying that "there is no inevitable economic cycle and we have found in a recent study by the Council of Economic Advisers that cycles don't die of old age."[58] A month later, President Clinton himself was moved to observe that the U.S. economy was performing so well that the concept of the business cycle may have been effectively repealed. In June 1997, the *New Republic* reported, under the headline "Bust Busting: The End of Economic History," that "top officials at the Treasury Department believe that, with the proper mix of policies and the absence of external shocks, the United States can prolong the current expansion indefinitely."[59]

The attitude of Alan Greenspan, the Federal Reserve Chairman, towards the new paradigm has been more difficult to discern. Greenspan seems to have hedged his bets. When he observed "irrational exuberance" among investors in December 1996, the stock market fell 2½ percent. On other occasions, he denied that the business cycle had been repealed and questioned whether stocks were not overpriced. Yet when asked to account for the long period of economic growth, Greenspan fell back on new paradigm explanations, claiming that information technology had "enhanced the stability of business operations" and that America was moving "beyond history." *Business Week* concluded that the Fed chairman had become an "avant-garde advocate of the New Economy." Unlike his 1920s predecessors, Greenspan saw no need to stem the

---

*Just as the 1929 crash and its aftermath destroyed Hoover's presidency, so the ascent of the U.S. stock market, from late 1994 to the summer of 1998, made Clinton's reputation. In late 1994, with the S&P index at around 450, fewer than 40 percent of those polled approved of Clinton's presidential performance. By the spring of 1998, with the S&P index approaching 1,200, Clinton's approval rating had risen to nearly 70 percent. Yet when the market dropped in August 1998, Clinton's approval rating fell back to 60 percent. By October 1998, both Clinton and the market had recovered. (Polls conducted by the *New York Times*.)

rise of speculation with either higher interest rates or stern warnings. As the guardian of the bull market, Greenspan's reappointment to office in 1996 was greeted with the same fervour as Treasury Secretary Mellon's in 1929.

The most striking similarity between the 1920s and 1990s bull markets is the notion that traditional measures of stock valuation had become obsolete. Once again it was argued that an investment in the stock market helped retain purchasing power during inflationary periods and that management was becoming more responsive to shareholders' interests. Abby Joseph Cohen of Goldman Sachs claimed that a longer business cycle and lower inflation justified an upward valuation in stock prices. In their *Securities Analysis,* Benjamin Graham and David Dodds wrote that "instead of judging the market price by established standards of value, the new era [of the 1920s] based its standards of value upon the market price." In similar fashion, consultants in the 1990s invented a concept named "market value added," which simply measured the difference between the market value of the firm and the amount of capital tied up in it. The higher the "market value added," the greater the firm is deemed to be worth.

The net asset value of a company—the value of its factories, machinery, and suchlike—became the most despised of traditional valuation tools. Dividend yields, which slipped to a historic low of less than 1½ percent, were also dismissed as irrelevant. At times even the price-earnings ratio, a measure favourable to speculative values, has looked too conservative. Discounting future cash flows was used to justify any price for fast-growing technology companies. In late October 1996, a headline in the *Investors Business Daily,* a stock market daily which published relative strength figures, asked and answered a question that vexed many minds: "Overvalued? Not If the Stock Keeps on Rising."[60]

The new paradigm, or new economics, of the 1990s provided the intellectual underpinning for the greatest bull market in American history. When stock prices fell sharply in October 1997, Abby Joseph Cohen of Goldman Sachs saved the day by advising her clients to increase their holding of shares. James Grant has suggested that the reappearance of the new era ideology was a sign that "markets make opinions not the other way round." In other words, the new paradigm ideology is simply a product of the bull market. As long as investors maintain their faith in a new era and ignore dissonant information, then stocks will continue to rise. In the short run, a rising market serves to cover up weaknesses in the economy. Consumers spend their stock market gains and ignore their rising debts, companies issue new shares or bonds to purchase other companies or finance capital expenditure, and governments enjoy rising tax receipts as the economy prospers. In this way the new era analysis becomes something of a self-fulfilling prophecy.

It has been estimated that between early 1990 and the spring of 1998 the rising U.S. stock market boosted household wealth by around $6 trillion. Capital gains realised from the sale of shares reached $184 billion in 1997. Profits on investments have supported the growth of consumer expenditure, which has risen faster than wages and enabled the savings rate to decline until it turned negative in 1998. Rising receipts from capital gains tax, $44 billion in 1997, also helped to produce a federal budget surplus in 1998. Escalating share prices encouraged the establishment of new businesses and boosted capital expenditure. The stock market was hailed as the "greatest wealth-creator America has ever seen." According to one analyst, it had become "a perpetual motion machine" (an unconscious echo of the legendary bubble company of 1720), in which every share price rise generated further rises. Yet in the past a point has always been reached where both speculation and credit arrive at the limits of their expansion. At that moment the business cycle reappears with a vengeance, the perpetual motion machine begins rotating in another direction, and the new era is consigned to history.

CHAPTER 8

COWBOY CAPITALISM: FROM BRETTON WOODS TO MICHAEL MILKEN

There is no way you can buck the market.

Margaret Thatcher (1988)

The foundation of the postwar economic system was laid in the summer of 1944 when delegates of the Allied powers (the British party led by Keynes himself) met at the Mount Washington Hotel in Bretton Woods, New Hampshire. Instead of reviving the old gold standard, they agreed that foreign currencies should be fixed in relation to the dollar, with the dollar convertible into gold at $35 an ounce. As the new system depended for its success on the control of capital movements between countries, it was marked by a deep antipathy towards the currency speculator. Echoing Roosevelt, the American Treasury Secretary, Henry Morgenthau, hoped that Bretton Woods would "drive the usurious moneylenders from the temple of international finance."*

*The freedom of the speculator was to be severely restricted by the Bretton Woods system. Keynes argued that in order to halt unwanted currency flows, "we [i.e., the authorities] may have to go so far as opening the mail." (Richard N. Gardner, *Sterling-Dollar Diplomacy in Current Perspective,* New York, 1980, pp. 73–76.)

For the next thirty years the speculator remained a figure of public obloquy, almost indistinguishable from the wartime black marketeer. In early 1946, after the market in grain futures was curtailed owing to shortages, President Truman declared that "grain prices . . . should not be subject to the greed of speculators who gamble on what may lie ahead of our commodity markets."[1] Truman denounced grain speculators as "merchants of human misery."[2] Such sentiments were even shared by the young Mrs. Thatcher, who announced to the House of Commons during the 1961 budget debate: "It is the speculators in shares that we want to get at . . . The person who is making a business of buying and selling shares, not to hold them for their income-producing properties, but to live on the profit he makes from transactions."[3]

When governments found their formal currency arrangements disintegrating, the speculator became a convenient scapegoat for the failure of policy. Before the war, Hitler had blamed the inflation and deflation of the Weimar Republic on foreign currency speculators, while both Lenin and Stalin cursed speculators for the Soviet Union's economic woes. Now the leaders of the so-called Free World joined in similar denunciations. During the Suez Crisis of 1956, the future prime minister Harold Wilson lashed out at speculating Swiss bankers, "the little gnomes in Zurich" in his celebrated phrase. The gnomes had their revenge in 1967, forcing Wilson's Labour government to devalue sterling. Four years later, when Nixon finally suspended the convertibility of the dollar into gold, thus bringing an end to the Bretton Woods system, he also condemned speculators: "They thrive on crises, they help to create them."[4]

Even in the period of largely floating exchange rates since 1971, intemperate attacks on currency speculators by politicians have continued. When Britain was once again forced to devalue its currency and leave the Exchange Rate Mechanism in September 1992, Lord Jenkins, a former Chancellor of the Exchequer, denounced the "predatory packs of salivating speculators"; to which the French finance minister, Michel Sapin, added that "during the Revolution such people were known as *agioteurs,* and they were beheaded."[5] During the Asian crisis of 1997, the prime minister of Malaysia, Dr. Mahathir Mohamad, described speculators as "ferocious animals," whose trade was "unnecessary, unproductive and totally immoral." In a more sinister fashion, he struck out personally at George Soros, the hedge fund manager, claiming that behind the speculators lay a "Jewish agenda" to return the developing nations to colonial status. The Malaysian government threatened to treat currency speculation as a capital offence, banned short sales on the Kuala Lumpur Stock Exchange, and later introduced currency controls.

In part, the immediate postwar attacks on speculators and their trade reflected a profound change in the attitude to moneymaking and the pursuit of profit. In an essay entitled "Economic Possibilities for Our Grandchildren" (first published in 1930), Keynes imagined a world in which increasing prosperity and material security would finally do away with the profit motive. During the period of strong and stable growth enjoyed by Western economies in the 1950s, it appeared that this vision might be realised. In *The Quest for Wealth*, a history of man's acquisitiveness published in 1956, Robert Heilbroner asserted that moneymaking in the current age was no longer esteemed:

> Opulence, the adulation of money-makers, and the wish for great wealth have given way, in part at least, to a new set of values: the camouflage of wealth, the contempt of "mere" money-makers, and even a certain disdain or disinterest in the goal of wealth itself.*

Heilbroner ascribed the anti-Mammonism of the period to the experience of the Great Depression, which represented not merely an economic failure but "the bankruptcy of the philosophic foundation of an age."[6] In the postwar world, the businessman was no longer flattered and admired as he had been in the 1920s. Instead, he became the dull, reliable, colourless figure satirised by Sloan Wilson as the "man in the gray flannel suit." This change of style was accompanied by a shift in corporate priorities. Other goals,

*According to Heilbroner, "one conclusion seems clear: if the acquisitive spirit of the pre-Depression days died of any one illness, it was from overexposure to the chill climate of a starkly acquisitive society." (Robert Heilbroner, *The Quest for Wealth*, New York, 1956, pp. 213, 221.)

such as stability, continuity, and responsibility towards employees and the community, predominated over the simple profit motive. According to Heilbroner, the individual quest for wealth had been replaced by a corporate ideal in which individuals took only a small share of their corporation's earnings, enjoying instead the prestige and security of employment with an established company. In the 1950s, these changes appeared so self-evident and enduring that Heilbroner concluded his study by pondering whether the further accumulation of wealth in the near future might bring a new economic motivation to displace Adam Smith's "invisible hand."

THE FINANCIAL REVOLUTION

When President Nixon suspended the convertibility of the dollar into gold on 15 August 1971, he brought to an end the Bretton Woods system of the previous quarter of a century, and ushered in a new era in the history of speculation.* Although the first financial revolution of the late seventeenth century had seen the expansion of paper debt circulating as money, all values remained ultimately tethered to gold. Gold represented the antithesis of speculative values. Whenever speculation got out of hand and a financial crisis appeared, everyone sought refuge in the precious metal. Only John Law, the land-bank projector and progenitor of the Mississippi Bubble, realised that the value of all money, including gold, rested ultimately on a consensus. After Law introduced a paper currency into France in 1720, Lord Stair, the English ambassador to Paris, commenting on Law's recent conversion to Catholicism (undertaken so that he could assume the official post of Controller General of Finances), wrote: "There can be no doubt of Law's catholicity since he has . . . proved transubstantiation by changing paper into money." For Stair and his contemporaries, Law's paper money was an act of faith, as bold as the belief in the miracle of the Eucharist. Finally in 1971, a year that coincidentally marked the

*The Bretton Woods system was not formally pronounced dead until the collapse of the Smithsonian Agreement in 1973.

three hundredth anniversary of John Law's birth, his vision was at last realised. The transition from *Credo* to credit was complete.

After the end of the Bretton Woods system, money became only a figment of the imagination, weightless and ethereal. In this new world where all monetary values were in flux, speculation—"the self-adjustment of society to the probable" in Oliver Wendell Holmes's phrase—was destined to play a greater role. In the past, the suspension of gold convertibility had been associated with uncontrolled eruptions of speculation (for instance, in France in 1720 and in the United States in the 1860s). During the turmoil surrounding the collapse of Bretton Woods, this was overlooked. Henceforth, all currency values would be a reflection of their perceived future values: the present would be as much determined by the future as the future by the present. And the grand arbiter of this confusing new system was the speculator.

One person quick to grasp the significance of these events was Walter Wriston, the head of Citicorp, who declared that "the information standard has replaced the gold standard as the basis of world finance."* A new financial revolution necessary to accommodate this momentous change was facilitated by advances in information technology. From 1969, details of banks' bond trading was provided by the Telerate machine, which became the electronic marketplace for U.S. Treasury bonds. Four years later, the British news agency Reuters introduced its Monitor Money Rates service, which created an electronic twenty-four-hour global marketplace for foreign currencies. Over the next few years, the computerisation of financial markets continued apace.†

Most commentators viewed advances in information technology as a boon. If markets were inherently efficient, they would become even more so when supplied with better information. They might

*Wriston added that in the new global financial marketplace, "information about money has become almost as important as money itself." (Adrian Hamilton, *The Financial Revolution*, London, 1986, p. 30.)

†Important advances in financial communications in this period include the introduction of automated trading on Nasdaq, the American over-the-counter stock exchange, in 1970; the establishment of Bloomberg's electronic bond information service in 1980, and the creation in 1983 of the Clearing Houses Automated Payments System (CHAPS) to settle monetary payments between banks.

even become rather dull, like a reliable motorcar.* In fact, there is little historical evidence to suggest that improvements in communications create docile financial markets or better-informed investment behaviour.† If anything, the opposite appears to be the case. In the past, the wider availability of financial information and improvements in communications have tended to attract impulsive new players to the speculative game: the first generation of daily newspapers stimulated the South Sea Bubble, the new "money market" columns of the British newspapers contributed to the mining mania of 1825, railways facilitated railway speculations in the 1840s, just as the ticker tape assisted stock market gambling in the Gilded Age and radio programmes in the 1920s excited a later generation of speculators.

More recently, the Internet has brought the stock market into the home, where it has thrived. Mobile phones, handheld trading devices, and on-line brokerage accounts have enabled investors to trade from anywhere in the world. This had led to the appearance of hordes of "day traders," amateur speculators who operate mostly from their homes, using their computers to access the cheap share-dealing services provided by on-line brokerages (they are called "day traders" because they close their positions at the end of each trading day).‡ By the summer of 1998, five million Americans had accounts with Internet discount brokerages and around a million of them were day traders. Average turnover on these on-line accounts was twelve times heavier than at conventional brokerages. Some traders reportedly carried out a thousand trades a day.

*In 1972, Donald Regan, head of Merrill Lynch and future Treasury Secretary, forecast that "by 1980 Wall Street will have lost lots of its distinctive flavor . . . The Street will be the scene of a lot less colorful action than we have witnessed in the past few years . . . When all the electronic gear is in place, will we still need a New York Stock Exchange?" (John Brooks, *The Go-Go Years*, p. 356.)

†As James Grant writes, "there is no observed improvement in the emotional stability of the average investor, notwithstanding dramatic advances in financial literacy or in the sophistication of computer software." (*Mr. Market*, p. xiv.)

‡Day traders also frequented the dozens of "day-trading firms" that sprang up across the country. These latter-day bucket shops required a minimum initial stake of only $25,000, which was often raised by taking out a home equity loan. An alternative stock market, called the Electronic Communications Network, enabled day traders to avoid the minimum transaction requirements at the older stock exchanges.

Because the Internet allows people to conceal their identity, the information revolution has generated an extraordinary amount of fraud, mostly of a low-level nature. Scattered across the worldwide web are literally hundreds of thousands of get-rich-quick investment scams.* Behind a veil of anonymity, crooked promoters "pump and dump" stocks through on-line investment forums. Perhaps more worrying than the appearance of fraud is the unsettling effect the Internet has had on investors' behaviour. Described by its early advocates as an "affinity group," the Internet has become a forum for herdlike speculation. Private traders spur each other on with messages posted on Internet bulletin boards. In some cases, on-line investors have developed unhealthy obsessions with individual stocks.† "Momentum investment," the mindless practice of buying and selling stocks as they rise and fall with the market, is said to be a sign of investors' reaction to "information overload."‡

Wall Street has joined with Silicon Valley to produce an investment argot for a virtual world: a world of *momos* (momentum stocks), *P & D* (pump and dump), *head fakes* (large traders creating

---

*E-mail facilitates the distribution of thousands of fraudulent schemes (a technique known as "spamming") which frequently offer investment returns of 100 percent on purportedly "risk-free" investments in fields such as wireless cable technology, bank securities, eel farms, etc.

†A classic case of investor obsession stimulated by the information revolution is provided by the run-up of Iomega, a computer hard disk manufacturer, in the spring of 1996. Iomega was the favoured stock of the "Motley Fool," a popular on-line investment forum, with its own dedicated bulletin board where "Iomegans," as they called themselves, could chat endlessly about their favourite company and its share price. An extraordinary cyber-cheerleading evolved: "Go, IOMEGA, Go! Go! Go!" ran one message observed by the author. Some Iomegans confessed to thinking of the company day and night, and a few invested their entire pension savings in its stock. A fierce battle developed on the bulletin board between the stock's bulls (or "believers") and bears, who were accused of spreading "untruths." Initially, the bulls were victorious. Iomega's share price went from under $2 in the spring of 1995 to over $27 a year later, on a price-earnings ratio of 169, at which point the company's market capitalisation exceeded $5 billion. The bubble soon burst, and Iomega's stock plummeted. By late 1998, it was trading below $4.

‡By the end of 1998, on-line day traders were estimated to account for up to 15 percent of the dollar volume of the Nasdaq exchange. Their speculations were largely responsible for the extravagant run-up of Internet stocks at the end of the year. Most day traders paid little attention to fundamentals. Sometimes they appeared not to know which stocks they were actually buying: When Xoom.com (stock symbol XMCM) was floated in late 1998, the stock of Zoom Telephonics (ZOOM) rose 27 percent on fifteen times normal daily turnover. And when shares

the illusion of a stock movement), *gapping up* (stock rises sharply), *scared money* (desperate traders closing their positions at the end of the day), *grinding* (taking small profits from many trades), *jiggles* (volatile stocks), and *noise* (disagreements among traders). The cyber-marketplace of the late twentieth century, with its *bashers* (bears) and *hypsters* (bulls), closely resembles the coffeehouses of Exchange Alley three centuries earlier, with their *bubblers, sharpers,* and *cullies.* The people and their practices remain the same, only the language and technology are new.

The lack of a positive relationship between improved information and financial sagacity was most evident in Japan during the "bubble economy" of the 1980s, when a nation of "information junkies," awash with financial data, nevertheless made some of the worst investment decisions in history (see the following chapter). Nor is it clear that advances in communications have produced any improvement in the performance of professional investors. Speedier communications have created conditions for greater feedback and more trend-following in the financial markets which offset any improvements in the operational efficiency of the markets. Self-fulfilling currency crises, provoked by panicking traders, have become the norm of the 1990s. The speedier the communication, the faster the contagion spreads.

THE REVIVAL OF THE LIBERAL ECONOMIC IDEOLOGY

Bretton Woods, Keynes's last significant achievement before his death in 1946, had failed for practical reasons.* By the early

in Ticketmaster (TMCS) soared 300 percent on their first day's trading, shares in an unrelated building maintenance and security firm, Temco Services (TMCO), climbed 150 percent.

The reckless activities of day traders caused concern. William Hambrecht, co-founder of Hambrecht & Quist, the investment bank, feared that they had introduced "mob rule" to the exchanges. On 27 January 1999, Arthur Levitt, Chairman of the Securities and Exchange Commission, remarked: "I believe that investors need to remember the investment basics and not allow the ease and speed with which they can trade to lull them either into a false sense of security or encourage them to trade too quickly or too often."

*The system had been unable to cope with structural trade deficits and the recurrent need by certain countries to appreciate or depreciate their currencies.

1970s, however, "Keynesianism" as a body of economic thought was also under sustained attack. For two decades, Milton Friedman, an economics professor at the University of Chicago, had been battling against Keynesian orthodoxy. Resurrecting the economic liberalism of the nineteenth century under the new guise of "monetarism," he argued that the market was fundamentally a self-correcting mechanism, and that government attempts to interfere with its operation—whether by introducing price controls to curb inflation or by compelling management to influence the level of unemployment—were doomed to failure. In *Free to Choose*, a popular introduction to free-market ideology that Friedman wrote with his wife Rose, he contended that all government intervention, however well-intentioned, had harmful side effects. For Friedman, markets were the best way to distribute information and provide incentives, regardless of the inequities that might emerge. In a 1973 interview with *Playboy* magazine, Friedman boldly asserted that all societies were structured on greed: "The problem of social organisation," he claimed, "is how to set up an arrangement under which greed will do the least harm; capitalism is that kind of system."

Friedman not only defended the speculator against the charge of causing the Great Depression; he was also highly sympathetic to the speculator's economic role. This much-maligned figure sought out future economic developments and fed them through to the current prices, thereby preventing shortages and contributing to the efficient distribution of scarce resources. Like the insurer, the speculator was prepared to assume some of the inevitable risks of the capitalist process. If he was motivated by a desire for personal profit, so much the better. In an essay entitled "In Defense of Destabilizing Speculation" published in 1960, Friedman claimed that speculation was castigated by economists because of "a natural bias of the academic student against gambling."[7] He suggested that speculation was unlikely to have harmful economic side effects, since so-called destabilising speculators (who sold when prices were low and bought when they were high) would inevitably lose money, while the counterparties would gain at the speculators' expense. A process of social Darwinism would eventually eradicate the destabilising speculator.* For Friedman, speculation in the futures market was a zero-sum activity which at worst supplied gaming activities to those who required the service.

Friedman was the most prominent of a group of American academics whose work contributed to the revival of economic liberalism. The work of other economists, interested specifically in the operation of financial markets, joined together to form a new body of economic thought, known as the Efficient Market Hypothesis (EMH). Exponents of the efficient market maintained that investors are rational agents seeking to optimise their wealth and that stock prices move randomly since at any moment they contain all information relevant to their price (i.e., they are only moved by new information, which, by its nature, is random).† While Friedman revived discarded nostrums such as the quantity theory of money, the efficient marketers resurrected ideas concerning equilibrium in the financial markets that harked back to Adam Smith's assimilation of Newton's theory of equilibrium (the "invisible hand" being the analogue of the "divine watchmaker"), and to Leibnitz's notion of the immanence of rationality in the world. During the 1970s, the Efficient Market Hypothesis spread throughout American universities and business schools, while businesses and banks began applying financial techniques founded upon its assumptions.‡ By the end of the decade, it had become the working

*This argument appears flawed. The activity of speculators may be destabilising, even if the speculators themselves are bankrupted by their actions. The failure of numerous Japanese speculators in the early 1990s, and the bad debts they have bequeathed the banking system, points to such a conclusion. Since in the long run a new generation will replace the failed speculators, the "survival of the fittest" argument is not applicable.

†Professor Paul Samuelson of the Massachusetts Institute of Technology, who had dabbled unsuccessfully in stock warrants, interpreted his lack of investment success as a sign of efficient pricing in the market: "the unpredictability of future prices from past and present prices is the sign not of the failure of economic law, but the triumph of economic law after competition has done its best." (Peter Bernstein, *Capital Ideas*, New York, 1992, p. 117.)

‡They include the Capital Asset Pricing Model, which "scientifically" calculates the required rate of return on investments, and the Black-Scholes model for pricing options, introduced in 1972 by two economics professors, Fischer Black and Myron Scholes.

ideology of financial capitalism—"holy writ" in the words of Warren Buffett.*

The efficient market school of economists (many of whose members received Nobel Prizes) were highly sympathetic to speculators. If markets were efficient and in constant equilibrium, and if price movements were always random, then the activities of speculators could be neither irrational in motivation nor destabilising in effect. Such a conclusion required the historiography of speculation to be rewritten, leading to a denial of the existence of "irrational bubbles" and replacing them, as we have seen, with the tendentious notion of the "rational bubble." While Friedman dismissed the idea that speculative excess caused the economic collapse of the 1930s, several economists of a historical bent attempted to show that the great speculative manias, such as the Tulip Mania and the South Sea Bubble, were mere legends. Insofar as share prices rose during these periods, they argued, it was for very good reasons.

Not everyone was convinced.[8] As Warren Buffett pointed out, "observing correctly that the market was *frequently* efficient, they [the efficient marketers] went on to conclude incorrectly that it was *always* efficient. The difference between the two propositions is night and day."† Paradoxically, the widespread acceptance of the Efficient Market Hypothesis may have served to make the markets

*Some commentators, including George Soros, have found the workings of the efficient market theorists, with their complex equations, to be more like those of the medieval Scholastics calculating the number of angels able to stand on the head of a pin than like those of the eighteenth-century rationalists (*Crisis of Global Capitalism*, p.128). Lewis Lapham complains that these "learned gentlemen speak and write an unintelligible language not unlike church Latin . . . Their function is ceremonial." (*Money and Class in America: Notes and Observations on the Civil Religion*, New York, 1989, p. 251.)

†If share price movements are truly random then it is impossible for an investor to outperform the stock market consistently. For this reason, supporters of the Efficient Market Hypothesis advise investment in stock index funds. Warren Buffett's phenomenal investment returns over nearly half a century have perplexed the efficient marketers. They argue that Buffett is an anomaly, a "three sigma event," so statistically abnormal as to be discounted from their theories. To this Buffett replied that he should endow a university chair to teach the Efficient Market Hypothesis: "What could be more advantageous in an intellectual contest—whether it be bridge, chess or stock selection—than to have opponents who have been taught that thinking is a waste of energy." (Berkshire Hathaway, Annual Report, 1985.)

less efficient: in the Panglossian world of efficient markets, investors were told that, theoretically, it was not possible to pay too much for financial assets. As a result, they were encouraged to bid up prices to unsustainable levels.*

THE DERIVATIVES REVOLUTION

Out of this new age of paper money, economic liberalism, and information technology came forth a flowering of financial creativity as profound and far-reaching as the earlier financial revolution at the turn of the eighteenth century. Nowhere was this activity more in evidence than in the field of financial derivatives. As we have seen, a derivative is simply a security created by contract which *derives* its value from an underlying asset, such as a share or bond. In the form of futures and options on shares and commodities, derivatives are as old as capitalism itself. Because derivatives, such as share options, require smaller down payments (normally around 5 percent for a three-month option) than the purchase of a "real" share, they were traditionally believed to encourage speculation. This prejudice was reflected in numerous government attempts to outlaw the derivatives trade, such as the Dutch ban on futures in 1609 and Sir John Barnard's Act passed by the British Parliament in 1734. In the new era of economic liberalism, however, the old stigma was removed and derivatives emerged at the forefront of financial innovation.

In 1967, Milton Friedman attempted to bet against sterling prior to Britain's forced devaluation, but was turned down by the Chicago banks on the grounds that his action would encourage speculation.

*In *Capital Ideas*, Peter Bernstein describes meeting with Myron Scholes, a leading EMH exponent, during the "nifty-fifty" boom of 1972. Bernstein asked Scholes whether the market was overvalued. Scholes denied such a possibility: if investors found the rate of return poor, he argued, they would refuse to buy stocks. Scholes had no belief in the ability of the individual to know more about the future than all the informed, rational investors. (In fact, at the time the market was severely overvalued and subsequently went into a steep decline.) This story is reminiscent of the old joke about two economists walking down the street. One observes a dollar bill on the sidewalk, but the other denies its existence, arguing forcefully that if the note had been there someone (i.e., a rational person) would already have picked it up.

Afterwards Friedman related his frustrating experience in print. His article attracted the attention of Leo Melamed, president of the Chicago Mercantile Exchange (known familiarly as the "Merc"), the smaller of the city's two agricultural futures markets.* Given Friedman's consistent advocacy of laissez-faire, his defence of speculation, and his distrust of government regulation, it was not surprising that Melamed, a fanatical believer in free markets, should seek him out to assist with plans to create the most radical futures contract in history.

After the collapse of Bretton Woods, Melamed approached Friedman and asked him to write a paper justifying the creation of a market for currency futures. The professor obliged, demanding a payment of $5,000 for his services (he is reported as saying, "I'm a capitalist, remember that").[9] Friedman had long argued against capital controls, in favour of floating exchange rates and the free movement of capital. In his paper for Melamed, entitled "The Need for Futures Markets in Foreign Currencies," he claimed that currency futures would have a stabilising effect on exchange rates and encourage the development "of other financial activities in this country."[10] Melamed's money was well spent. Permission was granted by the U.S. Treasury and Federal Reserve to establish the new International Money Market at the Merc, which opened in May 1972. The financial revolution had begun. Less than a year later, the Chicago Board of Trade opened a new exchange for trading share options.† Other derivatives markets opened during this period included gold futures in 1975, Government National Mortgage Association (Ginnie Mae) futures in 1975, Treasury bond futures in 1976, crude oil futures in 1978, and currency options in 1982.

---

*While the Chicago Board of Trade had dominated the massive corn market since the middle of the nineteenth century, the Merc was left to handle smaller scraps, trading futures in eggs and butter, onions (until these were outlawed in 1957 after some flagrant manipulation), and more recently pork bellies. In the 1960s it remained a quiet place, dominated by old Jewish families, where the "egg breakers," as the traders were called (*Business Week* called them "pork belly crapshooters"), spent much of their time playing cards and Ping-Pong or sitting around smoking.

†The new options market was dependent of the Black-Scholes options formula, which could be calculated using powerful handheld calculators.

In the past, a legal distinction had been made to distinguish the derivatives trade from mere gambling. It rested on the stipulation that the buyer and seller of a future must be able to contemplate actual delivery of the commodity at the end of the contract period. Gambling transactions, on the other hand, could only be settled with money. Yet in 1976, the Merc introduced a Eurodollar interest-rate futures contract (Professor Friedman rang the bell on the opening day). This was a significant innovation, since it was impossible to deliver an interest rate. This undeliverable derivative, however, was legitimated retrospectively five years later, when a sympathetic head of the Commodity Futures Trading Commission (the federal regulatory body created in 1974 to oversee the derivatives markets) declared that contemplation of delivery was no longer necessary for futures transactions and cash settlement was an acceptable alternative. This decision paved the way for the introduction of a plethora of index futures contracts at a number of exchanges. The first and most popular of the index futures, Standard & Poor's 500 index future (a more broadly based measure of the U.S. stock market than the Dow Jones Industrial Average), opened for trading at the Merc on 21 April 1982. Within a year the nominal value of S&P futures traded in Chicago exceeded the turnover on the New York Stock Exchange. Around the same time, the Chicago Board of Trade introduced options on futures—a derivative of derivatives.

This financial revolution was given further impetus in the early 1980s, when Sidney Homer, a brilliant bond specialist employed by Salomon Brothers, the investment bank, devised the idea of separating ("stripping" in technical language) bonds from their dividends and selling the two securities separately. This breakthrough enabled banks to turn a variety of previously illiquid assets into tradable securities (a process known as "securitisation"). Homer's insight was applied to the enormous U.S. federally guaranteed mortgage market and led to the creation of "synthetic" mortgage bonds, in which interest and principal payments were stripped and sold as separate bonds. The PO (Principal Only) bonds were divided into several tranches, with different repayment priorities. The final tranche, called Z-bonds, because they were the last to repay the principal, were highly volatile and known as "toxic waste" by the traders who handled them. They have been described as "among the most speculative instruments ever offered to American investors."[11]

Salomon Brothers invented many other new financial products in this period, including CARS (Collateralized Automobile Receivables), SPINS (low coupon debt securities which paid back on the rise and fall of the S&P index), and the gloriously named "Heaven and Hell warrant," a security whose payments varied under different circumstances. In 1981, Salomon Brothers also arranged the first debt "swap" (between the World Bank and IBM), which was followed by the rapid growth of the international swaps market.* Financial innovation continued into the 1980s with a multitude of new financial instruments: negotiable floating-rate notes, income warrants, puttable bonds, butterfly swaps, currency swaps, floor-ceiling swaps, interest-rate swaps, swaptions, synthetic equity, synthetic cash, and zero-coupon bonds. The offshore Eurobond market in London was a fount of creativity with its foreign bonds ("shoguns," "sushis," "down-unders," "kiwis," etc.), zero-coupon convertibles, dual currency yen bonds, and countless warrants bonds.†

By the end of 1996, the size of outstanding derivatives contracts was estimated at around $50 trillion, although since most of the derivatives trade was conducted away from the exchanges in the

*The earliest swaps (known as "plain-vanilla swaps") were relatively straightforward. They normally involved two contracting parties swapping interest payments on their debts, often denominated in different currencies, while each retained liability for the principal. In 1981, the World Bank borrowed in U.S. dollars and IBM borrowed in Swiss francs and deutsche marks and then both parties exchanged their obligations. It is also possible to "swap" floating and fixed (interest) rate liabilities.

†James Grant has listed some of the more fantastical oddities of this financially fecund decade: long-dated exchange-traded currency warrants, cumulative redeemable commodity-indexed preferred stock, subordinated primary capital floating rate notes, payment-in-kind preferreds, bonds with embedded options, currency exchange warrants, variable coupon renewable notes, variable spread floating-rate notes, floating-rate sterling notes convertible at the option of the holders into U.S. dollar-denominated floating-rate notes, guaranteed floating-rate notes with warrants to purchase ECU-denominated guaranteed retractable bonds, cumulative redeemable commodity-indexed preferred shares, duet bonds, synthetic floating-rate notes, and retractable facsimile bonds. (In *Minding Mr. Market*, pp. 134–44; and in *Money of the Mind: Borrowing and Lending in America from the Civil War to Michael Milken*, New York, 1992, p. 368.)

over-the-counter market, no one was sure of the figure.* The derivatives world lost none of its creativity in the 1990s. "Rocket scientists" or "quants" at investment banks were kept busy devising increasingly exotic financial instruments, such as Discrete Payoff Bull Notes, Principal Exchange Rate Linked Security, and Prime LIBOR Inverse Floating-Rate Notes. The new derivatives are explained in an arcane language of "forward-yield curves," "option-adjusted spreads," "duration," and "negative convexity." Few people, apart from their creators, understand either the language or how the financial instruments functioned.

Opinions differ as to whether the proliferation of new financial instruments stimulated speculation. Professor Merton Miller, the Nobel laureate who took a seat on the board of the Chicago Mercantile Exchange, maintains that derivatives are "essentially industrial raw materials" created to cope with uncertainty and financial volatility after the end of Bretton Woods and the 1974 oil crisis.[12] One man's insurance, however, might be another man's speculation. If a derivative position is hedged (i.e., when its risk is offset either by ownership of the underlying security, such as a share, or by a normal business risk, such as a foreign currency exposure), then it is insurance against potential loss. However, if the position is unhedged, then it is highly speculative.†

Anecdotal evidence suggested that players were not slow to exploit the opportunities for super-leveraged speculation offered by the new derivatives markets. This conclusion appears to be borne out by recent experience. Of the series of great derivatives disasters in the middle of the 1990s, only one, that of Metallgesellschaft (loss $1.5 billion), has been caused by the mishandling of bona fide hedging transactions. The others—Barings (loss £850 million), Orange County (loss $1.7 billion), and Sumitomo (loss $2.6 billion)—have

---

*Between 1990 and 1996 the notional amounts outstanding in the exchange-traded derivatives markets rose from $2.3 trillion to $9.8 trillion (an increase of 331 percent) and the OTC market grew from $2.3 trillion to $25 trillion (an increase of 729 percent). Figures provided by the Bank for International Settlements, published in Alfred Steinherr, *Derivatives: The Wild Beast of Finance* (New York, 1998), p. 214.

†An unhedged position in a stock index future is highly leveraged—roughly equivalent to buying the underlying shares on a 95 percent margin, a ratio of loan to value forbidden by federal regulations since the 1930s.

been the result of unhedged and unauthorised speculation.* Nick Leeson, a twenty-seven-year-old plasterer's son, displayed the speculator's traditional disdain for hierarchy by bringing down the Queen's bank, Baring Brothers, in February 1995. He did so by selling options and futures in the Singapore futures market, which created a total exposure of $18 billion, many times Barings' capital base. The escalating losses that caused the bank's failure came with a suddenness that only derivatives can produce. Several other high-profile cases of derivatives losses at American corporations appear to have been caused by a combination of aggressive pushing of derivatives by investment banks and speculative risk-taking by corporate treasurers. When Procter & Gamble sued Bankers Trust to recover derivatives losses of $102 million incurred in 1994, it produced a recorded transcript of a Bankers Trust derivatives salesman stating that he aimed to "lure people into the calm and then just totally fuck 'em."[13] Professor Miller dismisses these derivatives scandals as inconsequential "management failures."

THE REAGAN REVOLUTION

The full potential of the financial revolution was realised only when the political conditions were right. It took the better part of the 1970s for the revived free-market ideology to feed through from American universities to the political world. Milton Friedman, very much a *political* economist, played a key role in the process. In the 1960s, he advised Republican presidential candidates, including Richard Nixon. Later, he briefed Ronald Reagan, who, as President, showed off his economic proficiency by using his hands to draw charts of the money supply in the air.[14] During the 1970s,

*The Sumitomo losses were incurred by Yasuo Hamanaka, a forty-eight-year-old trader, who attempted to manipulate the price of copper futures at the London Metal Exchange. Known to fellow traders as "Mr. Five Percent" and "the Hammer," Hamanaka bought contracts for over 2.5 million tonnes of copper, a sum equivalent to America's annual copper consumption. He succeeded in pushing the price of copper from $1,800 a tonne in late 1994 to nearly $3,200 by the summer of 1995. When the manipulation ended in July 1996, the price of copper dropped $300 in one day's trading and a few months later it fell back to under $2,000. Hamanaka subsequently received a seven-year prison sentence.

Friedman visited Britain frequently, where his ideas were taken up by Mrs. Thatcher, then leader of the Conservative opposition. By the end of the decade, he was the best-known economist in the world: he had received the Nobel Prize in 1976; his face had graced the cover of *Time;* and he had presented a ten-hour television documentary on his views. On both sides of the Atlantic, Margaret Thatcher (elected in April 1979) and Ronald Reagan (elected in November 1980) were poised to put Friedman's economic philosophy in practice. A powerful alliance had emerged between economic liberals and Reagan Republicans; both agreed that government intervention in economic affairs was undesirable and that the judgement of the market was paramount.

Throughout Reagan's administration there was a profound, dogmatic distrust of regulation, which was seen as merely another malevolent aspect of "Big Government."* One of the first acts of Reagan's Justice Department was to drop the ten-year antitrust action against IBM. The regulatory structure of the 1930s, which had been designed to act as a counterweght to speculative excesses, was now allowed to decline.† The Glass-Steagall separation of investment and commercial banking was not rigorously enforced, the Securities and Exchange Commission's budget was reduced, and regulators everywhere were expected to be enthused with the spirit of the free market and deregulation.

Influenced by free-market economists such as Friedman and Arthur Laffer, Reagan rejected the Keynesian antipathy towards profit and actively encouraged the pursuit of self-interest: "What I want to see above all," he announced, "is that this remains a country where someone can always get rich."[15] As in the 1920s, income and corporation taxes were reduced, and the role of the entrepreneur

*Friedman was sceptical of Roosevelt's market reforms and advocated a more limited role for the government as a regulator. In his view, the regulation of the Securities and Exchange Commission over the American financial markets was inefficient, tending towards the maximisation of bureaucracy: "The urgent need today is to eliminate restrictions, not to add to them." (Milton and Rose Friedman, *Free to Choose*, London, 1980, p. 94.)

†According to the financial historian Robert Sobel, this combination of deregulation and lax supervision caused "the carefully regulated zoo of the 1950s . . . to be reconstituted as a jungle." (*Dangerous Dreamers: The Financial Innovators from Charles Merrill to Michael Milken*, New York, 1993, p. 83.)

was exalted. In the summer of 1981, Reagan broke the air traffic controllers' strike, ushering in an era of weak unions, declining real wages, and growing inequalities of wealth. While Reagan expressed the desire to create a nation where *someone* could become rich, what his laissez-faire policies actually created was one in which the financial operator could become wealthy beyond his wildest dreams. The rest of the population was promised an elusive "trickle-down" of wealth, as the rich spent the money they saved on taxes and new fortunes were expended on the consumption of luxuries.*

THE RISE OF THE TRADER

The 1970s were a decade of chronic financial instability. Floating currencies, rising inflation, stop-go economic policies, and declining growth rates produced unwelcome volatility that made the stock market a dangerous place for investors. The "nifty-fifty" boom of 1972, during which no price was deemed too high to pay for America's leading companies, was followed by a steep market decline. During a period of low growth and high inflation ("stagflation"), stocks did not arouse the speculative interest of the public. Although the Dow Jones Industrial Average had breached 1,000 in February 1966, by the spring of 1980 it was below 800. Faced with uncertainty, most private investors preferred to play it safe and enjoy the high interest rates paid on money market funds.

Those with a greater appetite for risk were able to speculate in commodities and precious metals, which offered the best hedge against the chronic inflation of the period. One person who availed herself of this opportunity was the wife of the governor of Arkansas, Hillary Rodham Clinton. In late 1978, the future First Lady embarked on a brief career as a speculator. Trading in cattle futures, soya beans, and live hogs, Mrs. Clinton turned an initial $1,000 stake into $100,000 ten months later, at which point she retired from the game. The derivatives contracts into which she

*The idea of the trickle-down effect, whereby the consumption of the rich would provide drops of nourishment for the less fortunate, resurrected Mandeville's thesis in the *Fable of the Bees* of private vices producing public benefits.

entered during this period were extremely risky, carrying an underlying value of over $3 million, which was roughly thirty times the net wealth of the Clinton household. The most remarkable aspect of this speculative foray, however, is that Mrs. Clinton achieved phenomenal success despite the fact that most of her trades were on the short side at a time when cattle prices doubled.*

Mrs. Clinton was not the only person looking to make a quick buck in the volatile commodities markets. In January 1979, after the Soviet invasion of Afghanistan, the price of gold rose to $875 an ounce. Six months later, Nelson Bunker Hunt and William Herbert Hunt, the sons of the Texas oil billionaire H. L. Hunt, together with several wealthy Arabs, formed a silver pool. In a short period, they amassed more than 200 million ounces of silver, equivalent to half the world's deliverable supply. The price of silver rose nearly tenfold, peaking at over $50. Once the silver market was cornered outsiders joined the chase, but a combination of changed trading rules on the New York metals market (Comex) and the intervention of the Federal Reserve lanced the bubble. The price of silver fell back to $10 in March 1980, bringing losses of over a billion dollars and eventual bankruptcy to the Hunt brothers.† During the silver bubble, an official at the Peruvian Ministry of Commerce, who was employed to hedge his country's silver production, lost $80 million by illicitly selling silver short. Although a relatively small sum for a sovereign nation, it was an omen: the "rogue trader" had appeared on the modern financial scene.

A number of institutional factors contributed to the rise of the professional market trader. During the 1970s, several leading U.S. investment banks, including Morgan Stanley, went public. Rather than cautious partners with unlimited liability and limited capital, these banks now had greater capital resources and answered to anonymous shareholders. Institutionalised speculation, known as

---

*Mrs. Clinton later ascribed her success to reading the *Wall Street Journal.* Victor Niederhoffer, however, was unconvinced: "The chances of achieving a 100-fold return in such a game," he writes, " is less than finding a snowball on a Little Rock sidewalk in August." ("First Speculatrix," in *Liberty*, VII, No. 5, July 1994.)

†In August 1988, the Hunt brothers were convicted of conspiring to manipulate the silver market. For an account of their attempt to corner the silver market, see Stephen Fay, *The Great Silver Bubble* (London, 1982).

"proprietary trading," became an appealing route to quick profits and large bonuses. Proprietary trading became even more attractive after Mayday 1975, when fixed commissions were abolished on the New York Stock Exchange. The rapid growth of "securitisation" (the process of turning illiquid assets into tradable securities) further enhanced the role of the trader-salesman.

By the early 1980s, traders were running Wall Street. John Gutfreund, the cigar-chomping son of a wholesale butcher, had risen from being a lowly municipal bond trader to become head of Salomon Brothers. Robert Rubin, the head of risk arbitrage at Goldman Sachs, became the firm's senior partner and later Treasury Secretary under President Clinton, following in the steps of Salomon's legendary trader William E. Simon, Nixon's Treasury Secretary. Another trader, the foul-mouthed Lew Glucksman, was appointed chief executive of Lehman Brothers, the prestigious white-shoe investment bank. (His brief and disastrous tenure at Lehman ended with the firm being taken over by American Express.)[16] The two most influential financiers of the 1980s, Lewis Ranieri of Salomon Brothers, who built the collateralised-mortgage business into a $1 trillion market, and Michael Milken, Drexel Burnham Lambert's junk bond guru, were both traders by training and inclination.

The trader also flourished outside the world of investment banking. Advances in communications encouraged the growth of hedge funds, private investment partnerships which evaded the SEC's regulation.* The most successful of these, the Quantum Fund, founded in 1973 by the Hungarian-born financier George Soros, produced average annual returns in excess of 25 percent from its leveraged positions in a variety of stock, bond, and currency markets. Alongside the hedge funds, "risk arbitrage" investment partnerships appeared in the 1970s. Highly leveraged like the hedge funds, they looked to profit from the sharp price movements associated with

*Hedge funds acquired their name because the original fund, set up by A. W. Jones in the 1950s, "hedged" its stock market exposure by balancing its long positions (i.e., shares it bought) with an equal number of shorts (shares it sold). The fund's portfolio was said to be "market neutral" (i.e., it would not rise and fall with the stock market). Nowadays, few hedge funds operate in this manner.

corporate takeovers. One of the most high-profile of the risk arbitrageurs was Ivan F. Boesky, the son of a Detroit bar owner, who set up his own partnership in 1975.

Egotistical, short-tempered, and flashy, the trader became a symbol of the 1980s: the "Master of the Universe," in Tom Wolfe's *The Bonfire of the Vanities* and the "big swinging dick" of Michael Lewis's *Liar's Poker* (the title of the book alluded to an alleged $1 million game of liar's poker between Gutfreund and John Meriwether, Salomon Brothers' chief trader). The trader was an international phenomenon, a product of deregulation and globalisation. In London, young traders employed by rapidly expanding American investment banks at the time of the "Big Bang" (the deregulation of the London Stock Exchange in 1986) earned six-figure bonuses. They were caricatured in the press as Porsche-driving "barrow-boys," and satirised in Caryl Churchill's play *Serious Money*. In pursuit of ever-larger bonuses, traders introduced a frenzied, brutal quality into the world of finance: "aggressive" became a synonym for ambitious in the curriculum vitae of the young banker, and *The Art of War*, a martial classic by Sun Tsu, the Chinese Clausewitz, became fashionable reading in financial circles. The trader's language was couched in violent metaphors. At Salomon Brothers, salesmen boasted of "ripping the faces off" their clients.

Capital no longer moved at a sedate pace; it whirled with the mesmerizing speed of a roulette wheel, and the trader had to keep up with it. In such an atmosphere there was no time to pause. "Lunch is for wimps," declared Gordon Gekko, the antihero of Oliver Stone's film *Wall Street*. Possibly no man worked longer hours than Michael Milken, head of Drexel Burnham Lambert's Beverly Hills bond department. Sleeping only three or four hours a night, Milken arrived at work before four o'clock in the morning in order to catch the opening of the market in New York, and handled up to a thousand transactions a day.* While Milken ascetically

*Where Milken led, his troops followed. One of his bond salesman boasted to the *Los Angeles Times* in 1984, "We get up at 4 a.m. and we don't go to lunch, we don't take calls, we don't talk about the ball game. No one in America works as hard as we do." (Cited by James Grant, *Mr. Market*, p. 240.)

avoided all stimulants except money, Ivan Boesky bolstered himself with endless cups of coffee to sustain his gruelling twenty-one-hour day. Hard work, a product of the trader culture, came to replace play as the motif of the super-rich. Gone was the extravagant idleness of the privileged described in Thorstein Veblen's *The Theory of the Leisure Class.* The new symbols of wealth in the 1980s—private jets for the wealthy, mobile phones for the less affluent—exemplified not repose but ceaseless striving.[17] In the era of global twenty-four-hour trading, money didn't sleep, nor did those who pursued it.

THE RISE OF MICHAEL MILKEN

By the early 1980s, the popular lessons of the Great Depression had worn thin. Under the influence of Reagan, business was once again venerated. Debt was perceived as tax-efficient rather than imprudent. In the capital markets, deregulation was replacing supervision. The individualistic pursuit of wealth had displaced the communal goals of full employment and equality of distribution. Yet for the first eighteen months of Reagan's presidency the bond and stock markets remained depressed as interest rates were raised to record levels in order to squeeze inflation out of the system. Commercial interest rates peaked at over 20 percent and the yield on long-term bonds climbed to over 15 percent. Finally, in the summer of 1982, the Chairman of the Federal Reserve, Paul Volcker, reduced the discount rate. The battle against inflation was now over. Half a century after the stock market nadir of 1932, the market began to rise.

While Mrs. Thatcher pioneered the privatisation of state-owned "public" corporations by floating them on the stock market, President Reagan witnessed privatisations in his country of a rather different nature. They involved taking "public" companies—those quoted in the stock market—and putting them back into private hands. The purpose of the leveraged buyout, or LBO, was to acquire a company with the maximum amount of debt. The interest and principal on the LBO debt was to be paid off as quickly as possible with the cash flow generated by the company. Once the leverage had reached a conventional level the company was normally put up for sale or refloated on the stock market.

The full potential of this type of transaction was first set before the public in the summer of 1983 with the flotation of Gibson Greetings Cards. Eighteen months earlier, former Treasury Secretary William Simon, together with a partner, had purchased Gibson for $1 million in equity and $79 million of debt. Yet when the company was offered in the stock market, its market capitalisation was $290 million and Simon's modest personal investment of $330,000 had turned into a fortune of over $66 million. The beauty of the deal lay in its timing. Simon had purchased the company when the stock market was in the doldrums, and sold it when interest rates were declining and the market had revived.

Falling interest rates and rising asset prices were not the only factors working in favour of LBOs. The fiscal system was conducive to leverage, since corporate interest payments were tax-deductible whereas dividend payments were not. This tendency was reinforced in 1981, when the Reagan administration persuaded Congress to pass the Economic Recovery Tax, allowing companies to accelerate depreciation charges, thereby reducing their tax bills and enabling them to take on more debt. Although the Federal Reserve prevented speculators from buying shares on a margin of more than 50 percent, there were no restrictions on the amount of leverage applied in a buyout. The participant in a leveraged buyout had several other advantages over the margin speculator: his interest payments were tax-deductible, he was not subject to margin calls (i.e., asked to provide more collateral when asset values fluctuated), nor was he personally responsible for the LBO debt, which was packaged as bonds and sold on to other investors. If the company went bankrupt he could walk away with little loss, but if the deal was a success, his gains were outlandish.

Although he was the son of an accountant, Michael Milken of Drexel Burnham Lambert preached a message heretical to accountants' ears. He advocated turning the balance sheets of companies upside down, replacing shareholders' capital with debt. Milken was employed by Drexel in 1970 as a trader in high-yield or "junk" bonds—loan securities which paid a higher rate of interest because their issuer's credit rating was low. He challenged the conventional wisdom that high-yield bonds were "speculative," in the sense of being more risky. This message was derived from an analysis which showed that the bonds of lowly rated companies—or "fallen angels," as Milken called them—offered good investment opportunities since high yields more than compensated for their historical rate of default. Investing in a portfolio of speculative bonds, he claimed, would produce better returns over the long run than a portfolio of triple-A-rated debt issued by the likes of General Motors.

Having successfully sold this idea since the early 1970s, Milken looked for new applications for his junk bonds. His first idea was to use them as venture capital for fast-growing businesses, such as Ted Turner's Cable News Network and McCaw Cellular, a mobile phone operator, along with a number of Las Vegas casino businesses. As Milken came to dominate both the primary (i.e., issuing) and secondary (trading) markets for high-yield bonds, a visionary side to his junk bond philosophy revealed itself. He claimed that he was able to distinguish between popular perception and reality. Bond-rating agencies such as Moody's, he complained, looked to the past rather than the future: "People and industries of the future are considered risky . . . Junk bond users are the industries of the future."[18] At other times, his vision was less exalted. Defending his bonds, he declared: "Everything we like is junk, junk food, junk clothes, junk records. Everything that stands the test of time is junk."[19]

Milken's instinctive salesmanship was as brilliant as his financial mind, which retained an encyclopaedic knowledge of companies' financial histories and market information. Had he confined his activities to the existing market in low-grade corporate bonds, supplemented with the issue of bonds for high-risk ventures, it is unlikely that his name would ever have attracted attention outside his professional field. Out of the mergers and acquisitions department of Drexel Burnham Lambert, however, came the idea of using high-yield bonds to finance leveraged takeovers of American public companies. In August 1984, Milken and Drexel made their first move into the field of hostile takeovers, backing T. Boone Pickens, the Texas oil tycoon and head of Mesa Petroleum, in his attempt to gain control of the giant Gulf Oil. Without actually having the funds necessary for the takeover, Drexel produced a letter stating it was "highly confident" of raising the capital through the sale of junk bonds. Although this bid failed, the "highly confident" letter symbolised Drexel's ability to finance deals of limitless size. The bank's first successful hostile bid came in April 1985, when a Milken-backed raider, Nelson Peltz, acquired National Can in a $465 million deal, involving leverage of eleven parts debt to one part equity. A few months later, Drexel client Ron Perelman captured Revlon, the cosmetics firm, in the largest hostile LBO to date. More successes soon followed. In April 1986, Kohlberg Kravis Roberts, an investment partnership specialising in LBOs, raised over $6 billion through Drexel to take control of Beatrice, a conglomerate whose interests ranged from Samsonite suitcases to Avis car rental.

Milken and his corporate raiders relished their position as outsiders to the corporate world. At the 1985 Drexel High Yield Conference, otherwise known as the Predators' Ball, the bank's chief executive, Fred Joseph, declared triumphantly that "for the first time in history, we've levelled the playing field. The small can go after the big."[20] In the manner of Jay Gould, the raiders applied a rhetoric of public service to their activities. They claimed that incumbent management, or "corpocracy" as they styled it, was inefficient and only concerned with its own security and the perquisites of office. Nelson Peltz went so far as to argue that American management was more communist than the Russians.[21] More bluntly, Sir James Goldsmith declared: "Takeovers are for the public good but that's not why I do it. I do it for the money." Yet the raiders' claim that they were promoting the "democratisation of capital" was hollow. At Milken's junk bond feast there was no vacant cover for the uninvited guest. Milken pursued his operations through a clique, whose membership was far more exclusive than the so-called establishment. Junk bonds were issued for a small number of corporate raiders, and sold to a small number of institutional investors. The group was so closely connected that it was nicknamed the "daisy chain."*

From his X-shaped trading desk in Beverly Hills, Milken commanded the financial and corporate worlds. He was revered by

*When his clients issued junk bonds, Milken frequently provided them with more funds than they required. The overcapitalisation of junk bond issues had several advantages: if a company experienced trouble servicing its bonds, Milken could arrange to restructure its debt, selling new bonds to his favoured clients. In Milken's world, favours were returned with favours. Occasionally "blind pools" were raised with junk bonds to finance unspecified future acquisitions.

clients and associates. "He only cared about bringing the truth. If Mike hadn't gone into the securities business he could have led a religious revival movement," claimed a former Drexel executive.[22] Another colleague asserted that "Michael is the most important individual who has lived in this century."[23] Contemporary descriptions of Milken as a "Messiah" preaching a junk bond "gospel" abound. As Milken's power waxed, he began proselytising on nonfinancial issues, rambling about the prospects of housing the world's population on floating hotels, lecturing his visitors on the risks of tampering with food packages, and pondering on human longevity.[24]

Yet there was a crude, bullying quality to the Drexel organisation which gave the outfit more the air of a Mafia family than a religious cult. Fierce "turf wars" were fought with other investment banks. Since Milken controlled around two-thirds of the junk bond market, no one could afford to alienate him, and companies which didn't play ball might find one of Milken's raiders, or even Drexel itself, appearing suddenly on its shareholder register with a potentially hostile holding.* By 1986, Drexel had stakes in over one hundred and fifty companies, and owned a junk bond portfolio worth several hundred million dollars. This gave Milken even greater power in his ceaseless quest to dominate the junk bond market. An anonymous colleague told Connie Bruck, author of *The Predators' Ball*, "Michael is interested in power, dominance, one hundred percent market share. Nothing is good enough for Michael. He is the most unhappy person I know. He never has enough. He drives people by insult. He drives everything—more, more, more deals."[25]

Although Milken had little interest in flaunting wealth, he had an insatiable desire to accumulate it. "In addition to being a talented creative genius," said one Drexel employee, "Michael is one of the most avaricious, ruthless, venal people on the face of the earth."[26] In the early 1970s, Milken had negotiated a generous compensation deal with Drexel, giving him the right to retain one dollar of every

*Connie Bruck maintains that after Wickes, a building materials concern, turned down an approach from Drexel, a Drexel client (Saul Steinberg) took a 10 percent stake in the company. Subsequently, Wickes issued $3 billion worth of bonds through Drexel. Bruck calls this "extortion." Drexel also attempted to pressure Staley Continental, a corn processor, into doing an LBO. When Staley demurred, Drexel bought 1.5 million shares in the company and demanded an investment banking relationship.

three he made for the firm. Hostile LBOs generated fees running into tens of millions of dollars for Drexel. Milken supplemented his Drexel income by running a number of private investment partnerships which participated in the more lucrative deals. On occasion, when clients issued bonds during a takeover, Milken demanded warrants (options to buy shares) as a sweetener. Instead of being distributed to the purchasers of junk bonds, these warrants were handed out to favoured clients, or retained by Milken's private partnerships and by Drexel.* "If we can't make money from our friends, who can we make it from?" Milken is reported as saying.[27] In January 1986, Milken interviewed Martin Siegel, a leading mergers and acquisitions adviser, for a job at Drexel: "If people here know how rich they are," he told Siegel, "they'll get slow and fat. You must never count your money; you have to keep driving yourself to make more."[28] In 1986, Milken kept $550 million of the junk bond department's $700 million bonus, making him the highest-paid individual in American history.

Sometimes, the wealth amassed by Milken's raiders was even greater. Ron Perelman, the Revlon raider, was reputed to have turned a loan of $2 million in the late 1970s into a fortune of nearly $3 billion a decade later. Although costs were cut after buyouts and management was pruned, corporate extravagance persisted. The former chief executive of Revlon, Michel Bergerac, observed that although much had been made of his supposed extravagance during the takeover, the new management under Perelman was if anything more luxurious. "These so-called raiders," complained Bergerac, "manage to get hold of one of these large companies and a mysterious process of osmosis seems to take place. They go to London to get their suits, they hire French chefs, they drink French wine, one plane is not enough for them and some of them have two or three planes. So all I can say is that either the demands of the job create these things or that the good life is contagious."[29]

Flushed with their newfound wealth, the "junk bond jillionaires," as one writer called them, and their bonus-laden financial advisers put on a show of wealth without parallel in postwar America. President Reagan's glitzy $6 million inauguration, in January 1981, set

*Warrants supplied by KKR after the takeover of Beatrice yielded profits of over $650 million, much of which was retained in Milken's family accounts.

the tone for a decade in which conspicuous consumption became a sign of the vitality of the American dream. Lavish parties were held at New York's cultural monuments. The Metropolitan Museum of Art, "Club Met" to one gossip columnist, was decorated with twelve thousand Dutch tulips and fifty thousand French roses to celebrate the marriage between the children of corporate raider Saul Steinberg and Larry Tisch, head of the Loews Corporation—a "baronial extravagance on the scale of Castile and Aragon in the fifteenth century," cooed *Vanity Fair*'s editor Tina Brown.[30]

For a while, Susan Gutfreund (pronounced Goodfriend), the wife of Salomon Brothers' boss, led "nouvelle society." Whether redecorating her Fifth Avenue apartment at a reputed cost of $20 million, booking two seats on the Concorde to fly a cake to Paris for her husband's sixtieth birthday, or sending out invitations styled "At Home" to a party at Blenheim Palace, the extravagances of "Social Susie" became the talk of the town. The former air hostess amused the world with her *gaucheries*. "*Bonsoir, madame*," curtseyed the native Texan on being introduced to the First Lady. "It's like living in a fairy tale," she told the *New York Times*. The value of the Gutfreunds' invitations, remarked Michael Lewis in *Liar's Poker*, seemed to rise and fall with Salomon Brothers' share price. "It's so expensive to be rich," she lamented a few weeks after the Wall Street crash.

As power shifted from the bankers to their clients, John Gutfreund was usurped as "King of Wall Street" by Henry Kravis (the title was bestowed by *Business Week* magazine). In society, Susan Gutfreund ceded place to Kravis's fashion designer wife, Carolyne Roehm. The second Mrs. Kravis was a tall and skinny Midwesterner, the definitive "social X-ray"—a type diagnosed by Tom Wolfe as suffering from *anorexia richiosa*. Her activities were followed insatiably by gossip columnists. Bent on self-improvement, she studied French in France and opera in Salzburg. She took up the piano and announced that she was a reincarnation of Brahms. While many of her husband's employees laboured longer hours for lower wages to pay off the debts incurred by his leveraged buyouts, Roehm announced to the press that she worked "like a slave," designing dresses embroidered with precious stones (a press release stated she was "crazy about diamonds"). A party she gave at the Metropolitan Museum was described by one guest as "Medi-chichi." The diminutive Kravis—according to his wife, he is "quite tall when he stands on his wallet"—affected a patrician air.[31] At his Manhattan office, he lunched off the finest Wedgwood china, had his shoes buffed while seated behind his mahogany desk, and one day was visited by Princess Margaret, who dropped in to admire a painting by Stubbs. An air of unreality hung over these inhabitants of nouvelle society. "Beauty and glamour are a state of mind," announced Carolyne Roehm's publicity material. Her husband might well have said the same of stock market values.

The boom in leveraged buyouts became the driving force behind the bull market of the mid-1980s. Conventional measures of value gave way to LBO valuations, known as "private market value,"which were calculated by examining how much cash ("free cash flow") a company generated and how much debt it could support. Professional "risk arbitrageurs," on the lookout for the next takeover, became the medium through which private market value was established in the stock market. Acting in unofficial collusion, arbitrageurs searched for vulnerable companies and took large stakes in them, thus putting them "in play." Members of the public followed the arbs' operations and imitated them, just as their forebears had followed stock market pools in the 1920s. Because the arbitrageurs and their followers had no loyalty to the company whose shares they owned, their activities made life simpler for the corporate raiders. When a bid was publicly announced, the raider's broker needed only to call round members of the arbitrage club to acquire control of a company. This process, known as a "street sweep," was most dramatically displayed in Robert Campeau's takeover of Allied Stores when, with a single telephone call, a Los Angeles broker named Boyd Jefferies acquired thirty-two million shares, or more than half the shares in circulation, giving Campeau control of the $4 billion company.*

Arbs risked losing large sums of money when they took a stake in a company if a bid was not forthcoming or fell through. For example, when Gulf Oil's bid for Cities Services collapsed in May

---

*This transaction was probably illegal since the arbitrageurs working through Jefferies appeared to be acting in concert. The SEC did not prosecute, but banned further "street sweeps." Jefferies was later convicted of securities fraud in connection with Milken. (See John Rothchild, *Going for Broke*, New York, 1991, pp. 86–90.)

1982, Ivan Boesky lost $24 million. Apparently, it was this loss that drove Boesky to build a secret network of investment bankers, which included Martin Siegel of Kidder Peabody and Dennis Levine of Drexel. Using inside information supplied by Siegel, Boesky made $28 million from Nestlé's acquisition of Carnation in 1984. Boesky was not the only one who wished to play the game with loaded dice: a *Business Week* study in the spring of 1985 showed that nearly three-quarters of takeover bids were anticipated by strong advances in share prices, a sure sign of insider trading.*

With his average annual investment returns of over 80 percent, Boesky was widely suspected of basing his speculations on insider information. On 18 May 1986, Boesky addressed an assembly at a California business school with words that defined the 1980s zeitgeist: "Greed is all right, by the way . . ." he announced to whoops of delight from the attendant yuppies. "I think greed is healthy. You can be greedy and still feel good about yourself."[32] This speech was not so much a call to arms as Boesky's perverse valediction to a life spent in pursuit of Mammon. For by the time he uttered his celebrated words, Boesky knew his time was up—six days earlier his chief informant, Dennis Levine, had been arrested on charges of insider trading in New York. On 14 November 1986, the Securities and Exchange Commission announced that Wall Street's most notorious arbitrageur had confessed to insider trading offences and was cooperating with investigators. Three days after "Boesky Day," the *Wall Street Journal* announced that Milken's role in the affair was under investigation. In reaction, the Dow Jones fell 43 points, junk bonds dipped sharply, and Ron Perelman abandoned his bid for Gillette. Although the game was not yet over, it had begun to turn.

**Business Week*, 29 April 1985, "Insider Trading: The Wall Street Epidemic That Washington Can't Stop." Some economists argue that insider trading is a healthy phenomenon as it helps to disseminate information to the public. They point out, correctly, that insider trading was perfectly legal until the antispeculative backlash of the 1930s. There are, however, sound reasons for banning insider trading. First, it makes the markets unfair by giving an advantage to "insiders" and their associates. Second, insiders are normally breaking the confidence of their clients, which in certain cases may actually lose clients' money. Third, insider trading forces up share prices. This rise may induce an existing shareholder, unaware of the inside information, to sell his stock when, had he waited, he would have received a larger profit. (For a defence of insider trading, see Daniel Fischel, *Payback*, New York, 1995.)

The market soon forgot the insider trading scandals. In January, President Reagan delivered an ebullient State of the Union address that caught the mood of the nation: "The calendar can't measure America because we were meant to be an endless experiment in freedom, with no limit to our reaches, no boundaries to what we can do, no end point to our hopes."[33] In sympathy with the notion of limitless aspirations, the Dow broke through the 2,000 mark for the first time. It continued upwards, despite a sharp fall in late January 1987, which brought a warning from the SEC chairman of an impending "first class catastrophe." Around the world a speculative froth was evident. In London, Saatchi & Saatchi, an advertising group best known for its services on behalf of the Conservative Party, launched an abortive bid for the Midland Bank, one of the country's largest commercial banks.*

A "FINANCIAL HITLER" ARRIVES ON WALL STREET

In America, mergers and buyouts rebounded after Boesky Day. Milken and Drexel faced growing competition from other Wall Street banks eager to muscle in on their LBO franchise. The world of junk bonds and hostile takeovers took on the attributes of a game, expressed in an esoteric ludic language: a target company was said to be "in play," if a "white knight" did not come to its rescue, management could thwart the predator with a "poison pill" or a "Pac-Man" defence (which involved making a counterbid for the predator), and if all this failed the chief executive could bail out with a "golden parachute" compensation package. A banker proposing a deal talked of "teeing up the concept," a high bid was a "hat trick," and a successful junk bond issue a "home run." The banker was rewarded with a small plastic-encased tombstone advertisement recording details of the completed transaction; it was known as a "deal toy." In the words of a Drexel executive, this was "Disneyland for adults."[34]

*Excess liquidity in the Japanese financial system buoyed the global bull market, bringing with it the familiar argument that new valuations were justified as "this time it's different." In the first nine months of 1987, Japanese investors spent $15 billion on large cap American shares, accounting for over a tenth of shares purchased on the NYSE. During the same period, the British FTSE 100 index climbed by nearly 50 percent, the Hong Kong Hang Seng index tripled, and Australian shares rose fourfold.

As the competition increased, the quality of the deals declined. Symptomatic of this development was the elevation of Robert Campeau, a Canadian property developer, to the rank of successful corporate raider. Campeau was a prize eccentric whose business success had been accompanied by increasing grandiosity, vanity, and quirkiness: he maintained two separate families, took elocution lessons, had his teeth capped, his face lifted, and his hair transplanted. A hypochondriac, he flew regularly to Germany for injections of sheep brains and travelled everywhere with large supplies of mineral water and fresh oranges. His unusual appearance was enhanced by a penchant for wearing porkpie hats with feathers sticking out. In New York, Campeau would call his bankers in the middle of the night and hold meetings with them in his hotel room dressed only in a pair of underpants. At one meeting, Campeau emphasised a point by picking up a fork and stabbing it through the tabletop. In fact, Campeau was a manic-depressive, given to throwing tantrums and delivering stream-of-consciousness tirades.* At such moments his eyes—the one part of his physiognomy untouched by the surgeon's knife—would bulge out of his head and his hands would shake. The Canadian business establishment rightly viewed Campeau with suspicion, and blocked his attempted takeover of a large financial institution at the beginning of the decade. In the giddy atmosphere of the 1980s, Wall Street was less fastidious.

In 1986, Campeau came to New York, where he took a suite at the Waldorf-Astoria, equipped himself with a lawyer from a prominent Wall Street partnership, and started looking for an acquisition. After much thrashing around, he finally set his sights on the department store sector. He decided to bid for Allied Stores, owner inter alia of Brooks Brothers, the preppy clothing store. Allied had sales of $4 billion, seventy thousand employees, and a market capitalisation of $2 billion—over ten times that of the Campeau Corporation.

*The fevered atmosphere of Wall Street in the second half of the 1980s attracted manic figures such as Campeau and Jeff "Mad Dog" Beck, a leading dealmaker employed by Drexel who fabricated, among other things, a heroic Vietnam War record. Later, Beck recalled his fantasy life on Wall Street: "Each of us in the deal game fed the next person's ambitions to the point of insanity; we were all magicians creating wealth and power from thin air . . . On Wall Street during the 1980s there were no boundaries to reality, and my creations took on a life of their own." (Bianco, *Mad Dog*, pp. 461–69.)

Campeau's advisers, led by Bruce Wasserstein, First Boston's "star" dealmaker, were unfazed by either the disparity in size between predator and victim or by their client's lack of experience in retailing (although Campeau talked vaguely of a "synergy" between real estate and retailing). Instead, First Boston offered to lend the aspiring department store magnate $900 million from its own coffers—a sum equal to the bank's entire capital—and to raise a further $600 million with a margin loan secured against Allied stock. Campeau even succeeded in borrowing the $300 million of "equity" he had promised to put into the $4 billion bid. On top of these loans, over a billion dollars' worth of junk bonds were issued to finance the acquisition. Because Allied did not generate sufficient cash to service the interest payments on these debts, First Boston issued on Campeau's behalf $250 million worth of "pay-in-kind" preferred shares (i.e., securities that paid dividends with loan notes rather than cash). The total bill for the acquisition of Allied came to $4.1 billion.

In March 1987, Allied succumbed to Campeau's bid. Its chief executive was dismissed, complaining bitterly of having been "blindsided by a trainload of clowns," although he got a $15 million "golden parachute." The bankers received fees totalling more than $500 million, and a "financial Hitler"—to use the description of one of his advisers—found himself in charge of America's second-largest department store group. The novel financial practices involved in the Allied takeover, in which banks staked their entire capital on strangers, debt could not be serviced without asset sales, bonds paid interest in yet more bonds, and advisory fees exceeded the equity investment of the investor, were hailed by Wasserstein as "the dawn of a new era of merchant banking."[35]

THE OCTOBER CRASH

On 25 August 1987, the Dow Jones Industrial Average closed at 2,746, up 43 percent on the year. Although sentiment remained bullish into the early autumn, with Morgan Stanley advising its clients to have 100 percent of their investment portfolio in stocks, the flow of funds to the market faltered. In preparation for a massive $35 billion issue of shares in Nippon Telephone & Telegraph,

Japanese investors started repatriating funds. As U.S. bond yields were rising on fears of inflation and the dollar was falling against the yen, Japanese investors were also losing heavily on their massive investments in Treasury bonds, which they now began to sell. This further depressed the price of bonds and made shares, trading on a multiple of twenty-three times earnings, look increasingly overvalued.

With the yield on Treasury bonds at over 10 percent by the beginning of the second week in October, there followed a spate of unsettling reports: Treasury Secretary James Baker was threatening to let the dollar go into free fall unless the German Bundesbank lowered interest rates; on Tuesday, 13 October, the market buzzed with the rumour that Congress planned to end the tax breaks favourable to leveraged buyouts; the following day, a larger than expected U.S. trade deficit was announced. On Friday, reacting to news that a tanker carrying the U.S. flag had been hit by an Iranian missile in the Persian Gulf, the market dropped 108 points, its largest points fall ever. The same day, the London Stock Exchange remained closed after a freak hurricane tore through southern England. Earlier in the week, Elaine Garzarelli, a research analyst with Shearson Lehman, had forecast on Cable News Network "an imminent collapse in the stock market." It was to prove, in the words of *Business Week*, "the call of the century."*

The international stock market crash of Monday, 19 October 1987, rose with the sun in the East. Hong Kong, Malaysia, and Singapore, followed by several of the European markets, were all down heavily while New York slept.† When the New York Stock Exchange

*There is reason to believe that Garzarelli, like Roger Babson in 1929, was fortunate in her timing. In an econometric analysis of the stock-options market prior to the October Crash, David Bates concludes, "there were no strong fears of a crash in the 2 months immediately preceding October 19, 1987—not even on late Friday afternoon, October 16." (D. S. Bates, "The Crash of 1987: Was It Expected? Evidence from the Options Markets," *Journal of Finance*, XLVI, No. 3 [July 1991], p. 1037.)

†Richard Roll argues that since the crash was international in scope (and some markets fell sharply before New York opened) it could not have been caused by U.S. program trading. He suggests some unknown international trigger. However, the international nature of the crash, partly preceding Monday, 19 October, is not inconsistent with the notion that it was primarily an American event. First, the steep fall in New York on Friday, 16 October, was

eventually opened at 9:30 on Monday morning, there were no bids for many of the large stocks. Half an hour later only twenty-five of the five hundred stocks in the Standard & Poor's 500 index, representing America's largest companies, were trading. If people were unable to sell shares, they could at least sell stock index futures at the Chicago Mercantile Exchange. Concentrated selling of futures, however, caused futures to drop to a discount to shares traded on the Big Board. In normal circumstances, arbitrageurs would have acted to close the gap by buying futures and selling shares, but this day the volatility was too great for arbitrage and the markets became uncoupled. Instead, a vicious circle operated as panic selling of futures caused the stock market to drop, which in turn induced further sales of futures. Shortly before noon, the press reported that the head of the Securities and Exchange Commission was considering a trading halt. People hastened to dispose of stocks while the market remained open.

The turbulence of October 1929 had been caused partly by the forced liquidation of margin accounts. In October 1987, an avalanche of computerised program selling was to blame. The sales were induced by "portfolio insurance," a fashionable and supposedly fail-safe investment strategy which dictated buying when stocks rose and selling when they fell. Funds managed by portfolio insurers had increased rapidly during the year, to reach an estimated $90 billion. In the three trading days before the crash, portfolio insurers unloaded nearly $4 billion worth of stocks on a falling market. On Black Monday, in the hour after one o'clock, they were responsible for over half the sales of the stock index futures at the Chicago Mercantile Exchange. Portfolio insurers were contracted to make their sales in the futures market, so that even when futures fell to a discount to the stock market, they continued selling there. Aggressive traders, anticipating these sales, jumped on the bandwagon and sold

---

sufficient to unsettle the smaller markets opening the following Monday in the East (Hong Kong, Singapore, etc.). Second, selling pressure from New York on Friday, 16 October, was transferred to London over the weekend. Third, the major markets experienced their steepest falls only after New York crashed on Black Monday. Japan fell only slightly on Monday, but crashed on Tuesday (down 15 percent), as did Australia (down 25 percent) and New Zealand. London divided its falls between Monday and Tuesday. (See Richard Roll, "The International Crash of October 1987," *Financial Analysts Journal*, September–October 1988.)

stocks short. By the market's close, portfolio insurers had sold the equivalent of $4 billion worth of stocks in the futures market, 40 percent of the day's total volume.*

The panic on that day was similar to countless former stock market panics. A trader at the Merc fled his post, withdrew his life savings from a bank in the foyer, and disappeared over the horizon in his Porsche.[36] Several other traders sold their seats at the Merc, whose price crashed along with everything else. In the White House, a senior administrative official was witnessed running down the corridor, shouting, "It's in free fall."[37] As in 1929, the technology of the market began to collapse. On the New York Stock Exchange, the automated trading system broke down (its printers could not cope with the flood of selling) and brokers were left unable to confirm trades. The new derivatives markets performed no better. Owing to extreme volatility, it became impossible to price stock options and the options market dried up.

When the markets closed, the indexes told the story: the Dow Jones Industrial Average was down 22.6 percent, the S&P 500 down 20.5 percent, and the S&P futures contract down nearly 29 percent. Turnover on the Big Board exceeded 600 million stocks, worth $21 billion, almost double the record set the previous Friday. A similar amount had been traded in the futures market. Two venerable New York Stock Exchange member firms, E. F. Hutton and L. F. Rothschild, failed, along with nearly sixty smaller brokers. For many the collapse of the market appeared to threaten a systemic financial crisis, possibly the end of capitalism. The financier Sir James Goldsmith, who had recently sold most of his assets in anticipation of a crash, compared his feelings at the time to "winning a rubber of bridge in the card room of the *Titanic*."†

*The finance professors who developed portfolio insurance were exponents of the Efficient Market Hypothesis and did not believe that their "informationless" trading could produce changes in share prices. This does not appear to be the case. In fact, "portfolio insurance" was a misnomer since the effectiveness of the insurance depended on market liquidity and during the panic liquidity disappeared.

†Goldsmith's liquidation of assets was not due to any particular financial prescience but was induced by his apocalyptic fear of the spread of AIDS. (Ivan Fallon, *Billionaire*, London, 1991, p. 438.)

Goldsmith's anticipation of doom was exaggerated. On Tuesday, 20 October, after a sharp initial decline and the temporary closure of the futures market at the Merc, the stock market climbed sharply. This rally was assisted by actions of the Federal Reserve, which provided extensive liquidity to the financial markets, in order to avert a banking crisis.* Several major companies, urged on by telephone calls from the White House, announced they would buy back their shares. Conspiracy theorists later suggested that the recovery was engineered by the authorities, who had closed the futures market at the Merc in order to manipulate stock prices.† Whatever its causes, the recovery effectively ended the panic. By the end of the year, investors who had held their stock positions since January were even able to record a modest profit despite having lived through the greatest crash (in percentage terms) in history.

Although a total of $1 trillion was knocked off American stock market values during the month of October, the panic of 1987 (unlike that of 1929) was not followed by an economic crisis. The reason for this, according to some commentators, is that the 1987 bull market was not really a "retail market" attracting ordinary members of the public, so when share prices collapsed the effect on public confidence and consumption was slight. Andrew Smithers, an English economist, offers another explanation. He claims that the crash of 1987 did not produce a recession because stock prices were not actually overvalued at the time. Using a measure of valuation known

*The Federal Reserve made large purchases of government securities, creating nearly $12 billion of new bank reserves. This caused the Federal Funds rate to fall by 75 basis points (0.75 percent). At the same time, bank loans to the holders of securities increased by around $7 billion.

†Tim Metz suggests that "only a broadly coordinated manipulation of stock and futures markets information and prices averted a stock market plunge on October 20 that could have rivalled, or even exceeded, that of the day before . . . [and that] some leaders and market makers at the New York Stock Exchange and the Chicago Mercantile Exchange collaborated to save the stock market by rigging stock information and prices." (*Black Monday*, p. 210.) More recently, Tony Dye, a British fund manager, has suggested that the U.S. authorities secretly intervened during the market turbulence of October 1997 by manipulating the futures markets to prevent a crash. (*Sunday Telegraph*, 22 March 1998.) If these interventions did occur, they raise the issue of "moral hazard" in the stock markets.

as the "Q" ratio, devised by the American Nobel laureate James Tobin, which compares the market capitalisation of companies to the replacement cost of their factories, plant, and other assets, Smithers shows that even at their peak in August 1987 share prices were only slightly above their long-term average.[38] If the mild aftermath of the 1987 crash remains an enigma to many, it was interpreted by the exponents of efficient markets as proof that speculative booms and stock market panics were rarely, if ever, the cause of depressions.*

POLITICAL VENALITY AND THE SAVINGS AND LOAN CRISIS

The leveraged buyout boom was made possible by the deep-seated laissez-faire attitude of the Reagan administration which dissuaded the Federal Reserve from applying margin restrictions on buyouts.† At some point principled laissez-faire gives way to a widespread acceptance of shortcuts in the pursuit of self-interest, and from there it is but a short step to outright dishonesty. As the Reagan years progressed a fog of corruption gathered over Washington, reminiscent of the Gilded Age or the Harding presidency in the early 1920s. By the spring of 1987, more than a hundred officials appointed to federal posts during the Reagan administration had been accused of misconduct.[39] Many of the nation's political leaders were prepared to sell themselves to the highest bidder in exchange for campaign contributions. Milken brazenly told the *Washington Post* in April 1986 that "the force in this country for buying high-yield securities has overpowered all regulation."[40] That year, Drexel raised half a million dollars in campaign contributions for Senator Alfonse D'Amato, chair of the Subcommittee on Securities of the Senate Banking Committee, who had

---

*For instance, Professor Peter Temin, an economist at the Massachusetts Institute of Technology, recently delivered a paper in which he claimed that the last time a stock market decline in the United States caused an economic downturn was in 1903. ("The Causes of American Business Cycles: An Essay in Economic Historiography," June 1998.)

†After the 1987 crash, any legislation restricting buyouts became unthinkable because of the threat it might pose to the stock market.

previously supported restrictions on hostile takeovers. After this donation, it was observed that D'Amato's disposition towards junk bonds "underwent a remarkable transformation."*

Political venality, dogmatic deregulation, and speculative opportunism combined explosively to produce the Savings & Loan scandal of the late 1980s. The Savings & Loan associations, known colloquially as "thrifts" or "S&Ls," were local banks originally created to provide mortgage loans to American homeowners—a role idealised in Frank Capra's movie *It's a Wonderful Life*, in which James Stewart played an honest and dependable thrift manager. By the early 1980s, however, many of these institutions were in trouble. In particular, they suffered from the deregulation of interest rates which obliged them to pay higher rates for short-term deposits (especially high during the Volcker squeeze on inflation), when they had already lent for long periods at low fixed rates.

The Reagan administration's prescription for the thrifts' ills was a large dose of deregulation. First of all, thrifts were freed from dependence on local customers' deposits and permitted to borrow funds wholesale from Wall Street money brokers. At the same time, federal deposit insurance on individual S&L accounts was raised to $100,000. Second, they were encouraged to diversify their loan portfolios to reduce their reliance on the local housing market. The Garn–St. Germain bill of 1982 removed restrictions on thrift loans, allowing them to invest in junk bonds, property deals, and almost any other speculative venture that took their fancy. On signing the bill, President Reagan commented, "I think we have hit a home run."†

---

*Congressman Timothy Wirth, who had previously suggested outlawing greenmail (a common practice of corporate raiders in the 1980s, greenmail involved purchasing a large hostile stake in a company and then selling the shares back to the company at a premium), received campaign contributions from Drexel employees and appeared as a guest speaker at Drexel's 1986 Predators' Ball. (Robert Sobel, *Dangerous Dreamers*, p. 169; and Stewart, *Den of Thieves*, p. 219.)

†A number of other restrictions were relaxed to help revive the ailing thrifts: The cap was removed on the maximum rates they were allowed to offer on deposit accounts; their capital requirement was reduced to 3 percent of assets; they were converted from mutual institutions into privately owned companies, and the minimum number of shareholders was reduced from four hundred to one. (Martin Mayer, *The Greatest-Ever Bank Robbery: The Collapse of the Savings and Loan Industry*, New York, 1992, p. 95.)

Important changes were made to thrift accounting rules. They were permitted to sell off bad loans without taking an immediate charge against profits (this was called euphemistically "loss deferral"). On the other hand, anticipated earnings on real estate investments could be reported. Property development loans of up to 100 percent of appraised value were permitted. In short, virtually every rule in the book of prudent banking was either flouted or struck off. Depositors might have been wary of these developments and removed their cash to safer havens had their deposits not been guaranteed by the federal government. Deposit insurance more than dulled depositors; it positively encouraged them to seek out the highest rates offered by the shakiest institutions—in the words of one commentator, it was "the crack cocaine of American finance."[41]

While depositors remained in a state of somnolence, Savings & Loan managers reacted swiftly to these changing circumstances. They proceeded to take the thrift out of thrifts. In California, seminars were held informing them "How to use the New Legislation to Get Rick Quick."[42] Formerly sober thrift managers started speculating in collateralized mortgage obligations—warned of the risks involved, one of their number retorted that "hedging is for sissies." Many Savings & Loans invested heavily in junk bonds. Thomas Spiegel, a former Drexel salesman who ran a California thrift, Columbia Savings & Loan, was particularly close to Milken, who took a large stake in his business. As the junk market took off, Spiegel expanded his bank's balance sheet from under $400 million in early 1982 to $13 billion five years later, of which nearly a third was invested in junk. Operating from an office in Beverly Hills close to Drexel's bond department, Columbia participated in all of Milken's biggest deals. Spiegel enjoyed the good life. He purchased two corporate jets and paid himself a $9 million salary in 1985.

Another junk-bond-buying bon vivant of the Savings & Loan world was David Paul, a former house builder, who ran the Centrust Savings Bank of Miami. Paul bought $1.4 billion worth of junk bonds and a similar amount of unrateable speculative bonds from Drexel, which had earlier helped finance his takeover of Centrust. Paul paid himself $16 million, took an apartment at the

Carlyle Hotel in Manhattan, and spent $1.4 million a year on a corporate jet, $13 million on a painting by Rubens and $8 million on a yacht (called *Le Grand Cru,* it came with gold-leaf ceilings and a Jacuzzi in the master suite). While the yacht and the art collection appeared as assets on the bank's balance sheet, junk bond losses went discreetly unreported.

The behaviour of the Texas Savings & Loan operators was even more unreal. They expanded their loan books by an average of over 1,200 percent a year, lending mostly on speculative property deals. Their business interests did not prevent them from enjoying the finer things in life. For instance, Don Ray Dixon of Vernon Savings took his wife by private jet and Rolls-Royce on a "market study" of French Michelin three-star restaurants (in return, she penned a report for the bank entitled *"Gastronomie Fantastique!"*). He also bought half a dozen jets, a vintage car dealership, and the sister ship to President Roosevelt's yacht. Another operator, Edwin "Fast Eddy" McBirney of Sunbelt Savings, fed his guests at his north Dallas home on lion meat and antelope, while presiding over the festivities dressed as Henry VIII with dry ice billowing around him. At another party at his penthouse suite in Las Vegas, McBirney allegedly diverted his bank's clients with an "enthusiastic lesbian romp" while prostitutes performed fellatio on favoured guests.[43]

Milken's web of contacts in the Savings & Loan world was complex. For instance, the Southmark Corporation, a conglomerate which issued junk through Drexel and bought the San Jacinto Savings & Loan Association of Houston in order to finance real estate deals, became the landlord of another of Milken's clients, Circus Circus, a Las Vegas casino operator. Southmark was connected with MDC Holdings of Denver, which owned Silverado Savings & Loan and also issued junk bonds through Drexel. McBirney's Sunbelt Savings held Southmark and MDC bonds in its junk bond portfolio.

By far the most notorious of Milken's many contacts in the thrift world was Charles Keating, head of Lincoln Savings & Loan of Irvine, California. A former swimming champion, Keating had once worked as a lawyer for Carl Lindner, the business tycoon and corporate raider. In 1978, he purchased from Lindner a large house-building company whose name he changed to American

Continental. Five years later, Drexel issued junk bonds and preferred stock for American Continental, retaining a 10 percent stake in the company for itself. With this money Keating bought Lincoln Savings & Loan. On taking control of Lincoln, Keating fired the thrift's senior management, increased its supply of funds from Wall Street money brokers in order to grow the bank rapidly, and commenced speculating in risky securities and property deals.

Keating put $100 million into Boesky's arbitrage partnership. In the spring of 1985, he backed Sir James Goldsmith's leveraged bid for Crown Zellerbach, the paper company. He made real estate deals in Texas and Arizona with the Southmark Corporation and Fast Eddy McBirney. In his dealings with Wall Street, Keating embarked on loss-making foreign exchange deals with Crédit Suisse, purchased the junkiest of junk bonds from Drexel, and speculated in stock options and shares using a supposedly fail-safe computerised trading system developed by Salomon Brothers, which nevertheless lost several million dollars. Facilitated by the deregulation and lax banking supervision of the Reagan years, Keating resorted to numerous accounting tricks to conceal his mounting losses. In 1986, he issued unsecured bonds for American Continental which he distributed to Lincoln's customers, many of whom believed, wrongly, that the bonds carried a federal guarantee.

Although reckless in his speculations, Keating displayed great care in cultivating politicians and regulators. He provided campaign funds to nine senators and several congressmen, and offered lucrative jobs to several of Lincoln's bank regulators and auditors. At one point, he even succeeded in getting a man heavily in debt to Lincoln appointed as commissioner to the Bank Board, the body ultimately responsible for regulating Lincoln's affairs. If he couldn't bribe bank regulators with employment, Keating threatened them personally with lawsuits. He hired the economist Alan Greenspan, later Chairman of the Federal Reserve, to support Lincoln's application to increase its "direct investments" to more than 10 percent of assets. (In a letter he must have come to regret deeply, Greenspan wrote to the California bank regulator that the management of Lincoln and American Continental was "seasoned and expert . . . [with] a long and continuous track record of outstanding success in making sound and profitable direct investments."*) When regulators discovered that Keating was concealing losses and had exceeded the regulations on direct investments, he used his friendly senators, later dubbed the "Keating Five," to browbeat the head of the Bank Board.†

For over two years, Keating successfully fended off the regulators. Finally, in the spring of 1989, Lincoln was taken over by the authorities. At a press conference held after the event, Keating announced: "One question, among the many raised in recent weeks, has to do with whether my financial support in any way influenced several political figures to take up my cause. I want to say in the most forceful way I can: I certainly hope so."[44] In similar manner, other thrift operators secured their freedom of action with political contributions. On his yacht Don Dixon of Vernon S&L held fund-raising parties for Jim Wright, the Speaker of the House, and several other leading Democrats.‡ "The Golden Rule," according to a lobbyist for the Texas thrifts, was that "he who has the gold makes the rules."[45] Never mind that the gold was borrowed with a federal guarantee.

By the end of the decade, the fastest-growing thrifts had accumulated staggering losses on their loan and investment portfolios—the bailout of Silverado Savings & Loan alone cost over $1 billion. Over eleven hundred thrifts failed as a result of their imprudent practices, and the American taxpayer was left to pick up the bill, amounting to around $200 billion. But for the presence of federal deposit insurance—the very policy which had encouraged their

---

*In another letter dated 13 February 1985, Greenspan claimed that Keating's management had turned Lincoln into "a financially strong institution" which would not pose any risk of loss to the federal insurer "for the foreseeable future." Greenspan was paid $40,000 for writing the two letters and testifying on Keating's behalf. (Mayer, *Bank Robbery*, pp. 140, 337.)

†Senator Alan Cranston of California, one of the "Keating Five," received nearly $900,000 from Keating (he also received campaign contributions from Drexel). The other members of this infamous group were Senators Donald Riegle, Dennis DeConcini, John Glenn, and John McCain (the only Republican among them).

‡Another Texas thrift operator, Tom Gaubert of Independent American, also supported Jim Wright. In return, Wright aggressively protected the thrifts. He accused the head of the Bank Board of abusing his expense account and a Texas bank regulator of homosexuality. Subsequently, the bailout of Independent American cost the American taxpayer $900 million. (Mayer, *Bank Robbery*, Chapter 9.)

reckless speculations—the collapse of the thrift industry would most probably have led to bank runs, followed by a credit contraction and asset deflation similar to that of the 1930s.

THE END OF THE DECADE

The junk bond mania continued into 1988. It was said that shortly after taking control of Allied Stores, Campeau, while on holiday in Florida, came across a Bloomingdale's store, whereupon he threw up his arms and declared, "This is the store I should have bought."[46] His bid for Bloomingdale's parent, Federated Stores, was launched in late January 1988; a contest developed, but Campeau had no limit. He secured the company at a cost of nearly $11 billion, with his own "equity" investment limited to less than $200 million. Bankers' fees for the transaction exceeded Federated's annual earnings. Shortly after the Federated takeover, Campeau ordered a lavish leather-bound book to be produced with photographs of his buildings and stores. In the introduction, America's greatest department store magnate expounded his vapid philosophy: "Because we can be no more than we aspire to be, we will aspire to be more than the best of what we are."[47]

The quality of junk bonds declined progressively as the gap between an LBO company's earnings and the interest payments on its junk bonds was whittled away. As a result, a slight decline in income would send the junk bonds into default and the company into bankruptcy. In order to conceal the fragility of this situation, Drexel and other investment banks issued more "accrued interest" securities, such as pay-in-kind and zero coupon bonds, which, because they paid interest with corporate paper rather than cash, delayed the initial impact of interest charges on a company's cash flow. The amount of equity invested in LBO deals also declined. James Grant calculated that in 1987 and 1988, equity investment in LBOs averaged less than 4 percent.[48] Some companies, such as Dr Pepper, the soft drinks manufacturer, went through multiple buyouts at ever increasing prices. Warren Buffett was reminded of a *New Yorker* cartoon in which a grateful borrower tells his bank manager, "I don't know how I'll ever repay you." On a more serious note, Buffett warned investors that "in the end, alchemy, whether it is metallurgical or financial, fails. A base business cannot be transformed into a golden business by tricks of accounting or capital structure."[49]

Ultimately, the health of the junk bond market rested upon an unwavering faith in Michael Milken. Unfortunately, the chief alchemist was removed from the scene just when his inspirational presence was most needed. Shortly after his arrest, Ivan Boesky had implicated Milken in order to lighten his own sentence. In September 1988, Milken and Drexel were charged with violating a number of securities laws, including those against racketeering, market manipulation, insider trading, and stock parking (i.e., executing false trades between parties in order to avoid taxes). After initial resistance, Drexel conceded to certain charges and agreed to pay a fine of $650 million and fire Milken. Milken initially proved more obdurate. In the spring of 1989, along with his brother Lowell and another Drexel associate, Milken received a ninety-eight-charge indictment which carried a potential maximum sentence of over five hundred years and limitless fines. Shortly after, in exchange for clemency for his brother, Milken arranged to plead guilty to a few minor felonies. A full trial, which might have provided a definitive exposition of Milken's role in the junk bond mania and ascertained the full extent of his criminality, was avoided. On 21 November 1991, Milken was sentenced to ten years' imprisonment. His fines totalled over $600 million.

At the time of his conviction, it was disclosed that between 1985 and 1987 Milken's cumulative earnings exceeded $1.2 billion. This revelation led the press to caricature the shy banker as "Money Mad Mike."* To many, Milken's ten-year sentence appeared a suitable punishment for his part in the "decade of greed." Naturally, his lawyers did not see it this way. Describing the case prepared against the financier by the U.S. Attorney's office under Rudolph Giuliani, Milken's lawyer, Arthur Liman, stated, "I am convinced that society needs a certain number of demons . . . The case took

Barron's labelled Milken "Mr. Greed of an historically greedy epoch, for analogs of which one must go back to the Gilded Age or the Twenties." (See Fischel, *Payback*, p. 181.)

on the characteristics of a heresy trial . . . [Milken had] become a symbol, the symbol of an era, and it was beyond any kind of control."*

While it is true that Milken was indicted for relatively minor offences (having escaped by plea-bargaining the more serious charges) and that, contrary to popular perception, the great bulk of his fortune was derived legitimately from his uncommonly generous remuneration package, Milken was not the innocent scapegoat portrayed by his legal team and PR advisers (whose budget ran to many millions of dollars). His total control of the junk bond market turned him and his fellow Drexel traders into bullies and braggarts. Corners were cut in the pursuit of profit. The lust for money and power created a collective adrenaline rush that fed upon itself, until Milken and Drexel became insatiable. Like Sir John Blunt in 1720, Milken overreached himself and brought about his own downfall. A greater degree of probity than Milken displayed has always been demanded from those who aspire to be great bankers.

Perhaps the best way to judge Milken's career is through the unfolding of events in the junk bond market. The leveraged buyout craze reached its zenith in early 1989 with Kohlberg Kravis Roberts' $26 billion takeover of RJR Nabisco, the food and tobacco conglomerate, an episode described by Anthony Bianco, a financial journalist, as resembling "*Der Ring des Nibelungen*, directed by Mel Brooks and starring a collection of ornery, steely-eyed midgets in the guise of gangsters."[50] *Time* magazine simply called it "A Game of Greed." The collapse of the junk bond world followed shortly after. In April 1989, Charles Keating's American Continental filed for bankruptcy. On 15 June, the day that Milken was sacked, Integrated Resources, a Drexel client, defaulted on its junk bonds (whereupon it became known as "Disintegrated"). In July, Congress passed a bill requiring Savings & Loan associations to dispose of their junk bond holdings. Two months later, the Campeau Corporation (not a Drexel client) admitted it could no longer pay the interest on its bonds. "It was as if," wrote the financial journalist James Stewart, "the nation's investors

*Sobel, *Dangerous Dreamers*, pp. 213–14. The view of Milken as the innocent victim of a popular backlash against financial excess has been the thesis of two revisionist accounts of the junk bond mania, Fenton Bailey's *Junk Bond Revolution* and Daniel Fischel's *Payback*.

had awakened from a decade-long dream and recognised finally that high returns could not be realised without increased risk."[51]

When the proposed buyout of United Airlines fell through in October 1989, the junk bond market collapsed and the Dow fell by 6 percent. A couple of months later, both the Campeau Corporation and Integrated Resources sought bankruptcy protection, along with the Jim Walter Corporation, a Kohlberg Kravis Roberts buyout. Its balance sheet heavy with depreciating junk bonds, Drexel Burnham Lambert found itself unable to roll over its short-term debts. Its numerous Wall Street enemies refused to come to Drexel's aid. On 13 February 1990, the bank that had epitomised the 1980s financial culture joined its clients in bankruptcy. During the next twelve months, two of Milken's largest junk bond buyers, Fred Carr's First Executive, an insurance company, and Thomas Spiegel's Columbia Savings & Loan, also failed. It was a sorry legacy for the empire of a man once hailed as the successor to Pierpont Morgan.

The corporate raiders had enjoyed lambasting incumbent managements, complaining typically that senior executives had no stake in the businesses they ran. Yet most of the raiders' stakes were composed of borrowed money. The debts were serviced by sacking workers and cutting other operating expenses, and by reducing ongoing investments. This might lead to increased efficiency as flab was cut from a company but it could also seriously weaken its competitive position, as has been the case with RJR Nabisco. When the timing was right, as with Perelman's takeover of Revlon and Kohlberg Kravis Roberts' acquisition of Beatrice, the gains for the raiders were mouthwatering. When the timing and execution were poor, as with Campeau's venture into the department store business, the losses for the creditors were excruciating.

The junk bond revolution was based on a profound asymmetry between risk and reward, with junk bond purchasers taking most of the risk and "takeover entrepreneurs" snaffling most of the rewards. In fact, the movement for leveraged buyouts represented the return of the large speculative margin loan through the back door. For instance, Robert Campeau acquired control of an $11 billion company with an equity investment of only $200 million. Since he actually borrowed the equity portion, the margin loan was close to 100 percent. Examined in this light, the returns of Kohlberg Kravis Roberts for its investors look less than impressive. Leon Cooperman, a Goldman Sachs partner, calculated that holding a selection of stocks on 85 percent margin during the bull market of the 1980s would have yielded annual profits of nearly 75 percent. Using similar leverage, KKR achieved returns for its investors of only 60 percent.[52] Yet these returns were sufficient to make vast personal fortunes for the firm's partners.

Once the figures could be examined, it became clear that, contrary to Milken's gospel, junk bonds had considerably underperformed investment-grade bonds. Not only were the returns lower, but the risks were far greater than Milken's initial analysis had suggested. The rate of default on junk bonds rose to around 9 percent in the early 1990s, more than four times the historic average.* The change in the rate of default demonstrates what George Soros has termed the "reflexivity" of the financial markets: as investors came to share Milken's belief that junk bonds provided better returns, their relative quality declined until they became the worst and most speculative investments. Milken's thesis for junk bonds resembles E. L. Smith's case for equity investment in the 1920s: both were based on sound statistical analyses of past returns, yet the validity of their conclusions was vitiated by subsequent manias. Commenting on Milken's original case for junk bonds (based on their historic outperformance), Warren Buffett observed, "If history books were the key to riches, the Forbes 400 would consist of librarians."[53]

Michael Milken received his sentence on the very day Mrs. Thatcher was toppled from power. It was widely expected that after the excesses of the 1980s, the speculative spirit would wane as it had done after the 1920s. In retrospect, the crash of 1987 sent out a radically different message to the events of 1929. The market's recovery appeared to show that buying and holding stocks was the best investment strategy, and that stock market crashes did not

*The total return for junk bonds in the 1980s was 145 percent, compared to 202 percent for investment-grade bonds and 207 percent for stocks. By 1990, over $5.5 billion worth of junk bonds issued by Drexel were in default. A year later, nearly a quarter of the smaller firms which issued junk bonds through Drexel had defaulted on their interest payments. (Stewart, *Den of Thieves*, p. 430.)

herald economic depressions. Instead, they provided an opportunity for bargain basement purchases by canny investors "buying into the dip." If a runaway stock market train hit the buffers at high speed, the Federal Reserve would always be there to sort out the mess. If the banks messed up, deposit insurance guaranteed that the taxpayer would end up paying. Portfolio insurers, it is true, suffered public censure and disappeared from the scene. Exponents of the Efficient Market Hypothesis kept their heads down, but for only a short while. A few years later, two number-crunching academics produced an analysis suggesting that the 1987 crash had been a chimera, a mathematical aberration, a chance event whose odds against recurrence were 10^{-160} to one: "Even if one were to have lived through the entire twenty billion year life of the universe," they concluded, "and experienced this twenty billion times (twenty billion big bangs), the probability that such a decline could have happened even once in this period is a virtual impossibility."*

*These fantastic odds are simply a convoluted way of stating that the size of the crash was unprecedented. (Cited by Melamed, *Escape*, p. 363.)

CHAPTER 9

KAMIKAZE CAPITALISM: THE JAPANESE BUBBLE ECONOMY OF THE 1980s*

By your patience, Aunchient Pistol, Fortune is painted blind, with a muffler afore her eyes, to signify to you that she is blind; and she is painted also with a wheel to signify to you, which is the moral of it, that she is turning and inconstant, and mutability and variation; and her foot, look you, is fixed upon a spherical stone, which rolls and rolls and rolls. In good truth, the poet makes a most excellent description of it. Fortune is an excellent moral.

Shakespeare, *Henry V*, Act III, Sc. 6

Central to the body of thought known as *Nihonjinron* (which roughly translates as "the theory of the Japanese") is the idea that Japan is unique. Perceived differences between Japan and the West were sometimes invoked by the Japanese authorities in order to hinder the import of foreign goods. For instance, Japanese intestines were said to be different from those of Westerners and therefore unsuited to foreign beef and rice. It was even claimed that American skis were useless in Japan because the snow was different. At other times, pointing out such differences became a barely concealed expression of Japanese cultural nationalism and xenophobia: the Japanese brain was said to have a heightened sensitivity to the sounds of nature and a more intricate understanding of social relationships. The Japanese distrusted Western-style rationalism as

*The term "kamikaze capitalism" was first used to describe the bubble economy by Michael Lewis in the *Spectator* (2 June 1990). It is irresistibly apposite.

being incompatible with the preservation of *wa* (social harmony). They recognised a distinction between *honne* (a private intention or thought) and *tatemae* (a public version of the truth), and considered both to be equally valid. Japanese reason was described as "wet," like the cloying rice of the national diet (which formed the glue of the community), while Western reason was "dry" and individualistic. Even in the ethical sphere, the Japanese were said to be different. They did not feel guilt, only shame on public revelation of misdeeds. At the root of all these differences, both real and spurious, lay a profound distrust of individualism, which found its counterpart in a strong attachment to community and deference to authority.

The Western model of capitalism is primarily individualistic: self-interest directs the "invisible hand" which holds the system together. Because self-interest cannot be directed by authority, Adam Smith described the market system as that most compatible with a state of civil liberty. The centrality of self-interest to Western capitalism dictates a number of economic policies: a confined role for government in economic affairs, a distrust of monopolies and cartels, and the protection of the individual whether operating as a tradesman, entrepreneur, capitalist, or consumer. Laissez-faire prescribes that markets should be left to find their natural level, while the law of comparative advantage enjoins governments not to protect their domestic industries from foreign competition.

Japanese capitalism is, in many respects, the antithesis of the Western model. Until the middle of the nineteenth century Japan remained a feudal economy, closed to the outside world, with no tradition of legal rights for the individual. When the Japanese authorities of the Meiji era decided to modernise their country following the arrival of American warships under Commodore Perry in the middle of the nineteenth century, they borrowed selectively from the West to build a new economic system. The hierarchy of the feudal system, however, remained in place. It was simply transferred from an agricultural base to a corporate industrial one. The peasant who had formally bowed to his feudal lord now served a corporate master. Even after the Second World War, it was common for a worker to be called by the name of his company. For instance, if he worked for the country's largest car manufacturer, he might be known to his friends as Toyota-san, Mr. Toyota. Employees were required to sing the company song, and even worship at the company founder's shrine. In exchange for their devotion and self-sacrifice, employees were rewarded by their companies with lifetime employment and promotion according to seniority. The primacy of the company in the Japanese system was recognised by the authorities, which encouraged the creation of industry cartels and huge industrial groups, known as *zaibatsu.* When the *zaibatsu* were partially dismembered by the American occupation forces after the Second World War, they were replaced by less formal groupings, known as *keiretsu,* in which outright ownership gave way to an intricate system of cross-shareholdings.*

In Japanese capitalism, the role of the authorities was traditionally wide-ranging, though undefined. Officials at the Ministry of International Trade and Industry (MITI) and at the Ministry of Finance controlled industries through an informal process known as administrative guidance, a system of persuasion and intimidation based on the bureaucrats' powers to license companies, provide tax concessions, distribute government contracts, and so on. In the postwar era, MITI decided which industries to support and which companies would enjoy a privileged position within an industry cartel and receive protection from foreign competition. The Ministry of Finance guarded the financial sector and ensured that cheap loans were channelled from Japan's thrifty savers to its cash-hungry and highly leveraged corporations. As interest rates were kept artificially low by these arrangements and companies generally paid only small dividends, returns for Japanese investors were poor. Indeed, the term "Japanese capitalism" is misleading since *capital* did not actually determine the nature of the system. The domestic consumer was similarly exploited by the Japanese system. Imports were restricted by a variety of measures, and it was common for Japanese manufactured goods to sell for a higher price in Tokyo than in New York.

The Japanese prided themselves that their system was less selfish and more stable than the West. They boasted that they were long-termist, while the West pursued only short-term gains. Japanese

*Cross-shareholdings increased in the early 1970s in order to prevent foreign takeovers of Japanese companies. By the late 1980s, they accounted for around 70 percent of all outstanding shares.

companies were more interested in market share than profitability, and paid more attention to administrative guidance and their *keiretsu* obligations than to their returns on capital. Under this system the role of the market was severely restricted. One Western commentator declared that the Japanese "have never really caught up with Adam Smith . . . They don't *believe* in the invisible hand!"[1] The individualistic pursuit of self-interest was deplored and a distrust of trade lingered. While money was recognised as the source of power in politics, samurai tradition emphasised the virtues of frugality. In prewar Japan, the nouveau riche were dismissed as *narikin,* a Japanese chess term for a pawn promoted to a queen—an object with no hierarchical right. Hierarchy remained the essence of the system: employees had a defined position within their corporate hierarchy, and companies were ranked within their *keiretsu,* which in turn took its place in the hierarchy of the Keidanren (the Federation of Economic Organisations).

Speculation is antithetical to a state-directed economic system such as existed in Japan. It is inherently short-termist and seeks the maximisation of gain, while the Japanese system was professedly long-termist and considered other economic objectives, such as the development of favoured industries, more important than mere profit. Speculation also involves the transference of risk, but after a stock market crash and numerous bank collapses in the 1920s and early 1930s, it was declared that the Japanese authorities would never again tolerate such failures. As a result, risk was socialised in Japan to a far greater degree than in the West. Nevertheless, speculation came to Japan in the 1980s. It burrowed so deep inside the Japanese system that when it departed, after a mere five years, the system was in ruins. Officials tried to pick up the pieces and reconstruct the old order, but their efforts were in vain. This was the real legacy of the bubble economy.

WINNING THE PEACE

Speculative euphoria is often a symptom of hubris. For this reason, we find great speculative manias at times when the economic balance of power is shifting from one nation to another. For instance, the Tulip Mania appeared in Holland shortly after the Dutch "economic miracle," which saw Amsterdam established as the entrepôt of the world. In similar fashion, a stock market boom occurred in New York at the beginning of the twentieth century, when the United States overtook Britain as the world's leading industrial power.* For more than three-quarters of a century America stoutly maintained its economic primacy, but by the middle of the 1980s its position was threatened by the growing might of Japan. Japan's share of world trade was over 10 percent, its trade surpluses were burgeoning, the nation's capital exports invited comparison with those of Britain in the nineteenth century, and Japanese per capita income was in the course of exceeding American levels. Japan's industrial companies dominated new technologies in consumer electronics and a number of other fields, and its banks were the largest in the world in terms of both assets and market value.

America was on the run. While Japan had its trade surpluses, America faced growing trade deficits. The Reagan administration also produced enormous budget deficits that were only sustained by the willingness of Japanese investors to sink their country's trade surplus into U.S. Treasury bonds. In Detroit, angry autoworkers destroyed Japanese cars in protest against imports. The *New York Times* warned that "today, forty years after the end of World War II, the Japanese are on the move again in one of history's

*There are a number of parallels between the bubble economy of the 1980s and the U.S. boom at the turn of the century. Like Japan in the 1980s, the United States had a huge trade surplus ($500 million in 1900). Just as Tokyo was heralded as a global financial centre in the 1980s, so New York was replacing London as the world's financial capital. Americans spoke of a "new era" of American greatness. In both periods, domestic speculative exuberance found an outlet in extravagant overseas purchases. In the early 1900s, Americans spent over $100 million on British shares, in particular buying up British shipping interests. As with Japanese acquisitions in America in the 1980s, this caused a furore in England, where it was claimed that the United States, with its boundless capital, was buying British shipping supremacy (the chairman of Leyland Lines said the price offered for his company was so high he could not refuse). When the boom subsided, British interests bought back control of International Mercantile Marine for less than a third of the original sale price. In a similar fashion, after the end of the bubble economy many of the Japanese "trophy" U.S. properties were sold back to Americans at lower prices. Alexander Dana Noyes called the U.S. boom of 1901 "as much a social and psychological phenomenon as a financial episode." The same might be said of Japan's bubble economy. (*Market Place*, p. 193.)

most brilliant commercial offensives, as they go about dismantling American industry."[2] Assailed by commentators who told them they were balefully short-termist and suffering from chronic individualism, Americans lost some of their self-confidence. It was claimed that the United States was threatened by an "economic Pearl Harbor."[3] A book entitled *Japan as Number One* became a best-seller on both sides of the Pacific.[4]

The Japanese also invested their trade surplus in purchasing U.S. assets other than Treasury bonds. American property was a particular favourite with Japanese investors. After the Mitsui Corporation acquired the Exxon Building in Manhattan for a record price of $610 million in 1986, it was reported that Mitsui's Japanese president had paid $260 million above Exxon's asking price in order to see his name in the *Guinness Book of World Records.*[5] Given the extravagance of many Japanese overseas acquisitions, this story appeared credible. As the decade progressed, the Japanese snapped up other icons of American capitalism, most notoriously New York's Rockefeller Center and Hollywood's Columbia Pictures. This deluge of Japanese capital revived the fierce xenophobia that Americans had formerly displayed towards their wartime adversaries. American anxieties over the "yellow peril," expressed in scaremongering works including Susan Tolchin's *Buying into America* (1988) and Daniel Burstein's *Yen! Japan's New Financial Empire and Its Threat to America* (1989), found their broadest audience with Michael Crichton's best-selling novel *Rising Sun,* which was published at the height of the "Japan is buying up the United States" hysteria.[6] Crichton told the *New York Times* that he had written the novel "to make America wake up."

American fears were matched by a revival of Japanese self-confidence, sweetly enjoyed after the deeply felt humiliation of military defeat and the long sacrifices undertaken to rebuild the shattered nation. A newfound self-assurance was evident in the posturing of Japanese politicians. In the autumn of 1986, Yasuhiro Nakasone, the newly elected Prime Minister, ascribed the success of the Japanese economy and the relative decline of the United States to his nation's racial homogeneity compared with America's racially mixed workforce. Such comments echoed the wartime propaganda that had asserted the superiority of the Yamato race.[7]

Several leading members of the government even publicly visited the Yasukuni Shrine, where the war dead were honoured, while Nakasone himself proclaimed that the "nation must shed all sense of ignominy and move forward seeking glory." Having lost the war and discarded its dreams of a Pacific empire, Japan had finally won the peace and emerged as an economic superpower.* Under the circumstances, hubris was perhaps inevitable.

ZAITECH: CORPORATE SPECULATION

Japan could not avoid being sucked into the vortex of the financial revolution that followed the breakup of the Bretton Woods fixed currency system in 1971 (an event, incidentally, which President Nixon blamed on Japan, whose chronically undervalued currency had undermined the system). In 1980, Japan liberalised its exchange controls. Even so, the pace of reforms was too slow for many American critics, who argued that continuing restrictions in the Japanese financial system were part of a deliberate policy to keep the yen below its natural level, thereby making Japanese exports cheaper. In fact, the liberalisation of the financial system was not simply the result of American pressure. Japan was obliged to reform its financial markets in order to recirculate the excess capital accumulated by its rising trade surpluses and sustained by its high savings rate. Although the Japanese authorities could not avoid the financial revolution, they hoped that reforms would enable Tokyo to emerge as a global financial centre, taking its rightful place alongside New York and London.

In the spring of 1984, the Japanese authorities agreed to allow foreign banks to deal in Japanese government bonds and enter the trust banking business. At the same time, controls on foreign exchange trading were removed. For the first time, Japanese banks were allowed to set their own rates of interest on large deposit accounts. As a result of these reforms, Japan's capital markets were quickly filled with the detritus of the financial revolution: Canadian

*During the second half of the 1980s, Japan was also described as a "creditor superpower," an "asset superpower," and a "financial superpower."

and Australian twofers, reverse dual-currency bonds, samurai and sushi bonds, instantly repackaged perpetuals, zero coupon bonds, square trips and double-dip leveraged leases, Euroyen bonds, and hara-kiri swaps.[8] Financial derivatives also came to Tokyo with the opening of futures markets for Japanese bond and stock indexes.

In the early 1980s, Japanese companies began supplementing their ordinary earnings with the extraordinary profits derived from *zaitech* (financial engineering). In 1984, the Ministry of Finance permitted companies to operate special accounts for their shareholdings, known as *tokkin* accounts. These accounts allowed companies to trade securities without paying capital gains tax on their profits.* Brokerages also offered a semi-legal service managing special speculative accounts for companies, known as *eigyo tokkin*, on which they guaranteed a minimum return above the current rate of interest.† The game was fixed to ensure they would emerge winners. In 1985, just under ¥9 trillion was invested in *tokkin* funds. Four years later, the figure had risen to over ¥40 trillion ($300 billion).‡

Zaitech speculation was facilitated by Japanese companies' access to the Eurobond market, the offshore capital market based in London. As part of the process of financial deregulation, in 1981 the Ministry of Finance gave Japanese companies permission to issue warrant bonds in the Eurobond market. These financial instruments combined conventional corporate bonds with an option (the "warrant") to purchase shares in the company at a specified price before the expiry date (normally set five years after issue). Since Japanese share prices were rising sharply, increasing

*From December 1980, Japanese companies were allowed to account the value of their investments at the *higher* of book cost or market price. Thus, companies were able to conceal their losses and flaunt their profits.

†Although *eigyo tokkin* accounts were not officially allowed, the Ministry of Finance turned a blind eye to them. Later, these accounts were at the centre of the loss-compensation scandal which plagued the leading Japanese securities firms in 1990. (See below.)

‡For the sake of simplicity, a constant exchange rate of ¥133 to the dollar is applied throughout this chapter.

the value of the warrants, companies were able to issue bonds with very low interest payments.* Warrant bonds were also attractive to their issuers for another reason. They were mostly issued in dollars that were subsequently exchanged in the swaps market for yen. Because the yen was expected to appreciate over the life of the loan, swapping a dollar liability for a yen liability could result in a *negative* interest payment by the company issuing the warrant bond. In other words, *Japanese companies were actually paid to borrow the money to finance their speculations.* Money raised from warrant bond issues could either be invested directly in the stock market or placed in an *eigyo tokkin* account with a guaranteed return of 8 percent. *Zaitech* was a game with no losers.

In the second half of the 1980s, the profits from corporate speculation soared along with the Japanese stock market. This created a dangerous circularity in the financial system: *zaitech* manufactured profits, causing share prices to rise, which further increased *zaitech* gains. By the end of the decade most of the industrial companies listed on the Tokyo Stock Exchange were engaging in *zaitech.* Over half the reported profits of the largest players—internationally renowned companies such as car manufacturers, Toyota and Nissan, and consumer electronics firms, Matsushita and Sharp—were derived from speculation.† Total corporate gains from *tokkin* accounts rose from ¥240 billion ($2 billion) in the year to March 1985, to ¥952 billion ($7 billion) two years later. Few cared that during the same period ordinary operating profits actually declined.[9] In certain cases, the speculative activities of companies came to dominate their business. A steel company named Hanwa, known as "the Gnome of the East," raised over ¥4 trillion ($30 billion) in the

*The valuation of Japanese warrant bonds created an absurd circularity: the faster Japanese shares rose, the more warrant bonds were worth—and the more warrants could be sold for, the faster shares rose. This situation recalls the earlier conversion of British government annuities into South Sea shares in 1720.

†For instance, Toyota raised ¥200 billion in 1986 for *zaitech* by issuing convertible bonds which paid a coupon of less than 2 percent. The following year, the car manufacturer made ¥150 billion in *zaitech* profits on investments totalling ¥1.7 trillion.

late 1980s for *zaitech* and its profits from speculation grew to exceed its earnings from ordinary trading activities by twenty times.*

Not all the new capital raised by Japanese companies in the late 1980s was poured into speculation. Warrant bonds also financed what has been described as "the greatest wave of investments in productive capacity the world has ever seen."[10] In the second half of the 1980s, capital investment in Japan amounted to $3.5 trillion, accounting for two-thirds of the country's economic growth. This massive burst of investment helped the Japanese economy pass through a difficult period when the stronger yen was causing both lower growth rates and declining returns on capital.† Some commentators have suggested that the Ministry of Finance deliberately called into being the bubble economy in order to supply cheap capital for Japanese industry at this critical time.‡ The capital expenditure of the bubble years created the illusion that Japan's economic miracle was continuing long after its real vigour had diminished, and produced a vast misallocation of resources into unproductive investments. By attempting to use speculation as a tool of economic policy, the mandarins of the Finance Ministry had opened a Pandora's box.

---

*In October 1990, Hanwa announced a loss of ¥20 billion on its stock market investments. By this date, Hanwa's leverage (the ratio of debt to shareholders' funds) had risen to over 1,200 percent.

†Many manufacturing companies which raised capital during the late 1980s used the proceeds to build overseas factories in order to circumvent the problems caused by the appreciation of the yen. Other companies invested in new plants in Japan in order to reduce the unit costs of their products. By 1990, business investment accounted for 22 percent of Japanese GNP, up from 14 percent in 1983. (See Zielinski and Holloway, *Unequal Equities*, p. 137.)

‡This point is made most forcefully by R. Taggart Murphy, who claims that "the bubble economy was deliberately manufactured by the Japanese Ministry of Finance and its sometime agents/sometime rivals at the Bank of Japan." (*Japanese Money*, p. 152.) In early 1988, an unnamed official at the Bank of Japan confessed: "We intended first to boost the stock and property markets. Supported by this safety net—rising markets—export-oriented industries were supposed to reshape themselves so they could adapt to a domestic-led economy. This step was then supposed to bring about an enormous growth of assets over every economic sector. This wealth effect would in turn touch off personal consumption and residential investment, followed by an increase of investment in plant and equipment. In the end, loosened monetary policy would boost real economic growth." (Cited by Tomohiko Taniguchi, *Japan's Banks and the "Bubble Economy" of the Late 1980s*, Center of International Studies, Program on U.S.-Japan Relations, Monograph Series, No. 4, Princeton University, 1993, p. 9.)

THE LAND STANDARD

The bubble economy, or *baburu* as the Japanese called it, was first and foremost a property boom. Land holds a special position for the Japanese. Its ownership continued to convey status in a society not long released from feudal servitude. Japan is a mountainous country where development land is relatively scarce. There were other reasons for high Japanese land prices. Punitive capital gains taxes—designed by the bureaucrats to encourage "long-termism"—taxed short-term property gains at 150 percent of profits. By discouraging the sale of land and creating an illiquid property market, the fiscal system actually stimulated land speculation.[11] Some Western commentators even suggested that high property prices—which turned the Japanese, in the words of Sir Roy Denham, a former European commissioner, into a nation of "workaholics living in rabbit hutches"—were part of a covert government policy to encourage savings which could then be ploughed back into the industrial machine.

Between 1956 and 1986, land prices increased 5,000 percent, while consumer prices merely doubled. During this period, in only one year (1974) did land prices decline. Acting on the belief that land prices would never fall again, Japanese banks provided loans against the collateral of land rather than cash flows. Towards the end of the 1980s, they increased lending against property, especially to smaller companies. The rising value of land became the engine for the creation of credit in the whole economy.* *Tochi-hon'i sei*, the land standard, had arrived.

In early December 1987 at a meeting of the Bank for International Settlements in Basel, Switzerland, representatives from the world's central banks gathered to set new international standards for banking capital. Because Japanese banks were protected from

*The same process had been at work in the United States during the 1920s. Until the McFadden Act of 1927, nationally chartered banks were forbidden to lend against property collateral. Afterwards they increased their property loans substantially, thereby contributing to the stock market and property booms. The failure of the Bank of the United States in December 1930, which triggered the national banking crisis, was due to the bank's overexposure to a falling property market. (See Grant, *Money of the Mind*, p. 211.)

failure by the Ministry of Finance, they had traditionally operated with a lower capital adequacy ratio (a safety cushion measured by the ratio of a bank's assets to its loans) than their Western counterparts. Foreign bankers were concerned that lower capital reserves gave Japanese banks an unfair competitive advantage in global banking and demanded that they conform to conventional international levels of banking capital. As a result, Japanese banks were obliged to raise their capital ratio to 8 percent by the spring of 1993.

An important concession, however, was secured by the Japanese representatives at Basel. As part of the web of cross-shareholdings peculiar to the Japanese system, their banks owned a large number of shares in other companies. It was agreed that a certain proportion of the profits on these shareholdings could count towards Japanese banking capital.* As a result of the Basel agreement, Japanese banks' ability to increase credit—in other words, to *manufacture money*—became linked to the level of share prices in the Tokyo stock market. Everything else being equal, if the banks increased their property lending, the value of land and shares (Japanese companies were increasingly valued according to their property assets) would climb, rising share prices would increase the value of the banks' cross-shareholdings, inflating their capital and enabling them to lend more. The world's central bankers had endorsed a circular arrangement by which credit creation could continue as long as stock prices rose. This was the "fatal flaw" of the bubble economy.†

*The agreement stipulated that 45 percent of the unrealised gains on the banks' shareholdings could count for up to half of their required capital reserves.

†The term "fatal flaw" was used by Christopher Wood to describe the Basel agreement (*Bubble Economy*, p. 27). In fact, the nature of this flaw was first recognised in the late seventeenth century. In 1695, an anonymous pamphleteer attacked land bank projectors who sought to replace a gold-backed currency with one based on agricultural rents. The author showed that as the stock of land remained fixed, increasing the supply of money would serve to drive up the value of land ad infinitum. John Law, a former land bank projector, introduced the same error into his Mississippi System in France between 1715 and 1720. As the Mississippi Company's share price rose, he increased the supply of paper banknotes issued by the Banque Royale (which he controlled). In his recent account of the Mississippi Bubble, Antoin Murphy refers to Law's confusion of money and shares as the "fatal flaw" in his system. (See Chapter 3.)

THE PLAZA ACCORD

In the mid-1980s, the economic policies of Japan were the opposite of those of the United States: Japan had a tight fiscal policy and a loose monetary policy, while America combined a tight monetary policy with a loose fiscal stance. High interest rates in the United States, intended by the Federal Reserve to keep inflation at bay, had the unwelcome effect of creating a strong dollar that hindered exports and increased the American trade deficit.* American exporters noisily demanded assistance from their government. Since the dollar was overvalued and the yen undervalued, floating exchange rates should theoretically have solved the problem. In practice, they needed a little prompting.

In September 1985, U.S. Treasury Secretary James Baker gathered the finance ministers of the world's leading economic powers at the Plaza Hotel in Manhattan. Spurred on by Baker, the ministers agreed to act in concert to push down the value of the dollar in relation to other currencies, in particular the yen.[12] A few months later, the dollar sank to under 150 yen, from an earlier high of 259. Viewed from another perspective, the purchasing power of the Japanese currency had risen by over 40 percent, and everything priced in dollars was that much cheaper to anyone with yen in his pockets. The great Japanese shopping spree—from Louis Vuitton handbags to van Gogh paintings—was set to commence.

There was, however, an immediate downside to the yen's appreciation. Ever since April 1949, when the American banker Joseph Dodge fixed the yen exchange rate against the dollar at 360, the Japanese currency had been consistently undervalued in the foreign exchanges. In the 1970s and early 1980s, higher rates of inflation in the United States than in Japan combined with a stable exchange rate to produce (in real terms) a continuous devaluation of the yen. This was of great assistance to Japanese exporters, the powerhouses behind the country's economic miracle. After the

*The U.S. current account moved from a surplus of $7 billion in 1981 to a deficit of $212 billion in 1985. In the same period, the federal government deficit rose from $74 billion to $212 billion.

Plaza Accord, the situation changed. Japanese goods in the international market were suddenly nearly twice as expensive. The threat to Japan's economy was palpable. In early 1986, as economic growth slipped below 2.5 percent, the talk was of *endaka fukyo* (the strong yen recession).* Exporters warned of a "hollowing-out" of the economy as the yen rose inexorably against the dollar. Urgent action was required and Japanese companies looked to the all-powerful Ministry of Finance for a solution. The ministry, in turn, put pressure on the (officially independent) Bank of Japan to reduce interest rates in order to stimulate the economy. During 1986, the Official Discount Rate was cut on four occasions until it reached 3 percent. Since the price of oil was falling and imported goods were cheaper due to the strong yen, the faster monetary growth that followed did not feed into consumer price inflation.† Instead, the price of assets—land and shares—started to rise.

By August 1986, the Nikkei index had reached 18,000, up nearly 40 percent since the start of the year. This sharp rise stimulated the public's interest in economic matters. A *manga* (comic book) on the Japanese economy, published by the *Nihon Keizai Shimbun*, Japan's leading financial newspaper, went to the top of the best-seller lists. At the end of the year, the *Far Eastern Economic Review* reported that "suddenly, stocks have become a national street-level preoccupation."

Against the background of a rising market, the government launched its long-awaited flotation of Nippon Telephone and Telegraph (NTT), the national telephone company. In October 1986, an initial 200,000 shares in the company were offered to the Japanese public (at the time, foreigners were forbidden by NTT's articles from holding its shares). Within two months, nearly ten million persons had applied for shares, even though the government had yet to announce the issue price. Popular demand was so strong that the shares had to be distributed by a special lottery. On 2 February

*In the first quarter of 1986, Japanese economic growth was negative (at minus 0.5 percent).

†While the discount rate remained at 2.5 percent in the late 1980s, the money supply grew annually by more than 10 percent, equivalent to twice the growth of GNP. See Koichi Hamada, "Bubbles, Bursts and Bailouts: Comparison of Three Episodes of Financial Crises in Japan," unpublished paper, September 1993, p. 16.

1987, NTT's shares floated freely on the Tokyo Stock Exchange at a price of ¥1.2 million per share. In the first two days of trading their price soared by 25 percent.

At the end of February, the Group of Seven Finance Ministers meeting at the Louvre in Paris agreed to stop the dollar from sliding any further against the yen. Following this agreement, Japanese interest rates were cut to a postwar low of 2½ percent (where they remained until May 1989).* The effect on share prices was electrifying: within a few weeks, NTT's share price was at ¥3.2 million, valuing it at over two hundred times annual earnings. The telephone company's market capitalisation was now more than ¥50 trillion ($376 billion), larger than the *combined* value of the West German and Hong Kong stock markets. Seeing the frenzy for NTT's shares, the company's chairman, Hisashi Shinto, remarked casually to a reporter: "One day people engaged in the money game are going to incur the wrath of God."†

The privatisation of NTT was reminiscent of the South Sea subscriptions in 1720: both privatisations were intended to improve the public finances; on each occasion the public applied for shares before being informed of the price; and a speculative bubble followed with both companies' share prices rising above "rational" levels. Most significantly, in 1720 and again in 1987, speculators were led to believe that the government would not allow the share price to fall. When the second tranche of NTT shares were issued in November 1987, the *Japan Economic Journal* observed that

> the popularity of NTT is attributed to individual investors' beliefs that since the government made the public offering, it

*R. Taggart Murphy finds a parallel between the Louvre Accord of 1987 and the decision of the Federal Reserve Bank of New York in 1927 to lower interest rates at the request of the British authorities in order to relieve pressure on sterling. In both cases, artificially low interest rates stimulated speculation. (*Japanese Money*, p. 180.) Professor Koichi Hamada concurs: "international coordination to keep the dollar from depreciating [after the Louvre Accord] imposed an extremely easy monetary policy [in Japan] that fuelled the land and asset price bubbles." (Hamada, "Bubbles," pp. 15–16.)

†Grant, *Mr. Market*, p. 303. The NTT chairman became one of the first to be called to account for the excesses of the "money game" when he was forced to resign for his part in the Recruit Cosmos scandal of 1988. (See below.)

> would not inflict losses on the people . . . individual investors consider they are buying Japan itself when they buy NTT shares. So they buy them without apprehension . . .*

When the Japanese stock market bounced back after the October crash, it was widely believed that political protection had been granted not just to NTT but to the stock market as a whole.

MONEY POLITICS

Japanese politicians were not solely guided by public duty in their desire to support the stock market. They also maintained a private interest in its continuing ascendancy. In Japan the conduct of politics had become an expensive business. It was calculated that the annual expense of maintaining a seat in the Japanese Diet was around ¥400 million ($3 million).[13] Cash was the primary source of power in Japanese politics: it bound factions together, purchased ministerial seats, procured favours, and bought votes. In the style of Tammany Hall bosses in the Gilded Age, Japanese politicians looted the stock market to fill their own coffers. During elections, "political shares" (*seiji kabu*) were pushed by securities houses. This enabled politicians, who had previously invested in them, to take profits and pay their election expenses, after which the shares were allowed to decline.[14] During the bubble years, shares became a supplementary currency for the conduct of the nation's money politics. This added further support to the notion that politicians would never allow the stock market to fall.

The deep involvement of politicians in the stock market was revealed to the public by the Recruit Cosmos scandal. In June 1988, a minor public official in the city of Kawasaki resigned after he admitted using inside information to buy shares in Recruit Cosmos, the property subsidiary of a fast-growing employment agency. Recruit's chairman was an ambitious businessman named Hiromasa Ezoe, who had made extensive gifts of shares to a number of

*Ibid., p. 304. In September 1988, the *Economist* cynically observed that there was "only one more tranche [of NTT] to sell, and then the market can be left to swim or sink by itself."

politicians, businessmen, and bureaucrats in order to forestall planned legislation detrimental to the interests of his company. In late December 1988, Takahishi Hasegawa, the newly appointed Justice Minister brought in to investigate the Recruit scandal, was forced to resign after only four days in office when it was revealed that he had received shares in the company. The Finance Minister also stepped down. A few months later, the Prime Minister, Nobura Takeshita, finally admitted to profiting by ¥150 million from the sale of Recruit Cosmos shares. Takeshita's political secretary, who had received the money on his master's behalf, hanged himself.* The net gradually widened to catch other big fish, including former Prime Minister Nakasone, the chairman of NTT, and the president of a major newspaper, the *Nihon Keizai Shimbun.* By the summer of 1989, nearly fifty politicians, civil servants, businessmen, and journalists had been exposed by the scandal. Western commentators wondered whether "crony capitalism" might not be an apt description of the Japanese system.

Recruit Cosmos was the greatest political scandal in postwar Japan. It showed political venality to be an integral aspect of the bubble economy. The rising stock market had initially reflected Japan's newfound feeling of economic prowess. The nation's growing self-confidence was appropriated by politicians for nationalistic purposes. Later, bureaucrats stimulated public speculation in order to assist Japanese companies in raising cheap capital during a difficult transitional period. A thriving stock market enabled the government to solve its fiscal problems by selling shares in an overpriced telephone company to naive investors caught up in the euphoria of the bubble. In the background lurked the systemic corruption of Japan's money politics, which utilised speculation to service its fathomless financial demands. Speculation ran amok because no one in a position of power had any interest in controlling it. The Americans, who feared that Japan threatened an "economic Pearl Harbor," were correct in one sense. The militaristic hubris that took Japan blindly into the Second World War found its

*He left behind an incriminating suicide note: "Behind the scenes of this peaceful democracy are the same bloody struggles to the death that were waged time after time by medieval warlords."

counterpart in the speculative hubris of the bubble economy. History was repeating itself, except this time a stock market farce replaced the tragedy of war.

VALUES IN THE JAPANESE STOCK MARKET

During the late 1980s, Japanese share prices increased three times faster than corporate earnings (which included the unsustainable profits derived from *zaitech* speculation). The Tokyo stock market flaunted some of the most overvalued shares in history: the textile sector sold for an average of 103 times earnings, services companies for 112 times earnings, marine transportation businesses for 176 times earnings, and fishery and forestry firms for a staggering 319 times earnings.[15] Japan Air Lines, in the process of privatisation, sold for over 400 times annual earnings. Western investors, who believed that such values were not justified, gradually reduced their Japanese shareholdings from the mid-1980s onwards. Their departure meant the market was no longer constrained by "Western rationalism," with its "dry" reasoning of discounted cash flows and credit analysis. The Japanese, on the other hand, with their tendency to accept the version of reality disseminated by authority, had no trouble justifying the lofty values found in their stock market.

A number of soothing explanations were given for high share prices: Japanese accounting practices understated real earnings, cross-shareholdings inflated price-earnings measures, etc.* Even the more conservative analysts, unmoved by claims that Japan was becoming the "locomotive of world growth" or that an explosion in consumer demand was around the corner, nevertheless pointed to the "weight of money" argument to justify further advances in share prices. According to this idea, since interest rates remained low and the rising yen discouraged investors from taking their money abroad, the Japanese people were left with no alternative but to

*In fact, cross-shareholdings did distort the price-earnings ratio as a measure of value. Zielinski and Holloway calculated that if the entire Tokyo market was regarded as a single company, with all cross-shareholdings consolidated, then the price-earnings ratio of the market would almost halve.

continue investing in the domestic stock market. This argument was reinforced by the abolition of tax-exempt postal savings accounts in April 1988, which released over ¥300 trillion ($2.25 trillion) for new investment. The massive flow of Japanese savings into the stock market combined with the scarcity of shares, caused by a gradual increase in the level of cross-shareholdings, became the most frequently cited explanation for stratospheric share prices.

The prevalent disregard for the fundamentals of value during the bubble years showed itself in a variety of ways. Shares of companies in the same sectors moved together, regardless of individual differences in earnings performance and prospects. The market rewarded increases in market share rather than rises in profitability. Some shares were hyped for no other reason than that they were affordable in relation to the multimillion-yen NTT share. Cheap shares, it was argued, would one day catch up with the more expensive ones.[16] Stocks not only rose on new issues (when the ownership rights of existing shares were diluted); they also climbed sharply when companies announced a bonus issue of shares (although by simply splitting its shares, the company did not create any real value). Shares continued rising despite the declining profitability of Japan's exporters and the hollowing-out of its manufacturing base. When Emperor Hirohito died in January 1989, they rose; when a small earthquake hit Tokyo six months later, they also rose.

Behind all the rationalisations for rising share prices lay the reality of an extraordinary real estate boom. Property prices climbed on an ever-increasing supply of credit. Total bank lending increased by ¥96 trillion ($724 billion) in the five years to March 1990. Over half this sum went to small businesses which invested heavily in the property sector. Loosely regulated consumer credit companies, the "nonbanks," increased property loans from ¥22 trillion in 1985 to ¥80 trillion ($600 billion) by the end of 1989. On occasion loans were provided for up to twice the collateral value of properties. As property prices climbed, the average lifetime earnings of a graduate salaryman (office worker) became insufficient to buy even a small apartment in central Tokyo. House buyers were forced to take out multigenerational, hundred-year mortgages.

By 1990, the total Japanese property market was valued at over ¥2,000 trillion, or four times the real estate value of the entire

United States. The grounds of the Imperial Palace in Tokyo were estimated to be worth more than the entire real estate value of California (or Canada, if you preferred). Low vacancy rates and the demand for office space from foreign financial institutions led to a building boom in Tokyo, where the number of cranes rising over the bay were eagerly counted (analysts talked of the "crane index"). When NTT opened a high-tech skyscraper in central Tokyo, with offices at over $3,000 a square metre eagerly taken up by foreign bankers, it became known affectionately as the "Tower of Bubble." With property in the Ginza district valued at ¥50 million a square metre, plans were hatched to build an underground city in Tokyo at a depth of a hundred metres.[17]

Inflation in the property sector had a direct impact on the stock market. The search for companies' "hidden assets" (which included both the value of landholdings and cross-shareholdings) became the fashionable pursuit of analysts. An economist at the University of Tokyo revived the Tobin "Q" ratio, which examined the ratio of stock prices to the market value of company assets. Japanese companies appeared cheap by this measure, since by 1988 they had latent capital gains or "hidden assets" on their balance sheets worth ¥434 trillion yen ($3.3 trillion) above book value.[18]

In a reversal of a trend common to most speculative manias, the trading prospects of high-tech firms were ignored in favour of the property on their balance sheets. The brokers called them "land plays." Even NTT was valued primarily for its land assets rather than as a telecommunications company. Propelled by its extensive landholdings, the market value of Tokyo Electric Power increased in 1986 by a greater value than that of all the stocks listed on the Hong Kong Stock Exchange. All Nippon Airways, another "land play," soared to a price-earnings ratio of nearly 1,200. More than three-quarters of the land owned by companies was kept for the purposes of capital appreciation.* The Japanese corporation, with

*For instance, New Japan Steel held 8,300 hectares of fallow land valued at over ¥8 trillion. When its president was asked what he intended to do with the land, he replied that he would sit on it since "our stock price has not yet risen to a four-digit figure." (Tsuru, *Japanese Capitalism*, p. 163.)

its cross-shareholdings and "hidden" land assets, had become a combination of investment trust and property company. In such circumstances, normal business activities were considered an irrelevance or, at worst, a drag on stock market values.

MANIPULATION IN THE JAPANESE STOCK MARKET

Although there were many predictions of a Japanese stock market crash—most notably by George Soros, the hedge fund manager, in a *Financial Times* article on 14 October 1987—it was Tokyo that best weathered the global stock market crash a few days later.* The day after the October crash, representatives of Japan's largest brokerages—Nomura, Daiwa, Yamaichi, and Nikko Securities, collectively known as the "Big Four"—were summoned to the Ministry of Finance. They were ordered to make a market in NTT shares and keep the Nikkei average above the 21,000 level.† Complying with this request, the brokers offered their most important clients guarantees against losses in order to encourage them to reenter the market. Within a few months, the Nikkei had recovered its losses and was progressing to new heights. In private, Ministry of Finance officials boasted that manipulating the stock market was simpler than controlling the foreign exchanges.

Among them the Big Four accounted for over half the turnover of the Tokyo Stock Exchange. The most powerful of their number was Nomura Securities, which during the bubble years became the most profitable company in Japan and amassed liquid assets of over $400 billion. Nomura had five million loyal domestic customers, mainly Japanese housewives, who daily put their savings into special Nomura piggy banks, played stock market computer games on Nomura software, faithfully followed Nomura's stock tips (no "sell" recommendations were ever issued), and every week handed over their money to one of Nomura's thousands of salesmen. Every

*During this period the top-to-bottom decline of the Nikkei was 19 percent, while the Dow Jones fell by 31 percent.

†On several previous occasions, in 1931, 1950, and 1965, the Japanese authorities had intervened to support a falling stock market.

month Nomura staff were given a sales quota to fill, and every morning they were told which stocks to push.

During the second half of the 1980s around eight million new investors entered the stock market, taking their total number to over twenty-two million. Although they owned only a small percentage of the market's total capitalisation (the majority of shares being tied up in corporate cross-shareholdings), private investors bought and sold more than a hundred billion shares each year. Encouraged to speculate by their brokers, private clients held a third of their stocks in margin accounts.*

Despite a traditional horror of gambling, which they see as a Chinese vice, two related national characteristics made the Japanese particularly susceptible to the lure of the stock market. First, they have a tendency to exhibit herdlike behaviour when pursuing a certain activity, whether at work or play. This was said to stem from the communal demands of rice farming, which had fostered a national *shudankizoku ishiki* (group consciousness). During the war, Japan was portrayed in government propaganda as "one hundred million hearts beating as one." After the October crash, the president of a securities house boasted that Japan had survived the period of volatility because it was "a consensus society—a nation that likes to move in one direction."† Second, the Japanese psyche is particularly prone to mood swings, shifting abruptly between elation and despair. These national weaknesses were exploited ruthlessly by brokers, who pushed a series of stock market "themes" which provided the focal points for speculation. The speculative crowd blindly pursued the "red lantern" (*akachochin*) shares that were enticingly placed before them.

The most prominent theme was the redevelopment of Tokyo Bay, which highlighted the property potential of many companies. It was followed by a series of stories hyping untried technologies, such as linear motor trains, superconductivity, cold nuclear fusion,

*In February 1987, all Japanese stock exchanges raised the minimum margin requirement from 50 to 70 percent (i.e., loans were limited to 30 percent of share collateral). Nevertheless, margin loans continued rising.

†This comment was typical of the "Japan is different" flannel put around during the bubble years to cover up manipulation and justify overpricing in the market. (Al Alletzhauser, *House of Nomura*, London, 1990, p. 17.)

and miracle cancer cures. After a Kobe prostitute died of AIDS in early 1987, there was a fever of interest in condom stocks. Despite the fact that three-quarters of Japanese adults already used rubber contraceptives (oral contraception being forbidden), the share price of Sagami Rubber Industries quadrupled. When Nippon Meat Packers was rumoured to have extracted an anti-AIDS agent from chicken bile, its shares rocketed.* Perhaps in anticipation of safe-sex alternatives, shares in pornographic film companies also climbed during the AIDS scare. In a report entitled *Theme Chasing: The Engine of the Tokyo Stock Market,* an American investment bank advised its clients: "A herd instinct is a sound survival instinct in an environment of excess liquidity."[19]

Through their large shareholdings in the press, the Big Four brokers were able to manipulate the information available to their clients.† During their weekly meetings, the same brokers were said to collude in choosing which shares to promote. As the stock market itself was awash with rumours and tips, brokers found their clients highly susceptible to manipulation. In the words of the *Far Eastern Economic Review,* the Tokyo Stock Exchange was "the most cynical, speculative and manipulable stock market in the world."[20]

Despite the inexorable rise of the market, the average private client made little money. He remained an outsider, fodder for the brokers and their favoured clients. "Churn and burn" was said to be Nomura's unwritten motto. Many private investors placed their money in investment trusts run by affiliates of the large brokerages. These trusts were churned mercilessly for commissions and produced average annual returns of less than 4 percent in the late 1980s, at a time when the market was rising by over 20 percent per annum.[21] The only reliable way to make money during the bubble was to be on the inside. Favoured clients—bankers, bureaucrats, politicians, rich individuals, and even *yakuza* (gangsters)—were informed

*The rise of Nippon Meat Packers was the result of outright manipulation by Daiwa Securities, which spread the rumour that the company's anti-AIDS products would shortly be approved by the U.S. Food and Drug Administration. Beforehand, Daiwa had accumulated nearly 18 million shares for its own account.

†Even the *Nihon Keizai Shimbun,* Japan's leading business paper with a circulation of nearly 3 million, was described as a "business tool to shape reality rather than a strict source of news and comment for businessmen." (Zielinski and Holloway, *Unequal Equities,* p. 71.)

beforehand which stocks the brokers intended to push. Brokers guaranteed the investment returns of insiders and compensated them for losses. Favoured clients who had lost heavily in the market were supplied with "ambulance shares"—stocks certain to rise—to heal their financial wounds. Since brokers habitually pushed stocks prior to the announcement of new shares issues, the information that a company was "underfinancing" became a licence to print money. Although there was a law against insider trading, no one paid any attention to it.*

THE SPECULATORS' WEB

The Japanese economic system was sometimes described as an example of network capitalism, with an "iron triangle" of politicians, bureaucrats, and corporations at its core. The bubble economy produced its own alternative network, with speculator groups, gangster organisations, banks, stockbrokers, and politicians joined together in the common pursuit of speculative profits. Since the majority of shares were tied up in long-term cross-shareholdings between companies and banks, it was relatively simple to manipulate share prices and corner stocks. A Tokyo Stock Exchange report claimed that one in ten listed companies was cornered between April 1987 and March 1989. Greenmail—the practice of buying into companies and demanding to be bought out at a premium—became increasingly common.†

Although Al Capone is reported to have avoided the stock market because he thought it a racket, the Japanese *yakuza* gangster of the 1980s was less fastidious. During this period the Inagawa-kai, Japan's second-largest crime syndicate, was run by Susumu Ishii, a

*Zielinski and Holloway describe the Tokyo Stock Exchange of the 1980s as "an inadequately regulated exchange controlled by a cartel of brokers and run for the benefit of listed companies." (*Unequal Equities*, p. 53.) Regulation of the stock market was in the hands of the understaffed Securities Bureau, which was not operationally independent from the Ministry of Finance.

†Greenmailers were said to have placed a hundred and fifty stocks in play. In March 1989, the American corporate raider and greenmailer T. Boone Pickens entered the Japanese market buying a 20 percent stake in Koito Manufacturing, an auto components manufacturer with connections to Toyota.

tall, distinguished-looking man with elegant manners and a reputation for intellectualism, uncommon among brash Japanese gangsters who generally favoured loud pinstripe suits and large American cars. Having recently completed a six-year prison sentence for illegal gambling activities, Ishii was seeking to reduce his gang's dependence on its traditional sources of income derived from drug running, brothels, protection money, and *pachinko* (pinball) halls. The bubble provided him with the perfect opportunity.

In early 1985, Ishii founded a real estate company, Hokusho Sangyo. This company was supplied with loans and loan guarantees by a large trucking firm whose president was linked to the powerful faction leader Shin Kanemaru, the "Don" of Japanese politics. Having provided himself with the necessary funds and political protection, Ishii began his ambitious speculations, funnelling around ¥170 billion ($1.3 billion) into the stock market. He built up large positions in a variety of concerns, including Tokyo Gas, Nippon Steel, and Nomura Securities. In 1987, his investment vehicle had earnings of over ¥12 billion, a fiftyfold increase on the previous year. He commissioned a new headquarters on land costing ¥15 million ($113,000) a square metre, and spent an estimated ¥10 billion ($7.5 million) on paintings by Renoir, Chagall, Monet, and others.

In the spring of 1989, Ishii attempted to corner the stock of the Tokyu Corporation, a large railway and hotels business. For this move, he received the assistance of two of the Big Four brokerages, Nikko and Nomura, which lent him ¥36 billion ($270 million) on the security of Tokyu's shares. The fact that Tokyu was also a Nomura client does not appear to have bothered the broker. Between April and November 1989, Ishii bought twenty-nine million shares in Tokyu: two-thirds of these supplied by Nomura and Nikko, while the remainder came from a shady Korean businessman, Ho Chung Yung, who was connected with Japan's largest crime syndicate, the Yamaguchi-gumi, and later became the central figure in the Itoman art fraud scandal. In the course of the operation, Tokyu's share price doubled.

Ishii became the model for the "corporate gangster" or "economic *yakuza*" who emerged during the late 1980s. In a society where public confrontation is a source of acute embarrassment, the *yakuza* used their powers of intimidation to muscle into every area of the bubble economy. They joined in many stock market corners and greenmailing operations, borrowed heavily from financial institutions (especially from the nonbank affiliates of the major banks), and acted as loan sharks to other speculators. Gangsters were also active in the property market, where *jiageya*—as they were called—intimidated smallholders into selling their properties by threatening them with firebomb attacks. Occasionally the game turned nasty. In the summer of 1985, a Nomura branch manager was beaten to death by gangsters who had sustained losses in a biotech speculation.[22] Three years later, the body of the president of Cosmo Securities, a well-known speculator and greenmailer, was discovered encased in concrete. He had been murdered by *yakuza* associates.

Outside *yakuza* circles there were an estimated forty powerful speculator groups which maintained interests in some two hundred companies. Half a dozen professional speculators (*shite-suji*) were rumoured to control shareholdings worth more than $5 billion apiece. The most prominent and powerful of these was Mitsuhiro Kotani, a self-made hotel and golf course operator and head of the Koshin speculator group. Towards the end of the decade, Kotani undertook a number of bold stock market operations, ramping, cornering, and greenmailing. Working closely with another leading speculator, Akira Kato, head of the Seibi speculator group, Kotani lured politicians, company directors, *yakuza*, and bank executives into his speculative web.

Kotani's modus operandi was to exchange stock tips for favours. Before ramping Janome Sewing Machine, he provided inside information to Toshiyuki Iwamura, a leading member of the ruling Liberal Party and former head of the Environment Agency. In return for bank loans of ¥15 billion ($112 million), he leaked the same information to employees and customers of Mitsui Trust. For his assault on Kokusai Kogyo, an aerial survey firm, he received the support of four directors of the firm to whom he lent money to buy Kokusai's stock. In exchange for a loan of ¥100 million, Kotani gave inside information to a leading businessman, Hirotomo Takei, the head of the Chisan group of companies and former president of a leading newspaper, the *Yomiuri Shimbun.** An aide to the former

*Both Iwamura and Takei were later convicted and sent to prison for failing to declare the gains from these operations, which totaled over ¥6 billion.

Prime Minister, Yasuhiro Nakasone, was also brought in on the deal. Kotani then turned to a branch manager of Sumitomo Bank, who persuaded some of his bank's clients to provide Kotani with loans of over ¥20 billion ($150 million) to finance the deal. The unofficial lenders were offered high rates of interest, and the bank manager received a generous commission.

Having successfully taken control of Kokusai Kogyo, Kotani found himself weighed down with debts. He attempted to solve his problems by manipulating the stock of a holiday tour company, Fujita Tourist Enterprises. For this operation, he demanded a ¥30 billion ($224 million) loan from the Janome Sewing Machine Company, on whose board he sat. When Janome's president demurred, he was told that two hit men had been employed in case the money was not forthcoming. Kotani also threatened to sell his own stake in Janome to gangsters. The president soon capitulated. Janome supplied the money and assumed responsibility for a further ¥187 billion ($1.4 billion) of Kotani's debts. To mark his absolute authority, Kotani placed orders for Fujita shares from the Janome boardroom and sent out the company's executives on his stock market errands. He proceeded to manipulate Fujita's stock by placing buy and sell orders through a number of brokers at escalating prices. In late April 1990, Fujita's share price shot up from 3,700 to 5,200. Once again Kotani received insider assistance from an employee of his victim. He was also supported by two construction companies, one of which contracted to buy the shares at their peak. More than any other individual, Kotani showed how easily traditional Japanese networks could be redirected for speculative purposes.

THE BUBBLE LADY

Since speculative manias tend to undermine established structures, it was fitting that in this male-dominated society the greatest private speculator should have been a woman. Born in 1930 into a poor family, Nui Onoue began her working life as a waitress in the entertainment district of Osaka, Japan's second city. Later, she became the mistress of a construction company executive, who helped her purchase two restaurants in the mid-1960s. For the following twenty years, Mrs. Onoue ran her restaurants without attracting notice. Then one spring day in 1987, she entered an Osaka branch office of the Industrial Bank of Japan and purchased over a billion yen's worth of the bank's discount bonds. Mrs. Onoue proceeded to borrow nearly three trillion yen ($23 billion), a sum roughly fifteen hundred times the value of her restaurants, which she invested in the stock market. She soon became the largest individual shareholder in a number of blue-chip companies, including the Industrial Bank of Japan and Dai-Ichi Kangyo Bank. She also took large stakes in Sumitomo Bank, Daiwa Bank, and NTT. Each shareholding was used as collateral for bank loans which enabled her to buy more shares.

Banks and brokerages fell over each other to do business with the "bubble lady." Despite rumours of her gangster connections and *burakumin* (low caste) origins, Mrs. Onoue's restaurant was visited by many leading financiers, including the president of the revered Industrial Bank of Japan. Yamaichi Securities even kept an employee in permanent residence at the restaurant. Unsurprisingly, this attention soon went to her head. She became an inveterate name-dropper, ordered senior bank executives around like servants, and telephoned junior staff in the middle of the night to command their immediate attendance. Known as the "Dark Lady of Osaka," Mrs. Onoue was a member of Mikkyo, an obscure Buddhist cult. Once a week, she held an all-night séance in her restaurant summoning the spirits to assist her speculations. Brokers were expected to attend these séances or risk losing her business. At dawn she would inform them of the names of the companies revealed to her. In the heady days of the bubble, such behaviour was accepted without question. With a fortune rumoured at half a trillion yen, she liked to boast that "with money all is possible."

A NEW GOLDEN AGE

The bubble economy promoted a massive increase in consumer expenditure as the Japanese people forswore their postwar frugality. Rising asset prices (producing what economists term the "wealth effect") combined with the stronger yen to stimulate a craze for foreign luxury imports. Cuts in income taxes increased personal spending power. Encouraged by low interest rates, people took out fresh loans against the equity of their homes. Credit card circulation increased almost threefold, and consumer debt per head rose to American levels.*

The consumers of the bubble economy were known as the *shinjinrui*, the "new people," to distinguish them from their hardworking, low-spending, and long-suffering forebears. The *shinjinrui* eschewed traditional fare as a *gurume buumu* (gourmet boom) arrived in Tokyo: new "French" restaurants served up *foagura* (foie gras) and *homard à l'armoricaine* (actually fried shrimps). Like the flappers of the 1920s, the female *shinjinrui* displayed a taste for shorter skirts and greater sexual display in their attire as part of the new *bodi-con* (body conscious) cult. They drank Moscow mule cocktails, despised salarymen for being *dasai* (styleless), spent their evenings in nightclubs, and consumed drugs, especially cocaine and ecstasy. An English stockbroker in Tokyo lamented that the Japanese wouldn't realise their shares were overvalued as long as they continued paying $300 for a glass of whisky-flavoured water in Ginza nightclubs.

Seibu Saison, the department store group owned by Seiji Tsutsumi, the brother of Japan's richest property owner, became a mecca for the *shinjinrui*. Long before the emergence of the bubble, Tsutsumi had anticipated a change in national taste and had coined the term *oishii seikatsu* (delicious life) to market imported foreign luxuries. In the autumn of 1984, Seibu opened a new department store in the exclusive Ginza shopping district, selling designer clothes by Yves Saint Laurent, Hermès, Gianfranco Ferre, and others. The store's greatest novelty lay on the eighth floor, where shoppers could buy shares, precious metals, and property. Other department stores soon followed suit. Tsutsumi also opened a new hotel at No. 1 Ginza whose decadent opulence might have made a robber baron blush. Its most expensive suite, supposedly modelled

*Consumer debt rose from ¥9 trillion in early 1980 to ¥67 trillion in March 1991. (Wood, *Bubble Economy*, p. 4.)

on the bedroom of the French actress Catherine Deneuve, contained a canopied bed covered with a silver fox quilt. Guests were offered a choice of seven stuffings for their pillows, including artificial pearls. The hotel's chef came from one of Tokyo's best French restaurants, and its cellars were stocked with the finest French wines.[23]

FUNNY MONET: THE BUBBLE IN THE ART MARKET

The art world of the 1980s was subject to the increasingly aggressive behaviour of its leading auction houses. Under new management since 1983, Sotheby's in particular worked hard to stimulate the demand for fine art. Potential customers were bombarded with glossy in-house magazines, and lavish parties were thrown to launch major sales. Sotheby's provided loans to buyers (the so-called Art Equity Loan), guaranteed prices to sellers and at times bought pictures for its own inventory. The auction house also went to great lengths to emphasise the investment potential of art and published its own "Art Market Index," which recorded price changes in the different collecting fields. According to the art critic Robert Hughes, the creation of confidence in the investment properties of art during the 1980s became "*the* cultural artefact of the last half of the twentieth century."[24]

In fact, there was little new about art as an investment. Towards the end of the nineteenth century, Henry Clay Frick, the American steel baron and art collector, observed with great satisfaction that "even during possession some paintings were seen to increase sometimes a hundred, a thousand fold more rapidly than the certificates of the best-managed joint-stock companies."[25] Unlike stocks, however, paintings have no theoretical value. They produce no cash flows, no dividend yields or price-earnings ratios to help collectors distinguish between prudent investment and rash speculation. Once a price for an artist's work has been established at auction, it sets the benchmark for all future valuations. As Hughes observed, "arts prices are determined by the meeting of real or induced scarcity with pure, irrational desire, and nothing is more manipulable than desire."[26] In the 1980s, the combination of ambitious Western auctioneers, promoting art with every trick in the book, and Japanese speculators, their wallets swollen with bubble profits, created the most extravagant art market on record.

It was only after the appreciation of the yen following the Plaza Accord that Japanese collectors became the dominant force in the global art market. In 1986, the dollar value of Japanese foreign art imports quadrupled. Their purchases became headline news in the spring of 1987, when a Japanese insurance company, Yasuda Fire and Marine, paid just under $40 million for van Gogh's *Sunflowers,* a figure nearly three times greater than had ever before been paid for a painting. The global stock market crash a few months later actually increased the demand for art, since Japanese investors became wary of international stocks. In the week after the crash, the world's most expensive diamond (for $6.4 million) and the world's most expensive printed book (the Estelle Doheny Gutenberg Bible for $5.9 million) were sold at auction. In both cases, the purchasers were Japanese.

The art market became progressively hotter, with the fifteen months from October 1988 to January 1990 described as "the most sensational that the art world has ever seen."* Among the many trophies shipped to Japan during this period was Picasso's *Les Noces de Pierrette,* an unfinished painting from the artist's Blue Period, picked up for $51.4 million by a flamboyant property dealer by the name of Tomomori Tsurumaki (a man given to lavishing $10,000 tips on art dealers). In December 1989, Sotheby's published "The Million-Dollar List," which revealed that during the previous month nearly sixty works had sold for more than $5 million each and a further three hundred paintings had fetched more than $1 million apiece. The art world called it the "billion-dollar binge." A few months later, Ryoei Saito, a paper manufacturer, bid

*Peter Watson, *From Manet to Manhattan: The Rise of the Modern Art Market* (London, 1992), p. 400. This was the period of the so-called Picasso Passion when six of the artist's paintings sold for more than $20 million.

$82.5 million for van Gogh's *Portrait of Dr. Gachet* and $78 million for Renoir's *Au Moulin de la Gallette.* (Saito even picked up a Renoir sculpture for a mere $1.6 million, as he said "for my backyard.") By the end of the decade, it was calculated that the price of French Impressionist paintings had risen by more than twentyfold over the previous fifteen years. During the same period, the Dow Jones Industrial Average had not even doubled.[27] Henry Frick's observation on the investment potential of art appeared to hold true.

Japanese art collectors were unsophisticated: a painting had to convey wealth and exclusivity and, above all, be easily recognisable. While the *shinjinrui* kept to their "bubble designers," such as Versace and Armani, the Japanese art speculators remained faithful to their "brand" painters, mostly French Impressionists and Post-Impressionists. When asked why he had spent over $300 million on late-nineteenth-century French paintings, Yasumichi Morishita (a moneylender known in his trade as the "pit viper") replied, "Impressionist paintings go better with modern decor."[28] This simple taste for iconic works both reduced the demands of connoisseurship, opening the market to all comers, and ensured that the speculative fervour remained concentrated, thus helping to promote the prices of selected artists. Masahiko Sawada, a car dealer turned gallery owner, once boasted to an arts magazine that he personally "controlled the prices of Renoir."

Finance companies provided margin loans for up to half the value of the artworks. Maruko, a real estate company, offered part shares in paintings: *La Juive,* a painting by Amedeo Modigliani, was valued at $12 million and divided into lots of $100,000. Maruko also set up a ¥5 billion fund to buy works by Picasso, Chagall, Renoir, and other masters. A spokesman for the company said that the fund's members, drawn from its established clientele of condominium and real estate speculators, "don't particularly care about the identity of the artist when deciding to purchase a share in a work of art. What they want is not a painting but a capital gain."[29] Paintings were also used as collateral to raise loans to buy shares and property. They became a branch of *zaitech,* another financial instrument for the bubble age.

THE GOLF CLUB MEMBERSHIP CRAZE

The confusion of investment with consumption that typified the art world in the second half of the 1980s was even more pronounced with Japanese golf club memberships. Played by nearly a third of all salarymen, golf was an important feature of the *shain ryoko* (company outing). The game had acquired a ritualised significance in Japan: The different ranks of prestige accorded to golf clubs allowed members to display their hierarchic status, while businessmen, politicians, and bureaucrats used their time at the club to expand their *jinmyaku* (network of connections), which formed an integral part of social and professional life.*

Since golf clubs were owned by their members, when land prices soared in the 1980s the property rights of club membership became increasingly attractive. In early 1982, the *Nihon Keizai Shimbun* launched the "Nikkei Golf Membership Index," calculated from the average membership prices at five hundred clubs. From a base of 100, the golf index reached 160 at the end of 1985. It doubled in the year after the Plaza Accord, suffered a "correction" in February 1987, but recovered to reach a peak of just under 1,000 in the spring of 1990. The golf index became a leading indicator for the illiquid Japanese property market. During the bubble, the cost of joining Tokyo's exclusive Koganei Country Club—restricted to Japanese males over thirty-five years of age—climbed from ¥100 million to ¥400 million ($2.7 million). Over twenty clubs cost more than $1 million to join. The total value of memberships in Japan was estimated at around $200 billion.[30]

The secondary market in golf club memberships was supported by a hundred registered and several hundred "unofficial" brokers who received a 2 percent commission on transactions. Brokers also solicited subscriptions for new clubs, of which over a thousand were under construction in the late 1980s. Banks provided margin loans of up to 90 percent against the collateral of membership

*Van Wolferen, *Japanese Power*, p. 333. Gifts of club memberships were frequently used as bribes to politicians.

certificates. These certificates were also used to raise money to invest in the stock market. The golf craze spread abroad. Japanese property developers bought most of the golf courses in Hawaii and started planning many more.* In September 1990, Cosmo World, a middling property company, purchased the Pebble Beach resort of hotels and golf courses in California for $831 million, a record-breaking sum that attracted a lot of attention from the "Japan is buying up the United States" doom mongers.

The booming art and golf markets with their brokers, "shares," market indexes, margin loans, "corrections," and corners parodied the manipulated and overpriced Japanese stock market. Both the art and golf markets involved a speculation in status as well as money. By combining the acquisition of status—Veblen's "trophies" of conspicuous consumption—with the frenzied desire for material improvement, the Japanese speculator resembled his seventeenth-century forebear: van Gogh's *Sunflowers* became the Semper Augustus tulips for a modern era.

Towards the end of the decade, the bubble's explosive growth was viewed with growing concern in certain circles. The Japanese saw themselves as a cohesive society of middle-class citizens. Yet rising asset prices and the unevenly divided spoils of speculation created egregious disparities of wealth. The fortunes of the richest fifth of the population quadrupled during the bubble years, while those of the poorest fifth actually declined. The *nyuu ricchi* (nouveau riche) with their fortunes in stocks or property had a counterpart in the *nyuu pua.* Moreover, it appeared that most of the bubble's profits accrued to insiders, while outsiders shouldered all the losses. Thus, the myth of classlessness was undermined. In the manner of traditional Western criticisms of speculation, the bubble was seen as eroding the work ethic by severing the connection between labour and reward. The *shinjinrui,* with their taste for luxury and credit, were increasingly resented by the older generation of

*Japanese investment in Hawaii during the bubble years was not confined to golf courses. They also invested heavily in commercial and residential property. Genshiro Kawamoto, a Tokyo property developer, was renowned for touring Honolulu in a rented limousine; he would stop outside any house that took his fancy and offer its occupant cash for the property.

frugal workaholics. In the type of language normally reserved for decadent Westerners, a Japanese research institute denounced the *shinjinrui* as "Epicurean egoists."[31]

Through their acts of speculation, the "new people" of the bubble economy were subverting the established social hierarchy, just as in the 1690s the "moneyed men" of Exchange Alley had weakened a feudal order based on the ownership of land. The social consequences of the bubble economy were not intended by the authorities, who when they belatedly decided to prick the bubble did so more for reasons of social control than for fear of its harmful economic side effects. The speculator had shown himself to be a *narikin*, a person without rank in the hierarchy of Japanese society. He posed a danger to the delicate structure of the system. Eventually, it became necessary to remove him.

THE END OF THE BUBBLE

As 1989 drew to a close, the Nikkei index was approaching the 40,000 mark, up 27 percent on the year, and nearly 500 percent on the decade. The price-earnings ratio of the stock market was at 80 times historic earnings, having peaked at 90 in 1987. Shares yielded a measly 0.38 percent in dividends, and sold for six times their book value. During 1989, shares worth ¥386.4 trillion ($2.9 trillion) changed hands, with daily turnover averaging around a billion shares. Outstanding margin loans approached ¥9 trillion ($67 billion), an eightfold increase since 1980. The last year of the decade had also witnessed some of Japan's most ambitious foreign acquisitions. Mitsubishi bought Rockefeller Center in Manhattan for over $1 billion, and Sony invaded Hollywood with its $3.4 billion purchase of Columbia Pictures.

Nomura Securities was forecasting that the Nikkei would reach 80,000 by 1995. Even the normally sceptical *Far Eastern Economic Review* was predicting another excellent year for 1990. Its analysis, however, overlooked a significant detail. At the end of the year, the governor of the Bank of Japan, Satoshi Sumida—a man seen by many as an ineffectual Ministry of Finance stooge—was replaced by Yasushi Mieno, a career central banker who liked to boast in public that he had never owned a share. Governor Mieno's personal mission was to prick the bubble. On Christmas Day 1989, he ordered another raise in the official discount rate (following an earlier increase in May). Four days later, the Nikkei reached its all-time peak.

The Japanese stock market did not collapse with a sudden jolt. There was no repeat of the two Octobers, 1929 and 1987. Instead, it gently let out air like a balloon left over from a Christmas party. By the end of January 1990, the Nikkei index had fallen two thousand points. Although many Japanese blamed the decline on short-selling by foreigners in the stock futures market that had opened the previous summer, its real cause was a sharp tightening of monetary conditions. As property prices continued rising in the early part of 1990, Governor Mieno—who publicly expressed a desire to see property prices fall by the curiously precise figure of 20 percent—lifted interest rates a further five times until they reached 6 percent in August 1990. With the yield on long-term bonds above 7 percent, compared to the average stock yield of under 0.5 percent, the Japanese stock market had nothing left to support it.

Having manipulated the market on the way up, the mandarins at the Ministry of Finance attempted with less success to control its descent. In early February, the margin requirement on stocks was reduced from 70 to 50 percent. Yet a few days later, on 21 February, the Nikkei fell a further 1,200 points. A month later, the Big Four brokers, under pressure from the Finance Ministry, agreed not to make any further issues of shares or warrant bonds until the market recovered. Shortly after, the Nikkei dipped below 30,000 for the first time in two years and the total capitalisation of the Tokyo Stock Exchange fell behind that of New York. The authorities continued their efforts to support the stock market: brokers were ordered to purchase stocks when the Nikkei fell below 20,000 in September 1990; margin requirements were reduced to 30 percent; life insurers were instructed to stop selling shares; the ban on new share issues was extended; funds were diverted from public pension funds and postal savings accounts into the stock market; and a number of accounting scams were introduced to discourage institutional shareholders from selling stocks.*

Brokers derisively referred to these efforts as the "price-keeping operation." They had little effect on the stock market, which revived briefly in October 1990—in a movement known as the "dead cat bounce"—and then continued sliding until it hit a low of 14,309 in August 1992, a decline of more than 60 percent from its peak.† As the Japanese authorities refused to allow the prices of stocks and property to sink low enough to find their clearing level (the point at which buyers equalled sellers), they frustrated the market's ability to clear away its own excesses—what Schumpeter called "creative destruction." Instead of alleviating the problems, the authorities' mismanagement succeeded only in drawing out the painful aftermath of the bubble (as we have seen, the same accusation has been directed at President Hoover's policies of the early 1930s). No longer were Western economics texts filled with wonder for the Japanese system and fulsome praise for its all-powerful ministries.

In the summer of 1990, the corruption that had simmered away during the bubble years burst forth in a series of financial scandals. Nomura and Nikko Securities became enmeshed in a scandal concerning the compensation of corporate clients for losses in their *eigyo tokkin* accounts, the speculative service run by brokerages for corporate clients which provided a guaranteed rate of return. Although officially illegal, these accounts had been privately sanctioned by the Finance Ministry. Their existence was symptomatic of a system which favoured insiders. Such arrangements became less acceptable after the stock market went into decline. Once again, a scapegoat was needed to purge the collective sins of the community. In June 1990, Yoshihasa Tabuchi, president of the mighty Nomura, was forced to resign for his firm's role in the loss-compensation scandal. It was the first of many ritualistic resignations in the financial world

*In 1992, it was announced that banks could defer writing off losses on their equity portfolios for another year and companies were no longer required to revalue their shareholdings to market value.

†On 1 October 1998, the Nikkei closed at a new low of 13,197, whereupon the authorities announced plans to ban short sales in the stock market.

intended to appease a vengeful public. The following year, it emerged that several brokers had avoided reporting losses by shifting them illicitly from one client's account to another, a practice known as *tobashi.* This time Daiwa and Cosmo Securities were implicated and their presidents obliged to step down.

In the summer of 1991, Fuji Bank was implicated in the forgery of certificates of deposit (credit notes) worth ¥260 billion. At around the same time, Mrs. Onoue was arrested after it was discovered that she had obtained ¥342 billion ($2.6 billion) worth of forged certificates of deposit from an employee of a small Osaka bank, and had used the forgeries to obtain loans from the Industrial Bank of Japan. In late October 1991, the chairman of IBJ resigned. A few months earlier, Mrs. Onoue had been declared bankrupt, thereby making the transition from being Japan's largest private investor to its greatest individual debtor.

Other leading speculators were also brought down by the deflation of the bubble. In 1992, Mitsuhiro Kotani was declared bankrupt with debts of ¥250 billion ($1.9 billion), having already been indicted for extorting money from Janome Sewing Machine Company. Subsequently, he received an eighteen-month suspended sentence for the "naked manipulation" of Fujita's shares (although the court declared that securities companies were "partly responsible" for his crime). By the time Kotani's web of speculation was fully unravelled, a high-ranking politician had been sent to jail, the presidents of two leading banks had been forced to resign, and several dozen others—among them politicians, gangsters, company directors, and stock market operators—had been implicated in his criminal operations.

Public disgrace came also to Sumitomo Bank, the most profitable Japanese bank in the late 1980s. Driven by its ambitious chairmain, Ichiro Isoda, known as "the Emperor," Sumitomo had taken the values of the bubble economy to its core, massively expanding its loans to the property sector and using *tokkin* accounts to enhance profits. The bank was deeply involved with Itoman, a trading company run by a former Sumitomo employee. When Itoman was enveloped in a scandal concerning forged painting valuations, illegal share support operations, and gangster-related property deals, Sumitomo was forced to bail it out at a cost of more than $2 billion. The bank was also linked to the gangster boss Susumu Ishii, after it was revealed that a Sumitomo branch manager had persuaded clients to make loans to Ishii to finance his failed corner of the Tokyu Corporation. Isoda took responsibility for this scandal and resigned in October 1990. For Sumitomo, the bubble's painful legacy continued. In 1994, *yakuza* murdered a Sumitomo manager in an affair connected with failed speculations, and the following year the bank reported losses of ¥280 billion ($2.1 billion) as a result of bad loans made during the bubble years.

Cosmo World's acquisition of Pebble Beach, in which Itoman had taken a stake, also turned sour. In early 1992, the company sold the California golf resort for a loss of more than $300 million. By then, the Golf Membership Index had sunk nearly 50 percent from its peak. As the trade in golf memberships diminished, many golf brokers went under. Cancellations from hard-up members brought demands for refunds that exceeded ¥10 trillion ($75 billion) in total. But many golf course developers had frittered away subscription funds in the stock market and now declared themselves bankrupt. Scandals soon emerged. The Ibaraki Country Club was raided by police after having sold nearly sixty thousand memberships, instead of an authorised two thousand.[32] Likewise, the Gatsby Golf Club, with its fateful allusion to the 1920s high life, was found to have illegally increased memberships by fifteen times its prescribed limit. It was also discovered that the gangster Ishii had raised ¥38 billion ($285 million) by selling fraudulent memberships in the Iwama Country Club, although this was a public golf course with no private membership rights.

The art market suffered a similar fate. Numerous Japanese art dealers were convicted of crimes ranging from tax evasion to racketeering. After Itoman collapsed in October 1990, it emerged that its property subsidiary had purchased thousands of paintings whose valuation papers had been forged. These paintings had been used as collateral for fresh loans in an attempt to circumvent the rules restricting loans to property. The leading art speculators ran into trouble. In March 1992, Masahiko Sawada, the man who tried to corner Renoir, was declared bankrupt with debts of over $600 million. His two thousand paintings were appropriated by a bankruptcy court. Yasumichi Morishita's gallery, Aska International, closed in 1994 and its collection of paintings, once valued at ¥30 billion, was taken by creditors. Because finance companies did not wish to realise losses on their loans by selling depreciated paintings, they crated them and stored them away from the public eye. As a result many famous pictures simply disappeared. When the National Gallery in Washington attempted to borrow Picasso's *Les Noces de Pierrette* for an exhibition in 1997, the museum was unable to locate either the painting or its current owner.

DECLINE AND FALL: THE COLLAPSE OF THE JAPANESE BANKING SYSTEM

The dream that Tokyo would emerge as a global financial capital declined along with share prices. Several large American companies, including General Motors, de-listed from the Tokyo Stock Exchange.* After turnover in the stock market ebbed to a tenth of its bubble peak, several foreign investment banks sold their seats on the exchange. Many of the famous Japanese overseas investments, including Mitsubishi's stake in Rockefeller Center, were put up for sale at knockdown prices. After the nationalistic hubris of the bubble years, Japan was in full retreat.†

The Japanese economy headed towards recession. Enormous capital expenditure—the product of cheap capital during the bubble years—had saddled the country with excess productive capacity. Consumer spending, the other great prop of the bubble economy, declined as the "wealth effect" reversed direction. The government announced a succession of fiscal boosts to stimulate

*By 1998, fewer than seventy foreign companies were listed in Tokyo. This was less than an eighth the number of foreign companies listed on the London Stock Exchange. In the same year, the total capitalisation of the London market exceeded that of Tokyo's.

†A vice president of the Ministry for International Trade and Industry acknowledged to the *Financial Times* (26 October 1992) that hubris had been to blame for the bubble economy: "We became overconfident, too bullish. We should learn not to become too pleased with ourselves. The Japanese are a very disciplined people, but they became intoxicated by the bubble and they somehow forgot their discipline."

the economy and revive the stock market.* Monetary policy—having been kept too tight for too long—was also loosened. The Official Discount Rate was successively cut until, in September 1995, it reached an all-time low of 0.5 percent. The rate remained unchanged until September 1998, when it was cut to 0.25 percent. Shortly after, foreign banks began offering *negative* interest rates on their yen deposits (in other words, Japanese depositors paid for the privilege of lending their money to overseas banks, which they considered safer than their own). Yet low interest rates failed to bring the market to life. As Keynes had observed during the Great Depression, in deflationary conditions monetary policy was no more effective than pushing on a piece of string.†

By late 1992 property prices in central Tokyo had fallen 60 percent from their peak. A banking crisis, caused by the banks' excessive exposure to the falling property market, loomed. At the time, analysts suggested that their bad debts might be as high as ¥60 trillion ($450 billion). Property prices continued falling throughout the middle of the decade, with commentators warning ominously of a debt-deflationary spiral similar to that of America in the 1930s. In August 1995, Japan experienced its first bank run of the postwar period, when depositors withdrew ¥60 billion from a stricken Tokyo credit union, Cosmo Shinyo. This was followed shortly after by a run on a large Osaka credit union and the collapse of Hyogo, a small bank in earthquake-struck Kobe, which became the first listed bank to fail in half a century. Lines of panic-stricken depositors jostling for place in front of tearful cashiers summoned up remembrance of earlier, seemingly less stable periods in the history of capitalism. Towards the end of 1995, the government was obliged to bail out several housing loan companies, known as *jusen*, whose losses of ¥6.4 trillion ($48 billion) came largely from gangster-related

*The first fiscal package was announced in March 1992. This was followed by a succession of boosts. By November 1998, it was estimated that since 1992 the government had announced ¥85,000 billion ($640 billion) worth of public spending packages. The *Financial Times* commented that Japan was experiencing "fiscal stimulus fatigue."

†Japan was suffering from what Keynes termed the "liquidity trap." As economic conditions worsened, the Japanese people reduced consumption and increased their already excessive savings. Their behaviour served only to prolong and deepen the crisis.

lending. In November 1996, the authorities allowed Hanwa Bank to go to the wall.

Twelve months later, Sanyo Securities became the first Japanese brokerage to fail since the Second World War. It was followed, in the middle of November 1997, by the closure of Hokkaido Takushoku Bank, Japan's tenth-largest bank. On 21 November, Moody's, the U.S. credit ratings agency, downgraded the debt of Yamaichi—one of the Big Four brokers. Yamaichi was rumoured to have concealed losses offshore. Rapidly the broker lost the confidence of the market and was unable to roll over its short-term debt. On 23 November 1997, exactly a hundred years after its foundation, Yamaichi Securities announced its closure. With estimated liabilities of ¥3,200 billion ($24 billion), it was the largest bankruptcy in Japanese history. A few days later, a Japanese stockbroker threw himself from the top of a Tokyo skyscraper. According to the newspaper reports, he had been unable to live with losses caused by Yamaichi's collapse.

Nine years after the collapse of the bubble economy, Japan teetered on the brink of a systemic collapse, its banking system weighed down with bad debts of an uncertain magnitude, its companies reporting record losses, and its consumers too frightened to spend. As the stock market declined, the banks' capital base, composed in part of the profits on their shareholdings in other companies, shrank. The "hidden assets" of the 1980s became the hidden losses of the 1990s. When the Nikkei briefly touched 13,000 in October 1998, it was estimated that among Japan's nineteen leading banks losses on cross-shareholdings had reached ¥5 trillion ($38 billion). In September 1998, Standard & Poor's, the U.S. ratings agency, estimated that bad loans in the banking system were around ¥150 trillion ($1.1 trillion) despite write-offs totalling billions of yen in the intervening years.* The resulting credit contraction threatened to deprive firms of working capital. By this date the post-bubble revulsion against stocks was so complete that over 60 percent of Japanese personal assets were committed to cash bearing interest of less than 0.5 percent per annum.

*In late 1998, the authorities belatedly reacted to the banking crisis by nationalising the Long-Term Credit Bank and announcing a ¥60,000 billion ($451 billion) programme, equivalent to 12 percent of gross domestic product, to recapitalise Japan's banks.

THE CRISIS OF THE JAPANESE SYSTEM

The Japanese bubble economy conflated notable features from several past speculative manias. The art and golf market booms recall the Dutch tulip speculations of the 1630s. Just as the first financial revolution produced a speculative boom in the 1690s, so the bubble economy of the 1980s was partly the result of the modern financial revolution following the collapse of Bretton Woods. Economies in the process of liberalisation appear to be especially susceptible to outbreaks of speculation. The warrant bonds issued by Japanese companies, with their conversion rights into ordinary shares, were reminiscent of the conversion of annuities into South Sea shares in 1720. In both cases, a circularity existed so that when shares rose, the value of conversion rights (of annuities in 1720 and warrants in the 1980s) appreciated, which in turn made the shares more valuable. The modish "theme" speculations—from miracle cancer cures to AIDS drugs derived from chicken bile—are redolent of the more absurd "bubble companies" of the South Sea year. Allowing Japanese banks to count their shareholdings as capital, thereby linking credit creation to share prices, re-created the same flaw that destroyed John Law's Mississippi System in 1720. Manipulation and corruption in the poorly regulated Tokyo Stock Exchange stimulated the kind of speculation common in the United States during the Gilded Age and the 1920s. Extravagant foreign acquisitions by Japanese corporations during the bubble economy were foreshadowed by American overseas purchases during the boom of 1901 when the United States overtook Britain as the world's leading economic power. In both cases, speculation was propelled by hubristic nationalism. The aftermath of the bubble economy, with its financial scandals, asset deflation, banking crisis, and prolonged economic malaise, finds its closest historical parallel in the American experience of the Depression years.

Perhaps more than anything the bubble economy illustrates the danger that arises when investors believe that market risk is shouldered by the government rather than by themselves (what economists refer to as the problem of "moral hazard"). Throughout the late 1980s, sceptics were told that the Japanese government would not allow share prices to fall and that Japanese banks and brokerages were "too big to fail." When the bubble collapsed a few years later this belief was revealed for what it was—an ignis fatuus that had led the banks to their ruin.

The problem of moral hazard is not new to the financial world. The Japanese authorities' support for an overvalued stock market harked back to 1720, when British shareholders believed that their government's sponsorship of the South Sea Company would protect them from loss. More recently, in the spring of 1997, there was a mad rush to invest in "Red Chips," companies operating in mainland China and quoted on the Hong Kong Stock Exchange. The main allure of the Red Chips was their association with Chinese politicians, who, it was argued, would not allow their share prices to fall once the former colony came under their control. In May 1997, the share issue at the flotation of Beijing Enterprises, a start-up operation connected to the Peking municipal government, was a thousand times oversubscribed, with the total value of subscription cheques exceeding the Hong Kong money supply. Yet a few months later, Beijing Enterprises was down more than 60 percent from its peak and the Red Chips had lost their sheen. The appearance of the "too big to fail" argument in speculative markets is a fairly reliable harbinger of crisis.

The Japanese economic system, with its emphasis on consensual values, was meant to be different from the freewheeling capitalism of the West. Despite the global financial revolution, Japanese corporations remained subject to a high degree of bureaucratic intervention. The bubble economy showed how the "fever" and "contagion" of speculation could infect even a tightly controlled economy, as long as its capital markets were relatively free. When the bubble economy ended in financial crisis, it proved impossible to return to the status quo ante. The essential components of the Japanese economic system—centralised industrial planning, administrative guidance, the authorised cartels of Japanese industry, cross-shareholdings, *keiretsu* groupings, lifetime employment, promotion by seniority, high personal savings, and the long-termist pursuit of market share above short-term profitability—were increasingly questioned and threatened with dissolution. In the hope of solving the financial crisis, the authorities were obliged to promise more deregulation and tighter supervision of the financial markets. With its characteristic disregard for tradition, speculation had brought its anarchic qualities into play and destroyed the Japanese system with its myriad restrictions. Just as Commodore Perry's "Black Ships" forcibly ended Japan's self-imposed economic isolation in the nineteenth century, so the aftermath of the speculative maelstrom is forcing Japan to converge with the Western economic model. In future, the invisible hand will assert itself. And Japan—the land of three seasons—will not be so different.

EPILOGUE

THE CASE OF THE ROGUE ECONOMISTS

... the ideas of economists and political philosophers, both when they are right and when they are wrong, are more powerful than is commonly understood. Indeed, the world is ruled by little else. Practical men, who believe themselves to be quite exempt from any intellectual influences, are usually the slaves of some defunct economist. Madmen in authority, who hear voices in the air, are distilling their frenzy from some academic scribbler of a few years back.

John Maynard Keynes,
The General Theory (1936)

Privatisations and stock market capitalism were essential components of the new world order after the disintegration of the Soviet Union. The opening of new stock markets from Warsaw to Mongolia, the free movement of capital, and the unfettered trade in foreign currencies that characterised the early 1990s were welcomed by economists and Western politicians alike. After centuries of controversy, it appeared that speculation had finally achieved respectability—according to the authors of a history of Wall Street, published in 1991:

> Now, however, no opprobrium beclouds the activities of those who seek stock that will show the greatest price increase over the shortest time period, precisely that for which the old-time speculators were condemned. Speculation has come of age; it can sit quite comfortably side by side with investment; and

> it is as legitimate and necessary as the securities markets themselves.[1]

In economics textbooks, speculators were now portrayed as benign economic agents who helped markets assimilate new information and made markets efficient. According to modern economic theory, speculators serve to increase the productive capacity of an economy by providing liquidity in the financial markets, thus reducing the cost of capital for companies. The benefits they bring are not confined to the domestic economy. Their resourcefulness and ingenuity take speculators abroad, where they bring liquidity to the stock markets of developing nations. Again, the effect of speculation is to provide capital for local companies, promote growth, and contribute to the optimal allocation of resources on a global basis.[2]

Speculators are credited with assuming the risks inevitable to the capitalist process. In the early 1950s, Professor Julius Grodinsky of the Wharton School of Business remarked that "investors in common stocks . . . are the genuine risk bearers in the system of capitalism and free enterprise . . . [as] nobody knows what future profits will be."[3] The speculator's appetite for growth stocks enables the entrepreneur to raise capital in the stock market (what has recently been called "IPO capitalism").* More companies are founded as a result. Speculators may lose money on occasion but the economy as a whole prospers by their activities. Professor William Sharpe, a Nobel laureate, has argued that the increased appetite of Americans for stock market risk in the 1990s was producing a more dynamic economy. Federal Reserve Chairman Alan Greenspan agreed. In November 1994, he announced: "The willingness to take risk is essential to the growth of a free market economy . . . If all savers and their financial intermediaries invested only in risk-free assets, the potential for business growth would never be realized."[4]

Speculators also scrutinise the policies of governments to judge whether they are sustainable or even wise. They make politicians accountable to the people. In an interview with the *Financial Times*

*IPO stands for "initial public offering," the American term for a stock market flotation.

in November 1997, the Chinese dissident leader Wu'er Kaixi claimed that the establishment of the stock market in China was creating a civil society: "The stock market has that magic power that makes people concerned about the country's economic policy . . . once the will of the people is awakened, they will not sleep again."[5] In the early 1990s, Britain was sunk in a recession that appeared to be without end. It was caused by her political masters linking sterling to a basket of European currencies dominated by the deutsche mark. Owing to the inflationary effects of German reunification, this policy inflicted on the British economy far higher interest rates than domestic conditions warranted. On Wednesday, 16 September 1992, the financier George Soros, manager of the Quantum Fund, came to the rescue of British industry by taking massive bets against sterling, thus forcing a devaluation and knocking Britain out of the European Rate Mechanism. This resulted in lower British interest rates and was followed soon after by economic recovery. "Black Wednesday," on reflection, became "White Wednesday," a day to celebrate.

Speculators also serve to discipline the behaviour of corporate managements, making them more accountable to their shareholders. They seek out value, rewarding companies which create value with high share prices and punishing companies that fritter away their shareholders' funds with low share prices. Out of this has emerged the cult of "shareholder value," the management fad of the 1990s, which asserts that executives' prime consideration should be their companies' share price. Because the interest of management is nowadays more closely aligned with shareholders through executive stock-option schemes, speculators effectively determine the level of management compensation. They hold the whip and will crack it when necessary.

TREND-FOLLOWING SPECULATION

These arguments in favour of speculation are predicated on the assumptions that markets are inherently efficient and that the actions of speculators are both rational in motivation and stabilising in effect. The Efficient Market Hypothesis rests on the observation that stock movements are unpredictable since, at any moment, shares reflect all information relevant to their value, so that their prices change *only* on the receipt of *new* information which by its nature is random. As we have seen, this so-called random walk theory is incompatible with the notion of stock market bubbles, since during bubbles investors react to changes in share prices rather than new information relating to companies' long-term prospects (what economists call the "fundamentals"). Such behaviour is termed "trend-following," and there is ample evidence that it has been a key feature of the financial markets in the 1990s.

In the American stock markets, trend-following speculation has recently acquired a new name: it is called "momentum investment" and has been popularised by best-selling investment books which advise buying stocks that are rising and selling those that are falling (these stocks are said to exhibit, respectively, high and low "relative strength").* Momentum investment has acquired a multitude of followers, particularly among the Internet day traders who use their immediate access to the market to execute lightning trades. This strategy has produced great volatility in individual stocks, especially those of high-tech companies, which have become the speculative "footballs" of the late twentieth century.

Recent experience suggests that foreign currency markets are also dominated to an unhealthy degree by the trend-following behaviour of professional traders who have the ability to create self-fulfilling currency crises. When a financial crisis afflicts an emerging-market nation, foreign exchange dealers rapidly reexamine the economic situation of its neighbours. They realise that if one of these countries were to suffer from a loss of confidence, interest rates would have to rise to protect the exchange rate. Higher interest rates, in turn, would exacerbate any fiscal weakness of the government, by increasing its cost of borrowing, and also cause local asset prices to fall, damaging local banks and businesses. The net result of these events might lead to a currency devaluation, possibly accompanied by a full-scale financial crisis if banks and local businesses have bor-

*The two leading investment books that propose momentum investing as the optimal investment strategy are James P. O'Shaughnessy's *What Works on Wall Street* and *The Motley Fool Investment Guide*, both published in 1996.

rowed excessively in foreign currencies. Thus, a nation which is otherwise sound can have its economy seriously damaged by a sudden and contagious loss of confidence. Having weighed these considerations, traders realise there is little to gain by continuing to hold the currency of such a country—selling the currency short becomes, in trading terminology, a "no-brainer."

The ability of trend-following speculators to create self-fulfilling prophecies was witnessed after the Mexican crisis of late 1994, when a crisis of confidence swept through other emerging markets. The so-called Tequila effect came to an end only after the United States and the International Monetary Fund arranged a massive bailout for Mexico. Just over two years later, the devaluation of the Thai baht, in the summer of 1997, sparked off currency devaluations and stock market crashes across East Asia, even though some economists asserted that the loss of confidence was not justified by economic "fundamentals."* However, as the Asian crisis brought high interest rates, bankruptcies, unemployment, and economic chaos to the afflicted nations, economic conditions soon changed and the loss of confidence was retrospectively validated.† It appeared that Soros's notion of reflexivity, where investors' perceptions serve to shape reality, was at work.

Efficient marketers claim that foreign currency crises arise only when governments pursue poor policies, such as Britain's excessively high interest rates in 1992 or Russia's failure to collect taxes in 1998. In particular, they argue that foreign currency pegs are an open invitation to speculators, who probe any weakness they can

*Jeffrey Sachs and Steven Radelet argue that the Asian crisis of 1997 was caused by foreign creditors acting not on economic fundamentals but on what they believed other creditors would do. ("The East Asian Financial Crisis: Diagnosis, Remedies, Prospects," Harvard Institute for International Development, spring 1998.)

†Dr. Mahathir, the Malaysian prime minister, presented his case against foreign currency trading to the IMF/World Bank meeting in September 1997: "When they [Western speculators] use their big funds and massive weight to move shares up and down at will, and make huge profits from other manipulations, then it is too much to expect us to welcome them . . . Other than profits to the traders involved there is really no tangible benefit for the world from this huge trade. No substantial jobs are created, nor products or services enjoyed by average people . . . I am saying that currency trading is unnecessary, unproductive and immoral. It should be made illegal."

find. Yet it is not only countries with currency pegs that have suffered from the herdlike activities of foreign exchange traders. Professor Paul Krugman of the Massachusetts Institute of Technology recently observed that the appreciation of the yen (an unmanaged currency) against the dollar from 120 in 1993 to 80 in 1995, and its subsequent decline to 120 in 1997, appeared to be the result of traders riding a trend rather than a reflection of changing economic fundamentals. The rise of the yen was extremely damaging to the Japanese economy at a time when the country could ill afford it.[6] George Soros has claimed that "in a freely fluctuating exchange rate system, speculative transactions assume progressively greater weight and, as they do, speculation becomes more trend-following in character, leading to progressively greater swings in exchange rates."[7]

DANGEROUS DERIVATIVES

According to most finance professors, derivatives perform a vital function in the capitalist system. In the age of floating exchange rates which has followed the collapse of the Bretton Woods system, derivatives enable businesses to hedge their risk exposure and increase production. Professor Merton Miller, a Nobel laureate and a zealous defender of derivatives, observed recently that "contrary to the widely held perception, derivatives have made the world a *safer* place not a more dangerous one."[8] Federal Reserve Chairman Alan Greenspan also enthusiastically supported the unregulated growth of the derivatives market.* Yet the economists' claim that derivatives are simply "risk management tools" does not withstand scrutiny.

---

*Greenspan has argued that derivatives create the most efficient mechanism for directing capital to the most suitable users at the lowest cost: "It is a system more calibrated than before to not only reward innovation but also to discipline the mistakes of private investment or public policy." In the summer of 1998, Greenspan claimed that "dramatic advances in computer and telecommunications technologies" had combined with "a marked increase in the degree of sophistication of financial products" to direct effectively "scarce savings into our most potentially valuable productive capital assets" (reported in *Barron's*, 28 September 1998).

Such is the baffling complexity of many new derivatives products that even George Soros has declared that he used derivatives sparingly because he could not understand how they function.* Financial risks that were formerly well understood have become arcane.† Soros and others have argued that many new derivatives serve no purpose other than to facilitate speculation—in particular, enabling fund managers to circumvent prudential restrictions on their investments.‡ What conceivable risk exposure, it has been asked, is a "LIBOR-cubed swap"—a security that multiplies by three times changes in the London Interbank Offered Rate, the rate of interest in the wholesale money market—designed to hedge?[9] And to what bona fide purpose is a "Texas hedge," a combination of two related derivatives positions whose risk is additive rather than offsetting?

Over-the-counter options may also pose a threat to the investment banks that issue them. At the end of 1996, ten U.S. banks had nearly $16 trillion worth of derivatives on their books. These banks must continually hedge their positions by buying and selling the underlying assets (i.e. shares, bonds, and currencies) from which the options derive their value. This activity, known as "Dynamic" or "Delta hedging," requires the banks to sell the underlying assets when prices decline and buy when they rise. Soros warned that Delta hedging sales during a market panic might

---

*In April 1994, Soros told the House Banking Committee that "there are so many of them [derivatives] and some of them are so esoteric that the risk involved may not be properly understood even by the most sophisticated investor, and I'm supposed to be one. Some of these instruments appear to be specifically designed to enable institutional investors to take gambles which they would not otherwise be permitted to take." (Cited by Richard Thomson, *Apocalypse Roulette*, London, 1998, p. 107.)

†Richard Thomson observes that a great deal of activity in the derivatives market is otiose: "the effect is to chop up risks that people are familiar with and understand quite well, only to repackage them into new risks that are at best poorly understood." (*Apocalypse Roulette*, p. 261.)

‡These suspicions were vindicated by the bankruptcy of the municipality of Orange County, California, in December 1994. Orange County's losses of $1.7 billion derived from the activities of its septuagenarian treasurer, Bob Citron, who had bought a variety of derivative bond hybrids, known as structured notes. Although Citron reportedly had the math skills of a schoolboy, he had turned to derivatives to avoid prudential restrictions on his investments and to leverage his portfolio.

cause a severe "financial dislocation." The effectiveness of Delta hedging depends on market liquidity, and the failure of portfolio insurance in October 1987 showed that liquidity might not be there when it was most desperately needed. The economist Andrew Smithers has argued that because this potential loss of liquidity is ignored, stock options are fundamentally mispriced. As a result, a severe market decline might precipitate bank failures. Smithers accused financial regulators of "catastrophe myopia."[10]

Commenting on the growth of derivatives in Washington in May 1992, Dr. Henry Kaufman, the former chief economist at Salomon Brothers, declared that he could "think of no other area that has the potential of creating greater havoc on a global basis if something goes wrong."[11] In 1994, Gerald Corrigan, the former head of the New York Federal Reserve Bank, who was responsible for overseeing the Fed's rescue operation in October 1987, warned that "the increasing complexity of financial markets could override the ability of the most sophisticated efforts to monitor and manage risk." A year later, Corrigan addressed a meeting of the International Monetary Fund: "There is little doubt in my mind that a repeat performance of the 1987 stock market crash would be more difficult to contain today . . ."[12] More recently, Alfred Steinherr, the author of *Derivatives: The Wild Beast of Finance* (1998), described derivatives as "the dynamite for financial crises and the fuse-wire for international transmission at the same time. Unfortunately, the ignition trigger does not seem to be under control."* The Federal Reserve, however, saw things differently and headed off moves to regulate the over-the-counter derivatives market.

HEDGE FUND MANIA

Hedge funds are the most purely speculative investment vehicles of the late twentieth century. Their managers trade in a variety of markets—foreign currencies, commodities, stocks, and bonds—around

*Steinherr notes that a survey of leading financial institutions conducted by the Group of Thirty industrial nations in 1997 put the likelihood of a serious disruption to the global financial system over the next few years at around 20 percent.

the world. They do not make long-term investments but aim to anticipate changes in the market's direction or ride a market trend (as the hedge funds' critics maintain). Although hedge funds have received the enthusiastic backing of the efficient marketers, several commentators believed that they were taking excessively large risks and contributing to the instability of the financial system.

Since hedge fund managers generally receive a slice of investment profits (normally around 20 percent) but do not suffer losses, they are encouraged to assume ever greater risks. Soros warned of the asymmetry of risk and reward in his profession. In May 1994, he called on central banks to regulate the giant hedge funds: "I think," he added, "there is an innate instability in unregulated markets . . . it behooves the regulators to regulate."[13] Dr. Henry Kaufman suggested that the unsound trading strategies of several hedge funds constituted what he called "the soft underbelly of the financial system." In April 1994, William E. Dodge, the chief investment strategist at Dean Witter Reynolds, expressed his worries about the lack of information concerning the size of individual transactions and the terms of trade: "The dimensions of investing in hedge funds have become so big that . . . if they fail, [they] would produce a systemic risk to the banking system and therefore endanger the financial structure of society."[14]

At the time, these warnings were ignored. Soros addressed his comments on the desirability of regulation to the House Committee on Banking in April 1994, but the Republicans' capture of Congress later in the year—assisted by generous campaign contributions from other hedge fund managers—killed off any further moves to regulate hedge funds. Alan Greenspan of the Federal Reserve also lobbied against hedge fund regulation on the grounds that it would only send the hedge funds offshore (where most were already registered in order to avoid the scrutiny of financial regulators). In fact, federal rules were actually relaxed in 1996, allowing an increase in the maximum number of investors at individual hedge funds from one hundred to five hundred. At the same time, a number of loopholes were exploited to attract less wealthy investors into the hedge fund game.

Freed from the threat of regulation, hedge funds increased in number from fewer than 200 in 1990 to around 1,200 by the summer of 1998. During the same period, their funds under management rose from under $20 billion to around $120 billion.* This figure understated their true influence since the balance sheets of many hedge funds were leveraged several times over with debt, and derivatives gave them the ability to create an investment exposure far greater than their capital. During the bull market, most hedge funds successfully used their leverage to produce the stellar returns that made them so popular on Park Avenue. In 1997, Americans invested an extra $40 billion in hedge funds.

"A WAKE-UP CALL"

Criticisms of hedge funds increased after the Asian crisis of 1997, when several funds were accused of colluding together to drive down markets. Dr. Mahathir Mohamad, the prime minister of Malaysia, claimed that hedge fund managers were the "highwaymen of the global economy." Although George Soros shrugged off Mahathir's accusations, denying that he had either contributed to or profited from the Asian crisis, the allegation that hedge funds were destabilising foreign currencies did not go away.† In the summer of

*Figures supplied by the *Economist*, 13 June 1998. A more recent report cited by the *New York Times* (1 October 1998) puts the number of hedge funds at the end of 1997 at 4,500 and their assets at $300 billion. Average leverage at hedge funds is estimated at five parts debt to one part equity.

†Subsequent research vindicated Soros's position and exonerated other hedge funds from responsibility for Asia's woes. Stephen Brown, William Goetzmann, and James Park argued that from June to September 1997 the hedge funds' exposure to the Malaysian ringgit was low and that many were in fact covering their short positions by purchasing the ringgit during the crisis. ("Hedge Funds and the Asian Currency Crisis of 1997," NBER Working Paper No. 6427, May 1998.) Two IMF researchers, Barry Eichengreen and Donald Mathieson, arrived at the same conclusion. They claimed that "macro" hedge funds (i.e., those that bet on currencies) were too few in number and the amount they control was too small (approximately $30 billion in the summer of 1998) to create a currency crisis. ("Hedge Funds and Financial Market Dynamics," IMF Occasional Paper 166, May 1998.)

1998, the Hong Kong government insisted that its currency and stock market were under concerted attack by a group of hedge funds and reacted by banning short sales of stocks and placing restrictions on the local futures market.

Russia's twin default and devaluation in August 1998 brought fresh difficulties to the profession. Several hedge funds had made large investments in high-yielding short-term Russian government debt in the expectation that the Western powers would bail out Russia (on the principle that Russia was "too big to fail.") When these bonds became almost worthless, hedge funds were forced to dump their other investments in order to meet margin calls from their creditors (a problem similar to that which afflicted American margin speculators in October 1929). These forced sales transformed the Russian crisis into a global one, causing stock and bond markets to collapse. Investors, who a few months earlier had considered no risk too great, fled to the relative security of American and German government bonds.

The great majority of hedge funds announced losses for August 1998—one fund, the aptly named "High Risk Opportunities Hub Fund," was forced into liquidation. Among the larger funds caught out by the Russian crisis were Soros's Quantum Fund, which lost $2 billion in August, and Long-Term Capital Management (LTCM), a recently established operation managed by John Meriwether, a former vice-chairman of Salomon Brothers. Meriwether had left Salomon after one of his bond traders was involved in an attempt to rig the market in U.S. Treasury notes in 1991 and subsequently established LTCM in the prosperous New York suburb of Greenwich, Connecticut—a town so popular with speculators that its exclusive seafront avenue was dubbed "Hedge Row" by the locals.

Among Meriwether's partners were two former finance professors, Myron Scholes and Robert Merton, who in October 1997 shared the Nobel Prize in economics for their contribution to the development of the derivatives market. At the time of the award, the *Economist* congratulated the professors for having turned "risk management from a guessing game into a science." Other commentators were less enthusiastic. Alan Abelson at *Barron's* viewed the award with a jaundiced eye. "The pair," wrote Abelson, "snared the rich honor and the tidy sum that goes with it for devising a formula to measure the worth of a stock option, thus paving the way for both the spectacular growth of stock options and their use as instruments of mass destruction . . . The two guys who artfully contrived the ultimate temptation that fuelled the crash [of October 1987] just won the Nobel Prize. Happy anniversary!"

Equipped with the brightest traders and the leading theoretical minds in the financial world, Long-Term Capital Management attracted investments from the cream of Wall Street, including David Komansky, head of Merrill Lynch (who along with 122 Merrill colleagues invested a total of $22 million), Donald Marron, chief executive of PaineWebber, and James Cayne, chief executive of Bear Stearns. Other investors included the Bank of China, Banque Julius Baer, a private Swiss bank, Michael Ovitz, the former Hollywood agent, and a number of partners of McKinsey & Co., the management consultants. With such a glittering roster of investors, LTCM became known as the Rolls-Royce of hedge funds.

The fund opened for business in early 1994. Its strategy, using mathematical techniques pioneered by Scholes and Merton, was to search for small valuation anomalies between various classes of bonds, dealing in bond derivatives known as "total return swaps." The firm specialised in what were called "convergence plays," going long and short on a variety of bonds in the expectation that their prices would converge. This was a backward-looking type of speculation based on an extrapolation of historic price patterns. LTCM also went in for "risk arbitrage"—the business made famous by Ivan Boesky—which involved trading shares in takeover situations. The equity positions of LTCM were characterised as "market neutral," meaning that it did not take bets on the overall movement of the stock market but went long and short on a variety of stocks. In theory, this should have protected it from any market downturn. Initially, its trading strategy proved highly successful: in 1995 and 1996, the fund produced investment returns of 59 and 44 percent, respectively. At the end of 1997, Meriwether was able to return $2.7 billion of capital to his original investors, retaining just under $5 billion for ongoing speculations. (Later, it transpired that the fund had returned this capital without reducing its exposure, thereby increasing its leverage.)

The hedge fund's glorious progress came to an abrupt halt in early September 1998, when Meriwether announced that LTCM had lost around $2 billion, around half of its capital, in the previous month. Putting on a show of bravado, Meriwether declared at the time that he continued to see "outstanding" investment prospects and would solicit investors for more funds. However, investors were not convinced and three weeks later it was announced that the Federal Reserve Bank of New York had arranged for a consortium of leading investment banks—including Komansky's Merrill Lynch and Marron's PaineWebber—to inject $3.4 billion into LTCM in return for a 90 percent stake in the fund. At the same time, it was revealed that the hedge fund had built up liabilities of around $200 billion on a capital base that had shrunk to less than $1 billion. Several American investment banks had provided loans at 100 percent of the value of collateral offered by LTCM (so-called zero-margin loans). The banks had lent bountifully without considering the other loans Meriwether and his partners were busy raising from their competitors. These loans, together with derivatives, allowed LTCM to build a position in the market estimated at $1.4 trillion. Soon after the bailout, several investment banks announced provisions against losses incurred from dealings with the hedge fund. Chief among them was UBS (formerly Union Bank of Switzerland), Europe's largest bank, which reported a loss of $686 million on a loan it had provided to Meriwether's partners (in true 1990s fashion, this was not a straightforward loan but an unhedged "structured equity swap").

Among the $541 million worth of investments LTCM made in U.S. stocks (a figure which excluded the fund's equity derivatives positions) was an $18 million stake in Bear Stearns, the brokerage firm, whose chief executive had a $10 million investment in LTCM. Revelations of the personal investments of Wall Street bosses in the hedge fund, the preferential treatment that the fund had received with its zero-margin loans, and the bankers' subsequent use of their shareholders' money to bail it out—thus preserving at least 10 percent of their personal investments—recalls the antics of Charles E. Mitchell and other Wall Street bankers in the 1920s. It is unfair, however, to suggest that Wall Street only came to the rescue of Meriwether in order to protect the personal investments of its top executives. The situation was, in fact, far more serious. It was suggested that the forced liquidation of LTCM's positions would have brought losses estimated at $14 trillion.[15] Such losses would have severely disrupted the world's capital markets and threatened the banks' own proprietary trading positions (which were highly leveraged and closely resembled those of the hedge fund). In the end, the risk was too great to contemplate and the bailout was swiftly arranged. Although there were no immediate resignations on Wall Street (only the chairman of UBS resigned), investors rapidly lost confidence in investment banks, whose shares declined by an average of more than 50 percent during the late summer and early autumn. Goldman Sachs, which a few months earlier had issued a report stating that hedge funds were safer than other forms of collective investment, was forced to delay its planned flotation. A few days after the bailout, Merrill Lynch announced 3,000 job cuts.

Among the more curious revelations to emerge from the affair was the news that the Italian central bank had made investments and loans to LTCM. It turned out that Meriwether had employed an Italian economist, Alberto Giovannini, who had previously worked for the Italian Treasury advising it on debt management, and that LTCM had made large purchases (estimated at $50 billion) of Italian government bonds. Such close arrangements posed the danger that insider information might be passing between the central bank and its hedge fund partner.

The Italian central bank was not alone in forsaking its traditional role as the guardian of monetary stability in favour of the attractions of speculation. In the early 1990s, the central bank of Malaysia, the Bank Negara, was an aggressive speculator in foreign currencies—an activity from which it retired only after suffering heavy losses. Throughout the 1990s, central bankers around the world have indulged in their own form of speculation: selling gold, a declining asset, and using the proceeds to purchase U.S. Treasury bonds, a rising asset. As this strategy was similar to that of many hedge funds, it was perhaps not so surprising to find a central bank among LTCM's backers. In early 1999, the Brazilian central bank announced that its new president would be a former managing director of Soros's hedge fund.

The standing of the U.S. Federal Reserve was also damaged by the LTCM affair. Among Meriwether's partners was a former vice-chairman of the Federal Reserve named David Mullins. A few years earlier, Mullins had been responsible for the Fed's investigation into the Salomon bond-rigging scandal which had precipitated Meriwether's departure from the bank. At the time, the Department of Justice accused two large hedge funds, Steinhardt Management and the Caxton Corporation, of collaborating in the manipulation (they subsequently paid a $70 million fine without admitting wrongdoing). Presumably, Mullins found no conflict of interest in later accepting a job at a hedge fund from Salomon's former vice-chairman. In Japan such behaviour would have been quite conventional. Indeed, the Japanese have a word to describe the custom by which a government official takes a job in an industry he has formerly regulated: they call it *amakaduri* or "descent from heaven."

Mullins's friend and former colleague Alan Greenspan was also embarrassed by events at LTCM. For several years, Greenspan had vigorously resisted calls to regulate both the derivatives markets and hedge fund activities. Only a couple of weeks before the bailout, Greenspan had insisted to Congress that hedge funds were, in his words, "strongly regulated by those who lend the money." Yet the leverage at LTCM showed clearly that this was not the case. Throughout the years of the bull market, Greenspan had delivered a series of opaque and ambiguous speeches, half warning of the dangers of speculation and half congratulating America on its economic revival. After the LTCM bailout, complaints were raised that Greenspan had failed to do enough to stem the growth of a stock market bubble caused partly by excessive monetary growth. The reputation of the man who not long before had been described by a member of Congress as a "national treasure" was beginning to look as fragile as the stock market itself.

Shortly after the bailout of Long-Term Capital Management, Paul Volcker, Greenspan's predecessor as Federal Reserve Chairman, asked. "Why should the weight of the federal government be brought to bear to help out a private investor?" No answer to Volker's question was forthcoming, except that both Greenspan and Treasury Secretary Robert Rubin insisted that technically there was no "bailout" since federal money had not been used.* A few years earlier, the Federal Reserve had passively stood by while Drexel Burnham Lambert, an investment bank with some five thousand employees and a history stretching back into the nineteenth century, was deserted by its envious Wall Street competitors and collapsed because of liquidity problems. Long-Term Capital Management, on the other hand, a mere four-year-old upstart with only two hundred employees but partners and investors drawn from a cabal of finance professors, central bankers, and the cream of Wall Street, was considered more important than Drexel and simply "too big to fail." Echoing Pecora's accusation of Wall Street's "heads I win, tails you lose" ethics in the 1920s, Representative Bruce F. Vento, a Democrat of Minnesota, accused Greenspan of having "two rules, a double standard: one for Main Street and another one for Wall Street." The Fed's involvement in the bailout of LTCM resembled the type of "crony capitalism" which the United States was continually decrying in Asian countries. Thus, at a crucial moment in the global financial crisis, the moral authority of the U.S. government and its ability to dictate economic policies to other nations were undermined.

Naturally, the hedge fund industry did not emerge unscathed by the crisis at LTCM. According to their apologists, hedge funds were in the business of risk dispersal. Yet Meriwether and his partners had concentrated risk in a manner similar to that of the negligent underwriters at the Corporation of Lloyds in the 1980s. In fact, the notion that speculators can effectively serve as insurers against financial risks is flawed. Whereas a life insurer can confidently write policies based on actuarial tables derived from slowly changing death rates, the speculator has only poor statistical information upon which to base his strategy. Moreover, the activities of other speculators are constantly changing conditions in the market, thereby making the past an unreliable guide to the future. In the end, the banks which "hedged" their positions with LTCM were

*Nor was it satisfactorily explained why an earlier offer for LTCM led by Warren Buffett of Berkshire Hathaway had been turned down. (Apparently Buffett's offer left no residual value for LTCM's partners or investors, who after the Fed-sponsored bailout still retained a 17 percent annual return on their original investment.)

obliged to take over their insurer in order to secure their own survival.

Liberal economists also claimed that hedge funds provided liquidity to the world's financial markets. Yet while LTCM teetered on the brink of collapse, the markets in which it operated—high-yield bonds, emerging-market debt, convertible securities, and mortgage-backed issues—became paralysed as liquidity dried up. The effect of this was to raise the cost of capital for corporations. Even after the bailout, the financial markets remained stormy due to a "flight to safety"—as investors eschewed long-term risks in favour of cash—bringing turbulence to the world's stock and bond markets. Many hedge funds had financed their speculations by borrowing cheaply in Japanese yen. After the bailout, these hedge funds were forced by their creditors to unwind their leveraged positions, causing a 20 percent fall in the dollar against the yen in one week in October. Never before had the world's leading currency markets exhibited such extreme volatility. At a hedge fund conference held in Bermuda shortly after the bailout (originally entitled "How to Handle the Flood of Assets Coming In" but hastily restyled "Crisis and Corrections: Implications for Hedge Funds"), Julian Robertson, head of the Tiger Fund, the world's largest hedge fund, joined Soros's call for greater regulation of the industry.[16]

The LTCM affair also raised questions about the fast-growing derivatives market. As we have seen, finance professors claimed that derivatives were seldom used for speculative purposes. Yet Meriwether's hedge fund, run by the world's leading "risk management experts," had used derivatives wantonly to build up the largest and most leveraged positions in the history of speculation. The leverage within LTCM was reported to exceed $100 of debt for every dollar of equity, and much of the partners' equity investment turned out to be borrowed money.

The near-bankruptcy of Long-Term Capital Management reflects the near-bankruptcy of the intellectual principles upon which it had been built. The flaw in the hedge fund's trading strategies was to assume that the historical relationships between various assets could be depended upon for future speculations. The hedge fund was so confident of its opinion that it took massive bets when its computers identified small divergences from the norm. The formula for pricing options, developed by Scholes and Merton, which lies at the heart of the modern derivatives world, is dependent on the similar assumption that past volatility is a reliable guide to future volatility. This assumption may be likened to driving a motorcar by looking in the rearview mirror—fine as long as the road continues straight but disastrous when you reach the first corner. In common with all the practical ideas generated by the Efficient Market Hypothesis, it is based on the belief that when financial theories are turned into practice there is no change to the underlying reality. This was the error of portfolio insurance in the 1980s and remained the error of the derivatives markets a decade later. If markets are not efficient but are subject to chaotic feedback loops, then the entire financial superstructure created around derivatives in the 1990s, with its $50 trillion worth of exposure, is based on shaky premises.

Even outside the field of options pricing, the teaching of the Efficient Market Hypothesis has insinuated itself into the practices of modern finance: the fads for "shareholder value" and corporate stock-option schemes, the Capital Asset Pricing Model (which "scientifically" calculates companies' cost of capital), and popular investment in stock index funds are all predicated, to a greater or lesser extent, on the assumption that shares are efficiently priced by the market. But if the hypothesis is false—e.g., because speculative euphoria does, in fact, drive share prices away from their "intrinsic" value—then these practices are in need of reform. Recently, James Buchan asserted that political economy is "in the same condition in which Scholastic learning found itself on the eve of the Discoveries. It is about to explode."[17] The crisis at Long-Term Capital Management suggested that the final refutation of modern economic theory might only be achieved by an implosion of the financial system. As the head of a risk management firm told the *New York Times*, the crisis was "a wake-up call." He chose his words well.

THE THIRD DEGREE

Unlike Merton and Scholes, John Maynard Keynes's personal (and successful) experience of speculation led him to the conclusion that markets were fundamentally inefficient. In his *General Theory*,

Keynes defined speculation as the attempt to forecast changes in the psychology of the market. He compared it to various parlour games—snap, old maid, and musical chairs. Switching his metaphor, Keynes likened speculation to a newspaper competition in which the competitors have to pick out the six prettiest faces from hundreds of photographs,

> so that each competitor has to pick, not those faces which he himself finds prettiest, but those which he thinks likeliest to catch the fancy of the other competitors, all of whom are looking at the problem from the same point of view . . . We have reached the third degree where we devote our intelligences to anticipating what average opinion expects the average opinion to be.[18]

Speculation which is a beneficial, indeed vital, component of the capitalist process has come to dominate the system to an unhealthy degree. To repeat Keynes's warning from the 1930s: "when the capital development of a country becomes a by-product of the activities of a casino, the job is likely to be ill-done." Momentum trading, trend-following currency speculators, overleveraged hedge funds, and corporate managements obsessed with daily fluctuations in share quotations are unlikely to produce the optimal distribution of scarce resources in the global economy. We have reached Keynes's "third degree."

Politicians and economists, pondering the problems caused by unfettered speculation, face an old dilemma. As Alexander Baring, head of the family bank lately brought down by Nick Leeson, remarked in 1825, any attempt to check speculation might be counterproductive: "the remedy would be worse than the disease, if, in putting a stop to this evil, they [the authorities] put a stop to the spirit of enterprise."

Governments have frequently attempted to control speculation by outlawing its tools and practices.* Yet on each occasion, speculators have found ways to circumvent regulations. They have also

---

*Although short-sellers are invariably blamed for the collapse of stock markets, the problem is really caused by long buyers during the preceding bull market who push stocks to unsustainable levels. No government has yet seen fit to ban stock purchases during a stock market bubble.

interpreted laws against speculation as a sign of weakness on the part of governments, which has caused them to step up their activities. Keynes whimsically proposed that speculation might be discouraged if people were forced to make investments, like marriage, for life (a solution which would have produced a lifetime of frustration for those unfortunate enough to make a poor initial choice). More seriously, he considered a penal rate of capital gains tax on short-term holdings. As we have seen, however, high rates of capital gains tax on short-term property investments in Japan actually stimulated the Tokyo property boom in the 1980s by reducing liquidity in the market. It is arguable that taxes on capital gains actually contribute to stock market bubbles since investors with large profits become reluctant to sell even when they believe stocks are overvalued. Keynes also suggested that a transaction tax be levied on U.S. share purchases on the grounds that "casinos should, in the public interest, be inaccessible and expensive."

Several economists argue that central bankers should consider asset prices along with consumer prices in their inflation targets. The problem with this suggestion is that nobody can prove definitively that share prices are rising because of speculative pressure rather than a genuinely improved outlook. As Alan Greenspan asked in December 1996, "how do we know when irrational exuberance has unduly escalated asset values?" Only in retrospect does the answer to this question become clear.

Furthermore, the central banker's main tool for controlling speculation is raising interest rates. As long as speculators continue to anticipate large profits from capital gains they are not deterred by high interest rates. And, as Keynes observed in the 1930s, raising interest rates to control speculation at the end of the business cycle damages the whole economy. The only other tool left to central bankers is to issue warnings to speculators to desist from their activities—what was called "moral suasion" in the 1920s. Time and time again, such warnings have been made by the authorities and on no occasion have speculators heeded a word.

During the Great Depression, American policymakers decided that speculation was best controlled by limiting the speculators' access to financial leverage. As a result, margin loans were limited by federal law to 50 percent of stock values. This policy has since broken down with the advent of financial derivatives, as the case of LTCM demonstrates in extremis. It has recently been proposed that derivatives should be subject to the same margin limits as conventional stock purchases. Restrictions on speculators' ability to achieve almost limitless leverage through the derivatives market might lessen the risk of systemic crisis in the financial world. Improved information in the almost unregulated derivatives world would also hinder the excessive accumulation of debt, such as occurred at LTCM.

The issue of speculation in emerging markets and the unfettered trade in foreign currencies is the most immediate and vexing problem faced by policymakers. Politicians and central bankers worry about how to achieve economic stability without inhibiting the flexibility necessary for growth. Yet flows of speculative capital into fragile emerging markets have not brought any visible long-term benefits. Indeed, it can be argued that they have actually hindered the evolution of the liberal market system in many countries. In this instance, speculation has been no friend of capitalism.

There have been a number of proposals, of varying degrees of practicality, about how best to deal with the problems of foreign currency instability. The reintroduction of capital controls, controls on foreign borrowing, improved accountancy and less cronyism in emerging markets, a tax on capital inflows into emerging markets, a tax on foreign exchange transactions, controls on hedge funds, the reform of the International Monetary Fund so it can perform effectively the function of lender of the last resort, and even the establishment of a world central bank are among the ideas floated by policymakers who appeared wrong-footed by the unexpected appearance of a world financial crisis. Dominique Strauss-Kahn, the French finance minister, has called for the construction of a "new Bretton Woods."*

*In *The Crisis of Global Capitalism* (New York, 1998), George Soros predicts "the imminent disintegration of the global capitalist system." His preferred solution to the problem of economic instability caused by uncontrolled capital flows is an international credit guarantee scheme, an end to freely fluctuating exchange rates, "some form of capital controls," and the transformation of the IMF into a world central bank with the power to act as a lender of the last resort.

Although a new system of fixed currencies would necessitate a degree of capital controls, there is no evidence that this would actually inhibit economic growth. In fact, the growth rates of Western nations have actually declined since the early 1970s. Providing currencies with fixed values would also obviate the need for derivatives, which could be allowed to wither on the vine without posing any further threat to the financial system. European businesses are the keenest supporters of the European single currency project because it saves them the cost and uncertainty of hedging their trading operations in the derivatives markets.* Investors in foreign countries might forgive capital controls and restrictions on the early withdrawal of investments if they had greater confidence that economic conditions in these countries would not be suddenly undermined by speculative currency attacks. A fixed currency system would also define the limits of speculation in the manner performed by the gold standard in the nineteenth century.

When the tide turns against the speculator there is an inevitable loss of liberty. In *The Road to Serfdom* (first published in 1949), the Austrian economist Friedrich von Hayek declared that state control of foreign exchange dealing was a "decisive advance on the path to totalitarianism and the suppression of individual liberty." Hayek believed that from a mixed economy there would be an inevitable progression to socialism. History has proved Hayek wrong. His analysis underestimated the power of speculation, even in quasi-socialist economies, to pull in the opposite direction. Speculation undermined the Bretton Woods system of fixed currencies and, more recently, it has destroyed the state-managed capitalism of Japan and other Asian nations. As an anarchic force, speculation demands continuing government restrictions, but inevitably it will break any chains and run amok. The pendulum swings back and forth between economic liberty and constraint.

DECEMBER 13, 1998

*A letter from a Labour MP in the *Financial Times* (25 November 1998) claims that the single European currency "is the only way Britain can protect itself from the ravages of currency speculation . . ."

NOTES

PREFACE: DEVIL TAKE THE HINDMOST

1 See L. Stuart Sutherland, "Sir George Colebrooke's World Corner in Alum, 1771–73," *Economic History* 3 (London, 1936).
2 Joseph A. Schumpeter, *Business Cycles: A Theoretical, Historical and Statistical Analysis of the Capitalist Process* (New York, 1939), p. 679.
3 Fred Schwed, *Where Are the Customers' Yachts? or a Good Hard Look at Wall Street* [1st ed., 1940] (New York, 1995), p. 172.
4 Bernard M. Baruch, *My Own Story* (London, 1958), p. 208.

1. THIS BUBBLE WORLD

1 *Satyricon* (trans. Michael Heseltine, London, 1913).
2 Jérôme Carcopino, *Daily Life in Ancient Rome* (London, 1956), p. 74.
3 *Curculio*, Act IV, Sc. II.
4 See E. Badian, *Publicans and Sinners* (Oxford, 1972), p. 104.
5 Ibid., p. 102.
6 Cicero, *Ad. Familias* XII, 10.2 (cited by Tenney Frank, *Economic History of Rome*, London, 1927, p. 282).

7 Polybius, *Rise of the Roman Empire*, Book IV, 17 (trans. Ian Scott-Kilvert, London, 1979), p. 316.
8 *Satyricon*, p. 257.
9 Mikhail Rostovtzeff, *The Social and Economic History of the Roman Empire* (Oxford, 1957), p. 472.
10 Richard Ehrenberg, *Capital and Finance in the Age of the Renaissance* (trans. H. M. Lucas, London, 1928), p. 309.
11 Ibid., p. 245.
12 Ibid., p. 241.
13 Violet Barbour, *Capitalism in Amsterdam in the Seventeenth Century* (Baltimore, 1950), pp. 95–122.
14 Ibid., p. 142.
15 Ibid., p. 44.
16 Fernand Braudel, *The Wheels of Commerce* (New York, 1982), p. 100.
17 Joseph de la Vega, *Confusion de Confusiones*, 1688 (in *Portions Descriptive of the Amsterdam Stock Exchange*, ed. H. Kellenbenz, Boston, 1957, p. 27).
18 Cited in *The Psychology of Gambling* (eds. Jon Halliday and Peter Fuller, London, 1974), p. 126.
19 Vega, *Confusion*, p. 11.
20 Ibid., p. 22.
21 Ibid., pp. 10 and 12.
22 Ibid., p. 18.
23 Benjamin Graham, *The Intelligent Investor*, 4th ed. (New York, 1973), p. 108; Warren Buffett, Berkshire Hathaway Annual Report, 1987.
24 *Autobiographical Recollections of Sir John Bowring* (London, 1877), pp. 110–13.
25 Jonathan Israel, *The Dutch Republic* (Oxford, 1995), p. 533.
26 Paul Taylor, *Dutch Flower Painting 1600–1720* (New Haven, 1995), p. 10.
27 N. W. Posthumus, "The Tulip Mania in Holland in the Years 1636 and 1637," *Journal of Economic and Business History*, I (1928–29), p. 462.
28 Ibid., p. 451.
29 Ibid., p. 455.
30 Ibid., p. 458.
31 Ibid.
32 Ibid., p. 450.
33 Ibid., p. 451.
34 Taylor, *Dutch Flower Painting*, p. 13.
35 Posthumus, "Tulip Mania," p. 436.
36 Taylor, *Dutch Flower Painting*, p. 13.
37 Posthumus, "Tulip Mania," p. 447.
38 Wilfrid Blunt, *Tulipomania* (London, 1950), p. 15.
39 Posthumus, "Tulip Mania," p. 452.
40 Taylor, *Dutch Flower Painting*, p. 47.

41 Blunt, *Tulipomania*, p. 17. This legend appears in modern descriptions of the Tulip Mania, including Zbigniew Herbert's *Still Life with a Bridle* (London, 1994).
42 See *Applebee's Journal*, 14 January 1721, and J. K. Galbraith, *The Great Crash* (London, 1975), pp. 148–50.
43 Peter Garber, "Tulipomania," *Journal for Political Economy*, 97, No. 3 (June 1989).
44 James Buchan, *Frozen Desire* (New York, 1997), p. 110.
45 Vega, *Confusion*, p. 18.
46 E. LeRoy Ladurie, *Carnival: A People's Uprising at Romans 1579–1580* (London, 1980).
47 Mikhail Bakhtin, *Rabelais and His World* (trans. Helen Iswolsky, Bloomington, Indiana, 1984), p. 9.

2. STOCKJOBBING IN 'CHANGE ALLEY

1 From "Discourses on the Public Revenues," 1698. Cited by J. G. A. Pocock, *The Machiavellian Moment* (Princeton, 1975), p. 439.
2 Defoe, *Essay upon Loans* [1710] (from *A Collection of Scarce and Valuable Tracts* [Lord Somer's], London, 1815, XIII, p. 36).
3 W. R. Scott, *The Constitution and Finance of English, Scottish and Irish Joint-Stock Companies to 1720* (Cambridge, 1912), I, p. 323.
4 P.G.M. Dickson, *The Financial Revolution in England* (Oxford, 1967), p. 465.
5 Scott, *Joint-Stock Companies*, II, pp. 285–86.
6 Ibid., p. 417.
7 Anon., *Angliae Tutamen* (London, 1695), p. 21.
8 Defoe, *Essay upon Projects* (London, 1697, reprinted Scolar Press, 1969), p. 13.
9 Scott, *Joint-Stock Companies*, III, p. 78.
10 Ibid., III, p. 95.
11 Ibid., III, p. 483.
12 Ibid., III, p. 33.
13 Thomas Shadwell, *Works* (London, 1720), IV, p. 435.
14 See Christine Macleod, "The 1690s Patents Boom—Invention or Stock-Jobbing," *Economic History Review*, 2nd Ser., XXXIX, No. 4 (1989).
15 Scott, *Joint-Stock Companies*, I, p. 345.
16 John Houghton, *A Collection for the Improvement of Husbandry and Trade*, June 1694, Issue 101.
17 Ibid., issue 99.
18 Dickson, *Financial Revolution*, p. 45.
19 Defoe, *Essay upon Projects*, p. 173.
20 Peter Bernstein, *Against the Gods* (New York, 1996), p. 90.
21 From *The Spectator* (ed. D. F. Bond, Oxford, 1956), II, p. 249.

22 Defoe, *Anatomy of Exchange Alley* [1719] (reprinted in John Francis, *Chronicles and Characters of the Stock Exchange*, 1849), p. 379.
23 J. M. Keynes, *The General Theory of Employment, Interest and Money* [1936] (London, 1973), p. 157.
24 Defoe, *The Villainy of Stock-Jobbers Detected* (London, 1701), p. 4.
25 From *A Discourse Concerning the Coining of the New Money Lighter* [1696] quoted by Buchan, *Frozen Desire*, p. 105.
26 *The Spectator*, IV, p. 5.
27 Keynes, *General Theory*, p. 154.
28 Dickson, *Financial Revolution*, p. 258.
29 Scott, *Joint-Stock Companies*, III, p. 247.
30 *Angliae Tutamen*, p. 16.
31 Cited by Scott, *Joint-Stock Companies*, II, p. 216.
32 John Evelyn, *Diary*, ed. E. S. de Beer (Oxford, 1955), V, p. 246.
33 Defoe, *Villainy*, p. 4.
34 Charles Kindleberger, *Manias, Panics, and Crashes*, 2nd ed. (New York, 1989), p. 24.
35 See John Carswell, *The South Sea Bubble* (London, 1993), p. 14; and Dickson, *Financial Revolution*, p. 518.
36 J. S. Mill, *Principles of Political Economy* [1848] (Toronto, 1965), p. 542.
37 *Angliae Tutamen*, p. 21.
38 Alexander Dana Noyes, *The Market Place* (Boston, 1938), p. 193.
39 *Angliae Tutamen*, p. 16.
40 Appleby, *Economic Thought*, p. 257.
41 James Grant, *Minding Mr. Market* (New York, 1993), p. 7.

3. THE SOUTH SEA SCHEME

1 Defoe, *Anatomy*, p. 378.
2 A full discussion of the Mississippi Bubble is beyond the scope of this book. For recent assessments of John Law, see Antoin E. Murphy, *John Law: Theorist and Policy Maker* (Oxford, 1997), and James Buchan, *Frozen Desire* (New York, 1997).
3 *The Weekly Journal or Saturday's Post* (known as *Mist's Journal*), 13 February 1720.
4 Archebald Hutcheson, *Some Seasonable Considerations* . . . 14 April (London, 1720).
5 Carswell, *South Sea Bubble*, p. 16.
6 *Secret History*, p. 429.
7 Dickson, *Financial Revolution*, p. 131.
8 Carswell, *South Sea Bubble*, pp. 108, 165.
9 Antoin E. Murphy, *Richard Cantillon* (Oxford, 1986), p. 165.
10 Adam Anderson, *The Origin of Commerce* (London, 1801), III, p. 102.

11 Scott, *Joint-Stock Companies*, I, p. 424.
12 Carswell, *South Sea Bubble*, p. 99.
13 Anderson, *Origin of Commerce*, III, pp. 103–7.
14 Scott, *Joint-Stock Companies*, I, p. 420.
15 Carswell, *South Sea Bubble*, p. 243.
16 *The Secret History of the South-Sea Scheme*, in *A Collection of Several Pieces of Mr. Toland* (London, 1726), p. 443.
17 Ibid., pp. 427–31.
18 Alexander Pope, *Correspondence* (ed. G. Sherburn, Oxford, 1956), II, pp. 48–51.
19 Ibid., p. 52.
20 Murphy, *Richard Cantillon*, p. 171.
21 Ibid., p. 168.
22 Quoted by Colin Nicholson, *Writing and the Rise of Finance* (Cambridge, 1994), p. 16.
23 *Secret History*, p. 446.
24 C. P. Kindleberger, *Financial History of Western Europe* (2nd ed., London, 1989), p. 182.
25 Dickson, *Financial Revolution*, p. 126.
26 E. Shemajah, *A Letter to the Patriots of Change Alley* (London, 1720), pp. 8–9.
27 Carswell, *South Sea Bubble*, p. 116.
28 William Fowler, *Ten Years on Wall Street* (New York, 1870), p. 450.
29 *Applebee's Original Weekly Journal*, 6 August 1720.
30 *Exchange-Alley: or the Stock-Jobber turn'd Gentleman*, 1720.
31 *Applebee's*, 5 August 1720.
32 Carswell, *South Sea Bubble*, p. 127.
33 *Mist's Journal*, 30 July 1720.
34 Carswell, *South Sea Bubble*, p. 144.
35 *Applebee's*, 27 August 1720.
36 Scott, *Joint-Stock Companies*, III, p. 328.
37 *Applebee's*, 1 October 1720.
38 Virginia Cowles, *The Great Swindle* (London, 1960), p. 143.
39 Pope, *Correspondence*, II, pp. 53–54.
40 Quoted in Halliday and Fuller, *Psychology of Gambling*, p. 281.
41 *Applebee's*, 15 November 1720.
42 Edward Gibbon, *Memoirs of My Life* (London, 1984), p. 49.
43 Ibid., p. 49.
44 Adam Smith, *Lectures on Jurisprudence* (ed. R. L. Meek, D. D. Raphael, and P. G. Stein, Oxford, 1978), p. 519.
45 See Dickson, *Financial Revolution*, p. 153, and C. P. Kindleberger, *Manias, Panics, and Crashes*, pp. 134–35.
46 Anderson, *Origin of Commerce*, III, pp. 91–92.

47 Schumpeter, *Business Cycles*, I, p. 250.
48 Neal in *Stock Market Crashes and Speculative Manias* (ed. E. N. White, Brookfield, Vt., 1996), p. 155.
49 Carswell, *South Sea Bubble*, p. 133.

4. FOOL'S GOLD

1 Frank G. Dawson, *The First Latin American Debt Crisis* (New Haven, 1990), pp. 41–42, 59–61.
2 David Kynaston, *The City of London: A World of Its Own* (London, 1994), I, p. 49.
3 Ibid., I, p. 47.
4 Dawson, *Debt Crisis*, p. 227.
5 Ibid., p. 105.
6 John Francis, *History of the Bank of England* (London, 1848), II, p. 27.
7 Dawson, *Debt Crisis*, p. 121.
8 Thomas Tooke, *History of Prices* (London, 1838), II, p. 142.
9 Ibid., p. 144.
10 Harriet Martineau, *The History of England during the Thirty Years' Peace: 1816–1846* (London, 1849), I, p. 357. Thomas Tooke, citing McCulloch's *Principles of Political Economy*, claims that ice skates were first sent to Rio in 1808. The tale is probably apocryphal.
11 F. B. Head, *Rough Notes* (London, 1826), p. 304.
12 Jane Ridley, *The Young Disraeli* (London, 1995), p. 31.
13 Benjamin Disraeli, *An Inquiry into the Plans, Progress, and Policy of the American Mining Companies*, first published March 1825. It soon ran to three editions.
14 Kynaston, *City of London*, I, p. 63.
15 Ridley, *Young Disraeli*, p. 33.
16 Ibid., p. 34.
17 Dawson, *Debt Crisis*, pp. 98–99.
18 This absurd venture is taken at face value by Clément Juglar in *Des Crises Commerciales et de leur retour périodique en France, en Angleterre et aux Etats-Unis* (Paris, 1889), p. 366.
19 Francis, *Bank of England*, II, p. 3
20 Anon., *Remarks on Joint Stock Companies by an Old Merchant* (London, 1825), p. 46.
21 William Smart, *Economic Annals of the Nineteenth Century 1821–1830* (London, 1917), II, p. 318.
22 Francis, *Bank of England*, II, p. 2.
23 Dawson, *Debt Crisis*, p. 163.
24 Ibid., p. 90.
25 Ibid., p. 100.
26 Smart, *Economic Annals*, II, p. 296.

27 B. C. Hunt, *the Development of the Business Corporation in England 1800–1867* (Cambridge, Mass., 1936), p. 35.
28 Martineau, *History of England,* I, p. 356.
29 *Parliamentary Debates* (Hansard), *New Series* (London, 1825), XII, p. 1.
30 Ibid., pp. 1048–1073
31 Ibid., pp. 1194–95.
32 Disraeli, *Inquiry,* p. 95.
33 *Parliamentary Debates* (Hansard), XII, p. 1076.
34 Dawson, *Debt Crisis,* pp. 108–10.
35 Thomas Joplin, *Case for Parliamentary Inquiry* (London, 1835), p. 13.
36 Ibid., p. 16.
37 *Parliamentary Debates* (Hansard), *New Series* (London, 1826), XIV, p. 200.
38 Tooke, *History of Prices,* II, p. 162. Kynaston discounts the story (see *City of London,* II, p. 70).
39 *Dictionary of National Biography,* XVII (Oxford, 1897), p. 1035.
40 Kynaston, *City of London,* I, p. 73.
41 Cited by Boyd Hilton, *Corn, Cash, Commerce* (Oxford, 1977), p. 227. Hilton claims this policy was "sado-masochistic."
42 Martineau, *History of England,* I, p. 364.
43 Ibid., p. 373.
44 Smart, *Economic Annals,* II, p. 334.
45 Dawson, *Debt Crisis,* p. 214.
46 Ibid., p. 119.
47 Head, *Rough Notes,* p. 279.
48 Ibid., p. iv.
49 Francis, *Bank of England,* II, p. 4.
50 Martineau, *History of England,* I, p. 352.
51 S. T. Coleridge, *Lay Sermons* (ed. R. J. White, London, 1972), p. 204.
52 Joplin, *Case,* p. 12.
53 S. J. Loyd, "Reflections suggested by a perusal of Mr. J. Horsley Palmer's Pamphlet on the Causes and Consequences of the Pressure on the Money Market" [1837], published in *Tracts and Other Publications on Metallic and Paper Currency* (London, 1858), p. 30. For other writers who have taken up Overstone's analysis, see John Francis (*History of Bank of England*), Walter Bagehot (*Lombard Street*), and especially Kindleberger (*Manias*).
54 Bagehot, *Lombard Street* [1873] (London, 1910) p. 139.
55 J. S. Mill, *Principles of Political Economy,* p. 543.

5. RAILWAY MANIA

1 J. A. Schumpeter, *Business Cycles,* I, p. 86.
2 W. T. Jackman, *The Development of Transportation in Modern England* (London, 1962), p. 406. As new markets opened up and the prices of transported goods fell, the value of land adjacent to canals rose.

3 J. R. Ward, *The Finance of Canal Building in Eighteenth-Century England* (Oxford, 1974), p. 107.
4 Ibid., p. 91.
5 Ibid., p. 136.
6 See Hunt, *Development of the Business Corporation*, p. 14.
7 Ward, *Finance of Canal Building*, p. 176.
8 See Leone Levi, *The History of British Commerce* (London, 1880), pp. 191–92.
9 Cited by John Francis, *History of the Railways* (London, 1850), I, p. 292.
10 Richard S. Lambert, *The Railway King 1800–1871: A Study of George Hudson and the Business Morals of His Time* (London, 1964), p. 62.
11 Francis, *Railways*, II, p. 139.
12 Ibid., p. 139.
13 Brian Bailey, *George Hudson: The Rise and Fall of the Railway King* (Stroud, England, 1995), p. 13.
14 Ibid., p. 55
15 Lambert, *The Railway King*, p. 157.
16 Ibid., p. 29
17 Ibid., p. 137
18 Bailey, *George Hudson*, p. 44.
19 Cited by Hunt, *Business Corporation*, p. 101.
20 *Times*, 22 October 1845.
21 *Times*, 25 October 1845.
22 *Times*, 27 October 1845.
23 *Economist*, 6 September 1845.
24 Robert Peel, *From His Private Papers* (ed. C. S. Parker, London, 1899), III, p. 188.
25 *Economist*, 6 September 1845.
26 *Economist*, 15 March 1845.
27 P. J. G. Ranson, *The Victorian Railway and How It Evolved* (London 1990), p. 83.
28 *Times*, 14 August.
29 *Times*, 28 July. Note the reference to the carnivalesque nature of the speculation. In his account of the railway mania, John Francis wrote that "the purlieus [of the stock exchanges] were like fairs." (*History of the Railways*, II, p. 183.)
30 *Times*, 2 July.
31 Hunt, *Business Corporation*, p. 105.
32 *Times*, 13 August; *Times*, 12 July.
33 Cited by D. M. Evans, *Commercial Crisis 1847–1848* (second edition, London, 1849), p. 15 n.
34 Francis, *History of the Railways*, II, p. 182.
35 *Economist*, 25 October 1845.
36 *Times*, 12 July 1845.
37 *Times*, 11 October 1845.

38 *Times,* 1 November 1845.
39 See G. R. Hawke, *Railways and Economic Growth in England and Wales 1840–70* (Oxford, 1970), p. 206.
40 Cited in *Times,* 9 August 1845.
41 Anon., *Ten Minutes' Advice to Speculators in Railway Shares* (Manchester, 1845), p. 5.
42 *Economist,* 16 August 1845.
43 Bailey, *George Hudson,* p. 60.
44 *Economist,* 6 September 1845.
45 Evans, *Commercial Crisis 1847–1848,* p. 167. Note how Evans compares the mania to the plague (see Chapter 3).
46 *Times,* 16 October 1845.
47 *Times,* 7 November 1845.
48 *Times,* 24 October 1845.
49 Lambert, *Railway King,* p. 189.
50 Tooke, *History of Prices,* V, p. 369.
51 *Economist,* 22 August 1846.
52 Thomas Carlyle, *Collected Letters* (ed. C. R. Sanders et al. Durham, NC, 1970–), XXI, p. 74.
53 Evans, *Commercial Crisis 1847–1848,* p. 35.
54 Francis, *History of the Railways,* II, p. 195.
55 Evans, *Commercial Crisis 1847–1848,* p. 73.
56 Ibid., p. 86.
57 *Economist,* 20 November 1847.
58 Bailey, *George Hudson,* p. 88.
59 Arthur Smith, *The Bubble of the Age: or, the Fallacies of Railway Investments, Railway Accounts, and Railway Dividends* (London, 1848). According to Smith, "the grossest and lowest tricks are daily resorted to by some Companies, to raise the shares, and make the traffic receipts appear larger."
60 S. Smiles, *Railway Property: Its Condition and Prospects* (London, 1849), p. 63.
61 Evans, *Commercial Crisis 1847–1848,* p. 126.
62 Bailey, *George Hudson,* p. 95.
63 Ibid., p. 102.
64 Ibid., p. 95.
65 Lambert, *Railway King,* p. 276.
66 Ibid., p. 280.
67 James Ward, *Railways for the Many, and Not for the Few,* 1847, p. 5.
68 See Richard Ehrenberg, *Die Fondsspekulation und die Gesetzgebung* (Berlin, 1883), pp. 70–73; and Ludwig Lesser, *Zur Geschichte der Berliner Börse und des Eisenbahnaktien-Handels* (Berlin, 1844).
69 Tooke, *History of Prices,* V, p. 373.
70 Nicholas Negroponte, *Being Digital* (London, 1995), p. 230.
71 Bill Gates, *The Road Ahead* (New York, 1995), p. 9.

72 *Forbes*, 4 December 1995.
73 Gates, *The Road Ahead*, p. 231.

6. THE GILDED AGE

1 J. S. Davis, *Essays in the Early History of American Corporations* (Cambridge, Mass., 1917), I, p. 33.
2 Fowler, *Ten Years*, p. 171.
3 Robert Sobel, *Panic on Wall Street: A History of America's Financial Disasters* (New York, 1968), p. 223.
4 Keynes, *General Theory*, p. 159.
5 Cited by A. M. Sakolski, *The Great American Land Bubble* (New York, 1932), p. 30.
6 William Armstrong, *Stocks and Stock-Jobbing on Wall Street* [1848] (reprinted in the *Magazine of History*, 1933, 45, No. 1), p. 12.
7 Fowler, *Ten Years*, p. 327.
8 Armstrong, *Stocks and Stock-Jobbing*, p. 24.
9 Fowler, *Ten Years*, p. 329. James Medbery called margins "the mainspring of speculation." (J. K. Medbery, *Men and Mysteries of Wall Street*, Boston, 1870, p. 59).
10 Fowler, *Ten Years*, p. 155.
11 Matthew Josephson, *The Robber Barons* (New York, 1934), p. 59.
12 Ibid., p. 28.
13 Fowler, *Ten Years*, p. 131.
14 Charles F. Adams, Jr., *A Chapter of Erie* (Boston, 1869), p. 4.
15 Fowler, *Ten Years*, p. 142.
16 Ibid., p. 489.
17 Medbery, *Men and Mysteries*, p. 161.
18 Cited by Sobel, *Panic*, p. 125.
19 Fowler, *Ten Years*, p. 281.
20 Ibid., p. 320.
21 Ibid., p. 243.
22 Cited by S. D. Cashman, *America in the Gilded Age* (New York, 1984), p. 41.
23 Sereno S. Pratt, *The Work of Wall Street* (New York, 1903), p. 140.
24 Medbery, *Men and Mysteries*, p. 205.
25 Boyden Sparkes and Samuel Morse, *Hetty Green, The Woman Who Loved Money* (New York, 1930), p. 139.
26 Henry Adams, "The New York Gold Conspiracy," in Charles Francis Adams, Jr. and Henry Adams, *Chapters of Erie and Other Essays* (Boston, 171), p. 102.
27 Medbery, *Men and Mysteries*, p. 241.
28 See Fowler, *Ten Years*, Chapter 18.
29 Ibid., p. 195.

30 Medbery, *Men and Mysteries*, p. 153.
31 Cited by Maury Klein, *The Life and Legend of Jay Gould* (Baltimore, 1986), p. 127.
32 Henry Adams, "Gold Conspiracy," p. 111.
33 Josephson, *Robber Barons*, p. 373.
34 Mark Twain and Charles Dudley Warner, *The Gilded Age* (Hartford, 1873), p. 397. The words *fever* and *lunacy* are, of course, frequently used to describe stock market behaviour.
35 Fowler, *Ten Years*, p. 387.
36 Henry Clews, *Twenty-eight Years in Wall Street* (New York, 1888), p. 115.
37 Henry Adams, "Gold Conspiracy," p. 113.
38 Ibid., p. 111.
39 Charles Adams, *Chapter of Erie*, p. 139.
40 Sakolski, *Land Bubble*, p. 291.
41 Josephson, *Robber Barons*, p. 94.
42 Sprague, *History of Crises*, p. 27.
43 Cited by Sobel, *Panic*, pp. 184–85.
44 Noyes, *Market Place*, pp. 19–20.
45 Pratt, *Work of Wall Street*, p. 43; and Clews, *Twenty-eight Years*, p. 97.
46 Josephson, *Robber Barons*, p. 351.
47 Noyes, *Market Place*, p. 42.
48 Medbery, *Men and Mysteries*, p. 128.
49 Ibid., p. 198.
50 Cited by Sobel, *Panic*, p. 209.
51 Medbery, *Men and Mysteries*, p. 210.
52 Armstrong, *Stocks and Stock-Jobbing*, p. 23.
53 Emery, *Speculation*, p. 100.

7. THE CRASH OF 1929

1 Bagehot, *Lombard Street*, p. 158.
2 Noyes, *Market Place*, p. 195.
3 Herbert Hoover, *Memoirs* (London 1953), III (*The Great Depression*), p. 6.
4 *North American Review*, 227 (1929), pp. 75–76.
5 Irving Fisher, *The Stock Market Crash—And After* (New York, 1930), p. 126.
6 Ibid., p. 176.
7 Cited by M. S. Fridson, *It Was a Very Good Year* (New York, 1998), p. 50.
8 Cited by J. R. Levien, *Anatomy of a Crash* (New York, 1966), p. 20.
9 James Grant, *Bernard M. Baruch: The Adventures of a Wall Street Legend* (New York, 1997), pp. 216–17.
10 Smith, *Common Stocks*, p. 81.
11 Graham, *Intelligent Investor*, pp. 315–21.
12 *North American Review*, 228, (1929), p. 156.

13 Ibid., n.p.
14 Barrie Wigmore, *The Crash and Its Aftermath 1929–1933* (Westport, Conn., 1985), p. 27.
15 *North American Review*, 228, p. 166.
16 Grant, *Baruch*, p. 221; John Kenneth Galbraith, *The Great Crash 1929* [1954] (London, 1994), p. 116; Frederick Lewis Allen, *Only Yesterday* [1931] (New York, 1957), p. 324.
17 Cited by Galbraith, *Great Crash*, p. 42.
18 Thomas Mortimer, *Elements of Commerce* (London, 1772), p. 400.
19 Fernand Pecora, *Wall Street Under Oath* (London, 1939), p. 93.
20 Galbraith, *Great Crash*, p. 103.
21 Ibid.
22 *North American Review*, 227, p. 406.
23 Gordon Thomas and Max Morgan-Witts, *The Day the Bubble Burst: A Social History of the Wall Street Crash* (London, 1979), p. 356.
24 Cited by Robert T. Patterson, *The Great Boom and Panic 1921–1929* (Chicago, 1965), p. 18.
25 *North American Review*, 227, p. 410.
26 Groucho Marx, *Groucho & Me* [1959] (London, 1995), p. 147.
27 Wigmore, *Crash and Its Aftermath*, p. 41.
28 *North American Review*, 228, p. 75.
29 *North American Review*, 227, n.p.
30 *Commercial and Financial Chronicle*, 9 March 1929.
31 *North American Review*, 228, p. 159.
32 Charles Mackay, *Extraordinary Popular Delusions and the Madness of Crowds* (New York, 1932), p. xiii.
33 See Gustave Le Bon, *The Crowd: A Study of the Popular Mind* (London, 1922), and Sigmund Freud, "Group Psychology and the Analysis of the Ego" (in *Collected Works*, trans. J. Strachey, London, 1955, XVIII).
34 Freud, *Collected Works*, XVIII, pp. 127 and 101.
35 Ibid., p. 96.
36 Fowler, *Ten Years*, p. 322.
37 Allen, *Only Yesterday*, p. 319.
38 Cited by Galbraith, *Great Crash*, p. 108.
39 Thomas and Morgan-Witts, *Bubble*, p. 226.
40 Martin Gilbert, *Winston S. Churchill* (London, 1976), V, p. 350.
41 Allen, *Only Yesterday*, p. 333.
42 Eddie Cantor, *Caught Short! A Saga of Wailing Wall Street* [1929] (repr. Burlington, Vt., 1992), p. 22.
43 Thomas and Morgan-Witts, *Bubble*, p. 368.
44 Noyes, *Market Place*, p. 342.
45 Pecora, *Wall Street*, p. 260.
46 Keynes, *General Theory*, p. 159.

47 Cited by C. P. Kindleberger, *The World in Depression 1929–39* (London, 1987), p. 106.
48 See Peter Temin, *Lessons from the Great Depression* (Cambridge, Mass., 1990).
49 Hoover, *Memoirs*, III, p. 30.
50 Murray Rothbard, *America's Great Depression* (Princeton, 1963), p. 295.
51 Wigmore, *Crash and Its Aftermath*, p. 337.
52 F. Scott Fitzgerald, *The Crack-Up* (ed. Edmund Wilson, New York, 1945), p. 21.
53 Allen, *Only Yesterday*, p. 338.
54 Cited by Jonathan Davis, *The Money Makers* (London, 1998), p. 3.
55 Galbraith, *Great Crash*, p. 50.
56 *Grant's Interest Rate Observer*, 15 August 1997.
57 *Grant's Interest Rate Observer*, 14 March 1997.
58 Cited in *Grant's Interest Rate Observer*, 17 February 1997.
59 *Grant's Interest Rate Observer*, 20 June 1997.
60 *Investors Business Daily*, 29 October 1996. Cited in *Grant's Interest Rate Observer*, 6 November 1996.

8. COWBOY CAPITALISM

1 Cited by James Grant, *The Trouble with Prosperity* (New York, 1996), p. 13.
2 Martin Mayer, *Markets* (New York, 1988), p. 11.
3 Hugo Young, *One of Us* (London, 1991), p. 46.
4 Robert Solomon, *The International Monetary System 1945–81* (New York, 1982), p. 186. Nixon accused speculators of "waging an all-out war on the American dollar."
5 *Economist*, 10 October 1992.
6 Robert Heilbroner, *The Quest for Wealth* (New York, 1956), p. 219.
7 Milton Friedman, *Optimum Quantity of Money and Other Essays* (Chicago, 1960), p. 286.
8 For an early attack on the Efficient Market Hypothesis, see David Dreman, *The Psychology of the Stock-Market: Investment Strategy Beyond Random Walk* (New York, 1977).
9 Cited by Gregory Millman, *Around the World on a Trillion Dollars a Day* (London, 1996), p. 109.
10 Leo Melamed, *Escape to the Futures* (New York, 1996), p. 177.
11 Martin Mayer, *Nightmare on Wall Street: Salomon Brothers and the Corruption of the Market Place* (New York, 1993), p. 153.
12 See Merton H. Miller, *Financial Innovations and Market Volatility* (Oxford, 1991) and *Merton Miller on Derivatives* (New York, 1997).
13 Frank Partnoy, *F.I.A.S.C.O.: Blood in the Water on Wall Street* (London, 1997), p. 33.
14 "Adam Smith" (pseud. George J. W. Goodman), *The Roaring '80s* (New York, 1988), p. 26.

15 Lewis Lapham, *Money and Class in America* (New York, 1989), p. 8.
16 See Ken Auletta, *Greed and Glory on Wall Street: The Fall of the House of Lehman* (New York, 1986).
17 See Anthony Sampson, *The Midas Touch* (London, 1989), p. 29.
18 Fenton Bailey, *The Junk Bond Revolution* (London, 1992), pp. 39–40.
19 Ibid., p. 284.
20 James Stewart, *Den of Thieves* (New York, 1991), p. 117.
21 Connie Bruck, *The Predators' Ball* (New York, 1988), p. 145.
22 Ibid., p. 25.
23 Anthony Bianco, *Mad Dog: The Story of Jeff Beck and Wall Street* (London, 1993), p. 323.
24 George Anders, *Merchants of Debt: KKR and the Mortgaging of American Business* (New York, 1993), p. 95.
25 Bruck, *Predators' Ball*, p. 302.
26 Ibid., p. 314.
27 Ibid., p. 285.
28 Stewart, *Den of Thieves*, p. 213.
29 Bailey, *Junk Bond Revolution*, p. 92.
30 Ibid., p. 99.
31 Ibid., p. 82. The same quotation is found in Dominick Dunne's novel *People Like Us.*
32 Bruck, *Predators' Ball*, p. 5. Boesky's words are paraphrased by Gordon Gekko in the movie *Wall Street:* "Greed is good, greed works."
33 Cited by Lapham, *Money and Class*, p. 182.
34 Bruck, *Predators' Ball*, p. 248.
35 Rothchild, *Going for Broke*, p. 93.
36 Tim Metz, *Black Monday* (New York, 1988), pp. 134, 165.
37 Steven K. Breckner, *Back from the Brink: The Greenspan Years* (New York, 1997), p. 50.
38 Andrew Smithers & Co., "The Economic Threat Posed by the US Asset Bubble," Report No. 92, July 1996, p. 8.
39 Lapham, *Money and Class*, p. 106.
40 Bruck, *Predators' Ball*, p. 266.
41 Martin Mayer, *The Greatest-Ever Bank Robbery* (New York, 1992), p. 20.
42 Ibid., p. 118.
43 James Ring Adams, *The Big Fix: Inside the S&L Scandal* (New York, 1991), p. 224.
44 Mayer, *Bank Robbery*, p. 221.
45 Adams, *Big Fix*, p. 228.
46 Rothchild, *Going for Broke*, p. 137.
47 Ibid., p. 211.
48 Grant, *Money of the Mind*, p. 426.
49 Berkshire Hathaway, Annual Report, 1989, pp. 16–20.

50 Bianco, *Mad Dog*, p. 428.
51 Stewart, *Den of Thieves*, p. 428.
52 Anders, *Merchants of Debt*, p. 58.
53 Berkshire Hathaway, Annual Report, 1990, p. 18.

9. KAMIKAZE CAPITALISM

1 Richard Dore in *Flexible Rigidities*, cited by John Dower, *Japan in War and Peace* (London, 1995), p. 307.
2 Cited by "Adam Smith," *Roaring 80s*, p. 136.
3 See Dower, *War and Peace*, pp. 292–93.
4 Ezra Vogel, *Japan as Number One* (New York, 1979).
5 See article by Ted Rall, "A Sprocket in Satan's Bulldozer: Confessions of an Investment Banker," *Might*, issue 6, October 1995.
6 See Ian Buruma, *The Missionary and the Libertine* (London, 1996), pp. 262–68.
7 Dower, *War and Peace*, p. 284.
8 See R. Taggart Murphy, *The Real Price of Japanese Money* (London, 1996), p. 113.
9 Robert Zielinski and Nigel Holloway, *Unequal Equities* (New York, 1991), pp. 145–46.
10 Taggart Murphy, *Japanese Money*, p. 168.
11 Christopher Wood, *The Bubble Economy* (Tokyo, 1993), p. 67.
12 See Taggart Murphy, *Japanese Money*, p. 139.
13 Karel Van Wolferen, *The Enigma of Japanese Power* (London, 1989), p. 134.
14 Brian Reading, *Japan: The Coming Collapse* (London, 1993).
15 Zielinski and Holloway, *Unequal Equities*, p. 85.
16 Ibid., p. 91.
17 *Japan Economic Journal*, June 1988, cited by Grant, *Mr. Market*, p. 172.
18 Shigeto Tsuru, *Japanese Capitalism: Creative Defeat and Beyond* (Cambridge, 1993), p. 162.
19 Cited by Grant, *Mr. Market*, p. 169.
20 *Far Eastern Economic Review*, 7 August 1986.
21 Al Alletzhauser, *House of Nomura* (London, 1990), p. 193; Zielinski and Holloway, *Unequal Equities*, p. 48.
22 Ibid., p. 206.
23 Lesley Downer, *The Brothers* (London, 1994), pp. 357–62.
24 Robert Hughes, *Nothing If Not Critical* (London, 1990), p. 396.
25 Josephson, *Robber Barons*, p. 343.
26 Hughes, *Nothing If Not Critical*, p. 396.
27 Peter Watson, *From Manet to Manhattan* (London, 1992), p. 427.
28 *Far Eastern Economic Review*, 18 January 1990.
29 *Japan Economic Journal*, 15 September 1990.

30 Wood, *Bubble Economy*, p. 60.
31 Jon Woronoff, *The Japanese Economic Crisis* (London, 1993), p. 163.
32 Wood, *Bubble Economy*, p. 60.

EPILOGUE: THE ROGUE ECONOMISTS

1 Walter Werner and Steven Smith, *Wall Street* (New York, 1991).
2 See Geert Bekaert and Campbell Harvey, "Foreign Speculators and Emerging Equity Markets," NBER Working Paper No. 6312, 1998.
3 Cited by Sobel, *Dangerous Dreamers*, p. 27 (from Grodinsky's textbook, *Investments*, 1953, p. 375).
4 Cited by Peter L. Bernstein, *Against the Gods: The Remarkable Story of Risk* (New York, 1996), p. 328.
5 *Financial Times*, 8 November 1997.
6 Paul Krugman, *The Accidental Theorist* (New York, 1998), p. 158.
7 Cited by Robert Slater, *Soros* (New York, 1996), p. 183.
8 *Merton Miller on Derivatives* (New York, 1997), p. ix.
9 Partnoy, *F.I.A.S.C.O.*, p. 140.
10 Andrew Smithers & Co., "Stock Options: An Example of Catastrophe Myopia?" Report No. 110, October 1997.
11 Mayer, *Nightmare*, p. 232.
12 Cited by Richard Thomson, *Apocalypse Roulette* (London, 1998), p. 256.
13 Slater, *Soros*, p. 232.
14 Ibid., p. 233.
15 Figure cited by *Economist*, 3 October 1998.
16 *Economist*, 17 October 1998.
17 Buchan, *Frozen Desire*, p. 182.
18 Keynes, *General Theory*, p. 156.

FOR FURTHER REFERENCE (WORKS NOT CITED ELSEWHERE)

M. Abolafia and M. Kilduff, "Enacting Market Crisis: The Social Construction of a Speculative Bubble," *Administrative Science Quarterly*, vol. 33, No. 2 (June 1988).

Gordon Allport and Leo Postman, *The Psychology of Rumor*. New York, 1947.

W. Brian Arthur, "Positive Feedbacks in the Economy," *Scientific American*, February 1990.

Fischer Black, "Noise," *Journal of Finance*, XLI, No. 3 (July 1986).

Shaheen Borna and James Lowry, "Gambling and Speculation," *Journal of Business Ethics*, vol. 6 (1987).

Reuven Brenner, *Gambling and Speculation: A Theory, a History, and a Future of Some Human Decisions*. Cambridge, 1990.

David Carrier, "Will Chaos Kill the Auctioneer," *Review of Political Economy*, vol. 5, issue 3 (1993).

Barry Eichengreen, *Globalizing Capital: A History of the International Monetary System.* Princeton, 1996.

Bill Emmott, *The Sun Also Sets: The Limits to Japan's Economic Power.* New York, 1989.

Eugene F. Fama, "Perspectives on October 1987," in Robert W. Kamphuis, ed., *Black Monday and the Future of Financial Markets.* Chicago, 1989.

Stephen Fay, *The Collapse of Barings.* London, 1996.

Leon Festinger, *A Theory of Cognitive Dissonance.* Stanford, 1957.

Benjamin Graham and David Dodd, *Security Analysis.* New York, 1934.

Bob Haq, ed., *The Tobin Tax.* Oxford, 1996.

Henry Howard Harper, *The Psychology of Speculation.* New York, 1926.

Bernard Hart, "The Psychology of Rumour," *Proceedings of the Royal Society of Medicine*, vol. 9 (March 28, 1916).

Robert A. Haugen, *The New Finance: The Case Against Efficient Markets.* Englewood, N.J., 1995.

Nicholas Kaldor, "Speculation and Economic Stability," *Review of Economic Studies*, vol. VIII (1939–40).

George Katona, "The Relationship Between Psychology and Economics," in S. Koch, ed., *Psychology: A Study of a Science*, vol. 6 (New York, 1959).

D. Kelsey, "The Economics of Chaos," *Oxford Economics Papers*, vol. 40, No. 1 (March 1988).

J. M. Keynes, *Collected Writings* (Economic Articles and Correspondence: Investment and Editorial), vol. XII, London and Cambridge, 1983.

Charles P. Kindleberger, *World Economic Primacy: 1500–1900*, Oxford, 1996.

—— "Asset Inflation and Monetary Policy," Banco Nazionale del Lavoro *Quarterly Review*, March 1995.

—— "Economic and Financial Crises and Transformations in Sixteenth-Century Europe," *Essays in International Finance*, No. 208 (June 1998), Princeton.

Michael Syron Lawlor, "On the Historical Origins of Keynes's Financial Market Views," in Supplement 26 to *History of Political Economy*, 1994.

Edwin Lefèvre, *Reminiscences of a Stock Operator*, New York, 1923.

Roger Lowenstein, *Buffett: The Making of an American Capitalist.* New York, 1996.

Robert K. Merton, "Self-fulfilling Prophecies," *Antioch Review*, vol. 8 (1949).

David Parker and Ralph Stacey, *Chaos, Management and Economics: The Implications of Non-Linear Thinking.* London, 1994.

Anna Pavord, *The Tulip.* London, 1999.

Edgar E. Peters, *Chaos and Order in the Capital Markets: A New View of Cycles, Prices, and Market Volatility.* New York, 1991.

Cliff Pratten, *The Stock Market.* Cambridge, 1993.

Charles Raw et al., *Do you sincerely want to be rich? Bernard Cornfeld and IOS: An International Swindle.* London, 1971.

David Roberts, *$1000 Billion a Day: Inside the Foreign Exchange Markets.* London, 1995.

Arnold Rose, "Rumor in the Stock Market," *Public Opinion Quarterly*, No. 15 (1951).

Robert J. Schiller, *Market Volatility.* Cambridge, Mass., 1989.

—— "Stock Prices and Social Dynamics," *Brookings Papers on Economic Activity* 2, 1984.

—— "Speculative Prices and Popular Models," *Journal of Economic Perspectives*, vol. 4, No. 2 (Spring 1990).

Eric Schubert, "Innovations, Debts, and Bubbles: International Integration of Financial Markets in Western Europe, 1688–1720." *Journal of Economic History*, vol. 48, No. 2 (June 1988).

S. M. Sheffrin, *Rational Expectations.* Cambridge, 1996.

William A. Sherden, *The Fortune Sellers.* New York, 1997.

Peter Tasker, *Inside Japan: Wealth, Work and Power in the New Japanese Empire.* London, 1987.

Jean Tirole, "On the Possibility of Speculation Under Rational Expectations," *Econometrica*, vol. 50, No. 5 (September 1982).

John Train, *The Dance of the Honey Bees.* New York, 1974.

Paul Volcker and Toyoo Gyohten, *Changing Fortunes: The World's Money and the Threat to American Leadership.* New York, 1992.

M. Mitchell Waldrop, *Complexity.* New York, 1992.

W. A. Weisskopf, *The Psychology of Economics.* London, 1955.

ACKNOWLEDGMENTS

This book would not have appeared in its current state without the generous assistance of friends and acquaintances. Chris Dennistoun and the late Jack Clark lent me books from their libraries. Alexander Marchessini sent me a copy of Niederhoffer's article on Hillary Rodham Clinton's speculative activities. Dominic Caldecott has amiably withstood years of pestering and has supplied me with books, brokers' reports, and much other invaluable information.

Several persons have sent me their unpublished papers, including Professor Koichi Hamada, Professor Peter Temin of MIT, Dr. Brian Mitchell of Trinity College, Cambridge, and Dr. Graham Storey. Professor John D'Arms read through the pages on speculation in ancient Rome, while Professor Robert Jay Lifton, Dr. John Kellet, and Dr. Harry Boothby discussed my material on the psychology of speculation. Anna Pavord instructed me about the tulipomania (a subject covered in her recent history of the tulip), and Nick Bennet read my chapter on Japan and made many useful points.

Two financial writers have greatly influenced my thinking on speculation in the 1990s: Andrew Smithers of Smithers & Co. (whose office sent me several reports) and James Grant of *Grant's Interest Rate Observer*, whose books and journal I have read with great pleasure and instruction.

The later drafts were read by Hamish Robinson, Professor Charles Kindleberger, Sir Raymond Carr, Dominic Caldecolt, Richard Windsor-Clive, and my father, John Chancellor. I owe a special debt to my former colleague, Pierre-Antoine Bernheim, who has left the world of banking to become a distinguished biblical scholar and publisher. Pierre-Antoine lent me many works from his extensive collection, patiently advised me, and carefully read the last draft.

One could not ask for better editors than Jonathan Galassi and Paul Elie of Farrar, Straus and Giroux. Gillon Aitken, my agent, has been both supportive and patient. Mrs. Drue Heinz kindly lent me her flat in New York in the spring of 1996.

My final and greatest thanks go to Antonia Phillips. It would be tedious to list her many kindnesses. As far as it concerns the reader, she has read several times every passage in the book and forced me to make many useful revisions that would otherwise have been left undone. Her time has been given at no small sacrifice to the progress of her own work. I only hope the finished book comes close to satisfying her exacting standards.

INDEX